The Lifetime Learning Companion

The Lifetime Learning Companion

Jean and Donn Reed

Brook Farm Books
Bridgewater, Maine, USA
Glassville, New Brunswick, Canada

This book incorporates material previously published in somewhat different form in *The First Home-School Catalogue* (1982, 1986); "efficient instruction elsewhere" (1984); *The Home-School Challenge* (1985); *The Home School Source Book* (first edition, 1991; second edition, rev., 1994); *The Home School Source Book*, third edition, 2000; *The Homeschooling Book of Answers*, by Linda Dobson; *Homeschooling: An Open House*, by Nancy Lande; and *Home Education Magazine*, *Harrowsmith*, *Nurturing*, *The New Nativity*, and other periodicals.

Portraits and cartoons by Chuck Trapkus, Rock Island, Illinois: Jean and Donn, pages 4 and 282; Donn and Gus, page 98; Gus walking Donn, page 104; cartoon with skunk, page 109; Gus, page 135; Jean with guitar, page 284. Clip art is from Dover Publications and Frank Shaffer.

Published simultaneously in Canada and the United States by Brook Farm Books, Box 246, Bridgewater, ME 04735, and Brook Farm Books, Box 101, Glassville, NB E7L 4T4, Canada.

Printed and bound in the United States of America.

Library of Congress Catalog Card Number: 2008905778

National Library of Canada Cataloguing in Publication Data

Reed, Jean, 1943-

The lifetime learning companion / Jean and Donn Reed ; illustrators, Chuck Trapkus, Jean and Donn Reed.

ISBN 978-0-919761-30-8

1. Continuing education. I. Reed, Donn II. Trapkus, Chuck III. Title.

LC5215.R455 2008 304 C2008-903190-3

DEDICATION — 1994

For Jean —

Whose constant inspiration, support, patience, hard work, and companionship have made this and all things possible; this book, like so many other parts of our lives, is hers as much as mine;

And for Cathy, Karen, Susan, and Derek —

Who have taught us far more than we have taught them; whose curiosity, interests, hopes and fears, increasing awareness, perceptions, and interpretations have all added to our knowledge of ourselves as parents and as people;

All five of whom have given me a life of warmth and meaning far beyond my reasonable expectations. I look back over our lives together, and am very glad we chose to do it all our way.

And our adventure continues …

DEDICATION — April 2009

For Donn, June 13, 1938 - December 21, 1995

Whose courage and vision have given us a living legacy of insight, liberally sprinkled with humor and filled with love. Who has been, and still is, the center of my life.

Who inspires me and supports me, now as much as ever, in all my endeavors. Donn, you were so much more than I ever dreamed of or expected in a husband and father, lover and friend, teacher and mentor, critic and playmate — my spiritual companion. You filled my life with inspiration, love, and companionship that has not been broken — even by death's summons. Although I can no longer hold your hand, I hold you in my heart. You are as much a part of me and this book as you always have been. I too look back over the years, and am very glad we chose to do it our way.

And for Cathy, Karen, Susan, and Derek —

Who held me through the dark days; whose love and support have kept me secure and encouraged me to continue doing what I hold most dear. Each of you, although far away, continues to teach me. I value your thoughts, opinions, and friendship more than you can imagine. Each of you continues to enrich my life beyond my expectations.

And yes, Donn, the adventure continues ...

ACKNOWLEDGMENTS

This book is dedicated to Donn and the kids, but it would not have been possible without the help and support of many others. To name them all would take a separate book.

Special thanks to David Albert for convincing me that I needed to catch up with the times and make this book and put the resources on the Web. And to Tim and Lillian Haas, for your much appreciated technical and editing expertise (keeping the egg off my face) and your generosity of spirit, all of which have made this book the best it can be. You've ensured that my education is still continuing. You are terrific!

Enduring thanks to my cousin Dr. Alfred Alschuler, now deceased, for helping me discover that I could write after the school system had discouraged the effort. And of course, thanks to Lillian Jones for her help, support, suggestions, and encouragement.

Many thanks also go to all my friends and neighbors who have kept me in contact with the world at large while I retreated to my cave and worked.

And last, but certainly not least, thanks to everyone who took the time to write with questions, concerns, and praise for past efforts. You have encouraged me to continue when I've felt overwhelmed. I owe you more than I can possibly express in mere words. I wish it were possible to list all your names, but you and I know who you are. I have saved each and every letter and card. This book is also dedicated to you and your families.

CONTENTS

FOREWORD

BY LINDA DOBSON

It's always an honor to be asked to pen a book's foreword. It is, however, a humbling experience to be invited to become even a minute part of this continuing labor of love first conceived by Jean and Donn Reed so many years ago.

I wish I could say I was aware of their early work while in grade school, but actually it was my grade-school-aged first child's education that set me on the path to discovering it. Kindergarten attendance was having a negative effect, rapidly changing this pleasant and loving person into a stressed-out, aggressive, and, most of all, unhappy child. Fortunately, I'd discovered homeschooling and, as I am wont to do, I set out to learn everything I could about it.

A generation ago, that was not as overwhelming as it has become today. Back then, a few large publishers had the good sense to publish the works of John Holt, David and Micki Colfax, and Raymond Moore. Other equally valuable material was being self-published; homespun, rough around the edges, relating firsthand knowledge and offering hopeful authors the opportunity to at least supplement the bank accounts of one-income families determined to stay home and take responsibility for the education of their children while living in a two-income society.

Much of that work has been lost, and of course time has changed many things. Homeschooling grew up alongside the World Wide Web, so it's natural for Jean to decide that her extensive lists of ever-changing resources should find a new home on the easily accessible Internet.

I am ever so grateful, for those of you currently homeschooling and for all of the homeschooling families yet to come, that time has not altered the truth of this book's content, and that Jean decided to devote the time, attention, and love necessary to allow you to hold this updated classic in your hands.

Yes, Jean has accomplished the work, but she has not done it alone. While Donn is not physically with us, Donn and Jean's minds and hearts continue to complement each other to inspire, support, and, hopefully, help your mind stretch in directions it may not have reached if not for being treated to the honest, intelligent, often humorous commentary that rings as true today as it did more than 20 years ago.

The book you hold in your hands now is a rare gift and a distinctive treat. Before you read, grab a cup of coffee or a nice herbal tea. Whether you are new to homeschooling or a seasoned veteran, discover how this family's homeschooling journey is at once powerful, yet tender; solid, yet flexible; intellectual, yet emotional. Let the inherent freedom in this educational approach also lead you to provide for your children an education that is worth having.

The Lifetime Learning Companion is also liberally sprinkled with thought-provoking quotes. One from Clifton Fadiman, author of *New Lifetime Reading Plan*, says, "When you reread a classic you do not see more in the book than you did before; you see more in *you* than there was before."

This classic now in your possession has stood the test of time. Read it. Reread it. Let it help you find in yourself what you need to embrace your family-centered, homeschool journey with wisdom and love.

RESOURCES IN THIS BOOK

RESOURCES NOT IN THIS BOOK

A NOTE ABOUT THE RESOURCES MENTIONED IN THIS BOOK

All the resources mentioned in this book you can probably find and purchase someplace on the web. For your convenience I have put them all on brookfarmbooks.com with information about the best places to purchase them. When we can give you the best deal, you can purchase directly from us. If you will get the best deal someplace else, I have done my best to give you all the information you will need. There are times you will find it more convenient to order from us if your choices are from a number of different sources (that information is on the web). I think you will find that frequently the deciding factor in this decision is the cost of shipping and handling. You'll figure it out.

A NOTE ABOUT THE RESOURCES NOT IN THIS BOOK

The *Home School Source Book, 3rd Edition,* had more than 3,000 reviewed resources. I've found this too much to keep up with in a book. You are better served by a combination of the best of the essays and updated material from *The Home School Source Book* and reviews of our all-time favorite resources in a smaller book, with the rest of the reviewed resources on the web where I can keep the prices current and make needed additions and changes more easily.

Our criteria for items we recommend are the same as for items we used ourselves: They must be fun, challenging, constructive, informative, and relevant to steady mental, physical, and moral growth.

We don't have a large company. Your orders will be processed personally, from opening the mail to sending out the orders. We may not be as efficient as computers, but we're friendlier.

TO ORDER MORE COPIES OF THIS BOOK

Additional copies of *The Lifetime Learning Companion* may be ordered from Brook Farm Books, P.O. Box 246, Bridgewater, ME 04735, or Brook Farm Books, Box 101, Glassville, NB E7L 4T4, for $19.95 plus $2 postage. All orders must be paid in U.S. funds; checks or money orders are fine. Visa/MasterCard orders are accepted through our toll-free order number: 877-375-4680. You may also purchase copies from your local bookstore. If they don't have it, they can order it through IPG in Chicago, Baker & Taylor, or their regular wholesaler.

BEFORE YOU GET CONFUSED, READ THIS INTRODUCTION!

Dear Readers,

This book contains the updated essays and commentaries, plus cartoons from the third edition of *The Home School Source Book*, that would have been in the fourth edition of *The Home School Source Book* if I'd chosen to put together another huge book. I've been called a "late bloomer" at times, but I think I've finally gotten the hang of modern publishing and communication. The updated resource and directory portion from the last edition of *The Home School Source Book* you'll find on our growing website: **www.brookfarmbooks.com**. Resources and prices are changing so quickly now that it is impossible to put out a really big book like *The Home School Source Book* with thousands of reviews, prices, and pieces of contact information and have it still be up to date when it comes off the press and gets to bookstores. Publishers put out new catalogs twice a year, and I do believe that I can do a better job of keeping the resources current by using the web. The new site will have a weekly blog and be the best place to keep up with all the exciting new resources I find, as well as pertinent commentary.

This book, like the third edition of *The Home School Source Book,* has my writing and Donn's. When I started writing I was stymied for a time figuring out how to make it clear who was speaking to you. When Donn wrote his last edition he used the first-person singular and plural, I and we, to indicate that he was speaking for himself, and for the two of us. When I began writing I soon realized that I, too, wanted to speak for myself, and use I, meaning me, Jean. I didn't want to fill the book with "he says" and "I say" or labels in the margins saying "Jean" or "Donn." I was stumped.

I should have remembered one of the major lessons we learned while homeschooling: Never underestimate your kids. When I finally posed this problem to the kids, Susan quickly pointed out the obvious solution. "Mom," she said, "you have a computer. Why not use two different fonts?"

"Well, why not?" I thought. I'd never seen it done, but that's never been an inhibiting factor for either Donn or me. I tried it and it worked well, but if you were to skip this introduction and start reading through the rest of the book first, I think you would be confused.

You will find my writing and most reviews of books and other resources in the typeface used for the majority of this page (Gotham).

Whenever you see a different typeface, you will know Donn is speaking to you. His essays and a few long book reviews are in Garamond; e.g., "When we began our 'experiment' in home-schooling in the early 1970s, part of our purpose was to determine what things and conditions are most useful, if not essential, in learning. What are the 'necessaries' of teaching at home — not just the physical materials, such as books and pencils, but the methods, the attitudes, and the objectives? What knowledge is really useful or essential in life, and what are the best ways of obtaining or imparting it?"

Many of you have come with us through the years as readers, customers, and long-time friends through correspondence. Some of you are about to meet us for the first time. The reason I need to write using separate fonts is because Donn can no longer do it.

For those of you who don't know, Donn died in December 1995 after a ten-year battle with cancer. He loved writing. He loved finding new and exciting resources and making them available to everyone. *The Home School Source Book* was his baby, and because he loved his work he did almost all of it. I was the coffee server, errand runner, chore doer, and everything else while he worked. I made doughnuts, gardened, did barn chores, hauled wood, played my guitar, and read. I eagerly awaited the next chapter, listened, gave comments, and helped only with packaging books and other minor chores. It was the way we worked together. It wasn't until he was very sick that we started my education into how to run the business. My first lesson was that most of the information I needed was in Donn's head. The transfer of information never was completed.

Over the intervening years I've had a massive midlife education in business, writing, publishing, and order fulfillment — the ultimate in adult homeschooling. By continuing Donn's work I feel that we are still working together; it's a continuation of our lives together in a new dimension. I hope you will find enjoyment and useful information within these pages and bear with me as I continue to learn.

A note about Internet addresses: Though not every listing in the book has a web address, most businesses and organizations do have them nowadays. Please note that web and e-mail addresses sometimes break across lines in listings. In these cases the break has been made after a period, slash (/), or underscore (_) in web names, or after a period or the "@" in e-mail addresses — so if it seems as if you've reached the end of a sentence in the middle of an address, read down to the next line for the rest of it.

Also, though I have included the "www" portion of web addresses in the listings, you can usually just skip it when typing addresses into your browser.

OUR BEGINNINGS

When Henry David Thoreau began his famous experiment in living at Walden Pond, his purpose, he wrote later, was to determine what things and conditions are essential to life. In most parts of the world, he said, only four things are essential for physical survival: food, clothing, shelter, and heat.

"At present day," Thoreau went on to say (mid-1800s), "and in this country, as I find by my own experience, a few implements, a knife, an axe, a spade, a wheelbarrow, etc., and for the studious, lamplight, stationery, and access to a few good books, rank next to necessaries, and can all be obtained at a trifling cost."

When we began our "experiment" in home-schooling in the early 1970s, part of our purpose was to determine what things and conditions are most useful, if not essential, in learning. What are the "necessaries" of teaching at home — not just the physical materials, such as books and pencils, but the methods, the attitudes, and the objectives? What knowledge is really useful or essential in life, and what are the best ways of obtaining or imparting it?

There were no books or magazines about home-schooling then, no directories or catalogs of materials, and we didn't know any other home-schoolers. We found and chose learning materials by hit or miss: browsing in book stores, buying discarded library books (still a good source), searching through garage sales and used-book stores, buying activity books in toy stores, borrowing from public libraries and, when we could, from schools.

When a school principal loaned us a school supplies catalog, we discovered wonderful possibilities we hadn't even suspected — books, charts, posters, toys, games, science kits, film strips, models, and much more. The rustic, rural lifestyle we prefer seldom generates much money (although we have no objection to money, in itself), but that period of discovery was one of the fortunate exceptions during which I was earning a good wage. We promptly spent several hundred dollars on our first order.

When the packages arrived, it was like a childhood Christmas morning for all of us. In the weeks following, we remained very happy with most of the purchases. Some items, however, proved to be very disappointing, and we began to learn that an item isn't necessarily good, or even worth the postage, just because it's offered for sale to "professional educators."

Once we discovered the scores of suppliers and hundreds of educational book publishers, our problem was no longer finding materials, but deciding what would be most useful. How we wished for a comprehensive guide to the materials available! It would have saved us hundreds of dollars, as well as hundreds of hours wasted in trying to use worthless materials.

We continued our search, gradually sifting the excellent from the moderately good and the worthless. Experience was certainly our best teacher.

As public schools continued to get worse, home-schooling became more common, and parents began coming to us for advice about teaching at home. In offering ideas and suggestions, we often discussed the need for a comprehensive directory of materials. One evening, after a couple had left with an armload of borrowed books and many pages of notes, Jean said to me, "No one else is doing it. Why don't you?"

I laughed, but she was serious, and the idea grew on me.

Even after teaching at home for more than ten years, we knew of relatively few families teaching at home. For years we knew nothing about the growing number of home-school newsletters and support groups. Guessing that the finished book would be about a hundred pages, and would take a month or two to finish, I began making notes. I wrote to publishers, government agencies, and the few home-school organizations I knew about. My notes grew. After eight months of researching, evaluating, and selecting, I had compiled nearly 240 pages of sources, resources, organizations, and publications. This was another period of very low income for us, so we decided to finance the publication by selling some of the listed items ourselves. After considering scores of titles, I finally called my book *The First Home-School Catalogue* — because that's what it was, the very first of its kind. I typed it on an ancient Royal and put illustrations in with Glue-Stick. I made fifty copies of the book on a photocopier and had covers printed. Jean and I collated the pages on our kitchen table, bound them, glued on the covers, and had the books trimmed at a print shop. In the spring of 1982, I mailed a few review copies, ran two small ads, and waited.

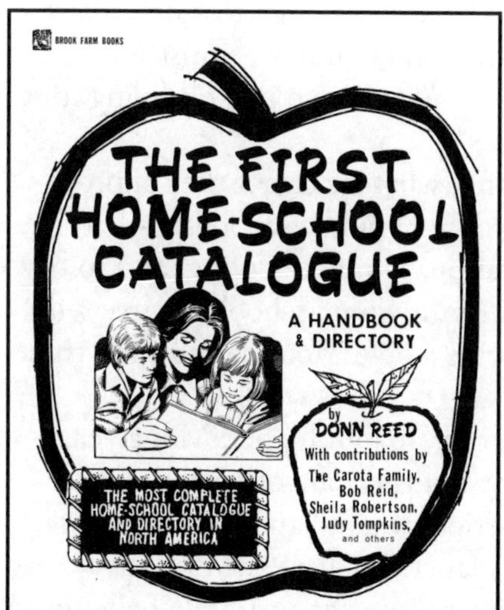

The response more than paid me for all my time and work. *The First Home-School Catalogue* seemed to be a welcome addition to the home-school movement. It was a very crude book, with no professional expertise whatsoever, but no one mentioned that, nor the many faults and serious omissions of which I was very aware. Orders for *The First Home-School Catalogue* came from all the Canadian provinces, from nearly all of the United States, and even from Spain, Greece,

Puerto Rico, Japan, Indonesia, and many other countries, and were quickly followed by enthusiastic letters of appreciation — "Thanks for the information," "Great," "Loved it."

"I like it very much," wrote John Holt. "A wonderful venture." *Mother Earth News* said its "listings, honest reviews, and advice ... should be invaluable to any home-schooling parent."

I was very happy with the positive response, but felt the high praise had been earned more by my intention than by an actual accomplishment. Almost immediately, I began planning extensive additions, revisions, and improvements. I published the second edition in 1986.

I had planned to call the next edition *The Second Home-School Catalogue,* but by then two other resource guides had been published (one in 1985, the other in 1986), each claiming to be the first; so, in weak self-defense, I kept my original title. It's true that imitation can be flattering, but an omission of polite acknowledgment reduces its sincerity.

The changing needs of our four children, the many new products available, and questions and suggestions from readers have all kept me searching and evaluating. Most home-school services and organizations freely exchange ideas and information, but, as in many growing movements, a few have become very competitive. Many new organizations have begun, most of them providing real and needed services, but a few apparently are trying to displace others. A few reviewers of books and other materials for home-schoolers, relying for a large part of their income on advertisers, praise and recommend everything sent to them, even when the products are contradictory in philosophy or purpose, sometimes without fully examining the material being reviewed. "He who praises everybody," wrote James Boswell, "praises nobody."

Jean and I believe learning materials should be fun, challenging, constructive, informative, and relevant to steady mental growth. We depend on orders from customers to continue the publication of this source book, but we absolutely will not sell or recommend any item that does not meet our criteria. This book lists a few items with which we don't agree, and you can't buy them from us, but we don't mind telling you where you can buy them if you want them. We also recommend many items we don't sell, sometimes because they are available only from other suppliers, sometimes because we can't give you as low a price as other suppliers can.

As you'll see, we have strong opinions. Whether you agree or disagree with us, you'll always know where we stand, and will not be misled by indiscriminate praise and false "objectivity." We want to make a living, but we want to make it honestly.

Most people who are not home-schooling, whether or not they approve of it, assume that its goals are similar to those of public schooling — to prepare young people for jobs or careers or further education, to make a living, and to be relatively good citizens of the society in which they live. Many home-schoolers agree with those goals, but believe that education at home will provide a better foundation than the public schools can.

We are among the many others who want to reach further, to aim higher. Money-earning skills are certainly useful and perhaps even necessary, but there are other skills of far greater importance. This is, and will continue to be, a period of rapid and radical change — in society, in government, and in the ecology of our planet. We have the duty, as parents and educators, to help our children prepare to meet those changes and challenges creatively and responsibly, and to help them develop skills and attitudes with which they can make positive contributions to the world. The ability to evaluate, to make responsible judgments, to resolve conflicts peacefully, and to create and maintain strong families will be of much more worth to our children and to the world than degrees in business management, welding, or engineering.

Of equal importance, we want our children to be happy now, as children. Childhood is important in and of itself; it shouldn't be spent only in preparation for adulthood.

In selecting learning tools and materials — to recommend, to sell, or to use ourselves — we always try to keep these objectives in mind — to find kits, books, models, and other learning materials that help us define and develop more fully the values and skills we believe are needed for happy, purposeful, creative lives, as children and as adults.

We hope you find this book useful. We welcome personal correspondence with all our readers. If you have any questions, comments, or suggestions, please write.

Donn and Jean Reed
Brook Farm, 1991

Are you feeling uncertain about your ability to homeschool? Does the idea of teaching your child to read make your stomach feel queasy? Do your poor high school algebra grades haunt you? Relax! Uncertainty in beginning a new challenge is normal. It's all right for you to learn right along with your children. As you read through our book you'll see how we met a variety of challenges and resolved various problems, and you'll find other books that will help you find the best way for your family to meet the challenges and adventures encountered when you and your children learn at home. Oh, yes, you'll learn too!

We too began with many doubts and fears, great expectations, and many more questions than answers. We had no models to follow. Neither our parents nor our own education had given us role models or patterns to follow, though both had given us examples we had no wish to emulate. Our goal was to instill in our children a lifelong love of learning, as well as the confidence in their own abilities to work and live in whatever manner they might desire, and to be people capable of making constructive contributions to the world around them.

Homeschooling can work for you. It worked for us. After twenty-four years of homeschooling, our last child took wing and left home. Do we wish we had done some things differently? Certainly — we were not perfect parents. We learned through the years by our mistakes as well as our successes. Was our homeschooling experience a success? Yes. All four kids have been off on their own for a number of years, some to college, some to work; some following lifelong dreams and others pursuing new interests.

Would we do it again? **Absolutely!**

Jean Reed
Brook Farm, 2000 and again in 2009

WHY WE TEACH AT HOME

When we were expecting our first baby, in 1966, there was very little literature about natural birthing. We had read enough to know that we wanted an undrugged birth, but we took for granted the "necessity" of birth in a hospital. All we asked was permission for me to be present during the delivery.

"Oh, no," the doctor said, "we have enough problems without having fainting husbands all over the floor."

So Jean and I decided, tentatively, to have the baby at home. (For the complete story see "Our Way" in "Birthing, Babies, and Parenting.") We studied everything we could find on the subject. Consequently, all four children were born at home. Cathy was born in a little log cabin in northern Vermont, forty miles from the nearest hospital. Karen was born in 1968, in our home, with six feet of snow drifted outside the windows. Susan was born in 1970 and Derek in 1972, both in a log cabin in the mountainous Central Interior of British Columbia, also forty miles from the nearest hospital.

Active fatherhood — that is, participating as a full partner in parenting — has many rewards, but one of the greatest is hearing that first little cry of "Hello" and cradling the new son or daughter even before he or she is fully born.

Jean nursed each of the babies for at least a year. For the first six weeks or more, we never put the babies down or left them alone; we always held them, carried them, and cuddled them. They never woke up crying, wondering where they — or we — were.

"It's good for them to cry," several neighbors and relatives told us. "It develops their lungs." Others told us, "You give them too much attention. It isn't good for them. They'll become too dependent on you."

We thought about these comments, but not in the way others may have wished. Babies *are* born dependent on their parents. They coo and gurgle when they are happy. They cry for attention when something is not right from *their* perspective. We always felt that our babies cried for a reason, and although we may not have understood why, their unhappiness was sufficient reason to do what we could to remedy the situation. Our convenience was not an issue.

The babies slept with us, despite the many warnings (from people who had never tried it) that "You'll roll on the baby in your sleep!" It never happened, of course.

When Cathy became hungry during the night, Jean had only to turn over, still half-asleep, help the baby find her nipple, and doze off again. No fumbling for the light switch, no grumbling at being awakened, no crying, no frustration.

There was only one instance when it didn't quite work — that is, not right away. I woke up enough to hear Cathy's murmur of hunger change to a cry of indignation, and I turned on the bedside light to see why Jean wasn't feeding her. Jean, still asleep, was trying with great determination to put her nipple into Cathy's ear. (A reader of *Nurturing Magazine,* in which part of this story appeared, wrote me, "Ah, the old nipple-in-the-ear trick — I've done it myself many times!")

The objections and fears many people have about home-birth are not greatly different from their feelings about home-school: "Something will go wrong," "You need the experts," "You're sheltering them too much," and so on.

Our main reason for having home-birth was that we loved our children (yes, even before they were born), and we wanted them to have the best start in life. We began teaching them at home for the same reason.

In education, as with birth, it was the narrow-mindedness and insensitivity of the "experts" and "trained professionals" that led us to realize we could probably do much better without their help.

We are confirmed do-it-yourselfers in many areas of life — childbirth, house-building, food production, etc. — and so we thought about teaching our children at home, but didn't have any definite reason for doing so, and assumed that contact with other children would be enjoyable and beneficial.

We had read some of John Holt's books (*How Children Fail, How Children Learn,* etc.) and various other books about education, but we thought that small rural schools might somehow have escaped the negative attitudes and academic failings most of the books described.

We were wrong. In nearly every instance, our children returned from school much poorer than they had been when they left home. The girls had learned to read and to enjoy books at least a year before entering school. Cathy and Susan soon learned, in the public schools, that reading was a very serious chore; they not only lost interest in reading, but actually lost a great deal of reading ability. Cathy became ill-mannered and bigoted. Susan developed a stutter. Far from being "broadened" by social contacts, they were coerced into becoming very narrow and intolerant.

Cathy had always enjoyed books, from the time she was old enough to look at them. Before she was two, she spent hours with her favorites, studying minute details in the pictures and asking us about the details in the pictures and the letters. By the time she was six, she was entirely familiar with the alphabet, basic phonics, shapes, and colors, and seemed to have an intuitive grasp of elementary psychology (but without knowing any of its jargon). She enjoyed working with us in the garden, the barn, and the kitchen. We talked about school, and decided to give it a try.

Each morning, we drove to the corner, where Cathy boarded the school bus and rode to the two-room schoolhouse twenty miles away. In the afternoon, we met her at the corner to bring her home.

Cathy liked school, she told us during the first weeks. She had many friends and she liked the teacher. Each day, she was eager to meet the bus, and came home with excited stories of new games and new friends.

In October she began sucking and chewing her lower lip, until it was always red and swollen. She stopped reading, and had no interest in books. She became bossy and whiny. The redness of her lower lip spread down toward her chin.

Cathy's teacher told us she hadn't noticed any problems. Cathy insisted there was nothing wrong; she got along with the other children, she still liked her teacher, and the work was very easy, even if a little boring. She continued to chew her lower lip, and often screamed at us and gave us belligerent orders. The other children no longer looked forward to the time she came home from school. Donn and I were puzzled and concerned, and weren't sure what we should do about the situation.

During the two-week Christmas vacation, Cathy stopped chewing her lip, and the redness almost disappeared from her lip and chin. Toward the end of her vacation, she looked into a few of her favorite books. She became more pleasant to live with, more friendly and agreeable and cooperative — as she had always been before she started school.

When she returned from the first day back at school after vacation, her lower lip was red and swollen. She refused to pick her coat up from the floor, and she was snappy and bossy.

We never returned her to that school. For the rest of that winter and through the following summer, she occasionally looked through her books, but had no interest in reading. We left her alone, and didn't try to give her any "school" work.

We moved, and in the fall Cathy entered a different school in the second grade. Despite having "missed" half of the first grade, she had no difficulties with second-grade work. Her teacher was pleasant, competent, and understanding. Cathy finished the school year with high marks and still had a pleasant personality. We concluded that the first year must have been an unfortunate exception.

Karen, like Cathy, had learned basic reading and math skills long before she entered formal schooling. Her first-grade teacher was one of the most loving and dedicated teachers our children ever encountered. Karen's first-grade experience was nearly everything we thought public education should be — a continuation of skills already learned and the introduction of new subjects and new concepts, both academically and socially. We could see Karen growing, rapidly and happily.

Cathy's third-grade teacher was often hoarse from yelling at her students. One of her favorite punishments for any misbehaving boy was to have him sit on her lap, making him the unhappy object of his classmates' coarse jokes and teasing.

What happens in the mind of a child for whom a customary act of affection becomes a dreaded punishment and humiliation?

I have vivid memories of visiting Cathy's class the day the school held Halloween parties. I went to Karen's class to deliver treats for their party and saw happy, costumed children having a good time. I knew Cathy's class would be different, but I was still unprepared for what I encountered. Her class was the only one in the whole school not having a party or wearing costumes. This teacher did not celebrate Halloween due to her religious beliefs, and therefore she would not permit her class to join in the festivities. I had no quarrel with this teacher's religion, or with her right to choose what to celebrate, but I felt that as a public employee, she had no right to force her personal decision on thirty children of varying beliefs. When I knocked on the classroom door, I could see through the window that the teacher was yelling. She beckoned to me to come in and pointed to a desk in the back of the room, all with hardly a pause in her ranting at one of the boys. I was dumbfounded.

The sound of the teacher's voice, her imperious stance, and the simple act of pointing to the desk without saying a word made me, even as an adult, cringe and want to disappear. I felt myself tumble emotionally back through time to my school days, gradually getting smaller and smaller. I sat at a child's desk stunned and intimidated. What was she doing to the minds of the children who spent five days a week with her?

As it happened, Cathy was a good student, academically and socially. She disliked the teacher's screaming and bullying, but was relieved (as we were) that she was never the object of the teacher's tirades. We felt it was a very unhealthy environment, whether or not Cathy was learning anything positive or useful. And she wasn't.

Given a writing assignment, Cathy wrote:

> One day I was sweeping the floor. I swept the edge of the counter, and I swept a spray can out. It said Spray broom. I sprayed the broom. The broom said Hi who are you? I'm Cathy I said will you come to the zoo with me? Of course I will I am your friend. So we went to the zoo. We saw a lion and it was loose. We told someone at the zoo. The end.

Not too bad, really. I know many adults who couldn't do as well. But it was much less than we thought should have been achieved in thirty hours a week, four weeks a month, nine months a year, for over two years.

Even worse, Cathy was bored.

"What did you do in school today, Cathy?"

"Oh, nothing. Just more second-grade work. I did it all last year. When will I start learning something new?"

From asking that question to becoming an eight-year-old dropout, with full parental approval and encouragement, was a very short step.

A dropout. No education? How would she get anywhere in life?

Cathy began "going to school" at home. Not yet free of our own educational conditioning, we eased ourselves into the formal teaching business by subscribing to a correspondence course from Calvert School. Each weekday, from nine in the morning until noon, Jean was Cathy's teacher. In those three hours, they easily covered more than two daily lessons, including arithmetic, geography, Greek mythology, art, literature, spelling, history, science, and composition.

At the same time, Jean was raising and teaching Susan and Derek. Karen was doing well in first grade in the public school. (I was taking life easy as an edgerman in a sawmill.)

As a hobby, Cathy studied dinosaurs and fossils, and this was only one of many areas in which we found Cathy was often the teacher and we were the pupils.

Ten weeks after leaving the public school, Cathy wrote:

> A JOURNEY TO THE PAST
>
> I found a time machine. I am going back to 120 million years ago. Dinosaurs roamed the earth and volcanoes erupted a lot. They liked it warm and wet and it never snowed. I saw a Stegosaurus, like a duck; it ate plants. It didn't frighten me but it was about 11 feet tall and four feet wide. I rode on a Triceratops, a three-horned dinosaur. I saw a Tyrannosaurus. I ran back to the time machine and I went to another part of the jungle. I saw a Teranodon, a bird without teeth. I had a ride on it. It took me to an Ankylosaurus and I took the Ankylosaurus home with me.

Did you notice she missed the "p" in "pteranodon"? You wouldn't miss it, of course; and I just looked in my dictionary for the spelling. But how much can you expect of an eight-year-old kid, only halfway through third grade? (If you missed it, don't feel bad. Microsoft Word's spell-check did too.)

In spite of a few good experiences with the public schools, we were finally beginning to learn our own lesson. For the next three years we taught all four of our children at home. Then Cathy wanted to try public school again, to be able to spend more time with others her age. After much discussion, we reluctantly agreed to let her try. Her teacher proved to be the second of the best teachers our children ever had in public school, and we never regretted Cathy's year with her.

For the times when the girls did decide to attend public school, we developed the policy that if the kids started the year in public school they were to stay all the way through the year unless we or they felt they were in harm's way, physically (which we felt was unlikely at that time), psychologically, or emotionally. We also discussed with the kids the fact that if they were in public school they had to follow their rules even if/when they made no sense.

The next year was quite different. Cathy's English and history teacher, with a master's degree in education, couldn't spell, punctuate, or construct a proper sentence. He taught his students to use colons and semicolons interchangeably. He taught them a punctuation device he called "dot-dot-dot," and met my objection with the explanation that the word "ellipsis" would be too difficult for eighth-graders to remember. He taught that capitalization of the first letter in a sentence is a matter of personal preference.

I haunted him, two or three times a week, after school hours and occasionally at class time, but wasn't surprised that it did no good. He wasn't overly anxious to discuss his methods, although he tried to assure me that his own training had been quite thorough, and that he certainly knew more about English and teaching than anyone without formal training in those subjects.

He did ask if I'd ever been an English teacher.

"No," I answered and thought to myself, "I may have a lot of skeletons in my closet, but that isn't one of them." I did admit I had done some teaching in a related field and even had a piece of paper from a university saying I was qualified to do so. The thought crossed my mind that a lot of certificates are written with more oink than ink, and even thermometers have a lot of degrees.

Cathy and her class were told to find Rio Blanco on a map of Brazil. She spent over an hour searching through her school atlas, our own atlas (which is better), and the Encyclopedia Britannica. Failing to find Rio Blanco anywhere, Cathy was finally convinced that the teacher had made another spelling mistake, and he later admitted it (with a shrug, and not seeming embarrassed). Cathy had learned a lesson, but not the one her teacher had intended. That wasn't the only hour of her life wasted by a teacher's careless spelling or sloppy handwriting.

I made a list of words the teacher consistently misspelled on assignment sheets and showed the list to the principal.

"What grade level," I asked, "should have complete mastery of the spelling of these words?"

He looked the list over and said, "Third grade. A fourth-grader who didn't know these words would be considered slow."

I said it seemed to be a great waste of time for the teacher, for his students, and for me — the latter because I often needed to correct the teacher's assignments before allowing Cathy to work on them.

The principal insisted I must be mistaken about the teacher's having misspelled the words, and suggested that Cathy had copied them incorrectly. I showed him the teacher's assignment sheets. He suggested I take my complaints directly to the teacher. I told him I had done so, several times, and was less than satisfied. He said he would have to side with his teachers, on the assumption that they would not be teachers if they didn't know what they were doing.

A few days later, the principal wrote me a letter (so he could put a carbon copy in his office files), saying that the teacher we had discussed (but whom he didn't name) was a Trained Professional (his capital letters), and therefore must know what he was doing. The Trained Professional's qualification to teach, he went on to say, was proven by the fact that he had been hired by the school board.

Mark Twain once remarked that God made a fool for practice, and then made school boards. That's a harsh judgment, and may be extreme. Was the mistake Twain's or God's? As far as I know, neither was a Trained Professional, except that Twain had a license to pilot a riverboat.

Jesus told the sick man to pick up his bed and walk. Henry David Thoreau advised his contemporaries to throw down their beds and run. Anyone who is only a Trained Professional — that is, who has nothing more to offer than his Trained Professionalism — has little chance of doing either.

Since that time, we have taught our children at home and have seen no reason to try the public schools again, although the girls did choose to go for a year now and then.

The kids have all been active, according to their ages and interests, in ball games, 4-H, youth groups, dances, overnight slumber parties, national exchange trips, and jobs in town. They have been concerned about global problems, such as hunger, human rights, and the death penalty.

School at home wasn't always easy, but whenever problems arose, we tried to treat them not as interruptions of our education, but as parts of it. In facing problems and working with them, we have learned more about ourselves, each other, and the world.

We're increasingly convinced that education at home has made our children happier, healthier, and stronger — physically, mentally, and spiritually. Our children have remained bright, curious, and creative — and, we hope, have helped us to remain so, too.

WHY THE MOVEMENT HAS GROWN, AND WHY IT WILL CONTINUE TO GROW

More than ten years ago [in 1984, so 25 years ago now] the United States National Commission on Excellence in Education said, "For the first time in the history of our country, the educational skills of one generation will not surpass, will not equal, will not even approach those of their parents."

Unfortunately, tragically, this statement is as applicable today as it was years ago, with too many professional educators and public schools still trying to figure out what to do about it.

"To be culturally literate is to possess the basic information needed to thrive in the modern world," says E.D. Hirsch Jr. in his best-selling book *Cultural Literacy: What Every American Needs to Know.* As evidence that far too many school students are not learning this necessary knowledge, Hirsch offers the steadily declining verbal scores on SAT tests and reports of the National Assessment of Educational Progress that student knowledge in key areas is shrinking.

A 1988 special edition of *Instructor,* a magazine for public school teachers, says, "Unfortunately, two recent surveys may back Hirsch up. The National Endowment for the Humanities assessed the study of history, literature, and languages in the nation's public schools and reported that 'America's elementary and secondary schools are failing to teach students about their shared past and culture.'

"In a related study [the article continues], Diane Ravitch, professor of history and education at Columbia University, and Chester E. Finn Jr., the U.S. Assistant Secretary of Education for Research and Improvement, analyzed a 1986 assessment of 7,812 high school juniors and gave them failing marks on their knowledge of literature and history."

This is also true for other subjects (and even President Bush recognized it, not that he improved the situation), and it is as equally applicable to the Canadian school system as it is to U.S. schools. I have tutored a number of students and been amazed by the low standard of work that is considered acceptable to pass a test or to proceed to the next grade level. I find it scandalous that the billions of dollars spent on education produce such mediocre standards and ultimately handicap many young people. I have never figured out why those in charge of the schools think that spending more money on the facilities will make a difference. It's not the modern buildings or labs that will improve the system but the teachers and the methods they use.

The public schools throughout North America are failing, even by their own standards, which most critics agree are misguided and poorly conceived at best. Too many children are being labeled "learning-disabled" and put into special remedial classes with "high-interest, low-vocabulary" readers and textbooks. Too many tenth-graders are reading on a third-grade level. How did they get to the tenth grade without learning to read?

The past decade has seen increased publicity in national newspapers and educational magazines about North America's failing school systems. I'm sure you have noticed that even the experts can't agree that the No Child Left Behind program or the mandatory testing of recent years will make a significant difference.

Yes, there are some good schools in existence. Yes, there are some excellent teachers in the public school system. Yes, there are students doing exceptionally well in the public school system. But do you want to trust your child to this system that is openly confessing its massive failure to educate, that is witnessing an increase in drug usage and violence? Many parents have decided they can't wait any longer. As a result, there has been growth in homeschooling every year.

More and more people are teaching their own children in their homes. Home-schooling families are well over a million strong and growing. Some parents have no particular quarrel with the public schools, but simply feel that children shouldn't be taken from the family at an early age, if at all. A reason given more frequently is the steadily declining level of academic instruction in the public schools.

More and more parents are no longer accepting the weak promises and weaker excuses of the schools. They want their children to receive a proper education, even if it means removing them from the schools.

> "Dear Mr. Reed,
>
> "I hope you receive this and are still in business! I saw your ad in an issue of *Nurturing Magazine* that I borrowed from a friend. Today is the last day of school for our three girls. Yesterday, they brought home the year's "work" — what a pathetic example of wasted time! Six pages of a notebook for the entire year's effort for science; maybe twelve pages for social studies. The story my sixth-grade student wrote had no punctuation or proper grammar. I have told the girls of my dissatisfaction. They like the social aspect of school — but I have to look out for their welfare. I don't feel they are getting an education that will help them in years to come. They need something better!
>
> "Yours truly, ..."

> "Jean,
>
> "I'm desperate and frightened. The school wants to pass my son on to the sixth grade ... but I know he can't read well enough. They don't want to hold him back because of his self-esteem. I think he would feel better about himself if he were given the time to learn the basics before going on, but the school doesn't want to do it. Will you help me get started with homeschooling?"

From a conversation with the mother of a public school student who will remain in the public school: "Jean, will you please tutor my daughter? She doesn't really know her basic math. The teacher allows the class to use calculators in the classroom, but I don't think my daughter really knows her multiplication tables or how to do long division, and she is going on to high school next year."

Not very many years ago, a grade level lower than 70 was failing. In most schools today, any grade over 60, and sometimes 55 or even 50, is accepted as a passing grade — and often that "passing" grade is achieved by comparison with a class average, rather than with the overall requirements of a course. If the class average is 50, a passing grade need be no more than 25.

I find this alarming. As parents we have every right to expect better standards, but it isn't usually feasible to change a school policy. In the past it was common for teachers to defend the system, but with increasing frequency, I hear from teachers that they have to spend a great deal of time each year working to bring students up to last year's grade level before they can begin to teach them at their current grade level. Here are two increasingly common statements I hear from teachers: "If I weren't a public school teacher, I would teach my children at home," and "Now that I have school-age children of my own, I'm leaving my job to teach them at home."

Most school suppliers' catalogs have a high percentage of "high-interest, low-vocabulary" readers — books written on a reading level several years below the grade for which they are intended. In such catalogs, notations such as "Interest level, grades 11-12; reading level, grades 3-4" are common. There has always been some need for such books, especially in teaching remedial reading to the few students who somehow got behind, and in teaching adult illiterates, but now the failure of the public schools is making it necessary for nearly half of all textbooks, in nearly all subjects, to be written with "high interest" and "low vocabulary."

There are numerous reports of high school students not knowing the basic facts (e.g., not knowing that the United States fought against Japan in World War II, or not knowing who won the war). And it doesn't stop with the high schools. From speaking with college professors and from my own reading, I have learned that colleges are dumbing down freshman courses and offering remedial courses to incoming students just so they can keep up the flow of incoming students and the revenue they generate.

College students have similar problems. A journalism student at USC didn't know if Germany had been an enemy or an ally of the U.S. during World War II. A junior at UCLA thought Toronto was a city in Italy; another guessed that Stalin was the U.S. president just before Roosevelt; and another thought Lenin was a drummer with the Beatles before Ringo Starr.

"We have a situation," said the director of the U.S. National Council for Geographic Education, "where Johnny not only doesn't know how to read or add, he doesn't even know where he is."

A newspaper article written by a college graduate reported, "The body of a man found in the Saint John River last week is still trying to be identified."

A newspaper editor showed me a letter he had received from a recent high school graduate asking for a job as a "sprots writter."

What's the good news about public schools? They'll still take a child off your hands for six to eight hours a day year after year, and are much cheaper than babysitters.

Learning problems frequently come from problem teachers who seek to excuse their inability to convey knowledge to their students by saying the students are hyperactive, retarded, disturbed, or disabled, or — more recently — have Attention Deficit Disorder.

One of the students in an adult literacy class I taught some years ago was a man with a measured IQ of 50. Previous teachers had tried briefly to teach him, but were quick to decide that he was incapable of learning, and therefore not worth the time it would take to work with him. He was living away from home, and the high point of each day for him was "writing" — dictating — a letter to his mother. One day, I typed the letter he had just dictated to me, then asked him to read it to me. None of the symbols meant anything to him, although I'd been working with him for several weeks. I pointed out the letters that spelled MOM, naming them and sounding them, then pronouncing the word again. "This is the word that means *your mom,*" I told him. He repeated the sounds and the word after me, lovingly, wonderingly, studying the letters. I moved his finger, tracing the shapes of the letters as I said them. Then I guided his hand, with a pencil in it, to draw the letters. He printed **M O M** over and over for hours. With that word as his personal key, he progressed from total, "hopeless" illiteracy to a sixth-grade reading *and writing* level in less than six months. He could read comic books, magazines, newspapers, street signs, a driver's manual, and thousands of books. The psychologists and educators who had pronounced him incapable of learning decided their tests had been wrong, and were baffled when his IQ still tested at 50. Retarded? Disturbed? Attention Deficit? When I read those weak excuses for the schools' failures, I have a definite Belief Deficit.

Over the years we've heard many more disturbing tales from parents who took their diagnosed ADD children out of school, gave them time and attention, and discovered the problem wasn't the children, but the system.

Teachers today are rated as much for their accuracy and punctuality in keeping attendance records as they are for their achievements in providing an environment in which students can learn. In most cases, the teachers themselves are not at fault, at least when they begin their careers. They have high ideals and higher hopes, but they are soon beaten down by the quasi-scientific theories of statisticians and pompous educational psychologists who can't get past the first four letters of analysis.

An article in the national home-school magazine *Growing Without Schooling* (December 1983) told of a Minnesota judge who ruled that a mother's actual ability to teach is unimportant if she isn't legally "qualified." The mother had offered her daughter's educational progress as evidence of the effectiveness of her teaching, but the judge ruled that if the mother doesn't have legal certification, then her being a good teacher in fact is irrelevant.

In the same state, according to an article in *Learning Magazine,* several teachers who had been out on strike were given up to thirty-three credits needed for the renewal of their teaching certificates, "on the theory that the teachers learned communication and political organization skills during the walkout."

Time reported in October 1983 that "when one-third of Houston's public school teachers took a competency exam last spring, some sixty percent failed the reading section."

A study titled "What's Happening in Teacher Testing," released in 1987 by Chester Finn Jr. of the U.S. Department of Education, says 28 percent of the applicants to teacher education programs are being rejected, and that 17 percent of teacher graduates who apply for teaching licenses are being turned down. In spite of this, says the report, passing scores are still set so low that many "incompetents" are being licensed and subsequently hired. And do you suppose it's changed during the intervening years?

Joseph Weizenbaum, a professor of computer science at MIT, in an interview published in *Science Digest* (August 1983), said, "[F]ully half of all math and science teachers are operating on emergency certificates." That is, when there aren't enough qualified instructors to go around, unearned certificates are given to teachers whose training is in completely different and often unrelated fields.

The same school authorities who issue these "emergency certificates" would undoubtedly scoff at mail-order diploma mills that will sell a phony Ph.D. for a few hundred dollars. Is there really any difference?

Although the quotes above are dated, the problems still exist and are still unresolved. I believe the increased publicity about inadequate schools and incompetent teachers is helping some very dedicated people within the system to make changes, but slowly. How long can you wait?

It's probably still true, as we've been told for so long, that high school graduates earn more money than dropouts, but it's not always because they're better educated. It's often because employers also have been taught that there is magic in the graduates' parchment coupons with the Olde Englishe lettering. Indeed, a few decades ago, there may have been some magic there, but today most of it is no more than clumsy legerdemain.

Thank goodness homeschoolers are no longer oddities. An increasing number of homeschooled children are now young adults. I have read their stories in *Home Education Magazine* and *Growing Without Schooling* (no longer in print but available through FUN Books: www.fun-books.com/gws.htm) and met many young adults who have had school at home and gone on to college or into the workforce or created their own businesses. They are a very impressive group of self-assured young people. To the best of my knowledge these grown homeschoolers have not met with admissions or employment obstacles they could not overcome. As with everyone else, there are sometimes problems, but school at home has only extremely rarely been one of them, and that is rapidly changing. Colleges and employers are losing faith in the fancy pieces of paper given to those who spend their years in public education. More than ever, who you are and what you can do are what matters.

Public schools teach students how to pass tests — by memorizing facts and formulas, by guessing, or by cheating. If most teachers did not announce tests days and weeks in advance, then tell their students what to study in preparation, and even what questions to expect, and on what pages they should look for the answers, and then just as often give a "pre-test" for practice, many more students would fail. Even with all this rigorous coaching, most students would still fail if the test were unexpectedly postponed for two weeks, during which time everything would be forgotten again. It's only by such hocus-pocus that too many teachers are able to help most students "pass" their tests; the marks are duly recorded, and the year is considered a success. Next year, two or three months will be spent in "review" of last year's subjects before a new field or higher level can be introduced.

Sixty, forty, even twenty years ago, "average" students learned more and retained more than most of today's top students. "But we have more subjects to cover," protest the teachers. That's true, but so what? The larger range of subjects supposedly being presented is no excuse for dim mediocrity in all of them.

The academic failures of public schools are unimportant beside their much greater failure to provide an environment in which children can grow in moral strength and integrity. Most parents, whether or not they consider teaching at home, are worried about drugs, violence, promiscuity, and teenage pregnancy.

Several magazines and newspapers have repeated a comparison of two surveys of public school teachers:

In 1940, the most serious problems they had to deal with were talking without permission, chewing gum, making noise, running in the halls, getting out of turn in line, and wearing improper clothing.

In 1980, their major concerns were rape, burglary, robbery, assault, arson, bombings, murder, suicide, vandalism, extortion, drug and alcohol abuse, gang warfare, pregnancies, abortions, and venereal disease.

These "problems" are the fault of society in general, not of the schools and teachers, but they are not doing enough to change them.

I find it interesting that not one of the problems mentioned in either survey was academic. It's 2009. Have these problems been addressed? Are any of them under control? How many of these will you or your children have to deal with if you teach your children at home?

On an administrative level, the schools try to produce obedient, unquestioning citizens, good consumers, and productive (but not necessarily creative) workers.

On a social level — admittedly usually not through deliberate design — the schools promote religious intolerance, racial bigotry, drug abuse, sexual promiscuity, lying, cheating, emotional insincerity, philosophical skepticism, fake sophistication, and intellectual apathy.

When we began to homeschool, my parents were firmly opposed to our decision to do so. My father wrote to us, "Your lessons on morality are fine for your homeschool, but they have no validity in the real world."

Obviously we disagreed, but his statement seems to reflect the opinions of a disproportionate segment of society. Corporate advertising, popular music, television, and the majority of public schools are bombarding our society with the dictum "If it feels good, do it."

"You can't shelter your children forever," the self-appointed experts tell us. "They'll have to be exposed to these things sooner or later."

That's true, we answered; we can't shelter them forever — nor do we want to. We just want to shelter them until they are strong enough to face these issues by themselves without being overwhelmed by them. Most adults would have great difficulty in resisting a daily barrage of sex, drugs, and violence. How, then, can we expect our children — who are still learning to examine, evaluate, and judge — to put such "problems" into their proper perspective?

A distressed parent recently explained to me that she was taking her child out of public school because of notes her daughter had brought home from her teacher. These notes told the children to beware of local pedophiles, giving personal details and descriptions of their cars. Her child became frightened of all men with blue cars. I do not believe we should have to define the word *pedophile* to our six- and seven-year-old children or that they should live with that type of fear unnecessarily.

Such issues and problems are facts of life, particularly in the cities, and our children need to be aware of them and to be prepared to deal with them, but they don't need — and should not have — daily or even frequent exposure to them. Such problems are symptoms of an unhealthy society, a society with an illness that, we hope and believe, isn't fatal, but is certainly dangerous and highly contagious.

"As any parent knows, teaching character is a difficult task," William J. Bennett, former Secretary of Education, told the National Press Club in Washington, D.C., on March 27, 1985. "But it is a crucial task because we want all our children to be not only healthy, happy, and successful, but decent, strong, and good. None of this happens automatically; there is no genetic transmission of virtue. It takes conscious, committed effort. … Not all teachers are parents, but all parents are teachers, the indispensable teachers. And, as teachers, parents always have had the first and largest responsibility for educating their children.

... And in some cases parents discover that their children are unlearning in school the lessons they have learned at home."

To protect our children from the harmful influences of a chaotic society until they are better able to handle them is not only our right, but our duty and responsibility — even if it means (although of course it doesn't) that they receive no academic education at all.

Hardly a day goes by without an article about home-schooling in a major newspaper or magazine. Publications that promote and celebrate family closeness are becoming much more numerous. There are now hundreds of home-school newsletters, organizations, and support groups.

Professional educators are beginning to realize that all their training and certification are not helping them teach, and that most parents could educate their own children far better, and in less time, than the schools can. The teachers may have to find other work — or throw out their schedules and formulas and remedial classes and get back to real teaching.

Drawing from our experience with our own children, the multitude of books with homeschooling stories, and the many articles in homeschooling publications and some national publications that have appeared in the last five years, it is now possible to make some general comparisons between public and home education. I clearly see that learning basic skills at home is done in less time, leaving more time for developing other interests, which creates a broader spectrum of learning. Learning at home is individualized, leading to a higher retention of material covered because the material is usually more creatively presented and related across the curriculum, linked to individual interests and to life itself. Homeschooling parents generally make a strong effort to involve their children with the community and activities outside the home, giving homeschooled children the ability to relate well to all ages (and not just their peer groups). Many homeschoolers are going on to college, and according to the Home School Legal Defense Association, are generally scoring higher on the SATs and other tests than the average student in public school. Other homeschoolers have created their own businesses or followed their creative interests into the arts. Best of all, I see children developing with a deeper sense of themselves as individuals; maturing into responsible, caring adults; and pursuing their own goals with a great respect for those around them and the world at large.

"WE WOULD BETTER WAIT AND SEE"

"We would better wait and see," our provincial Minister of Education was quoted as saying, referring to the possibility of closing the public schools if 3,000 janitors, secretaries, and bus drivers decided to strike.

A staff writer for the *Telegraph-Journal* of Saint John, New Brunswick, went on to tell his readers about the Treasury Board's efforts to ensure that many non-teaching employees would be forced to work in the event of a strike: "The board has been only successful in having 132 non-teaching employees designated essential."

Did he think the board should have been more than successful? Wasn't success enough? Perhaps the adverb was meant to be an adjective, to modify the number of employees, "only 132," rather than to diminish the board's success.

The 132 employees whom the Treasury Board designated as "essential" should have been congratulated. Apparently, it wasn't their jobs that were essential, but the 132 employees themselves. Kings, queens, prime ministers, and presidents will all be replaced someday, so even they are not essential, but the writer brought to our attention 132 people with a sinecure greater than that of the Twelve Disciples — at least in the opinion of the Treasury Board.

Part of the problem, according to the chief negotiator, was that for more than six months the Treasury Board "constantly refused to negotiate in a serious tone."

According to all of my several dictionaries, "constantly" means "happening or continuing all the time; happening repeatedly." Those Treasury Board members must have been as busy as naughty schoolboys writing their penances on the chalkboard: "We will not negotiate in a serious tone, we will not ..." and so on, over and over, for six months.

The chief negotiator didn't say that the Treasury Board had refused to negotiate, but that it had refused to do so "in a serious tone." Did the board make flippant remarks? Giggle during meetings? Make faces at non-essential employees?

"The only reason Charlie got to be Minister of Education," a neighboring farmer told me recently, "is that he sat behind me in grade school and copied all my answers."

Another question pops up constantly, in a serious tone: If the school employees, whether essential or non-essential, go out on strike, and the schools are all closed, and the students spend the day watching *Sesame Street* and cleaning their fingernails, will it make any appreciable difference in the education of tomorrow's writers, educators, and politicians?

We would better wait and see.

PERMISSION TO TEACH AT HOME

Alice began to feel very uneasy. To be sure, she had not as yet had any dispute with the Queen, but she knew that it might happen any minute. "And then," thought she, "what would become of me? They're dreadfully fond of beheading people here." — Lewis Carroll

Homeschooling is now permitted in all U.S. states and all of Canada. Requirements and conditions vary from extremely lenient to very strict, with the majority in between but leaning toward the more permissive.

Just a few years ago Donn suggested that you begin with a copy of the Education Act for your state or province, which your public library would have or be able to get. Now that homeschooling is widespread I think it's more practical to contact the nearest group, whose members will be familiar with the state or provincial laws and be able to advise you about the best way to deal with those laws. Your local group also will know if your local officials are easy to deal with, what they will expect from you, and what you can expect from them. Many groups have detailed "legal packets" with both general and specific information and suggestions. If you're unable to find local support, write or call a statewide group. The advantage of starting with a support group instead of the Education Act is that you will avoid having to interpret the legal jargon. Your local group will know with whom you should speak and how to deal with the formalities. In the last big edition of *The Home School Source Book* I had about 14 pages listing support groups by state, province, or country, and I'm sure I missed some — and I'm equally sure that there are many more groups in existence today. Today the very best place to find all that information up-to-date is on the Internet. To attempt to include a thorough listing in print would be a waste of my time and yours; this information sometimes changes rapidly, and once this book goes to the printer you would be stuck with unreliable information. The very best places to begin your search are www.nhen.org (the National Home Education Network) and www.homeedmag.com (*Home Education Magazine*). You'll find much more than you thought possible, and both of these sites are reliable and exciting places to begin your search.

You can also ask your Department of Education for a copy of all laws regarding home education, but don't get into a lengthy dialogue, and don't take the word of teachers, principals, or education officials as infallible. Sometimes they don't know the laws, but will gladly offer opinions or even guesses as if they were facts. Sometimes, they have been known to lie. (A couple in one state was told that homeschooling is allowed only in the first four grades, and another couple in the same state was told that homeschooling is allowed only after the first four grades. In fact, it's allowed there on all grade levels.)

John Holt's ***TEACH YOUR OWN,*** the only one of his books specifically about home-schooling, has many invaluable suggestions for dealing with officials and the law, as well as extensive information, with examples, about many other aspects of home-schooling. (See "Homeschooling and Education" on our website for more detail.)

Another excellent source of general information is **HOME EDUCATION PRESS,** P.O. Box 1083, Tonasket, WA 98855, which publishes the national bimonthly *Home Education Magazine* and offers a free Resource Guide. Write them or find it online at www.homeedmag.com.

The **NATIONAL HOME EDUCATION NETWORK** (NHEN), P.O. Box 1652, Hobe Sound, FL 33475, is a group representing all homeschoolers. NHEN is creating a giant data-base with listings of audio and video recordings, books, online and distance learn-ing schools, curriculum and resource distributors, e-mail lists, events, magazines and newsletters, speakers, websites, support groups, and more. A group to represent and help us all. Online at www.nhen.org; you can e-mail them at info@nhen.org.

Our Story

Two of the cardinal points in our home-schooling are that individuals are always more important than government, and that individuals can effect meaningful changes in society. Might does not make right, and we want our children to know it. We tell them that freedom is a very fragile and elusive condition. We agree with Thomas Jefferson that eternal vigilance is the price of liberty, not only in a broad, political sense, but also in our immediate, personal lives; not only against foreign governments, but against soft-drink ads, religious fanatics, and repressive forces in our own government, including a few education authorities.

If the government has particular rules and regulations regarding subjects taught or hours observed, we'll try to meet them — if such compliance doesn't interfere with the education of our children. If the government comes to us to discuss, negotiate, or offer a compromise, we're willing to listen and participate and consider. We don't want broadside confrontation with school officials. But if the government comes to us with orders and demands, as if it is right simply because it is stronger, then we resist. That which is demanded may be right, but the demand, as such, is wrong.

We are convinced — not by anyone's scripture, but by observation and reason — that teaching our own children is not merely a privilege to be granted by the government, but is an intrinsic right. Whether that right is God-given or a sine qua non of natural, universal law (not forgetting that they may be one and the same), the instruction to render unto Caesar only that which is Caesar's is completely pertinent, both literally and symbolically. As Emerson wrote in "Self-Reliance," "We cannot consent to pay for a privilege where we have intrinsic right."

We never asked for permission to teach at home. A request for permission would imply a willingness to abide by the response, whether positive or negative. The request might be denied, and then where would we be? We have no such willingness, so we usually just go about our business, and expect the government to do the same.

But people who build their home in the woods and don't put their children on the rural school bus don't blend into the woodwork, even if they dress conventionally and drive an ordinary eight-year-old car. Word gets around, although it's often like the old game of Telephone, in which the players sit in a circle and a message is whispered from one to the next and finally back to the one who began it, usually becoming considerably distorted as it passes through one head after another.

Although the following correspondence is dated, it is typical of what can be expected from educational authorities:

Office of the Superintendent of Schools
Fredericton, New Brunswick
October 27, 1980

Dear Mr. Reed:

It is my understanding that you have recently moved to this area from British Columbia. It has been brought to my attention that you have four school-age children for whom you are responsible. The Province of New Brunswick requires any person from seven to fifteen years of age inclusive to be in attendance at school. I have included the appropriate sections for your information.

59(1) In sections 59 to 66 inclusive "child" means any person from seven to fifteen years of age inclusive.

59(2) Except as provided in this section, every child shall attend school in the school selected by the school board in that school district provided for in section 5.

59(3) Where

(a) in the opinion of the Minister, a child is under efficient instruction elsewhere,

(b) a child is unable to attend school by reason of his own sickness or other unavoidable cause,

(c) the child is officially excluded from attendance under sections 45, 46, or 53,

(d) the child has completed the course prescribed for grade twelve, or

(e) the Minister certifies in writing to the school board that the child should be exempt from school attendance, the child shall not be required to attend school.

59(4) A school attendance officer shall examine every case of non-compliance with subsection (2) within the district for which he is employed.

59(5) When the examination warrants it, the school attendance officer shall notify in writing the parent of a child of the fact and the consequence of non-compliance.

59(6) Upon receipt of the notice mentioned in subsection (5), unless the child is excused from attendance as provided by this Act, the parent shall cause the child to attend school forthwith.

59(7) A parent who violates subsection (6) is guilty of an offense and on summary conviction is liable to a fine of twenty dollars for the first offense and forty dollars for each subsequent offense and in default of payment is liable to imprisonment in accordance with subsection 31 (3) of the Summary Convictions Act, or to both fine and imprisonment. 1966, c25 s.47.

Unless you receive special permission from the Minister of Education to exempt your children from the public school system, you must enroll them without further delay.

Yours truly,
Garth Hathaway

When the superintendent wrote, "It has been brought to my attention," he didn't say by whom. Certainly not by us. In these days of neighborhood watchers and satellite surveillance, there seems little need of our volunteering to the government what our intentions are.

Not knowing what kind of nut he might have to deal with, the superintendent let loose with both barrels, sections and subsections, including the penalties of fines and imprisonment for non-compliance with the rules. With the exception of 59(3) (a), "in the opinion of the Minister, a child is under efficient instruction elsewhere," there was no mention of the child receiving an education, but only of his obligation to attend school, or, rather, my obligation to cause him to do so.

The superintendent offered no arguments about the need of learning or the general advantages of dispelling ignorance, only the potential threat of losing my money or my freedom — or both — if I didn't comply without further delay.

"Thus the State never intentionally confronts a man's sense, intellectual or moral, but only his body, his senses," wrote Henry David Thoreau. "It is not armed with superior wit or honesty, but with superior physical strength."

My visceral inclination, held in check by reason, was to write back that I feel the government has no business interfering in the education of my children, and to refuse to answer questions or entertain an assessment of our books and program. However, we must refrain from the satisfaction of self-righteous paranoia. Government isn't always bad, nor are the public schools. Whether or not the school authorities are right, most of them sincerely believe they are. To challenge their beliefs or their authority is no better than waving the seat of one's pants at a mad bull.

We've known parents who have responded to such reminders of the government's strength with counter-threats, accusations, and ultimatums. Usually, it's fruitless. What would we have gained? Nasty letters, more threats, and probably loss of the one thing we wanted most — the opportunity to teach our children at home.

We were certain that our children were "under efficient instruction elsewhere," so the next step was to convince the Minister of Education. Since he and I were not yet on speaking terms, I wrote back to the superintendent, with extensive details of our kids' previous education, including specific courses and books, to indicate that we were taking the matter seriously, and listing many of our educational materials — "more than 2,000 volumes, including an encyclopedia, various reference books, dictionaries, and atlases; non-fiction works on art, music, philosophy, psychology, medicine, astronomy, history, literature, religion, science, botany, and biology; novels, short stories, and essays; posters, charts, flash cards, records, cassette tapes, a microscope, chemistry sets, and electronics kits; models of the human body, vital organs, and the solar system; and a world globe and a moon globe" — to point out that we had spent a great deal of money as well as thought, and also implying that our school's inventory, per capita, was superior to that of most public schools.

In closing, I wrote, "I hope this information will be of use to you. If you have any further questions about Brook Farm School, please do not hesitate to write or to visit us at any time. Thank you again for your concern, and for any help you are able to give us."

I didn't "request permission" to teach at home, but neither did I underline that omission.

I used the name "Brook Farm School" frequently in the letter (and earlier had had letterheads printed) to impress upon the Minister and his representatives that ours is a "real" school, not just a home with books. Subsequent letters from school authorities were addressed to Brook Farm School, and authorities usually used the name in referring to our educational program.

Many home-schooling parents are "invited," in a peremptory manner very like a court summons, to present their case in person before a school official or board. Failure to comply may mean automatic dismissal of the request for exemption. Those in this situation should prepare themselves with as much material as possible — laws, precedents, examples, educational theory, etc. — and proceed cautiously, a step at a time.

Some home-school writers feel it's best not to invite officials to one's own home, but in our experience it has always worked out well. We think it's almost always best, if possible, to invite the superintendent or examiner to our home — and to get the jump on him, by inviting him before he invites us. "To look over our materials" is a good pretext, and not untrue. It has saved us the bother of collecting material, leaving home, tapping our feet in a waiting room, and facing the lion in his own den. People, like most other animals, are usually more at ease on their own territory; we feel more comfortable in our own home. The visiting official is aware that he's a guest, and even if his basic attitude is hostile, he'll be less antagonistic than if we were in his office.

Not all school officials are suspicious or opposed to home-schooling. Most of those who have come to examine our materials and our children have been curious, friendly, and cooperative, and our visits have been genuinely friendly, with no need for verbal fencing. Officials in person are often much more human than in their letters or on the phone. They never know when their letters may be taken from the file, or by whom, so in their letters they'll be careful not to depart from the most conservative and official position. If they know they're speaking off the record, they may be freer and more helpful. (Two visiting officials admitted to us that if they were not working for the school system they would definitely teach their own children at home.)

In *The Power of Non-Violence,* Richard B. Gregg refers to disarming an antagonist with love and sympathy as "moral jujitsu." True peacefulness is not a tactic, but an attitude of being, so inviting an official to our home is not really equivalent; however, the changes in our relationship can be so marked that it might certainly be a kind of psychological jujitsu.

On the few occasions we were visited by an officious Mrs. Grundy and a suspicious Mr. Crabapple, we invited them in graciously. We introduced our children to them, and included the children in our discussions. Sometimes the officials wanted to talk with the children, to see if they could speak with some semblance of knowledge and intelligence; other times, they suggested that we might talk more freely if the children were excused. We explained that the children found adult conversation, particularly about education, stimulating and informative, and that they might as well stay. Besides, we said, we had to get back to our studies soon, which let the officials know that they were interrupting a serious school. We invited them into the kitchen (less formal than the living room and therefore more relaxing), offered chairs, and put examples of the kids' work on the table. Without asking, we served tea or coffee, and one of the kids passed a plate of cookies. The informality and the homey warmth was somewhat contagious. We stood by the visitors' shoulders occasionally to point out something in the material in front of them, causing them to look up at us — the eternal pose of a student with a hovering teacher, to reawaken a little of their own childhood conditioning toward authority. We tried to keep them slightly off balance — "jujitsu" — but not uncomfortably so. If they relaxed, then we did, too, but we stayed on guard, not wanting to lose any psychological advantage we had gained.

We seldom attacked the school system. It would only have made them more defensive and then more offensive. We just told them of our own materials, methods, and objectives. We knew we'd never convince the officials that our standards were superior to theirs, so we didn't try; instead, we tried to help them see that our educational program was good, not only by our standards, but also by theirs.

We read books and magazines about public education so we can talk the officials' language, use their terminology, and relate to their frames of reference. We can win and let them think they have won, but not by lying or deceit. Being imprisoned or having our children kidnapped by the state would certainly defeat our purpose, but avoiding either of those circumstances by deceit and subterfuge might defeat our larger purpose.

As the officials talked, even if they were telling us that we were depriving our children of all the advantages of life, we remained friendly (outwardly, at least), which confused them. Anger, no matter how thoroughly provoked it might have been, would have been taken as a sign of weakness, and as cause for a stronger position on their part. If they began a long harangue, we excused ourselves to get more of the children's work, and talked about it as if we hadn't interrupted a speech about something else.

We felt an attitude of firm commitment was of prime importance. If we had any doubts or reservations about our methods or materials, or about our ability to teach, we didn't let them show. Our manner exuded self-confidence and calm determination. Usually, school officials were as desirous of avoiding a serious confrontation as we were. Once they realized we wouldn't change our position, even under heavy pressure, they always gave in.

This approach won't work all the time, for everyone, but it has worked well for us, and many readers have said it worked well for them.

DEPARTMENT OF EDUCATION
Office of the Minister
February 3, 1981

Dear Mr. Reed:

I have arranged for the Coordinator of Elementary School Programs in my Department and the School Supervisor in Districts 30 & 31 to conduct an assessment of the instructional programs that you are providing in your home for your four children. It is my understanding that the Supervisor has discussed these programs in some depth with you and that he has communicated this information to the Coordinator.

It is reported to me that the instructional programs that you are using with your four children are adequate and that you have a good supply of books and materials.

In light of the positive report that I have received, I am willing to approve the exemption of your four children from attendance at public school for the current school year. You should make an application to me during the coming summer before the opening of school in September.

Yours very truly,
Charles G. Gallagher
Minister of Education

BROOK FARM SCHOOL
Glassville, New Brunswick E0J 1L0
August 15, 1981

Dear Mr. Gallagher:

As you requested, we are informing you of our intention to teach our children at home again this year. Thank you for your attention and consideration.

Yours truly,
Donn Reed

OFFICE OF THE SUPERINTENDENT
September 30, 1981

Dear Mr. Reed:
You will recall that the School Supervisor came to visit the Brook Farm School to determine the suitability of your curriculum for your four children. You were subsequently given permission by the Minister of Education to teach in your home-school instructional program for the school year 1980-81.
Unless you plan to enroll these students in the school system, approval from the Minister of Education must be received for exemptions covering the 1981-1982 school year.
Please enlighten me with respect to your intentions relative to the education of your children for the 1981-1982 school year.

Yours truly,
Garth Hathaway
District Superintendent

BROOK FARM SCHOOL
Glassville, New Brunswick E0J 1L0
October 10, 1981

Dear Mr. Hathaway:
Thank you for your concern.
We wrote to the Minister on August 15, informing him of our intention to teach our children at home again this year, but have not received a reply.

Yours truly,
Donn Reed

The following August, I wrote again, telling the Minister that we intended to continue teaching at home. We received no answer, nor any more letters from the Superintendent asking us to enlighten him with respect to our intentions relative to the education of our children. Although my letter had been one of declaration rather than of application, I felt it was close enough to the Minister's instruction to have fulfilled my obligation. No one had objected to my wording — not to me, anyway — so I assumed the absence of further inquiry was not because I had offended them.

The following year, feeling that the Department of Education was behind in its correspondence and owed me a letter, I wrote neither application nor declaration. There the matter stood for half a dozen years. We received letters from other home-schoolers in the province who were being harassed by the Department of Education or by their local school boards, but we received no more letters and no more assessments, and our children never had the privilege of being tested by school authorities.

We decided our file must have been misplaced, or the authorities had given up on us as a lost cause.

Then, after being ignored by the authorities for several years, we received a letter explaining that home-schoolers in the province were now in the charge of a new special branch, and asking us to fill out and return a long questionnaire. The questions seemed reasonable and non-threatening, so we answered them. A few weeks later, the administrator of the new special branch came to visit. We had many similar ideas about education, and she had no objections to our home-schooling, and she liked our homemade cookies.

Probably the cookies had nothing to do with the letter we received a few weeks later from the Minister of Education, granting exemption of our children from public school for the current school year, saying that our supplies seemed adequate, and telling us to apply again next summer if we planned to continue this practice.

We no longer felt ignored, but the renewed official stamp of approval didn't have any noticeable effect on the efficiency of our instruction elsewhere. Probably the department had been changing from human files to computer files, and it took six years for modern technology to bring us out of limbo.

Most of our experience has been limited to places where the grounds for exemption are not clearly or rigidly defined (as with New Brunswick's ambiguous phrase, "efficient instruction elsewhere"), or where home education is more or less well-accepted (such as British Columbia, where many people live more than several miles beyond any school bus line). Even in such areas, officials may bluster and threaten, and sometimes impede education, but they're not immovable obstacles.

In the past a few states made no statutory allowance at all for home-schooling. If we were in such a place, our approach might not work, but our attitudes would still be the same, so we'd probably try it anyway. I prefer not to wave flags (or the seat of my pants) at bulls, mad or not, but I also agree with Kahlil Gibran, who says in *The Prophet* that "if it is a despot you would dethrone, see first that his throne erected within you is destroyed." (Gibran's statement still applies, even though — thank goodness — homeschooling is now legal in all 50 states.)

"Unjust laws exist," wrote Thoreau in "Civil Disobedience." "Shall we be content to obey them, or shall we endeavor to amend them, and obey them until we have succeeded, or shall we transgress them at once?"

Across the United States and Canada, home-school support groups have lobbied and petitioned state and provincial governments with great success, causing restrictive education laws to be significantly modified, but many home-schoolers are still subject to laws they feel are too intrusive and demanding. "Men generally think," Thoreau said, "that they ought to wait until they have persuaded the majority to alter them. They think that, if they should resist, the remedy would be worse than the evil. But it is the fault of the government itself that the remedy is worse than the evil. ... As for adopting the ways which the state has provided for remedying the evil, I know not of such ways. They take too much time, and a man's life will be gone. I have other affairs to attend to."

So do we all.

We cannot change all the unjust laws, nor constantly risk our freedom even by resisting them all, but we must begin somewhere. Let us begin with those laws that affect us most personally and deeply.

To live outside the law, you must be honest. — Bob Dylan

Five of my ancestors were on the Mayflower, and twice that number dropped their hoes to join the fighting in Concord and Lexington. Maintaining the tradition of their spirit, I simply do not accept the authority of any person or government to force me into an action I believe is wrong. We would be very polite and tactful, but our final position would still be that no government has more right than we to determine our children's upbringing and education. If possible, without extreme danger of completely losing that for which we would be fighting, we would join Washington, Thoreau, and Gandhi in resisting the state's unwarranted demands. If necessary, we would emulate my Mayflower ancestors and go to another place where the demands were fewer and the restrictions more democratic. Exodus to escape persecution has several worthy precedents.

Home-schooling should never be just an avoidance of the problems in or created by the public schools. It should also be a positive contribution to the improvement of the society in which we live. By insisting upon our right to choose the place and method of our children's education, we are helping to prepare a slightly better world for them, and we are showing them, by our own example, how they can make similar contributions.

We must be clear, however, about the difference between moral right and legal right. Government, at its root and in its simplest form, is neither more nor less than a contract among individuals for their mutual benefit and protection. The need for some form of government, and the corollary need for some means of enforcing it, is obvious. However unjust or immoral an individual law may be, the basic principle of law per se is just. Disobedience of a law willfully or on a whim, simply because it is disagreeable or inconvenient, or because of greed or cowardice, strikes not only at the law but at the foundations of society itself. "Action from principle," wrote Thoreau, "the perception and the performance of right, changes things and relations; it is essentially revolutionary. ... Cast your whole vote; not a strip of paper merely, but your whole influence."

Your whole influence, and ours, will bring us all a little closer to true democracy, and beyond — to that time and place when people are governed not by the wishes of the majority or the dictates of the minority, but by what is right and true.

Another Type of Opposition

You may or may not find school authorities opposed to your plans to homeschool. This type of opposition isn't always the hardest kind to deal with. When your parents or in-laws feel you are about to do something irresponsible and catastrophic to their grandchildren, it's more personal and can put incredible strain on otherwise good and important family relationships.

Speaking from our experiences, I know how difficult this problem can be. If possible, strive to keep it from becoming a major issue that will destroy your relationships. Time is on your side. When your parents or in-laws see what your children are learning, and the kind of people they are becoming, they will eventually change their minds. Prepare yourself: It may not happen soon. For years some of our relatives would send fancy clothes, games, sports equipment, and toys, but they would not send needed educational supplies — not even good books. The family opposition we faced didn't really disappear until our kids were well into their teens. Only then did the attitudes change and become supportive. We all regret those missed years of closeness and harmony.

HOMESCHOOLING AND EDUCATION

CHANGING THE WORLD, ONE HOMESCHOOLED STUDENT AT A TIME — DEVELOPING YOUR LONG-TERM GOALS — IDEAS TO THINK ABOUT — RESOURCES — LEGAL ISSUES

If your plan is for a year, plant rice.

If your plan is for a decade, plant trees.

If your plan is for a lifetime, educate children. — Confucius

I firmly believe we are changing the world, one homeschooled student at a time. With every young adult who goes from homeschool to college, work, or other pursuits, we are broadening the definition of "meaningful education" and challenging the existing attitudes about the efficacy of standardized public schooling.

Whether we are consciously aware that our homeschooling creates pressure on the public educational system to change or are doing so only to meet our personal goals, we are influencing the way people think about education now and in the future. What we do today, with our children, is changing and challenging the community around us and society at large. As we quietly go about the daily business of raising and educating our families, we should be aware that our actions have repercussions beyond our immediate goals.

We are changing not only some attitudes about education, but also attitudes regarding parental responsibility and parenting. At a time when many feel it is important for women (in particular but not exclusively) to get out of the house and "make something" of themselves, we are living the "family values" that too many people just talk about. We are creating strong foundations for our children and ourselves.

There will always be those who are resistant to change or actions that vary from the norm. If you are new to homeschooling and find resistance or skepticism, remember that you are not alone. There are hundreds of thousands of parents just like you enjoying the time and privilege of sharing the learning adventure with their children.

Never doubt that a small group of thoughtful citizens can change the world. Indeed, it is the only thing that ever has. — Margaret Mead

Don't be dismayed at the lack of regulation textbooks in this book or on our website. You won't find many of them. Our kids never liked them. We never liked them. They reminded us of commercial baby food — they fill a need but on the lowest possible level. At best, some make reasonable reference books. You will find books you and your children will enjoy that will transform your learning into a creative adventure.

Right Where You Are

Much has been written about raising and homeschooling children in urban vs. rural environments. There certainly is a wealth of resources available to families in and around cities. But the question comes up: Can homeschooled children raised in a rural or wilderness environment find their way in modern society, comfortably?

I believe so. All our children were born in either rural or wilderness areas of the U.S. or Canada. All are now grown and found ways of living within this modern society. As they would tell you, there are advantages and disadvantages. Donn and I would say the same. I don't think it makes any difference where you live when children are young. Young children spend the first years of their lives exploring and learning about their immediate home surroundings wherever they are. It is easy to find stimulating books, toys, and games for the young ages, and the surrounding area is a playground ripe for exploration. As children get older they do need contact with a wider, more varied world. We used magazines, books, and limited television to bring the world to us because we felt the kids needed to see that there are many ways of living and thinking, and that the world was a lot bigger and different from where we lived. We traveled when we could and encouraged the children to travel and visit relatives.

There weren't any homeschooling families in some of the places we lived, so our kids grew up feeling set apart from others their age. In some cases this wasn't a bad thing, but we did have to make an effort to connect them with other children. Homeschooling today has grown, so it is easier for you to connect with other homeschooling families. Homeschooling is well enough accepted in most places that homeschooled children can take part in activities without prejudice.

We did find that the kids went through periods when they really wanted to be with other kids their age, and that is difficult in very isolated areas. It was difficult for the kids because they couldn't go next door or down the block and find a friend. It was difficult for us because driving a long way for a birthday party was a bit of an inconvenience. At one point it meant that during the winter months we needed to Ski-Doo two miles to our truck, hope it would start, and then drive six miles up to the main highway — with another forty miles to town. On the other hand, without all the distractions of today's fast-moving society — the TV, video games, computer games, and such — the kids had to develop their inner resources. They had unhurried time to follow their interests and time to daydream, time to read just for the fun and adventure of it, and lots of time to play together. When your society of peers is mainly your brothers and sisters you have to find ways to get along. All of us had to work together to get chores done, put food on the table or away for the winter, and care for our animals whether they were for food or pets. They had puppies and kittens, baby pigs and kid goats and lambs. They didn't have organized sports, but they had acres to run in and play their own games. They watched us milking and knew exactly where their milk came from. Sometimes if they were lucky they could catch their breakfast egg as it was laid. They learned to respect other life forms at a very early age. They also learned the life cycles of birth and death firsthand. Donn and I felt lucky because our lifestyle gave us time to play and explore with them.

Yes, our kids missed out on some things, but I believe that what they gained as inner resources has given them the advantage of knowing themselves well. I can't imagine any of them being bored or feeling that there is nothing to do. They know how to pursue their own goals and dreams, and I think that the more concentrated time they spent playing together in creative play has helped them develop good social skills.

I find it interesting and not too surprising that none of our kids has chosen to live the way we did. I think for the most part they were happy children growing up with unusual freedoms. Having "been there, done that," they moved on to explore a different way of living for themselves. I can remember times when my parents in particular thought we would ruin our children by depriving them of a more normal upbringing and interaction with other children. I think our children grew up with added dimensions.

It is good to have an end to journey toward; but it is the journey that matters, in the end. — Ursula K. Le Guin

Learning to Think Long-Term

Be forewarned: You may have young children now, but they won't always be at home and your full-time concern. We are discussing learning resources for "kids," but the more I hear from the growing number of parents whose homeschooled kids are adults now, the more I realize that many of these parents are moving on to higher education for themselves, following dreams that have been dormant or have sprung anew through the homeschooling process. Don't hesitate to dream for yourself too — and plan — or start or restart your own journey. You can and will inspire your children by your actions.

My Favorites That You Might Not Consider

You may think the first few entries here should go in a section about parenting or family living. I don't, and you're free to disagree with me. I'm putting them here because how we raise our children is, or should be, so integrated into how we homeschool that we need to be clear about our parenting philosophy before adding the role of educator.

These are challenging times politically, ecologically, and socially. The weapons of mass destruction are realities that we have to live with and are the inheritance we hand to our children. We, as a people, as nations, cannot continue indefinitely destroying our world and others who live in it. Just as I believe we are changing the face of education one family at a time, I believe that to give our children more than despair we must change what we can, starting within our homes and our hearts in the hope that they will do better.

It is possible to kill a million people without personally shedding a drop of blood. It is possible to destroy a culture without being aware of its existence. It is possible to commit genocide or ecocide from the comfort of one's living room. — Derrick Jensen

This quote left me speechless and scared when I read it, but there is hope. It is in the future with our children.

Humane: having what are considered the best qualities of human beings. The following two books delve deeply into the most desirable qualities we seek for ourselves, our children, and the future well-being of our world.

***ABOVE ALL, BE KIND: RAISING A HUMANE CHILD IN CHALLENGING TIMES,* by Zoe Weil.** Weil could just as well have called this book Your Life Is Your Message. She says, "More than anything you will ever say to your children, your life — the choices you make and the values you embody — will be their biggest teacher." How do you do this? Weil uses a four-step process to help make evaluations and decisions.

I got this book thinking it was about family living. I am so glad I was wrong. The scope of this book encompasses families, communities, and all the people whose lives we touch through the ripples of our actions. Did you know that it would require four earths for everyone on the planet to live the lifestyle of North Americans? This book offers facts like this that will alarm you, and you will find information to help you research the subject so you can make your own evaluations and make a change for the better.

Weil has written chapters to cover the early, middle, and high school years with thoughts and suggestions for what values each age can assimilate, the problems encountered, parenting challenges, and best of all some solutions you can use. Here is an excerpt from the chapter about the middle years:

> "Our children are growing up in a culture that often glorifies disrespect. They watch cartoons with rude heroes and hear insulting talk show hosts on the radio. They are growing up in a society in which corporate theft is becoming the norm. They are living in a nation in which politicians are assumed to lie. Children need to learn why such behaviors are not humane. They must understand the harm that is caused by deceit. Even when your own children are honest and respectful, they will still need your help to maintain their convictions and their virtues in today's world."

The book ends with stories of young adults who have learned how to make a difference in their world and consequently the world at large. There is a questionnaire you can use to help you think about your life and the changes you would like to make, and a place to write about what you will do about it. There is also a long list of organizations you can go to for information and concrete ways you can make a difference.

This book is a thought-provoking tool.

THE NATURAL CHILD: PARENTING FROM THE HEART, **by Jan Hunt.** Hunt very clearly puts forth the premises of this book in the first chapter. Here are a few of her points: "We understand that all children are doing the very best they can at every given moment. We trust that though children may be small in size, they deserve to have their needs taken seriously. We know that it is unrealistic to expect a child to behave perfectly at all times. We recognize that 'bad behavior' is the child's attempt to communicate an important need in the best way she can. We learn to look beneath the child's outward behavior to understand what he is thinking and feeling. We see that in a very beautiful way, our child teaches us what love is." If you are having trouble accepting these concepts, this book will help you find your way to a peaceful and rewarding acceptance, or make you decide not to read it.

Another reason this book is here is that I believe that part of our duty as parents is to educate our children for the future, and we want a peaceful future for them. How we raise them, the unspoken values they learn even before we can communicate with words, is very important. In the foreword, Peggy O'Mara of *Mothering* magazine writes: "Margaret Mead ... said, 'The most violent tribes were those that withheld touch in infancy.' To me, it is very simple. The propensity to act aggressively is related to unmet needs. When we objectify our babies and manipulate their legitimate needs to meet our own comfort level or prescription for living, we may unknowingly put them at risk. We can instead choose to surrender to the mystery of our baby's needs and the surprises he or she brings just as we would surrender and adapt to the surprises brought by a new love."

At first I wasn't sure why Hunt begins her book with the topic of child abuse and the cycle of violence it tends to perpetuate, but perhaps it is to clear the way so that even those with a history of abuse can find their way through the book and find peace in their own lives as parents.

This book can help you find the balance between discipline and spoiling, much in the same spirit as A.S. Neill draws the line between freedom and license in his book *Freedom, Not License.* You will find examples of how to deal constructively with misbehavior and difficult situations. The book progresses from infancy into adulthood, offering examples of problems and possible solutions. There is an emphasis on forgiveness — forgiving your child during trying times and forgiving yourself too, with the understanding that we are human and imperfect. It's likely that you will not find the perfect example of your own problems, but you will learn the attitudes to develop so that you can cope and find your own constructive solutions. You will find advice about coping with your own preconceived and unconscious conditioning from your upbringing and how to make the changes you would like. Hunt has a lot to say about the inherent problem of rewards and finding an alternative to spanking, and there are very sane suggestions for coping with our seemingly hurried lives and making time for our children to just be children.

Although Hunt is an unschooling parent and there is much about parenting in general, you will quickly realize that her attitudes and suggestions are applicable to all styles of parenting, and so contribute to all styles of homeschooling. Her parenting ideas are what we used years ago, although we didn't find that unschooling worked for us all the time. I like to think that unschooling in Hunt's style would work for everyone, but I can't convince myself that it would. Maybe someday it will be possible. I hope so.

Because you are reading this book I'm assuming that you are looking for answers and suggestions to meet your goals as a parent and as a homeschooler. When we become parents we should be parents before anything else, before being a teacher, a cellist, a homemaker, etc. Hunt's book is one to keep handy. Read it once to set yourself on the right track. Pick it up again any time you're feeling stressed or need reinforcement.

***THE QUESTION IS COLLEGE,* by Herbert Kohl.** It's fair to wonder why I'm putting college before kindergarten in this next review when the only thing you may be concerned with right now is clean diapers. I am doing it because whether we actually discuss our philosophy of living and goals in relation to our children's education or not, our everyday actions have a direct effect on our children's future. This first book will help you form an overview of living and education that will help guide you through the years.

Before considering specific resources it's important to think about where you want your homeschool journey to take you and your children. You need some idea of your long-term goals or you'll waste time and effort and encounter more obstacles than necessary. *The Question Is College* will stimulate and help clarify your thinking. Kohl is more concerned with the attitudes toward living you would like your child to end up with than about academic skills and college attendance.

This book is not against college, but questions whether there is a genuine need for it. It was written primarily for high school students, not parents, but in a homeschooling family, the concerns of one affect the other. This book isn't intended for parents of young children, but reading it while your children are young will help you create a philosophy about learning and living that will be of enormous benefit.

The preface to Kohl's new edition begins:

> What do I want to do when I grow up? For many people that childhood question persists throughout life. At 5 it can lead to wild fantasies and lifelong dreams. ... And in middle age, it has the sadness of an incomplete life. Yet the question persists as long as the imagination is alive. What, of all the possible things that people do, would I love to do?

Donn and I have always felt that the journey from childhood through adulthood should be enjoyed in and of itself, progressing into a satisfying way of life and personally meaningful work. Unfortunately, when parents first think of homeschooling they are all too often thinking of the skills they've been conditioned by upbringing and society to accept as needed to succeed in life. The skills we teach our children are, all too often, a reflection of what we think we needed to succeed in life. We should remember that our children's needs will be different. To fulfill their dreams we should strive to give them the most versatile tools possible along with the confidence to know they can learn whatever is necessary along the way. Our culture equates a college degree with success. Kohl's book will give you good reasons to look beyond the common equation: college = success = money = happiness. He does not accept the premise that your life's work need be dull. Therefore, in homeschooling, we should seek out the greatest opportunities for exploration and discovery possible. I think a copy of this book should magically appear with the birth of every first child.

HOME EDUCATION MAGAZINE, P.O. Box 1083, Tonasket, WA 98855. Publisher since 1983 of the national bimonthly *Home Education Magazine*. I don't know how they do it month after month and year after year, but this magazine has managed to stay fresh and interesting even to this old-timer. Kudos to you, Mark and Helen Hegener! If I had to choose only one homeschool magazine to read, this would be it. The content is representative of the diversity within the homeschool movement, with a top-notch staff of regular columnists, plus articles by parents with information and ideas to share. You can find many other online and offline services at www.homeedmag.com; their e-mail address is info@homeedmag.com. HEM's free "Pocket Field Guide to Homeschooling" answers most major questions about homeschooling; write to request single copies or enough for your group, or download it from their website. You'll find up-to-date networking and message boards where you can find support and new resources and ask questions about most of your homeschooling concerns. Fun to read and full of ideas to think about.

THE AMERICAN HOMESCHOOL ASSOCIATION (AHA) is a service organization created in 1995 to network homeschoolers on a national level and to provide news and information about homeschooling. Current AHA services include an online discussion list providing news, information, networking, and resources; a free e-mail newsletter; and a website (www.americanhomeschoolassociation.org) providing categorized links to the most helpful and informative pages of homeschooling information on the Internet (including a collection of columns from *Home Education Magazine* by Larry and Susan Kaseman, authors of *Taking Charge Through Homeschooling: Personal and Political Empowerment,* addressing issues such as working for homeschooling freedoms, curfews, "homeschooling" programs in the public schools, user-friendly homeschooling records, tax credits and homeschooling, homeschoolers playing public school sports, the question of credentials, the school-to-work program, homeschooling legislation, doing the minimum to comply with homeschooling laws, and much more). It is a showcase of the best writing on a wide variety of topics, from sources all across the Internet.

***THE FIRST YEAR OF HOMESCHOOLING YOUR CHILD: YOUR COMPLETE GUIDE TO GETTING OFF TO THE RIGHT START,* by Linda Dobson.** This book starts off acknowledging all the doubts, fears, and questions you may have about beginning homeschooling. Then it goes on to make you feel comfortable and competent to deal with these uncertainties whether your child has been in school before or you are beginning this journey before your child has attended public school.

Those of us who have homeschooled our children over a long period of time know how important it is to develop a philosophy about learning at home. We understand how important it is to be flexible and recognize each child's learning style. Linda offers some clear guidelines and sound recommendations to help beginners. There is a very clear overview of a variety of approaches and very practical suggestions for using them.

In this book you will see that it is possible to homeschool children under a variety of circumstances. You'll find examples of two-income families juggling time and needs, those who choose to homeschool because of medical or other special needs of parents or children. You'll find stories of families who homeschool for academic reasons or just because they want to spend more time together.

Along with learning from Linda's years of experience, you'll learn from many others who contributed their insights into the question "What do I wish someone had told me during my first year of homeschooling?"

Thank you, Linda. This is an outstanding and wonderful contribution to the growing body of homeschooling literature.

***THE HOMESCHOOLING BOOK OF ANSWERS,* by Linda Dobson.** Finally! A book with more answers than questions. How can that be? Read on! Drawing from years of experience homeschooling her own family, time spent helping other homeschoolers through workshops, and her extensive body of written work about homeschooling, Linda has posed more than 80 of the most important, most frequently asked questions about homeschooling and asked more than 35 of homeschooling's most respected voices to contribute answers. Issues of structure, expense, socialization, dealing with officials, resources, and many more are answered here. Reading this book is like attending a homeschooling forum and hearing the most experienced people in the field express their ideas and opinions. Best of all, each question is answered by at least two people so you can consider differing points of view and form your own conclusions. I found it interesting to see where contributors agreed (without any consultation) and where they differed. The greatest value of this book lies not in the number of questions that are answered, but in the rich diversity of answers. You will come away from this book knowing that there are as many ways to homeschool as there are homeschooling families. These "expert" answers come from a combined total of more than 500 years of personal experience, experimentation, observation, and the courage to pursue personal dreams and values. This is a book for all homeschoolers. Reading it will empower you as you experiment and find the best learning style for you and your family.

In the book, Linda asked several of us to address the following frequently asked question: "I hated school! How can I possibly teach my child?" This was my answer, slightly altered to fit this book:

> Homeschooling is a fantastic challenge! If you didn't want a challenge I don't think you would be homeschooling or considering it. It is also one of the most fantastic opportunities. But what if I don't think I know enough to teach my child? The obvious answer to this question is to learn right along with your child or find someone willing to teach a particular subject for you.
>
> I can't think of one valid reason we should know everything we would like our kids to learn before starting to homeschool. Some things we can learn about before actually beginning to do them. Some things are learned best by doing them. Some things require a combination of approaches. I believe homeschooling needs the combination of both approaches.
>
> Only very young children believe their parents know everything, but kids ask the craziest questions, and by the time they are 5 or 6 they certainly know we don't have all the answers, and they love and respect us and have learned from us anyway.

Except for the time I attended public school, I've never felt that admitting ignorance about something was shameful or wrong. One of the most important things we wanted our kids to learn was that the only really stupid thing you can do is not ask a question when you don't understand something. In our homeschooling we found that admitting we didn't know something put us on equal footing with our kids and they respected that; we could then search for the answer together. Whenever you search for tools or materials so you can learn something together with your children, you double your rewards. By saying "Let's find out," you'll have the fun of doing something important together *and* learning something new.

I hated school. Period. I was a terrible student. The idea of teaching our kids scared me just about witless. But I never wanted our kids to go through the humiliation and fear I experienced, and that gave me courage. At the other end of the spectrum, Donn did well in school, found it an all-right experience, but felt it could have been much better. From opposite ends of the spectrum we had a common goal. We wanted something better for our children.

In the first month that Donn and I were together we met a family using the Calvert School correspondence program. Whenever we went to visit, the kids met us at the door bubbling over with excitement, immediately wanting to show us what they were learning and doing. Their excitement was tangible. It was our first glimpse of something that would shape our future.

Since that time hundreds of parents have written and told us that they've felt homeschooling gave them a glorious second chance to go back and learn many things they had missed in school. You may be challenged if you were a poor student in some subjects and you take your whiz-kid teenager out of school, but there are numerous great books to help you. If the material your child needs to learn is important, then you'll find the resources you need. You may just get more education in the process!

Are you wondering what a normal homeschooler or homeschooling family is like? Linda Dobson asked the following question in *The Homeschooling Book of Answers.* "All I ever read about in the newspaper is exceptional kids doing exceptional things. Are there any 'normal' homeschoolers?" This was my answer:

Normal! What's normal? Who is normal? Are you normal?

Exceptional people will make the headlines. Exceptional kids will make bigger headlines. Homeschooled children are essentially no different than children in public schools. Like people everywhere, we all have our strengths and weaknesses. If there are any significant differences it's because homeschooling can allow all children, gifted or not, to grow more freely and pursue an interest to the point of excellence.

Our four children may resent me for calling them "average, normal kids," but that's what they are. Just like kids all around the world they've argued and fought, played, failed at some things, and done some outstandingly great things. They're not geniuses, yet they have done some exceptional things because they had the freedom to investigate and follow their special interests.

Susan, who never considered herself to be a great, or even good, writer, won a provincial writing contest because it centered around a subject she cared about. She was also placed in an honors English class in college. Cathy spent hours studying dinosaurs in third grade and acquired exceptional knowledge in the subject. Derek got hooked on sharks in about fourth grade and read everything we could find for him. He read through everything in the provincial library and we had to search the Library of Canada and then enlist friends and relatives to find resources to help satisfy his insatiable curiosity. He began reading at high school and college levels because he really cared about what he was learning. Karen finished her entire high school studies in two years, tackling all twenty-eight subjects in *High School Subjects Self-Taught,* including some advanced courses we tried to dissuade her from doing. We couldn't see that she would need them. We were wrong, of course. She's used what she learned, and has been glad she did it all.

Not everyone needs to go to Harvard, or wants to. Not everyone can write a symphony at age eleven, win a national spelling bee, or be outstanding in a particular field of knowledge. Most adults don't make headlines; it's the exceptions who do. If we don't have exceptional kids, that's all right. The point of homeschooling is not to compete for headlines, but to give our children as much freedom and enjoyment as possible in their living and learning, and to help them prepare themselves for their own future.

***LEARNING AT HOME: A MOTHER'S GUIDE TO HOMESCHOOLING,* by Marty Layne,** mother of four homeschooled young adults. *Learning at Home* is a personal book. Marty's insights about interacting with her children should be used by all parents and teachers even though it was written primarily for homeschooling parents. What makes this book exceptional are Marty's observations about the interaction between parents and children. She has an acute awareness of how children learn best and how to help them. Marty shares her insight into how to see and work through the conditioned responses we all subconsciously carry from society, our own upbringing, and our schooling in order to create a harmonious homeschool environment. The book begins by taking a close look at the answer to the very common question "Can I do this — teach my child at home?" You'll find Marty has the unique capacity to help you sort out your inner thoughts and motivations and recognize your fears (and learn how to deal with them), and to impart confidence. You'll find numerous comments and suggestions for creating a learning environment to suit yourself and your children, and the emphasis is always on how to relate and respond to your children, and how to best meet their needs and your own. Yes, Mom and Dad, you have to take care of your needs too; that's a strong part of Marty's message. Being a good mate and parent presents many challenges. Add teaching (working with, guiding, whatever you want to call it), and you've added to those challenges exponentially. Unless you're superwoman or superman you're going to find your life, at times, more stressful than is reasonable. Marty's chapter on burnout — how to recognize it, what to do about it, and (most constructive of all) how to prevent it — is the best I've seen. This is a book designed for real people. She recognizes that parents as well as kids have times when they are grumpy, that there are times when the kids get bored or are unhappy, and she offers some interesting observations about why these times happen and some ideas for improving the situation.

Along with all this sagacious writing about critical issues, you'll find chapters about helping your child learn to read, write, and do arithmetic; the importance of including the arts (music, art, dance, and drama); and using all of life as a curriculum. Many of us have read about homeschoolers becoming accomplished musicians at a young age, going to prestigious colleges, or doing other remarkable things. Marty makes the important point that homeschooling can "allow time to pursue an interest and reveal talent but can't create it." Thankfully, Marty recognizes that not all children develop remarkable talents or abiding interests, and points out that there are important talents our society does not recognize: "We tend to recognize only outstanding gifts that fall in recognized categories like art, music, drama, or sports. We are not willing to recognize talent for something like happiness, listening to others, being a warm person, taking delight in a rainy day." I particularly value this observation because more important than any talent or recognition, living well with ourselves and those around us is one of life's true goals and rewards. There is so much depth to this book that it's worth reading and rereading.

If you are considering homeschooling it will help you decide if this is really what you want to do and how to do it successfully. This book also has great value to those who have been homeschooling for a while, because Marty has given so much thought to issues that frequently cause problems in daily homeschooling, and clearly states ways to help you deal with them.

The end of the book contains several very useful appendices, with a list of read-aloud books, a bibliography, help in setting goals, and addresses for U.S. and Canadian support.

***AND THE SKYLARK SINGS WITH ME: ADVENTURES IN HOMESCHOOLING AND COMMUNITY-BASED EDUCATION,* by David H. Albert.** David's astute observations and comments about modern educational methods used in the public schools are important, but they aren't what impressed me most. The Alberts, more than the families in any other homeschooling accounts I've read, integrated their freestyle homeschooling with other people and resources in their surrounding community. This called for a change in lifestyle, and David calls that "hard work." Their striving to connect their children with people who were passionate about what they were doing, and who were willing to share and foster the interest of young children, demanded that they expand their network of friends and acquaintances and explore options through newspapers and by calling strangers. This wasn't always easy, but the results were immensely rewarding. The children's interests were respected and their horizons expanded. Their intellectual growth flourished, and because this learning took place within the family and expanded into the community at large, the children formed relationships with people of all ages based on common interests and needs, as opposed to the public school standard of peers based solely on age. Many books emphasize "values," but mostly within the family. David and his wife talk about imparting the values of community interaction — not just for social contact with people outside the family, but because this interaction makes activities outside the family more than just isolated incidents: They become a foundation and model for the future.

While David is cognizant of the precocity of his own children (and you will be well aware of this too), you will quickly see that the most important aspect of his story is how he and his wife labored to observe, respect, encourage, and only occasionally direct their children. The observations, ideas, and suggestions given for encouraging personal and intellectual growth are worthy models for all of us.

You'll find many insightful comments about how children learn throughout the book. I heartily endorse his suggestion that you read James Loewen's *Lies My Teacher Told Me* and Howard Zinn's *People's History of the United States* so that you can incorporate varied perspectives about history and its depiction into your own presentation of the subject. I agree with David's idea of repeatedly making math relevant to young children, thereby enabling them to discover its usefulness in making sense of their world. I particularly liked his statements about encouraging early reading and the use of phonics: "Having kids read at ever-younger ages may be high on the agenda of parents with heady images of escorting their sons and daughters off to Harvard, but given the content of most young children's reading material, learning to read is small potatoes compared with the fascination of an anthill." He goes on to point out that the choice of whether to use a whole-language or phonics approach to reading should be determined by each child's need at the time — and that this may change over time. He points out that his daughter Meera was not interested in having a word sounded out phonetically, but wanted the word said and explained (if necessary). She would then memorize it if it was useful. "What I am cautiously suggesting is that heavy emphasis on phonics might get some children to read earlier, but not necessarily better, provided 'late' readers are not stigmatized and their self-confidence damaged for not reading on someone else's time schedule. The problem with either phonics or whole-language approaches to reading is that they are each all too often tied to both a timetable and a content not of the child's own devising."

David disagrees with using E.D. Hirsch's cultural literacy and Core Knowledge books as standards for yearly content, and while I feel strongly that a common cultural knowledge is important, I agree that these books can become simply another set of artificial standards with emphasized data unrelated to a child's life, which makes the content just something to be regurgitated, not an integrated relevant set of useful knowledge.

At the end of the book he concludes that "to educate a child well is to enable her to find her destiny as well as our own. This can only be accomplished successfully, I am persuaded, by allowing her to find the freedom to listen to and be exhilarated by the harmony of her own inner voices and those of the world around her so that, like Blake's schoolboy, she comes to know that 'the skylark sings with me.'"

This is a book to inspire you throughout your homeschooling journey. An added bonus is a list, at the end of each chapter, of resources the Alberts found most useful.

***HAVE FUN. LEARN STUFF. GROW.* is also by David Albert.** The title could have been *LIVE! Don't Be Afraid to Try. Have Fun!* I had the fun of reading this book before it went to press, and I thought I'd share with you my end of the correspondence with David about this book.

> David,
>
> Thanks for bringing me back to the other side of my life with a great read. As you know, I've spent the winter as director of a ski school, spending my days outside teaching others to ski and now and then being humbled with my face in the snow.
>
> Getting back to the homeschooling part of my life on a full-time basis has called for a bit of transition. During the winter my body was generally more agile than my mind by the end of the day. Sitting at the computer and writing calls for a role reversal.
>
> When I first picked up your new book I thought it was another homeschooling book when I read the title! Well it is, and then again it isn't, and then again, it is. It begins with a glass-half-full–half-empty metaphor. That should make a reader stop and think right there. We all develop, consciously or not, an outlook on life and relationships, and the fact that you put that challenge right up front is appropriate. Those with the (half) empty outlook will either think more about it or retreat.
>
> This book is a delightful mix of philosophy, metaphor, storytelling, and how to homeschool in freedom, and it's not just about freedom for the kids.
>
> The chapters about math and spelling should be mandatory for all parents and teachers. As a self-confessed math phobic I dearly wish someone had figured out the "best" way to not teach math when I was "doing time" in the public school system. I'm going to have to try the unspelling myself. If it will work with me it will work with anyone. I have always learned best from my failures.
>
> Thank you for sorting out for me the roots of the "video" obsession some kids have. It's bothered me for some time but I couldn't quite wrap my mind around it. Control is the issue. It makes sense. I am grateful that you have put it all in perspective too. Who wants their kids playing violent games, even if they

are "only" games? It's an oxymoron, but I am fiercely opposed to teaching or supporting violence (should we add intolerance here too?) in any way.

In reading this book I came away feeling that as a parent, homeschooling or otherwise, one of the best teaching/learning tools available for you and your children is how you learn within the context of your own life.

Thanks too for another great addition to my homeschooling library.

Jean

All right. I admit to being a David Albert fan.

***HOMESCHOOLING AND THE VOYAGE OF SELF-DISCOVERY: A JOURNEY OF ORIGINAL SEEKING,* by David H. Albert.** A unique, wise, witty, literate, useful, philosophical, and thought-provoking journey for homeschooling parents and thoughtful educators. There isn't a comparable work available for those seeking to enrich and expand their homeschooling horizons into a life-altering experience for themselves and their children.

David asks the most magnificent questions that will provoke you into turning ideas on their heads, but he doesn't always give you the answers. Instead, you are invited and challenged to find your own. He has the unique ability to find the kernel of truth in a quagmire and let it shine for us. I consider reading this book a major step forward in my own continuing education.

***THE UNSCHOOLING HANDBOOK: HOW TO USE THE WHOLE WORLD AS YOUR CHILD'S CLASSROOM,* by Mary Griffith.** This book kept me awake even at a very late hour. I enjoyed and learned from the creative ideas presented by her many contributors about how they expanded their children's knowledge and enjoyment in their learning activities. I liked her broad definition of a classroom. This book begins with suggestions and thoughts about unschooling that can help you decide if it's something you want to do — and can do. It continues on to cover all the subjects expected by schools and interesting unschooling approaches used by her contributors. The variety of approaches adds depth and interest and offers good suggestions. At the end of each chapter is an example of how that chapter's subject would be covered throughout an unschooling day, along with a list of very good resource books.

***THE TEENAGE LIBERATION HANDBOOK: HOW TO QUIT SCHOOL AND GET A REAL LIFE AND EDUCATION,* by Grace Llewellyn.** Probably the best, most accurate review of this book was in *Bloomsbury Review:* "This is a very dangerous book. It contradicts all the conventional wisdom about dropouts and the importance of a formal education. It is funny and inspiring. Do not, under any circumstances, share this book with a bright, frustrated high-schooler being ground into mind-fudge by the school system. The writer cannot be responsible for the happiness and sense of personal responsibility that might come from reading this book." Grace Llewellyn has compiled a fantastic array of ideas and resources for a very comprehensive unschooling education, in all the standard subjects and scores of non-standard ones — science, math, social sciences, English, languages, the arts, sports and athletics, outdoor jobs and activities, travel — through books, personal contacts, jobs, apprenticeships and internships, volunteering, social and political activism, and more. She offers very encouraging advice throughout the book, and illustrates her arguments with dozens of real-life stories (many borrowed from *Growing Without Schooling)* of kids who have done it. Even a home-school with more structure than Grace advocates will find the numerous ideas and resources invaluable; for the truly unschooled teenager who is serious about doing more than watching TV, it will be an invaluable guidebook.

I have one major reservation, and a few minor ones. Like many unschoolers, Grace seems to think that any and all resources (people, places, etc.) are good — except the child's own parents. The first thing to do after making the decision to quit school, Grace advises the teenaged reader, is "celebrate your audacity with deep chocolate ice cream" and then, step two, "consult your parents." Some parents might feel they should have something to say about such a momentous decision, but Grace doesn't seem to have much sympathy for them. "You might get this over with after dinner tonight," she says, "or you might acclimate them slowly to the idea." At least she realizes that some old fogies may be a little slow. "Fortunately," she adds, "with a little care and planning, you will probably be able to help them see the light." Ah, yes, we remember it well — our kids, at the age of 13 or 14, suddenly wise and mature, trying to help us see the light — and we, stubborn and over-protective, always in the way of their freedom and happiness, trying to keep them from frying their brains or wrapping themselves around a tree. Our own "fortunately" is that they soon saw the light and grew out of this phase almost as quickly as they had grown into it, and we continued our lives together as friends and family. Overprotective or not, we still think that most kids of 13 or 14, and even some of 16 or 17, are not ready to take on the entire world on their own terms alone, with no consideration for their parents' opinions, guidance — and yes, even a few rules now and then. There are exceptions, of course, but even for them there is seldom any excuse for presenting parents with ultimatums and sudden declarations of independence.

My minor reservations about the book have to do with some of Grace's recommended reading for the newly liberated teenager. We happen to agree with most of her choices, but a few of them seem to encourage a "liberation" with which we cannot agree. Poe, Gibran, Thoreau, the Bible, Blake, Shakespeare — excellent choices. But Grace also recommends *Rubyfruit Jungle,* by Rita Mae Brown, with the parenthetical note that it's "sexually explicit, offends a lot of people," which is putting it very mildly. She recommends *The Color Purple,* by Alice Walker, without mentioning that it's largely about incestuous rape, sexual promiscuity, and infidelity. She does admit that Tom Robbins' *Even Cowgirls Get the Blues* is "rated R — some sex, some drugs," but her idea of some is a long way from the book's nearly total preoccupation with random promiscuity and constant drug use. Grace's list of "poetry" looks okay, except "poetry by Sappho," which is of course explicitly lesbian.

In what she calls "a short list especially tailored for searching teenagers," I think she could have made better choices than these.

These reservations are concerned with a tiny part of the book, and shouldn't keep you from buying it and using it, but keep in mind that the author has her own orientation and opinions, and you may not always agree with her.

P.S. A reader recently pointed out that Grace has no children of her own. Our reader wondered if Grace would be as liberal with her own children at the expense of parental judgment. Me too.

***FUNDAMENTALS OF HOMESCHOOLING: NOTES ON SUCCESSFUL FAMILY LIVING,* by Ann Lahrson-Fisher.** Ann continues her legacy of practical approaches to homeschooling in this book, which follows her first, *Homeschooling in Oregon* (still available from Ann at ann@nettlepatch.net), in which she basically says "relax." Ann stresses (is that the right word to use after telling you to relax?) the importance of play — children playing and parents playing with their children. Her advice about talking together and listening to each other is a theme that runs throughout the book. She explores family issues and good ways to cope with them at various ages. All her main points show you how to connect within your family and with the community around you. You will also find good resources listed that you won't find anyplace else and practical ways to use them. Reading this book will add new depth to your homeschooling experience.

I was reading the other day about some kids whose mom had decided not to engage them in the rat race. No after-school activities, no music lessons, no playdates, and only one hour of TV a day. After an initial period of the "I don't know what to do's" her kids learned to play — really play. They invented their own games and read and told stories, rode their bikes, played ball, and just hung out — happily. I wouldn't go so far as to drop time with friends or the music lessons if the kids enjoy them, but I agree that the time to just play or do nothing is valuable. It's part of childhood, or should be. I can remember days when time seemed elastic and the afternoons would stretch out seemingly forever, and not in a bad way. I don't seem to have that sort of time as an adult. This is going to sound oxymoronic, but perhaps even now, as an adult, I should schedule in some time to do nothing or just lie outside and watch the clouds.

So far I haven't made mention of **JOHN TAYLOR GATTO**'s large body of work. He was voted teacher of the year and then left the school system because he felt it failed too many students. If you have a chance to read his work he will give you extensive reasons for leaving the public school system — and he's fun to read.

***HOME LEARNING YEAR BY YEAR,* by Rebecca Rupp,** is good guide for creating your own curriculum for grades pre-K through high school. This book follows the public model but will allow you to tailor your homeschool to your child's needs. I think it will allow you to create a compromise between recreating a "public school" atmosphere at home and the unstructured "unschooling" approach. Becky includes a useful listing of resources to support her suggestions.

Where to Find Curriculum Materials and Related Resources

We do not offer curriculum packages, but you will find a list of organizations that do later in this chapter. When you begin to look for resources you'll look at the world with new eyes — starting with yourself. You know much more about finding and using resources than you think you do. You've been showing your children how you live and learn in this world since they were born. You started the minute you first smiled and talked to your baby. Family unity, good values, curiosity, and learning to satisfy it aren't taught so much as shown by example. Some things you can't buy, and those are some of the most important gifts you can give your child.

Very young children use their surroundings to explore and learn. You can start the same way. Your own house is full of resources! Your best tool is yourself — your love, playfulness, laughter, and encouragement. Older children will need books and materials that may be harder to find. Successful homeschooling is not as much a matter of how much you spend as how creatively you use what you have. According to several surveys, the average spent per homeschooled child is $500 per year. I'm sure we never spent that much. Use your library card (and don't forget to check for library discards), visit yard sales, invest in cheap workbooks — and, occasionally, you can find good, inexpensive books at Wal-Mart. It's amazing how much paper you'll use. Check your local newspaper office and print shop for rolls of newsprint and odds and ends left over from printing jobs. If you're part of a support group, make a list of books you'd like to borrow or are willing to lend, organize a book sale, or create a group resource library.

Look for homeschooling magazines and books, preferably by an author you know and trust, that review other books and products. Ask other homeschoolers who share your learning philosophy what they like. I also suggest you include *Home Education Magazine* because you'll find reviewed resources, how-to articles from different points of view, and news you should know about.

Donn did the very first of all the homeschool catalogs years ago because we learned by trial and some expensive errors that all that is hyped as educational ain't necessarily so, and he wanted others to benefit from our mistakes. Donn included a caveat concerning goods from "professional educators" in the last edition of our book, and it is more important now than ever. Commercial companies have discovered the "new" homeschool market, and some are working very hard to foist their standard material onto homeschoolers by changing their advertising. Brook Farm Books (the mail-order part of our business) is a known supplier for homeschoolers, and we have been inundated with promotional literature from publishing companies and suppliers of professional teaching materials urging us to carry their products. We don't take advertising and refuse to be influenced by any "special deals" these companies may offer. Many reviews in various publications are subsidized by the manufacturer or publisher of the product. It's called co-op advertising. A publication puts in an ad or sometimes writes a product review, and the publisher or manufacturer of the product contributes money toward the cost of publication or offers a better discount to the supplier if they sell the item. Caveat emptor. Some homeschooling publications will advertise almost anything to bring in revenue. Don't discount all paid ads — some of the books and products are excellent — but use your discretion.

When we began homeschooling, I felt very insecure. We used the Calvert School correspondence courses for a couple of years until I felt ready to follow our own course of study, guided by what we felt the kids should learn and what they wanted to learn. I know from corresponding with many of you that you would like to start with this type of security. Many of you also have to contend with periodic testing, which usually means you feel you must compromise between following your own path and satisfying officialdom. Therefore, if you want to compromise between a ready-made curriculum like the Calvert School and complete responsibility for all choices, there are several generally useful sources we recommend you use as guides — but not bibles.

LIVING IS LEARNING curriculum guides are designed to be useful to all homeschoolers. These guides have all the basic information about what is usually taught for a particular age group. What makes them different from the World Book guides (free and listed below) is that Nancy Plent has included many good resources for finding the information you want to teach and special suggestions for unschooled learning, such as how to do it, how to keep useful records (for yourself and for school or state), and much more. Nancy offers a multitude of other good materials as well, so ask about her other pre-K through high school resources. From Nancy Plent, Unschoolers Network, 2 Smith St., Farmingdale, NJ 07727.

***THE COMPLETE HOME LEARNING SOURCE BOOK: THE ESSENTIAL RESOURCE GUIDE FOR HOMESCHOOLERS, PARENTS, AND EDUCATORS COVERING EVERY SUBJECT FROM ARITHMETIC TO ZOOLOGY,* by Rebecca Rupp.** Rebecca has spent years finding resources and sharing them through her column for *Home Education Magazine* and in her earlier books. This is a mind-boggling collection of the good learning tools she's found. As Donn said in the last *Home School Source Book,* "It's a little difficult for the author of a resource guide to review someone else's resource guide, unless there are major disagreements in subject matter or philosophy. … I don't think I disagree with any of her choices, although only a small number of them appear in this book. That means you can consult both books with little chance of duplicated reviews."

TYPICAL COURSE OF STUDY. Available for the U.S. and Canada. This small booklet is not a step-by-step guide. It will provide general guidelines compiled from an analysis of many educational programs. Each grade level has a listing of general goals for social studies, science, language arts, health and safety, and mathematics. If you want more specifics see the Core Knowledge Series. This is free from World Book International, Educational Products Dept., 14333 Ash Ave., Flushing, NY 11355-2110, or World Book Educational Products of Canada, Georgetown Warehouse,

34 Armstrong Avenue, Georgetown, ON L7G 4R9. Online at www.worldbook.com/wb/Students?curriculum.

You will find more good basic homeschooling books on our website.

Legal Issues

I don't like politics. I don't like protests, meetings, lawyers, school principals (on principle), or school boards. Donn and I put years into being politically active, and we finally felt we had done enough. We just wanted to raise our family in peace and not deal with any more public issues, but we have always felt we have a responsibility to ensure freedom of education for those yet to come. Like it or not, we all need to be constantly aware of what legal decisions are being made. There are a number of political groups working, within and outside the homeschooling community, to increase regulation of homeschooling. I feel that every homeschooling parent should take the responsibility to understand what these groups are doing, and to ensure that everyone's freedom to homeschool in his own way is protected. We should all make a contribution. Those who invest nothing shouldn't be surprised if that's all they get.

TAKING CHARGE THROUGH HOME SCHOOLING: PERSONAL AND POLITICAL EMPOWERMENT, **by Larry and Susan Kaseman.** "Empowerment," say the authors, "includes identifying options and realizing that we can make choices and act on them, that we can take charge." Taking charge begins with making one's own choices about education (or anything else), which in itself is a political action, but the freedom to choose can be regained and held only by being politically active; i.e., by being aware of laws and lawmaking trends that affect homeschooling, and by taking an active part in influencing those laws. This is a very clear, comprehensive explanation of the many ways in which laws are made and how they can be influenced, and should certainly be read by anyone faced with legal or social opposition to home-schooling. Although the greater part of this book is concerned with political involvement, I think the Kasemans' suggestions regarding the everyday experience of home-schooling are just as important and useful, and make this a very valuable book even for those who don't feel ready to become politically active, or for whom just the decision to teach at home is sufficient challenge.

I think this book is more important now than ever. Although homeschooling is now legal across North America and there are more homeschoolers than ever before, there is also a stronger movement to regulate and control it than ever before. If you don't believe this or are just unaware of this move toward governmental regulation, read *Home Education Magazine*. Having won our freedom to teach at home, we now need to protect it. $12.95 plus $2 shipping and handling from Koshkonong Press, 2545 Koshkonong Rd., Stroughton, WI 53589.

Canadian Resources

BROOK FARM BOOKS, Box 101, Glassville, NB E7L 4T4. This is our Canadian address. Phone: 506-375-4680; toll-free ordering: 877-375-4680. E-mail: jean@brookfarmbooks.com. As soon as I can get this book off to the press for printing our website will become active with new exciting additions.

THE WONDERTREE FOUNDATION acts as an umbrella school and will help you design a course of study for your child. You'll find them online at www.wondertree.org, or write to Wondertree Foundation for Natural Learning, Box 38083, Vancouver, BC V0B 2C0 Canada; 604-224-3663.

CANADIAN INTERNET NEWSLINE: The Association of Canadian Home-Based Education is a national organization dedicated to helping all Canadians who wish to teach at home. There are no political or religious affiliations, no hidden agendas; just friendly help and support. You will find them at www.flora.org/homeschool-ca. It's got it all: legal requirements for all provinces, helpful resources, and much more.

***SCHOOL FREE: HOME BASED EDUCATION IN CANADA,* by Wendy Priesnitz,** one of Canada's leading homeschooling advocates and pioneers. This book provides an overview and sampling of experiences of homeschoolers across Canada, plus basic legal information. 140 pages including index. To order this book go to: www.life.ca/hs.

HOMESCHOOL AND MORE is a very good catalog of Canadian resources. Gertrude DeBoer, 29 Donald Dr., Charlottetown, PEI C1E 1Z5.

Correspondence Schools

Check out brookfarmbooks.com for a selective listing of correspondence schools.

Finding Support

Some home-school support groups meet periodically to socialize and exchange views on home learning experiences, difficulties, and successes. Others have picnics, camp-outs, group tours, and regular meetings. Some have libraries, to be shared by members. Many have information packets that include resource guides and pertinent legal information useful to members and newcomers. Most publish newsletters with information and sometimes articles about home-schooling in their respective areas. Some groups are very active politically, presenting a unified front to legislators and school officials in seeking changes favorable to home-schoolers.

Many of the larger homeschool groups have initiated yearly conferences with speakers and workshops with special features for parents and specific programs for their children. Many groups (large and small) have yearly book fairs where you can peruse and purchase books and other learning materials. Some of these book fairs have a used book sale where you can buy, sell, and swap resources. These conferences are wonderful places to meet other homeschoolers and exchange ideas. This is one of the striking advances that have occurred since we began homeschooling.

We always lived in areas where there were few, if any, other home-schoolers, to say nothing of a support group. In fact, we had been teaching at home for a number of years before we learned that any support groups existed. We would have welcomed such a group, and undoubtedly would have joined, but at the same time we'd have been somewhat cautious about our identification with them. We might wear buttons proclaiming "I'm a home-schooler" when attending a support group meeting or camp-out, but never when visiting our neighbors or going to town. In relating to our neighbors, we have always been very casual about our home-schooling, wanting to be known as people who happen to be home-schooling rather than as home-schoolers. There's a big difference. Home-schooling, although interwoven throughout our lives, is still not the most dominant facet of our being. We also do many other things, none of which would be an adequate definition of our entire lives. Although we're glad to answer questions and to share information, we're not attempting to recruit converts to a new religion, and we carefully avoid any evangelistic stance that could easily antagonize people who would otherwise be friendly and interested (or not interested). We don't want our home-schooling to be a barrier between us and our neighbors. If the subject comes up, we're very open about our home-schooling, but we don't feel it's proper or even advantageous to answer our neighbors' comments about their children's problems in school with a smug reminder that our children don't have those problems. Self-righteous, proselytizing home-schoolers can quickly become as boring as recently reformed smokers and drinkers. Besides, the only home-schoolers who don't have problems of their own don't have children.

Most support groups invite all home-schoolers in their areas to join; a few insist upon agreement with certain religious doctrines or educational philosophies. If you don't agree with the requirements of the group nearest you, start another. Put a note on the supermarket bulletin board and a small ad in the local paper with your phone number, and you're bound to discover many others who share your views.

In rejecting the professional experts, we try to remember that amateur experts may not have all the answers, either. We read and listen, weigh and consider, and then take the course that seems best to us.

I urge you to keep in contact with at least one local, state, or provincial group to gain access to up-to-date information. Because the homeschooling laws are being challenged and changed, and because of the push for national standardized testing, in and out of the schools, it is imperative — for your own welfare and your freedom to homeschool in the manner of your own choosing — that you keep yourself informed and, I hope, involve yourself in the maintenance of homeschooling freedoms for everyone.

*** **IMPORTANT!** ***

Homeschooling is legal in all states and provinces. Although the Department of Education is listed for each state, we strongly urge you to seek information and help with your questions about homeschooling from your local support group first. They will have up-to-date information about legalities. They will know the best way to deal with the formalities involved in meeting homeschooling requirements. Experience over the past years has shown (as Donn stated earlier in this book) that some professional educators and some people at the Department of Education do not thoroughly understand the regulations, and many people have been given incorrect information.

The last edition of *The Home School Source Book* had seventeen pages of contact information for support groups in the U.S., Canada, and worldwide. Experience has taught me that very few groups contact publications like ours to notify us of address or contact changes, so I have had come to the conclusion that it is impossible to keep this information up to date. I'm now referring you to www.nhen.org (see below) for local support groups so you will get the most recent and reliable information. Below I've listed what I think are the best sites.

Organizations

NATIONAL HOME EDUCATION NETWORK (NHEN), P.O. Box 41067, Long Beach, CA 90853; info@nhen.org; www.nhen.org. A proactive group with a very solid base of longtime homeschoolers, leaders in the field, individuals, and many other homeschooling groups. NHEN's mission statement says it wants "to encourage and facilitate the vital grassroots work of state and local homeschooling groups and individuals by providing information, fostering networking, and promoting public relations on a national level. Because we believe there is strength in a diverse network of homeschoolers, we support the freedoms of all individual families to choose home education and to direct such education." NHEN is creating a giant database of all resources related to homeschooling. This is a group to represent and help us all. Write for information or check out their website.

Read this paragraph if you have children attending public schools or colleges as full- or part-time students. Military recruiters are pushing for access to high school and college students. If your child is in a public institution, find out if they share student information with the military. Some schools share and others don't, and you should be aware of the policy.

Military Homeschooling Families

If you're a military homeschooling family and would like to connect with other military homeschoolers around the world, several e-mail lists are available to you. The military section of the NHEN website lists them with brief descriptions: www.nhen.org/nhen/pov/military. NHEN now has a form at the website that enables people to become points of contact for their area: www.nhen.org/nhen/pov/military/form_military_contact.asp. If you have only e-mail access to the web, contact military@nhen.org to be listed as someone willing to help in your area!

Also available to you is a super resource from Valerie Star Moon, a longtime military homeschooler with experience to share: groups.yahoo.com/group/Mil_homeschool_book.

Useful Odds And Ends

No self-respecting homeschooling book would be complete without including **JOHN HOLT** and his work. Pat Farenga has carried on John's work and you can find both John's and Pat's work at www.holtgws.com.

Ann Zeise's **A TO Z HOME'S COOL:** homeschooling.gomilpitas.com. This site can be viewed in Spanish (tinyurl.com/nmst) and French (tinyurl.com/nmsv).

BEST OF HOMESCHOOLING: www.besthomeschooling.org has a wealth of information on just about all areas of interest to homeschoolers and suggestions of where to go if you don't find what you're looking for. It's noncommercial and low-key, and you'll want to bring a cup of coffee or tea with you when you sit down to explore this site. I hope your drink doesn't get cold while you're fascinated with all you find here.

NEW AND USED BOOK BUYING COMPARISONS: Before going to Amazon.com for books that have been out a while, try www.DealOz.com, which tells you the many places you can find a book and a total price that includes shipping.

Sign up as a teacher with **SCHOLASTIC** to earn points towards free books. www.scholastic.com/teacher. You can also inquire about "educator" discounts at your local bookstore.

SHAY SEABORNE has some great essays on her website. "Confessions of a Homeschool Exclusionist" is a must-read: www.synergyfield.com/exclusionist.asp.

Because I Was Curious

You can find interesting statistics about homeschoolers done by the National Assessment of Educational Progress at nces.ed.gov/pubsearch/pubsinfo.asp?pubid=2006042. Various sections seem to be done in four-year cycles. I expect that their data is accurate with the exception of the number of homeschooling students, because many homeschoolers aren't counted for a variety of reasons. Here's what I found most interesting:

The results of the 2003 NHES survey reveal that the weighted estimate of the number of students being homeschooled in the United States in the spring of 2003 was 1,096,000, a figure that represents a 29 percent increase from the estimated 850,000 students who were being homeschooled in the spring of 1999. In addition, the estimated homeschooling rate — the percentage of the student population being homeschooled — rose from 1.7 percent in 1999 to 2.2 percent in 2003.

In 1999, three reasons for homeschooling were the most frequently cited: 49 percent of homeschooled students had parents who cited the ability to give their child a better education, 38 percent had parents who cited religious reasons, and 26 percent had parents who cited a poor learning environment at school.

Finally, the 2003 report also investigates the sources homeschoolers used to obtain curricula or books for home education. A majority of homeschooled students had parents who used one or more of the following sources of curricula or books for their children's home education: a public library (78 percent); a homeschooling catalog, publisher, or individual specialist (77 percent); a retail bookstore or other store (69 percent); and an education publisher that was not affiliated with homeschooling (60 percent).

Some students also used distance learning media. Forty-one percent of students who were being homeschooled in 2003 had engaged in some sort of distance learning. Approximately 20 percent of homeschooled students took a course or received instruction provided by television, video, or radio. About 19 percent of homeschooled students had taken a course or received instruction provided over the Internet or by e-mail. An estimated 15 percent of homeschooled students took a correspondence course by mail designed specifically for homeschoolers.

Home School, Home-School, or Homeschool?

Usually I prefer "home-school," with a hyphen, although "public school" doesn't have one. I haven't thought up any impressive etymological arguments yet. I try to be consistent in spelling and punctuation, but if my word processor insists that there are only ten spaces left on the line, I usually drop the hyphen and the intervening space rather than carry six letters over to the next line. I admit that's not consistent, but it's economical. I often hear or read "I home-school my children," but I've never heard "I public-school my children." I think the form with the strongest support so far is "homeschool" — one word, no hyphen. Would it surprise you to learn that some people take this problem very seriously? There are a lot of home-schoolers around, but I don't recall much reference to public-schoolers. A few people have written long arguments for one form or another, and I won't be very startled if some national organization soon puts it to a vote. The home(-)school movement may be divided by a hyphen more than by any other major issue. If you stare at the words long enough, none of them makes much sense. The same trick works with most of the arguments.

If you've noticed the variations in spelling home school, home-school, or homeschool, here's my explanation: Donn always preferred "home-school," and I've left his spelling in his work. I prefer "homeschool." It's just my preference, or maybe it's that I'm a lazy typist and leaving the hyphen out is easier. In quotes by other writers I've left the spelling the way it was originally written.

I'm curious — does anyone know if any group has voted on the proper way to spell home school/homeschool/home-school? I think the weight of common usage has decided the issue in favor of "homeschool," no hyphen, but I'm willing to hear arguments if someone is still inclined to belabor the point.

Regardless of your choices, you are always homeschooling.

HOMESCHOOLING AND "CULTURAL LITERACY"

Reflections on the book *Cultural Literacy: What Every American Needs to Know,* by E.D. Hirsch Jr.:

I went to school in southern Vermont in the 1940s and 1950s, and Jean went to school in suburban Illinois and a private high school in Colorado, just five years behind me. Three of our children — Cathy, Karen, and Derek — stayed at home with us through most or all of their "high school" education, and therefore have similar, if not superior, backgrounds. When we discuss key events in history or major works of literature, we usually understand each other very quickly; we learned the same basic information, and don't need to give each other long parenthetical explanations of our reference points before continuing a general discussion.

Our daughter Susan attended The Meeting School, a supposedly Quaker "alternative" boarding high school in southern New Hampshire, for two years. At least, it was founded by Quakers. She and I visited the school before her enrollment, and were very impressed by the informality, the large library, and the spacious grounds. The expectations Jean and I had of "alternative education" were that it would encompass most standard subjects, such as English, math, history, science, etc., but in a non-standard manner: i.e., without rote learning of dead facts without reflection, without quarterly exams, without grading of papers and performance, and so on. We soon realized, after Susan felt well established in the school and happy with many new friends, that the school's definition of "alternative," especially in some subjects, was very different from ours, and often depended largely on what the students felt like studying. Theoretically, that's the basis of "invited learning," and in theory I'm all for it. In practice, I need to see it working; if it isn't, I favor a little uninvited learning.

In one U.S. history course, Susan chose to concentrate on the role of women in U.S. history, which we thought was fine. A study of the important, but largely forgotten or ignored, roles of women in U.S. history should certainly give the student new perspectives on old concepts. Susan's final term paper on the subject, prepared with regular advice from a faculty adviser and awarded an A+, was an emotional defense of "rising feminism" through the ages, hardly touching any "historical" issues except that women have always been mistreated by a male-dominated society. Another student chose to study American history through its music, which we thought was a good idea; we suggested (through Susan) that he begin with Alan Lomax's *Folk Songs of North America,* which is almost a history course in itself. He began his "study" with Bob Dylan's later, "electrified" rock music, decided it was too tame, and devoted the rest of his time, including a four-week intercession, to being a Grateful Dead groupie, following the rock group from city to city, sleeping in his car and skipping meals so he could pay for rock concert tickets. And so on.

All the students chose what we thought would be excellent behind-the-scenes approaches to history, and ended with little or no knowledge at all of even the most basic facts of U.S. history, such as the causes of the Civil War or of the two world wars, the significance or even the existence of the Monroe Doctrine, and relations between the United States and other countries. To the question, "Did you study U.S. history in school?" all the students will answer, "Yes," but their various impressions are more faulty and incomplete than those of the six blind men trying to determine what an elephant is.

There are very good examples of the importance of Hirsch's message — that being "culturally literate" is to possess a large amount of shared knowledge of basic information about our world and our culture. Without that shared knowledge, says Hirsch, communications fail, and then the undertakings; and that, he adds, is the moral of the story of the Tower of Babel.

Shared knowledge is neither more nor less than a kind of language that has evolved in our culture over many, many years; it provides a short-cut to effective communication.

If our family is sitting around the TV discussing a news item about some U.S. activity in the Middle East, someone may comment that it seems to be in violation of the Monroe Doctrine; for all of us, except Susan — through absolutely no fault of her own — many years of U.S. history and policy-making are summed up in that one reference, including many of the problems preceding Monroe's administration as well as more recent activities such as the never-declared Korean War. For someone unfamiliar with the Monroe Doctrine, a lengthy explanation may be necessary to make it relevant to the present discussion, and by that time everyone else has wandered off to play Ping-Pong.

The second example is my allusion to the six blind men. For most children of my generation, it's a familiar story; for many children growing up in the '70s and '80s, it's a mental blank. If you know the story, my point is made quickly and picturesquely with fewer than a dozen words; if you don't know the story, I must either tell it to you or use ten times as many words to communicate my thought to you.

Hirsch blames much of our society's decreasing shared knowledge on Jean-Jacques Rousseau and John Dewey, although he concedes that their ideas may have been carried to unreasonable extremes by their adherents. Until about 1960 or a little earlier, children's stories, literary heroes, and school subjects across the country were very similar, as were basic courses in secondary schools and universities, and such short-cuts in communication as I've described were easy and common. Then many leading educators decided that children were being made to memorize too many facts without being taught how to think about them. Public education changed almost overnight to emphasize "thinking skills" and "communication skills." At first, this seemed to be an important advance, but gradually people began to see that although children might have been learning how to think, they had nothing to think about. Publishers and teachers, not wanting to be accused of teaching dead facts, reduced history and science and literature to the bland consistency of vanilla pudding. Magazine articles complained that Johnny and Janie couldn't read, but no one seemed to realize that Johnny and Janie no longer cared about reading because their storybooks and textbooks were as exciting as yesterday's oatmeal. Today's students are still being taught "how to think," and are still being given very few facts or ideas to think about. They're absorbing their cultural knowledge from television and rock music because no one else is telling them anything of interest. There is very little on television about the Monroe Doctrine, and rock groups seldom sing about the Renaissance or the Reformation. Hollywood no longer makes movies about Joan of Arc or King Arthur or Lewis and Clark or the Oklahoma Land Run. The people and events of the past that were a part of our everyday lives — in books, movies, radio programs, and even early television programs — are no more than blank faces and meaningless dates to most children today.

A friend in New Jersey wrote, "I told my husband I thought 'cultural literacy' was just what everybody knows. He just looked at me, and didn't say anything." That, of course, is the point: Cultural literacy *used to be* what everyone knew. Each day now, fewer and fewer people know the same things. "We have ignored cultural literacy in thinking about education," says Hirsch, "precisely because it was something we have been able to take for granted. We ignore the air we breathe until it is thin or foul."

Since reading Hirsch's book I encounter constant reminders of its truth. In discussing our model of the solar system with a neighbor, an intelligent adult who finished the ninth grade of school, I discover that he doesn't know the planets go around the sun. Pointing at the model's sun, he thinks it's the moon.

Adult acquaintances in Vermont, learning that we once lived in British Columbia, say, "Really? Why did you go all the way to South America?"

Hirsch has been most seriously criticized for his book's 63-page appendix, an alphabetical listing of words, phrases, book and song titles, historical and geographical references, aphorisms, and quotations Hirsch says "literate Americans know." Critics ignore Hirsch's own disclaimer that the list is meant to be suggestive rather than definitive. Not every literate person, Hirsch says, is familiar with every item in his list, and, although he and two colleagues worked hard to make their list as complete as they could, Hirsch invites interested readers to suggest amendments and additions to the list. Although I haven't tried to "score" myself on his list — hardly his purpose in presenting it — I've looked it over, testing myself at random, and would guess that I am completely familiar with about half, somewhat familiar with another fourth, and completely ignorant of the other fourth. I can easily come up with several references I think he missed (or perhaps chose not to include).

Conversations and correspondence among educated, "literate" people are rife with references and allusions that often convey paragraphs or even volumes of meaning in a few well-chosen words. Much more than idle whim directs many authors to borrow from the Bible, Shakespeare, and other great literary works for their titles. Readers are given extra measures of meaning in the books if they are familiar with the chosen phrases in their original contexts. Derek recently wrote a very good book review of John Steinbeck's *Of Mice and Men,* not knowing that the title had been borrowed from a poem by Robert Burns. I sent Derek to *Bartlett's Familiar Quotations,* in which he read the words in their original context; he then rewrote his review, having quickly reinterpreted Steinbeck's book in light of his new understanding of the title. *East of Eden* is another Steinbeck title that comes to mind; a very good book, even if one doesn't recognize the origin of the title — but how much more meaning will be found by the reader who realizes that Steinbeck is drawing a loose parallel with the banishment of Adam and Eve from the Garden of Eden, along with the implicit implications of toil and shame and sorrow?

"Learning without thought is labor lost," said Confucius, seemingly in agreement with Rousseau and Dewey, but, he added, "thought without learning is perilous," which I think is Hirsch's contention. We want our children to know how to think, of course, but without the lessons of history, the examples of good literature, knowledge of other peoples and cultures, and basic information about the physical world around them, their ability to think won't help them emerge from a personal repetition of the Dark Ages. We don't want to teach our children *what* to think, but *how* to think, and to do that, we must help them find facts and information and ideas to think about. Word games and puzzles in logic are no substitute for information and ideas about the "real world" of the past and present and — if we're ready — the future.

In our home-school, we've tried to cover everything. It's a star we'll never reach, of course, but still worth aiming for. Just a few of the subjects we've entertained at Brook Farm School are reading, 'riting, 'rithmetic, geography, history, science, art, music, mythology, literature, languages, psychology, ethics, religion, philosophy, humor, home economics, physical education, civics, politics, government, citizenship, commitment, integrity, self-reliance, sympathy, empathy, responsibility, map reading, typing, biology, and physiology. We also toss in a little astronomy, physics, chemistry, botany, and woodworking. We discuss and evaluate astrology, palmistry, dream interpretation, and telepathy. We talk about marriage and divorce, birth and death, abortion, the death penalty, drugs, alcohol, and the world's health and hunger problem.

We occasionally refer to our home-schooling as "elementary and secondary education in the liberal arts." As immigrants to Canada but not forgetting our American background, and with two of our children born in each of the two countries, our home-schooling has included the history, literature, and culture of both countries, which are, after all, very similar and in many ways inseparable, having both sprung from Western Europe, bringing with them shared laws, history, literature, and tradition. As E.D. Hirsch makes us look back over the years, wondering if we have helped our children acquire "cultural literacy," we realize that his phrase is a more concise way of saying what we've been saying right along. Our children have, and are continuing to acquire, much of the basic information that used to be shared knowledge, and that Hirsch hopes will be restored not only to everyone's formal education, but also to everyone's thinking and communication.

One important omission in his list of "what literate Americans know" — which Hirsch could not have foreseen — is the phrase "cultural literacy" itself. Besides conveying a meaning far beyond a basic competency in reading and writing, the phrase now represents a new way of looking at education. In discussing educational theories and practices with other educators, I feel the conversation would be as difficult without a shared knowledge of Hirsch's ideas as it would be without a shared knowledge of the basic ideas of Rousseau, Dewey, and John Holt. "Cultural literacy" has become an important part of cultural literacy.

You will find related reviews of The Dictionary of Cultural Literacy: What Every American Needs to Know, by E.D. Hirsch Jr., Joseph Kett, and James Trefil, and A First Dictionary of Cultural Literacy: What Our Children Need to Know, by E.D. Hirsch Jr., on our website. Of A First Dictionary of Cultural Literacy, Donn said, "This book is even more controversial than Hirsch's other two, but I think those who object that "Hirsch is telling us what to teach our kids" are like medieval kings who beheaded messengers who brought bad news. Would you rather have Clinton (or George W. Bush) or a national committee tell you what your child should know? If we don't set some standards for ourselves (not values for everyone, just ourselves), we will not achieve our goals. Public educators agree more and more with the opinion home-schoolers have had for years — that today's kids are not being educated. Taking them out of school is no solution if they aren't being educated at home. This book presents Hirsch's concept of the core body of knowledge that has been (and should be) the framework of American society and culture, particularly for children through the sixth grade. More than 2,000 concise, understandable entries are presented in 21 sections, ranging from the Bible and mythology to geography, history, and mathematics to the sciences, health, and technology. Richly illustrated with photographs, drawings, charts, and maps. Like the lists in *Cultural Literacy* and *The Dictionary of Cultural Literacy,* this one is meant to be suggestive, not definitive, and readers can easily adapt it to their use. We think it's a very useful skeleton for all parents and teachers — especially home-schoolers — to use as a basic reference in designing a curriculum, in stocking a home library, or both before and after the children have learned to read. The suggestions in this book give children many things to think about while they're learning to think.

Then there is the Core Knowledge Series, edited by E.D. Hirsch Jr. There are six books in this series: *What Your First* [*Second, Third, Fourth, Fifth,* or *Sixth*] *Grader Needs to Know,* subtitled, "Fundamentals of a Good First- [Second-, Third-, etc.] Grade Education." Each book is a very comprehensive, almost encyclopedic outline of basic information for each respective grade level in language arts, fine arts, history, geography, mathematics, science, and technology. The mathematics sections don't have "lessons" as such, but their very detailed summaries of all the basic facts, information, and skills that are most desirable will serve as excellent skeletons (or cores, as the series title suggests) around which to build your materials and activities. All the other subjects — such as nursery rhymes and Aesop's fables in the first-grade book through stories and poems and more advanced literature selections in the higher grades — are very good, but will need to be supplemented with other similar materials (more literature, more biographies, etc.). The series seems to be similar in some ways to Saxon's approach to math, using an incremental method of teaching, presenting very basic information at first, and then slowly building on this information, year by year, to give a more complete picture without bombarding the child with so much information that it can't be remembered or used. We have reservations about a few details, but in general we're very favorably impressed by the books. If they had been published when we were still teaching young kids, they would have made it much easier for us to design our own curricula. The arithmetic and math sections of these books — supplemented with some of the other early-learning books we recommend — can easily be all that's necessary to prepare for *Essential Mathematics* (or Saxon's Math 76, if you prefer a more academic program), with no need for the monotonous drill in standard school textbooks. Each book in the series is now in paperback.

BUT —

Having praised and recommended the Core Knowledge Series, I have to remind you that the books were *not written* by E.D. Hirsch Jr., but were edited by him, and I sometimes wonder if he was watching *Sesame Street* at the same time. Most of the books in the series are well done and need no apology, but the first, *What Your First Grader Needs to Know,* is one of the most poorly written books of its type that I have ever read. As I read it, I scribbled out eight pages of notes, of which I'll give you a little sampling:

Many sentences are not properly punctuated; commas, in particular, are often missing. Throughout the book, many sentences begin with conjunctions (and, but), apparently to "simplify" the reading by dividing one sentence into two. The writer frequently jumps from third person to second person, then back again.

Several words and phrases need explanation; e.g., in a story about "Brer Tiger," the apostrophe is missing from "Br'er," and there is no explanation that the word is a colloquial abbreviation of "brother." There is no pronunciation guide for non-Hispanics of "Medio Pollito" (MAY-de-o po-YEE-to). There are several inane statements, such as "A written sentence starts out with a capital letter that says, 'Hey, a new sentence is starting'" and "A paragraph is made of several sentences *that talk* about the same thing" (my emphasis). "Rhyming words" are referred to as "rhyme words."

"Since it is a northern country, Canada is cold in the winter," says the book, ignoring the fact that many parts of Canada are warmer than some parts of the United States. Should the reader infer that Antarctica is warm because it's a southern continent?

World religions are tossed around as if they were cute nursery stories, with no mention of their place in world history, and with no regard for their real substance. Buddha "sat beneath a tree for 98 days! Don't you think that is a long time to keep quiet?"

People crossed from Asia to North America on a "bridge," the book says, with no explanation of a land bridge and how it differs from a man-made bridge.

"It may seem strange to you, but for thousands of years only a few ships from Europe had 'bumped into' North or South America." Most small children will take "bumped into" literally, like bumping into a table. Why not "found" or "discovered"?

"Some [of the Native Americans] wanted so much to be thought brave that they clashed [?] with the men of other tribes. They called it 'going on the warpath.'" Is that a direct translation from an Indian language? An old John Wayne movie?

"One reason that [sic] Mozart was so good at music was that his father's job was teaching music, so you might say that music was in Mozart's family." Does this idiocy need a comment?

In "The World of Plants," "a seed is a little plant in a box with its lunch." "Let's pretend you are a tree, to see how a plant works." Sure, and then let's pretend you're a typewriter, to see how an editor works.

"The Pilgrims were very religious people," says the book, and I don't disagree, but what does "very religious" mean to the average six-year-old? "They came to *our country* [my emphasis] to worship in a way that was not allowed in England." What way? Why not allowed?

"Even though [Washington] would have preferred to be at his home, Mount Vernon, with his wife, Martha, he agreed to become President and was in office for eight years. This is why he is called the Father of His Country." Whoops, lost me again. Because he left his wife for eight years? Because he was in his office for eight years?

I agree with you, of course. The influence of the public school is very damaging to a child's mind. I'd certainly like to teach my children at home, but my neighbors wouldn't understand.

Supposedly this book was written *for* first-graders and not by them, but how can you tell? If there were some other book I could recommend in its place, I'd do so, but I don't know of any. I still think it's a good core for a first-grade curriculum, but don't be surprised if you sometimes feel like throwing it on the floor and jumping on it.

WHEN YOU HAVE SPECIAL NEEDS

The Little Prince said, "It is only with the heart that one can see rightly. What is essential is invisible to the eye."

There are numerous resources for the gifted and disabled. You could spend a lot of time investigating everything I've found and still wonder which items are really useful for you. I've limited the listings here to items and organizations I know and trust based on what have I learned from parents homeschooling gifted children and children diagnosed with ADHD, severe dyslexia, or other physical, psychological, or emotional problems. You will find more aids on the website.

First and foremost: If the "professionals" and "experts" give up on your child or tell you he will never read or learn independent skills, don't believe everything they say. I'm not suggesting you deny there is a problem. I'm simply passing on what I have learned from parents who have shared their special stories with me. These parents have met incredible challenges and found that their children with special needs also have special gifts and can do far more than the "professionals" think they can. These parents have found that they need to be more creative in their parenting.

These parents say patience — a lot of it — is essential. Also, children with special needs especially benefit from being read to. If these children can't read for themselves, you can open up a world they are unable to enter without your help. All children want to do the things they see other children doing. When you read to these special children, you are providing them with an example. Reading can become a goal for them, but without the pressure to perform. Many children who are unable to read on their own at the "normal" time learn to compensate with excellent memories, and can hear and retain incredible amounts of knowledge and information.

Along with patience and imagination you will need flexibility to accommodate and stimulate these minds that march to the beat of their own drummers.

Don't give up. One mother wrote to me: "I have particularly noted over the years that what is impossible today comes magically later on. It has happened time and time again, and is a good plug for 'waiting until they're ready.'"

***THE WILDEST COLTS MAKE THE BEST HORSES,* by John Breeding, Ph.D.** I recommend this book to all parents dealing with hyperactive children, whether or not they have been diagnosed as ADD, ADHD, etc., by a school or perhaps a "professional." Breeding writes convincingly against the use of mind/mood-altering drugs. Actually, he really scared me. The statistics are terrifying, and I believe a sign of a society that has failed in helping parents and teachers do the most basic of caring for young children, particularly those children we think of as "hard to handle." Breeding says, "It is a great violation of the human spirit that we give toxic, mood-altering drugs to hundreds of thousands of our precious children. Things have to be seriously out of balance for this to occur." He suggests that to begin the process of raising our children we must look at our own conditioning. This is consistent with the thinking of Jiddu Krishnamurti, who writes so eloquently on education. Mind you, I have found gaps in Breeding's reasoning, and I disagree with some of his thoughts. I think he's in outer space some of the time, and yet I find much of his analysis of the way our society raises children to be in line with my own thinking. I do not agree that we need to heal all of our own past wounds to be good parents or raise our children compassionately. We do need awareness of our conditioning and a willingness to rethink our actions and reactions. I hope you can find this book in your library so that you can decide if it's worth purchasing before you pay someone for it. For some of you it will be well worth the price, and for some it will only be worth borrowing and reading once.

An interesting article in *Newsweek* on September 17, 2007, caught my attention. Titled "You and Your Quirky Kid," by Lorraine Ali, it was about children who are different and learn differently from the norm. It discussed the challenges and rewards of living with these children, and I think the consensus from parents was that the rewards at least balanced the difficulties of the challenges.

One point stood out to me in particular: A formal or professional "diagnosis" can by a mixed blessing. If a child is truly dysfunctional and medication or very specialized education will help, it may be a good thing to know exactly what you are dealing with. For children who are marching to their own drummer but not truly dysfunctional, Ali says that putting some kind of label on a child can make it harder for parents, siblings, and the child. Some children are very high functioning in one or more areas and deficient in others, but not "sick" or in need of a "fix."

Ali knows what it is like for these different children and says, "School is the most brutal frontier for these kids and as we all know, anything from a lisp to a bad haircut is grounds for persecution." I was pleased that the article included suggestions such as finding a school that is geared toward helping these kids. Note was made of Landmark College in Vermont, which works with ADHD kids. All Kinds of Minds (www.allkindsofminds.org) states its goal as "helping parents, teachers, and students appreciate differences in learning is the first step. Helping them celebrate the differences is the goal." If you have a child who has trouble learning in the conventional manner, I suggest you look at the resources on the site.

"Depression in a 3- or 4- year-old?" says Lawrence Diller, a pediatrician and author of *Running on Ritalin*. "What is that? I can't see any reason for it. Every doctor who's ever prescribed a psychiatric drug to any kid is doing a balancing act between the needs of the kid and the needs of the system."

My thoughts on the subject: Perhaps we should be medicating the system, either the school system or the medical establishment, but certainly not our children at that age.

Notes About Sign Language

If you are hearing-impaired or have a hearing-impaired child, I'm sure you know the difference between ASL (sometimes referred to as Ameslan), SEE, and PSE. If you're not hearing-impaired but you're interested in learning sign language, you should know that ASL (American Sign Language) is the standard. It qualifies as a foreign language in many school districts. The grammatical construction is unlike English. The books listed here are all ASL. SEE, which stands for Signing Exact English, is easier to learn, but is not used by the deaf community. PSE is referred to as Pidgin Signed English. It falls somewhere between ASL and SEE.

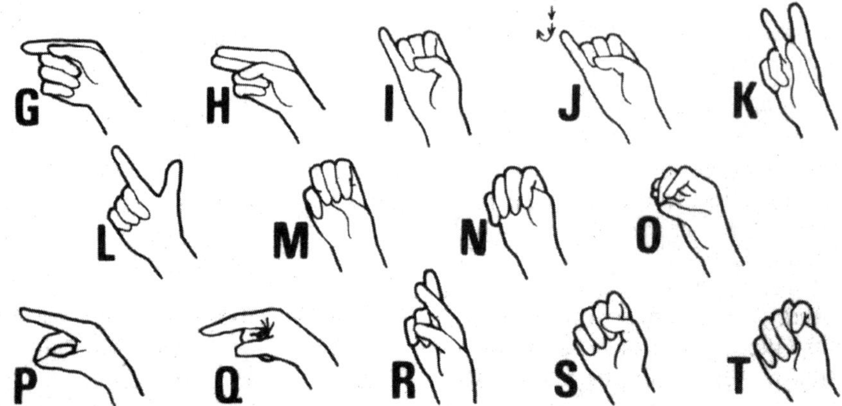

Our three girls began studying Ameslan — American Sign Language for the deaf — after reading about Helen Keller. They frequently told each other "secrets" with it, very pleased that Jean and I didn't know what they were saying. Cathy entered a 4-H speaking contest with the subject of Nim, a chimpanzee who signs to humans and other chimpanzees, and illustrated her speech with appropriate signs. (She won two first prizes and one second.) Since then, Cathy has been in several situations in which knowledge of Sign Language has been an asset: counselor in a girls' summer camp where one of the campers was deaf, working in a public library where several customers were deaf, and occasionally meeting deaf people in her travels who have been very glad to meet someone who could speak with them. More recently, Jean has studied Ameslan, and has had occasion to use it. Whether or not Sign Language will ever be of actual practical use to you or your children, it's fun to learn and to use — and it helps one to think of what it must be like to be dependent on Sign Language for communication.

I loved learning sign language. I studied it at a community college with a teacher who had lost her hearing later in life. Although she could speak English very well, the class was conducted in sign language only. Those first couple of classes were a real challenge! I made deaf friends, and the more I learned of their language the more fascinated I became. It may look simple, and much of it is, but don't be deceived. Sign language is made up of many signs and, like all languages, involves more than simply spelling out words. The more you learn, the more complex it becomes: The grammatical structure is unique, and facial expression and body language play a complex role. If you or your kids have only a casual interest in learning sign language, much can be learned and enjoyed without getting into the complexities. There is a video of signed poetry (and I wish I could remember the name of it!) that is worth watching even if you're not interested in learning the language. Literally, it is pure poetry in motion, a true art form, and extremely moving — no spoken poetry I know of compares.

For the Deaf and Hearing-Impaired

GALLAUDET UNIVERSITY PRESS, 800 Florida Ave. NE, Washington, DC 20002; gupress.gallaudet.edu. Many books for all ages, including books about deafness, sign language, parents with deaf children, and deaf parents; signed English dictionaries; sign/word flashcards; coloring books captioned with signs; first books using signs; children's fiction about children with deafness, and more.

DEAF HOMESCHOOL NETWORK. Great help for hearing parents of deaf homeschoolers is available from Marilyn Agenbroad, 116 Jerome, Silverton, OR 97381; 503-872-8451; agie@ncn.com. There is a $6 charge for her newsletter.

DEAF MOMS HOMESCHOOLING NEWSLETTER. For deaf parents homeschooling hearing children. Write: c/o Vanessa Kramer, 602 S. West St., Carlinville, IL 62626-2110.

WGBH in Boston, a PBS affiliate, offers promising help for deaf children. Cornerstones, a kit designed by and for teachers of the hearing-impaired combines video, text, and web-based exercises to guide elementary school students through basic reading exercises. Lesson guides, printable flash cards, and online games and video clips are included. Check it out at www.pbskids.org/lions/cornerstones.

The manual alphabet is not difficult to learn and is a good introduction to signing. ***THE POCKET DICTIONARY OF SIGNING,* by Rod Butterworth and Mickey Flodin,** contains the alphabet, along with numbers and simple signs, all presented in alphabetical form. There's a very good introduction to the basic hand shapes used. A good basic dictionary. 223 pages.

***THE PERIGEE VISUAL DICTIONARY OF SIGNING,* by Rod Butterworth and Mickey Flodin.** The most comprehensive alphabetized guide to American Sign Language available. Includes history of signing, tips, inflection, synonyms, precise pictures of each sign, and much more. Organized by alphabet, not subject. 478 pages.

***THE JOY OF SIGNING,* by Lottie Riekehof.** Excellent and well illustrated. Contains many useful signs for everyday conversation. I have this one and have used it a lot.

Christine Wixtrom, founder and president of the nonprofit **ASL ACCESS,** homeschooled her children for 14 years, and she e-mailed me to say that her organization will assist your public library in acquiring ASL videos — that you can borrow. On her website, www.aslaccess.org, you can search for the type of material you are looking from among the two hundred titles available. The videos are not for sale from the site, but you will find a list of vendors and publisher where you can buy them. Chris recommends Harris Communications. Subject matter crosses the educational spectrum and beyond. Most videos have a voice-over so you can enjoy and learn with ease. For more information, call 703-799-8733; fax: 703-799-4896; for TTY 703-799-4896; e-mail: cwixtrom@gmail.com. When I spoke with Christine I learned that 95 percent of the ASL videos checked out of libraries are by checked out by hearing people. You might like to mention that if your library is reluctant to get the material for you.

Blind and Dyslexic

RECORDING FOR THE BLIND AND DYSLEXIC offers recorded books: literature and educational material, including textbooks, on tape. 20 Roszel Road, Princeton, NJ 08540; www.rfbd.org.

THE NATIONAL ASSOCIATION FOR THE VISUALLY HANDICAPPED, 305 E. 24th St., New York, NY 10010, offers an excellent series of free publications for the visually impaired (all ages) and free newsletters for youth ("In Focus") and adults ("Seeing Clearly").

THE BRAILLE INSTITUTE, 741 N. Vermont Ave., Los Angeles, CA 90029-9988, offers a publication called *Expectations*, an anthology of children's literature produced annually in Braille. www.brailleinstitute.org.

PARENTS ACTIVE FOR VISION EDUCATION is highly recommended. Find out more by going online to Homeschooling With Special Challenges (www.hsc.org/chaos/specialchallenges) and clicking on the link to Parents Active for Vision Education.

Autism

HOME SCHOOLING CHILDREN WHO "AUT" TO BE HOME: home.earthlink.net/~tammyglaser798/authome.html. This website is a wealth of helpful information you can use.

Gifted

***THE GIFTED KIDS' SURVIVAL GUIDE: FOR AGES 10 AND UNDER,* by Judy Galbraith.** This upbeat and informative perennial best-seller answers bright kids' questions about why they think and learn the way they do. Includes advice from hundreds of gifted kids. Illustrated.

***THE GIFTED KIDS' SURVIVAL GUIDE: A TEEN HANDBOOK,* revised and expanded, by Judy Galbraith, M.A., and Jim Delisle, Ph.D.** Contains a wealth of information and support for gifted teens. Galbraith and Delisle have spent years working in this field, and this book was written especially to help gifted teens make the most of their potential. They write about what it means (and doesn't mean) to be gifted, how to have more control over your life, perfectionism, mistakes, goal setting, gender issues, stress, how to talk to parents, and much more. In this book, gifted teens have contributed their own thoughts about growing up, their education, and their choices (the good ones and the bad ones). At the back of the book is a useful listing of additional resources for parents and teens. This book is up-to-date and suggests web listings to explore. Highly recommended.

***THE SURVIVAL GUIDE FOR PARENTS OF GIFTED KIDS: HOW TO UNDERSTAND, LIVE WITH, AND STICK UP FOR YOUR GIFTED CHILD,* by Sally Yahnke Walker.** The subtitle just about says it all! Authoritative information about giftedness, gifted education, problems, personality traits, and more. Friendly and inviting. You'll be glad you read this one.

General Resources

NATHHAN (NATional cHallenged Homeschoolers Associated Network) is a marvelous nonprofit organization dedicated to providing encouragement to families homeschooling children with special needs. You will find help and caring support for yourself as well as for your children. NATHHAN publishes some of their own resources and lists many others. Families share their experiences. You will learn how to create a support system and discover new as well as tried-and-true methods of teaching and living well with children who live with challenges. They even have a lending library! There is some Christian content, but if you are not a Christian please don't disregard this valuable resource. NATHHAN, P.O. Box 310 Moyie Springs, ID 83845; 208-267-6246. nathanews@aol.com; www.nathhan.com.

The **DIRECTORY OF AMERICAN YOUTH ORGANIZATIONS** (out of print, but your library might have a copy) includes some listings just for disabled young people, but a note at the front of the book says that many organizations feel disabilities do not present any barriers that would limit participation. If you don't ask, you'll never know.

LINC (Learning Independence Through Computers) is a resource center that provides opportunities for children and adults with disabilities to use computer technology to achieve independence. LINC "is committed to the principle that every person with a disability should have access to the benefits of computer technology, regardless of ability level, age, income, or national origin." More than 40 affiliates across the country. LINC, 1001 Eastern Ave., 3rd Floor, Baltimore, MD 21202; www.linc.org.

SUCCEEDING WITH LD, **by Jill Lauren, M.A.** The common label LD can mean anything: learning difference, learning difficulty, learning disorder, learning disability. However, you will learn (from reading these 20 true stories by people, ages 12 to 62, who have overcome the labels and the difficulties) that it is possible for those with LD to live a satisfying and successful life. You will find straight talk about learning problems and the resulting emotional difficulties, and how these difficulties were overcome. Answers to common questions about LD plus a resource list for students, parents, and teachers. Inspiring.

Camp opportunities for the disabled can be found in ***PETERSON'S SUMMER PROGRAMS FOR KIDS & TEENAGERS***, reviewed in "Family Living — Simple Living?"

If you are looking for information about dealing with ADHD using alternative methods, check out this site compiled by Teresa Gallagher: www.borntoexplore.org. You'll find great support material here.

If you would like to give someone you care about the opportunity to explore and enjoy music, ***SOUND CHOICES*** (reviewed in the music section of the "Arts and Activities" chapter, page 239) has resources for music therapy, and includes resources for the physically disabled and hearing- or sight-impaired.

Textbooks geared to children with learning disabilities are available from **AGS** (American Guidance Service), 4201 Woodland Rd., P.O. Box 99, Circle Pines, MN 55014-1796; 800-328-2560. Free catalogs.

LEARNING DISABILITIES RESOURCES has a useful free catalog. P.O. Box 716, Bryn Mawr, PA 19010.

NICHCY (National Information Center for Children and Youth with Disabilities) has many good resources. P.O. Box 1492, Washington, DC 20013-1492.

LIVING WITH CHRONIC OR TERMINAL ILLNESS

Some may feel that this is an inappropriate chapter to include in a homeschool book. I haven't seen this type of information available specifically for homeschoolers, which is precisely why it is here. We frequently read about celebrities who are dealing with serious illness or death, but the truth is that, eventually, everyone must learn to cope with these issues. We assume that old people will get sick and die. We expect that, but it isn't just old people who have serious medical problems. I hope with all my heart that you are not reading this because you have a child, a spouse, or another loved one with a chronic or life-threatening disease, but if you are, there is help and comfort to be found. Illness and dying are a normal part of all life cycles. It can be difficult, scary, and a great privilege to be a part of this passage.

To those of you who have had to deal with life crises, or are dealing with them now, I know the agony as well as the unbelievable and wonderful depth of relationships that can develop as you move through this experience together. I've seen relationships torn apart because of the stress this kind of crisis can create. You do not have to let this tear you apart. There is help and there is hope. It is possible to win all the battles and know you have been victorious in spirit — even in the face of death.

For those fortunate enough to have lived to this point in your lives without this kind of struggle, I hope you will find ways to help others. There are many ways you can make a significant difference. You do not need to feel or act like a hero to be one. You can become someone's hero by being a friend, helping with errands, or doing seemingly small chores; sometimes being a good listener is all that is needed. Sometimes people who are sick have trouble asking for help. Don't wait to be asked to do something. Look and see what needs to be done. You can also volunteer time at your local hospital visiting with patients. Ask the staff and the patients what is needed — sometimes it's just a friendly visit. You could read to patients, or just talk. If you have a talent, share it. Make music in the halls, or put on a play in the pediatric ward. If you want to help, you will find a way.

Bill Moyers did an excellent series of shows for PBS called *On Our Own Terms*. I highly recommend this series, which illustrates the many options that are available for end-of-life care. You'll see stories of the dying (of various ages) and their families that demonstrate the courage, beauty, and peace that can be achieved with the right care and support system. You'll also see medical professionals and volunteers working to improve the current system. Someday each of us must face and deal with these issues. Being as comfortable with death and dying as we are with birth should be natural, but in our society this isn't so. Watching *On Our Own Terms* as a family or with extended family can help you all learn to discuss these personal issues with more comfort.

In the "Family Living" chapter I write about expressing feelings: "Sorrow and hurt are harder. We tend to want to shelter our children from the hard things in life, but they will learn to cope with their own inner lives and feelings better if they begin to understand these feelings through our experiences and examples." This is especially true of expressing our grief. Death and dying in our society are coming out of the closet, but there is still a long way to go. There is nothing easy about coping with the loss of someone you love. Children sometimes feel guilt or anger along with their grief. We really need to help them find a way to express — preferably talk about — these feelings. Healing comes more easily if internal feelings are expressed and talked about so that they are understood.

About ordering the books in this section on our website: For those of you dealing with chronic or terminal illnesses, if you can afford to pay full price for these books, that would be nice. If it will put a strain on your already overloaded budget, please let me know, and I will gladly get them for you at our cost. This is one of my ways to begin repaying the many people who helped us.

Need help with transportation to a consultation or treatment? If your insurance won't pay, contact the **AIR CARE ALLIANCE** (888-260-9707; www.aircareall.org) or the **NATIONAL PATIENT TRAVEL CENTER** (800-296-1217; www.patienttravel.org). There's a similar service for cancer patients called the **CORPORATE ANGEL NETWORK** (866-328-1313; www.corpangelnetwork.org).

YOUNG PEOPLE AND CHRONIC ILLNESS: TRUE STORIES, HELP, AND HOPE, **by Kelly Huegel.** Huegel was diagnosed with Crohn's disease at age 12. She tells us that her book deals only with chronic, lifelong illness, but I think it offers a wealth of information about coping on a daily basis that can apply to most young people with either chronic or terminal illness. The first section of the book contains the personal stories of young people coping with hemophilia, diabetes, epilepsy, asthma, cancer, inflammatory bowel disease, juvenile rheumatoid arthritis, congenital heart defect, and lupus. You'll find honest talk about their reactions to diagnosis, their feelings of fear and isolation, their struggles and dreams, and their sometimes difficult relationships with family and friends. The second section has very straightforward suggestions for learning to manage your illness, working with your doctor, talking about your illness with friends and family, fear of hospitals, and more. You will find lists of support groups and organizations as well as places to find up-to-date information about your illness.

CAMP SUNSHINE is for terminally ill children and their families — a place specially designed to give comfort, respite, support, and joy to the whole family. Located on Sebago Lake in Maine, the year-round program is free of charge to all families, and includes 24-hour onsite medical and psychosocial support. Bereavement groups are also offered for families who have lost a child to an illness. 35 Acadia Rd., Casco, ME 04015; www.campsunshine.org.

At **STARBRIGHT WORLD** (www.starbrightworld.org), teens can find information about their disease, chat with others coping with the same problem, and a lot more. There are opportunities for families listed there too.

***WE ARE NOT ALONE: LEARNING TO LIVE WITH CHRONIC ILLNESS,* by Sefra Kobrin Pitzele.** Harold S. Kushner, author of *When Bad Things Happen to Good People,* said: "This is the most practical book on chronic illness I know. It is clear, complete, personal, and extremely helpful. I highly recommend it." Although written for adults facing this difficult, life-altering problem, the book delves into the repercussions for the whole family and how to deal with them as constructively as possible. There's an extensive appendix for finding helpful organizations, products, services, and financial help in the U.S. and Canada. I like Pitzele's frankness; there isn't anything she doesn't discuss. Her journal excerpts have depth and warmth; while personal, they express what many cannot put into words. Pitzele was diagnosed with lupus, but this book deals with the problems faced by everyone with chronic illness.

***LOVE, MEDICINE, AND MIRACLES,* by Bernie S. Siegel, M.D.** Many doctors today rely increasingly on one or two of three ways of dealing with serious illness: drugs, radiation, and surgery. For many patients, none of these treatments works. Bernie Siegel tells about scores of "terminally ill" patients who gained partial or complete recovery after discovering the unity of their minds and bodies, an understanding that allowed them to heal themselves. He discusses the ways in which anyone can achieve the same understanding and healing. This is not a "new age," faith-healing message, but a sober examination of realities the medical establishment would rather not recognize. Reading Siegel will give you a different view of the medical profession. It can also awaken the healer within you.

Donn used this book as a means to help himself, to take as much control of his situation as possible. I learned from this book how important it was to support his efforts and how I could best help him. It gave us the tools to work together. This book and the one below introduce new ways to heal yourself, while acknowledging the usefulness or necessity of conventional treatments at times. Once you read one book by Siegel you'll want to read his other works.

ELISABETH KÜBLER-ROSS has written extensively on the subject of death and dying. She has extraordinary insights, and her books are well worth reading. They are found in almost all libraries and bookstores. If you can't find them, write to us for a list. We'll get them for you if you want them. ***DIALOGUES ON DEATH*** and ***DYING AND LIVING IN THE FACE OF DEATH*** are a couple of her titles.

The great need for healing and closure after losing someone you have loved deeply is an important part of continuing with your own life. There are various things you can do to help yourself and those around you. If death is not sudden, if you have some time to plan, visit this website: www.naturaldeathcare.org. This group sees death as a natural part of life. They feel strongly that care for the dying, whenever possible, should take place at home. You'll also find information about caring for the body after death, creating your own ceremonies, dealing with bureaucratic details, and much more.

Hospice

Do you know what hospice is and does? Here are some key points:

- Hospice concentrates on keeping patients free of pain and discomfort.
- Hospice offers more than just medical help. Patients and families can find help in spiritual, emotional, and practical matters.
- The patient is in charge of his or her care.
- Hospice involves the whole family as well as friends in end-of-life care and counseling before and after a loved one's death.
- Hospice offers advice and aid to caregivers.

For information write to the **NATIONAL HOSPICE AND PALLIATIVE CARE ORGANIZATION,** 1700 Diagonal Rd., Suite 625, Arlington, VA 22314; www.nho.org; or call the Hospice Helpline at 800-658-8898.

HOSPICE FOUNDATION OF AMERICA: www.hospicefoundation.org. Information about how to select a hospice or how to be a hospice volunteer.

You can research advance directives and making end-of-life decisions at **www.compassionandchoices.org.**

HELPING CHILDREN COPE WITH THE LOSS OF A LOVED ONE: A GUIDE FOR GROWNUPS, **by William C. Kroen, Ph.D., LMHC; foreword by Maria Trozzi,** director of the Good Grief Program at Boston Medical Center. "To be able to grieve appropriately and cope with loss before, during, and after a death enables a child to grow up free of guilt, depression, anger, and fear. When we can help our children heal the pain of the deepest emotional wound — the death of a loved one — we are giving them important skills and understanding that will serve them the rest of their lives." Being empowered to help our children will also help us to grieve fully and to heal. This is the best book I've seen for adults who want to help children — from infancy through adolescence — cope with grief. Kroen answers our questions as parents, enabling us to help our children with their questions and emotions. Sensitive, with excellent suggestions for giving comfort and guidance.

You can register to be a possible bone marrow donor. Contact the **AMERICAN BONE MARROW DONOR REGISTRY** at 800-745-2452 or www.abmdr.org or the National Marrow Donor Program at 800-627-7692 or www.marrow.org for more information.

SOMETHING TO REMEMBER ME BY, **by Susan Bosak with Laurie McGaw,** is a very special book. It's here because although it deals with death, this book is also for the living — to keep alive in memory the special people who have touched our lives. The most important thing in all our lives is the love we give and receive, and it is the one and only true lasting legacy. From the book jacket: "It's the little things, the simple things. It's the big, warm smiles and warm snuggly hugs. It's the moments that make memories ... it's a gift that both young and old can give each other. It's the most important gift we can all give. *Something to Remember Me By* is a celebration of the gift of love, and of memories and legacies across generations." Throughout this universal story of a grandmother and her granddaughter over the years, you will find delight for your eyes through the illustrations, it will touch your heart, and it will leave you with a smile and tears. The message is simple: Share the moment. Take the time, now; for what you do today will be your legacy.

Although the story is about a grandmother and granddaughter, you can expand on the ideas presented to include any important family relationship. Each hardcover book comes with a 24-page Reader's Companion with ideas of things to do together; of greater importance are the opportunities to discuss relationships, intergenerational bonds, and, if appropriate, death. The last few pages of the guide have a wonderful list of books with intergenerational themes for children and resources for adults.

***MY GRANDMA DIED: A CHILD'S STORY ABOUT DEATH AND LOSS,* by Lory Britain, Ph.D.** A simple story, well illustrated. From the introduction: "Children who can name their feelings and find creative ways to deal with their losses are far healthier emotionally and physically." This book was written to allow you to insert your own personal beliefs about death. The author suggests that you let your child know that others may believe differently, teaching tolerance. There are ample opportunities to discuss with your child the feelings that come with grief. There are suggested activities (your child can even color right in the book) and advice for providing help if your child is not dealing well with loss. This is the best book on the subject that I've found.

***ALWAYS MY GRANDPA: A STORY FOR CHILDREN ABOUT ALZHEIMER'S DISEASE,* by Linda Scacco, Ph.D.** This book has a very warm, intimate feel to it, and the story is one that parents and children can easily relate to: A young boy and his mother live through the time when Grandpa begins to lose his memory and his ability to care for himself. Both mother and son have to learn to cope with the difficult situations and emotions that result from this, and they help each other by talking about their feelings. At the end of the book are some very sound suggestions for parents finding their own way through this experience with their children and their own parents.

A Personal Journey

There are some similarities between living with cancer or any serious illness and homeschooling. There is a dramatic learning curve, changes of plans, new routines, and changes in personal relationships.

In November 2005 I was diagnosed with breast cancer. I caught it early. I caught it with a self-exam. All I can say about this is just do it regularly. It scared me. It scared me nearly witless sometimes. I felt fine. I didn't feel sick, and it was hard to accept that there was something in my body, which has been very healthy over the years, that could make me very sick and maybe kill me. I've learned a lot of new lessons. Cancer in all forms seems to be becoming an epidemic in our society. Maybe what I've learned can help you.

I was scared. First I learned that it is all right to be scared but that you can't let it paralyze you in mind, body, or spirit. This diagnosis of cancer can haunt you awake or in your bed. I had to learn to segregate dealing with it, or it could have taken over my life completely. You need the support of family and friends. I talked to Donn. I talked to Donn a lot. I was angry, not at Donn, but with the fate that took him years ago so that he wasn't here for me when I needed him as I had been there for him. There was also a inner knowing that he was there in his own way and that all I really needed to do was let go and look inward without words. A small comfort when your mind won't let you sleep. In day-to-day living I had my kids and a very dear friend who immediately said she would come with me to appointments and through whatever came along, anytime.

Donn and I were always very self-reliant. I learned that there are times this is totally inappropriate. There are times when you really do need others, and it is a privilege for all parties involved to be part of the giving and taking.

I learned that it is essential to do your own homework. You have to live with the consequences, so don't take anyone's word for anything. Check it. Check it again. Get a second opinion. Get a third opinion. Talk to everyone you know who has had to deal with the same diagnosis. Join a support group if you can. It helps to know there are others coping — and how they cope.

Never take the word of a specialist. He sees with tunnel vision. Talk to an oncologist or at least someone in a different specialty before making decisions.

Listen to your inner voice/self. You know yourself best, and you have to make the decisions and live with them.

Take your time even when you feel you don't have any. Take a deep breath — and let it out. And do it again until you feel calm. You cannot think clearly while your mind and body are feeling panicked.

Take charge. Collect all your medical records as you go. Take a friend or spouse with you as witness, second pair of ears, secretary, question asker. This is extremely important, as you just can't take in all the information doctors will (sometimes) casually throw out at you.

Take care of yourself in some special way. Make sure you take time to do something that pleases you. Stay connected to your friends and family. Don't withdraw or hide. Work hard to keep your life as normal as possible. I was working as director of a snowschool (for those of you who don't know this relatively new term, it replaces "ski" school and includes snowboarding). and was out and teaching every day that I possibly could. It was an activity I loved, and it absorbed me totally so that there was no room for worry. Psychologically there was no illness when I was out there working with the kids — just me and the kids and the snow and the fun. It gave me a spot of sanity. It was a retreat, and while physically demanding it was emotionally rewarding and calmed my spirit. My general manager and the staff were great support.

If you look at the whole scenario it can overwhelm you. Take it on one step at a time. To stay sane, focus on what you can do.

Remember this if nothing else: Take charge of your treatment options. You are not like everyone else. For me the standard treatment was surgery, chemotherapy, radiation, and then one of the follow-up drugs. It didn't happen quite that way. I had one round of chemo (of the four prescribed) and it just about killed me, literally. I had an allergic reaction to the anti-nausea drugs, a toxic reaction to the chemo itself, and a period of being psychotic. You don't need all the details, but I just said "no more." Strange things happened, like patches of my normally grey (used to be blonde) hair turning jet black from the root to the tip. I still have little or no memory of a few days.

They tried to convince me there were other chemo formulas they could try, but I just couldn't tolerate the thought of allowing someone to poison my body in any way again. There was very reluctant agreement with me, because this is the treatment that's the "standard." They did concede, finally, because they really couldn't guarantee me that if I survived physically I would still be all there mentally — still be me. It took weeks before my mind functioned more or less normally (and maybe it isn't all there still! How would I know? Like Alzheimer's, maybe I don't know what I've lost) and months to make a comeback physically. Of course they wanted to start radiation immediately since the chemo wasn't an option. Being a good girl I went for a consult. The doctor was very good. I liked him and knew from references that he was very good. I heard all the good news and all the bad effects and he said he would "fix" me. I said I wanted time to think about it. That seemed to bother him. I wrestled and fought with this decision for about 48 hours. This was what I was supposed to do, but I just couldn't find a good reason to justify six weeks of this treatment that didn't guarantee me anything but a local fix — and a mastectomy would do that without all the short- and long-term side effects. I had so much wonderful support that it was with some regret that I upset my family, many friends, and the doctors by refusing the radiation. I opted for the mastectomy, and I am so glad I didn't listen. I am fine now. Although I know it could come back, I am refusing to let it take up any more of my life — with the exception of regular checkups.

Cancer has changed my life in ways similar to the changes that came with homeschooling. It took over my life. It revolutionized my perspective and my priorities. One of the few constants in life is Change. For some people, or under some circumstances, changes can make us uncomfortable. Change challenges us. It can make us afraid. Now if you think about that for a bit you'll realize that sameness makes us stagnate. We need change to challenge ourselves and to make us break out of our shells and grow. Homeschooling can and will do this for us like other major happenings in our lives. Challenge and change, homeschooling and illness are what you make of them. It can be a good thing.

This chapter is dedicated to Donn, Gus, and my Dad and Madge, who in their dying taught me many valuable lessons about living and loving. I thank them all. Death is the end of life as we've known it, but not of our relationship.

USEFUL MAGAZINES AND CATALOGS

Most magazines are cheaper than an equal weight in textbooks, and many are much better. These are some of the most helpful on the market today. We read some of them all the time, some of them occasionally, and some of them never. When subscribing, we try to order magazines at different times of the year, so the renewal notices don't all show up at the same time. Fortunately, a few subscriptions have been gifts from relatives. Magazine publishers will usually be glad to send advertising brochures; some will send samples or enter a trial subscription. Please send an SASE for price and subscription information. Many specialized magazines (science, history, etc.) are listed in those chapters.

I find it interesting, after so many years of being involved with homeschooling, that my two favorite homeschool magazines, *Home Education Magazine* in the U.S. and *Life Learning* in Canada, still exist and are still my favorites. They have managed to grow to meet new demands while staying fresh and interesting to read. I do mourn the passing of *Growing Without Schooling*.

Magazines

CONNECT. A publication dedicated to creative thinking, synthesizing science and hands-on math for grades K to 8. Articles about new products, ideas to investigate, multidisciplinary approaches, literature links, and excellent book reviews. Designed for classroom and group use, but you can adapt the material to suit yourself. Synergy Learning International, P.O. Box 60, Brattleboro, VT 05302; 800-769-6199; info@synergylearning.org; www.synergylearning.org.

THE EDUCATION REVOLUTION. A magazine published by the Alternative Education Resource Organization that will keep you abreast of major developments in alternative education around the world, including major homeschooling news. Mentions camp opportunities; lists and describes related organizations and current activities, teaching jobs and internships, and conference news; and more. Write for subscription information: AERO, 417 Roslyn Rd., Roslyn Heights, NY 11577; 800-769-4171 or 516-621-2195; info@educationrevolution.org; www.educationrevoltion.org.

HOME EDUCATION MAGAZINE. If you can afford only one homeschooling publication, you shouldn't miss this one. It's the best. P.O. Box 1083, Tonasket, WA 98955-1083; 509-486-1351; info@homeedmag.com; www.homeedmag.com. See "Homeschooling and Education," page 42, for more.

HOME EDUCATOR'S FAMILY TIMES. Christian-based with a liberal view. Many good resources and articles. P.O. Box 6442, Brunswick, ME, 04011; www.HomeEducator.com/FamilyTimes. These people put on the largest homeschooling conference in New England (mid-July in Boxboro, Massachusetts). I've been a number of times and loved it. Lots of workshops, great speakers, and plenty of entertainment for the kids.

LIFE LEARNING, Life Media, P.O. Box 112, Niagara Falls NY 14304-0112, or 508-264 Queens Quay W, Toronto ON M5J 1B5; 800-215-9574; www.lifelearningmagazine.com. In the words of founder and editor Wendy Priesnitz, "*Life Learning* magazine is an intelligent, high-quality, professionally edited and produced magazine written by and for unschooling families who trust themselves and their children to learn freely and naturally what they need to know to live successful, happy lives."

THE LINK: THE HOMESCHOOL NEWSPAPER. Free online or in print as a newspaper for homeschoolers. Lots of news, good book reviews, and resource ads. A wealth of information just for the asking. 741 Lakefield Rd., Suite J, Westlake Village, CA 91361; www.homeschoolnewslink.com.

MOTHERING MAGAZINE. One of the leading international magazines devoted to natural childbirth, breastfeeding, child-rearing, and midwifery. Covers family issues, pros and cons of vaccination, dental care, discipline, childhood illnesses, and baby supplies. Bimonthly. P.O. Box 1690, Santa Fe, NM 87504; 800-984-8166 or 505-984-8116; www.mothering.com.

NURTURING. An international journal to encourage attachment parenting. If you really want to be close to your children and understand their needs and how to fulfill your needs too, you will treasure this magazine. You'll find articles on birth, breastfeeding, emotional issues, and health. Of all the magazines for parents I've seen, this one comes closest to representing our feelings and philosophy about raising children. Ads for baby- and parent-friendly products. Write for sample issue: P.O. Box 58067 (Inglewood), 12621 118th Ave., Edmonton, AB T5L 4Z4; www.nurturing.ca.

QUEBEC HOMESCHOOLING ADVISORY NEWSLETTER, 1002 Rosemarie, Val David PQ J0T 2N0, is an excellent resource for those living in Quebec in particular as well as across Canada.

READER'S DIGEST, Reader's Digest Rd., Pleasantville, NY 10570, or 1100 René Lévesque Blvd. West, Montreal, QC H3B 5H5; www.rd.com.

SMITHSONIAN MAGAZINE. The Smithsonian Institution in Washington, D.C., has the greatest collection of Americana in the world and much more. The magazine covers everything from the far reaches of space to fossils. We've had the pleasure of a gift subscription from one of my aunts since the early '70s, and I always look forward to getting it. *Smithsonian* has provided a window into the world when we have lived in very isolated places, with its strong focus on art and conservation, intelligent articles, and great photography. P.O. Box 420113, Palm Coast, FL 32142-9143;

www.smithsonian.com. ***MUSE*** is a child's version of *Smithsonian*. It offers a diversity of articles, puzzles, contests, and more just for kids ages 8 to 14. P.O. Box 9304, La Salle, IL 61301.

UTNE READER. Articles, editorials, reviews, letters, and selections from more than 1,000 independent small-circulation magazines, journals, and newsletters. Offbeat, upbeat, politically aware. Bimonthly. Utne Reader, 12 North 12th St., Suite 400, Minneapolis, MN 55403; www.utne.com.

For Kids

There's something special about a magazine that arrives addressed to a child; although it comes regularly, it's still an unanticipated surprise.

BOOMERANG! A monthly 70-minute "audio magazine" that you can download as an MP3 file or receive in the mail on CD, with feature stories about geography, history, and current events; mysteries; letters to the editor; interviews; and jokes. For kids 6 to 12 (more or less), professionally written from a kid's perspective and reported on by kids. P.O. Box 261, La Honda, CA 94020; 800-333-7858 (credit card orders only); boomerang@boomkids.com; www.boomkids.com.

CHILDREN'S BOOK-OF-THE-MONTH CLUB, Book of the Month Club, 1225 S. Market St., Mechanicsburg, PA 17055; 717-918-2665; www.cbomc.com. Mostly very good books for ages 6 months to 12 years. Shipping costs may be high.

COBBLESTONE PUBLISHING COMPANY, 30 Grove St., Suite C, Peterborough, NH 03458-1454; 800-821-0115; www.cobblestonepub.com. Cobblestone offers a variety of excellent publications targeting specific areas of interest, including some books for teaching with primary resources: ***CALLIOPE,*** world history; ***APPLESEEDS,*** social studies for younger kids; ***FACES,*** world cultures and geography; ***COBBLESTONE,*** American history, ***DIG,*** archaeology; and ***ODYSSEY,*** science. Cobblestone also produces three magazines in conjunction with *Smithsonian* magazine: ***CLICK*** introduces the universe to children ages 3 to 7; ***ASK*** is for curious kids ages 7 to 10, with outstanding photography, cartoons, contests, and projects; and ***MUSE*** offers a diversity of articles, puzzles, contests, and more just for kids ages 8 to 14. The company also publishes fiction magazines for a wide range of ages: ***BABYBUG*** is for ages 6 months to 2 years. Sturdy cardboard format makes it easy to handle. Stories, rhymes, bright pictures. ***LADYBUG*** is for ages 2 to 6. Stories, poems, songs, games, and more. Comes with activity sheet and special section for parents. ***SPIDER*** is for ages 6 to 9. Stories, poetry, articles, artwork, and activities for independent young learners. ***CRICKET*** is for ages 9 to 13. Lots to read: stories, folktales, fantasy, science fiction, history, biographies, poems, science, sports, and crafts — and, of course, humor. ***CICADA*** is for ages 13 and up. Literary magazine with fiction and poetry.

HIGHLIGHTS FOR CHILDREN. This is one our favorites. Creative writing, poems, and seasonal activities for ages 6 to 12. Sometimes they publish submissions by kids. Approximately $26 a year. P.O. Box 2182, Marion, OH 43306-8282; www.highlights.com.

Highlights now has a couple of new publications for children ages 7 to 10 (more or less). Request information about ***PUZZLEMANIA*** and ***MATHMANIA,*** P.O. Box 4002862, Des Moines, IA 50340-2862.

SKIPPING STONES is the best multicultural magazine for kids that I've ever seen. It's full of excellent and exciting prose and poetry by and about children from every imaginable background. There are book and video reviews; contributions from city and country kids telling of their hopes and dreams, their living conditions, and the problems they cope with on a daily basis; pen pals from around the world; bilingual pages; photos by and about kids; and more. Exciting! Ask for information on their low-income subscription allowance if you need it, or a multiple copy discount. P.O. Box 3939, Eugene, OR 97403-0939; info@skippingstones.org; www.skippingstones.org.

STONE SOUP: THE MAGAZINE BY YOUNG WRITERS AND ARTISTS. Just what it says it is. Contributors through the age of 13 may submit stories, poems, and artwork. Stone Soup has been publishing quality children's art and writing for more than 25 years. Each piece published is accompanied by a picture of the contributor. A great gift for a child who wants to be a writer or artist. Write for current subscription rates. P.O. Box 83, Santa Cruz, CA 95063; subscriptions@stonesoup.com; www.stonesoup.com.

The National Wildlife Federation offers ***ANIMAL BABY*** for ages 0 to 4, ***YOUR BIG BACKYARD*** for ages 3 to 7, and ***RANGER RICK*** for ages 7 and up. 11100 Wildlife Center Dr., Reston, VA 20190-5362; www.nwf.org/magazines.

Aimed at kids 8 to 18, **WWW.YOUNGBIZ.COM** offers professional advice and many success stories to inspire and guide ambitious young people on the path to becoming successful entrepreneurs. The company behind the site also runs workshops in the U.S. and Canada.

Catalogs

ANDERSON'S BOOKSHOPS, P.O. Box 3832, Naperville, IL 60567-3832. One of the best catalogs of children's books. Everything reviewed on their website: www.andersonsbookshop.com.

BITS & PIECES, P.O. Box 30140, Salt Lake City, UT 84130-0140; www.bitsandpieces.com. Puzzles from simple to complicated to unique.

BLACKSTONE AUDIO, P.O. Box 969, Ashland OR 97520; 800-729-2665; www.blackstoneaudio.com. Excellent selection of audiotapes and CDs. Worth investigating.

BOOKS ON TAPE, 400 Hahn Rd., Westminster, MD 21157; 800-548-6574; www.booksontape.com. They say they have the largest selection of unabridged audiobooks. I don't know if that's true, but you can check it out.

CARSON-DELLOSA, P.O. Box 35665, Greensboro, NC 27425; www.carsondellosa.com. If you're looking for good workbooks, try this catalog.

CBC RADIO CATALOGUE, Georgetown Terminal Warehouses Ltd., 34 Armstrong Ave., Georgetown, ON L7G 4R9. schools.cbc.ca/catalogue.html. List of programs available to the public. They offer some interesting listening. Fortunately the recorded material is better than the PR letter I received, which had the following information: "The independent stores that decided to carry CBC Audio have done particularly well, and they indicated that audio did not sell well for them."

CHINABERRY, 2780 Via Orange Way, Suite B, Spring Valley, CA 91978; 800-776-2242; www.chinaberry.com. Children's books sorted by reading level and books for adults, too, with marvelous reviews. Many other interesting items.

CONTINENTAL PRESS, 520 E. Bainbridge St., Elizabethtown, PA 17022; 800-233-0759. Inexpensive workbooks and test prep books for grades K through 12 in all subjects, including special needs.

CURIOSITY KITS, Action Products International Inc., 1101 N. Keller Rd., Suite E, Orlando, FL 32810; www.apii.com. Lots of creative play and learning materials.

DOVER PUBLICATIONS, 31 E. 2nd St., Mineola, NY 11501-3582; 800-223-3130; store.doverpublications.com. Hundreds of good books for children and adults at low prices. Ask for the children's books catalog. Check with them about their shipping rates — it may be cheaper to buy these books from us. Anything you can order from Dover, we can get for you.

WWW.DHAUDIO.COM is a useful link to a huge variety of audio material you can rent, download, or buy on tape, CD, Mp3, and videos. The material you can link to covers the whole spectrum of what we read and watch.

FOLLETT EDUCATIONAL SERVICES, 1433 Internationale Parkway, Woodridge, IL 60517; 800-621-4272; www.fes.follett.com. Used textbooks from most major publishers in very good condition at reasonable prices, plus teacher's editions, workbooks, dictionaries, reference books, and classroom paperbacks (literature).

F.U.N. NEWS. Published by the Family Unschoolers Network, edited by Nancy and Billy Greer. F.U.N. News is full of good commonsense ideas for all homeschooling families. The focus is on unschooling, but there are too many good articles and reviews, relevant to all of us helping our children learn, to dismiss it as an "unschooling" and therefore useless publication to those using a more structured approach. Your kids will enjoy the special projects, and you'll definitely enjoy this upbeat newsletter. Computer information, timely articles, good resource page, book and magazine reviews, and more. New issues are no longer being published, but back issues are still available, and some of the articles are available for free on their website. F.U.N., 1688 Belhaven Woods Ct., Pasadena, MD 21122-3727; fun@FUN-Books.com; www.unschooling.org, www.FUN-Books.com.

HEARTH SONG, 6519 N. Galena Rd., P.O. Box 1773, Peoria, IL 61656-1773; 800-325-2502; www.hearthsong.com. Creative and interesting toys and games. Decent prices. I'll be using this one for sure.

HOMESCHOOL AND MORE ..., 44 Price Street, Petitcodiac, NB E4Z 4R5; www.homeschoolandmore.ca. Excellent Canadian home-learning resources.

KAPLAN EARLY LEARNING COMPANY, P.O. Box 609, 1310 Lewisville-Clemmons Rd., Lewisville, NC 27023; www.kaplanco.com. A great variety of educational materials: toys, games, books, paints, and more.

KEY CURRICULUM PRESS, 1150 65th St., Emeryville, CA 94608; www.keypress.com. High school math textbooks, computer software, and more.

KLUTZ, 450 Lambert Ave., Palo Alto, CA 94306; www.klutz.com. Super catalog of fun and interesting kits, books, and games for kids. Great for birthdays and holiday gifts, or anytime.

KNOWLEDGE UNLIMITED, 2310 Darwin Rd., Madison, WI 53704; 800-356-2303; www.thekustore.com. Very good learning materials.

LIGHTER SIDE, P.O. Box 25600, Dept. LD, Bradenton, FL 34203-5600; www.lighterside.com. Funny and unusual gift ideas.

MILLIKEN PUBLISHING, 3190 Rider Trail South, Earth City, MO 63045; www.millikenpub.com. Good workbooks. Reasonable prices.

NIENHUIS MONTESSORI USA, 140 E. Dana St., Mountain View, CA 94041-1508; montessori.nienhuis.com. Montessori materials.

PARENTING PRESS, P.O. Box 75267, Seattle, WA 98125; www.parentingpress.com. Lots of good books about raising kids. We've reviewed some of them.

PBS HOME VIDEO, 2100 Crystal Dr., Arlington, VA 22202; www.shoppbs.com. Catalog of videos from public broadcasting.

PLAY FAIR TOYS, 1690 28th St., Boulder, CO 80301; www.playfairtoys.com. Very good toys, including three-foot dinosaur models, a human skull model, and Lincoln Logs.

THE PLAYSTORE, 508 University Ave., Palo Alto, CA 94301; www.playstoretoys.com. Beautifully made toys, games, costumes, and more.

SCHOOL ZONE, 1819 Industrial Dr., Grand Haven, MI 49417; www.schoolzonecatalog.com. This company has some of the very few workbooks of which we thoroughly approve. They're clear and easy to understand, they stick to basic principles and explain them well, and they present exercises that make learning fairly easy and even fun. The books are graded, but most of the materials can be used without regard for the grade level intended by the publisher. Workbooks are available in math, grammar, spelling, reading, phonics, handwriting, number readiness, and several preschool activities. Prices are reasonable, and the service is prompt and efficient. They now offer CD-ROMs for young children and I'm sure they're good, but I don't think young children should be learning this way (see "Computers," page 227).

SKY PUBLISHING CORP., P.O. Box 171, Winterset, IA 50273-1517; www.shopatsky.com. Books and many other resources about astronomy.

SOCIAL STUDIES SCHOOL SERVICE, 10200 Jefferson Blvd., P.O. Box 802, Culver City, CA 90232; www.socialstudies.com.

SPILSBURY PUZZLE CO., P.O. Box 1408, Ottawa, IL 61350-6408; www.spilsbury.com. Puzzles, games, and more.

SPIZZIRRI PUBLISHING, P.O. Box 9397, Rapid City, SD 57709; www.spizzirri.com. Great science, art, and bilingual workbooks.

THE STRAND BOOK STORE, 826 Broadway (at 12th St.), New York, NY 10003-4805; www.strandbooks.com. All kinds of books both new and used.

TIN MAN PRESS, P.O. Box 11409, Eugene, OR 97440; www.tinmanpress.com. This small catalog of creative language arts material is promoted for the gifted, but I think it's good for everyone's kids.

TREETOP PUBLISHING, P.O. Box 320725, Franklin, WI 53132; www.barebooks.com. Great blank books.

ZANER-BLOSER, 1201 Dublin Rd., Columbus, OH 43215-1026; www.zaner-bloser.com. Handwriting resources.

THE HOME SCHOOL SOURCE BOOK, 3RD EDITION, had a large section of free and almost free resources. These can change so quickly that I've decided not to put that section in this book. I suggest you go to the library or check Amazon.com for books of free stuff. Your state and the federal government also have numerous publications either free or for very little money. You can also order the 3rd edition of *The Home School Source Book* from us for $10 and use the listings there.

STRUCTURE

Having concluded before we started teaching at home that the loosely structured approach is definitely best, we were sometimes dismayed to find that it wasn't working, and it's hard to find an instruction manual for something that isn't supposed to have instructions. Until the kids were about six or seven, they were certainly eager to learn anything and everything around them. After that, sometimes they were eager to learn, and sometimes they'd go out to lunch for two or three weeks. We watched and waited, and told each other that they'd soon get tired of old Donald Duck comics or television and would return to doing something productive. Maybe they just needed a break. Usually, they did tire of their early retirement, and began reading, thinking, drawing, making things, and asking us twenty questions a minute about anything at all, but occasionally it looked as if they'd settled down for a long winter's nap.

"Hey, look, kids," we'd say, "we're having school at home. That means you're supposed to be learning something."

"Okay, Dad. What do you want us to learn?"

"What causes gravity? What makes the Aurora Borealis light up? Why was Mona Lisa smiling? What does x represent if five times x to the fourth power equals eighteen? How do you drive a nail without mashing your thumb? How can you collect a dozen eggs in the barn and deliver twelve eggs to the house? How high is up? Things like that."

"Dad, have you read this story about when Donald Duck and his nephews went to Yellowstone Park and —"

"Okay, then, where is Yellowstone Park?"

"You mean there really is a Yellowstone Park?"

"That's all, folks. Back to the drawing board. Notebooks, pens, pencils, eager minds, and smiling faces. Nine o'clock tomorrow morning. All drinks of water, toilet trips, and forgotten books to be remembered before then."

"Really? Okay, Dad! We were wondering if you were going to help us learn anymore, or if you were too busy."

"That's what I thought you were wondering. Is that about the time the Beagle Boys think Donald Duck has a buried treasure under a geyser? Let me borrow it when you're done with it."

So our unschool would become a home-school again, and we'd have fairly regular hours, and lots of discussions, and real Assignments For Tomorrow, and after a while we'd try the unschooling again. After all, how can I write a book about how well unschooling works for us if it doesn't? The kids just never realized what a responsibility they had to my readers.

School, as we all know, is a box or series of boxes in which children are required to sit for several hours a day, while government-inspected teachers attempt to transfer information out of books into the children's heads.

Home-school was around a long time before school, and often consisted of nothing more than a borrowed book and the light from a fireplace. Sometimes, just the fireplace. Some people did quite well with this arrangement, and went on to become president or to invent the phonograph. At that time, most of the unschools were not different from the nonschools. Instead of spending years in preparing to learn how to make a living, people went out to make a living. Or stayed at home to make a living.

The industrial revolution reduced the number of job opportunities, so a different kind of child labor had to be invented. School was the answer. The government told parents they were too stupid and ignorant to teach their children anything, and the parents were too stupid and ignorant to realize the government was wrong, so the children tucked baked potatoes into their pockets and trotted off to school. A few people still became presidents and a few still invented things, and everyone had a piece of paper certifying that he had spent a lot of time behind a desk, so schools were considered to be Good Things.

Gradually the parents got smarter and noticed that their children were getting dumber. Although some were still growing up to be presidents or to invent things, most of the presidents were stupider, and so were the inventions, so a few parents re-invented home-schools. The children were taken out of school to be taught at home. Unfortunately, the parents had been taught in schools and thought school methods were the only methods, so the home-schools were not much different from the schools, except that fewer students were smoking dope or getting pregnant or both. They still learned to be almost as stupid and uninventive as they had in the public schools.

Most home-schools had a structure as rigid as that of most public schools, with the entire day planned in detail — so many minutes for spelling, so many for math, so many for standing in line, so many for getting out your books and sharpening your pencils, hold up two fingers when you have to go to the bathroom, and so on — with regular testing, grading, and even "homework" to be done in the evenings.

Many of the new home-schoolers were fundamentalists, who were usually very concerned with authority and obedience, which they felt couldn't be maintained without a rigid teaching structure and lots of what they called strict discipline. The fundamentalists frequently recommended an intricate system of rewards, bribes, punishments, and psychological games — not only for schoolwork, but even for such daily chores as making the bed. Punishments included spanking, forfeiture of meals, and withholding of play privileges; rewards included food treats, games, special trips, and even money. The fundamentalists didn't realize that such rewards and punishments not only undermined their goal of discipline, but usually indicated that discipline had already broken down. Or maybe it was too late, because now they had to try to maintain control over children who had unwittingly been taught that everything has its price. It must be discouraging to know that sinfulness has been a dominant characteristic on both sides of your family ever since Adam and Eve ate the fruit of the tree of knowledge.

A few public-schoolers and a few home-schoolers, who had read *Robinson Crusoe* or *Mowgli of the Wolves* and had heard of Jean-Jacques Rousseau, decided to chuck the whole works and have unschools. The unschools had no lesson plans, no assigned subjects, and no guided study, and the students could go to the bathroom without raising their hands. The unstudents unlearned several of the things they had learned in the schools and home-schools, and were allowed to sit at desks if they wanted to, read books if they wanted to, and get jobs as construction workers or hairdressers or magazine editors if they wanted to.

Sometimes unschooling is referred to as the invited learning approach. I think the idea is that when the kids decide they want to know something, they invite someone to teach them. Otherwise, they are protected by the First Amendment from any obligation to learn anything. Adults have no moral right to intrude on children's lives without invitation.

In New York City, parents don't have any legal control over their children who have reached the age of sixteen, but they are responsible for all contracts and crimes of their children who have not reached the age of eighteen. Many parents have found that this creates some very interesting situations.

Back to unschooling. The prefix "un" was meant to communicate the unschooling parents' rejection of stiff structures and canned curricula. The term "unschool" has the drawback of saying what it is not, but not saying what it is. "Unhorsed" gives the impression of an impromptu flight from the back of a horse, but it doesn't say if the unrider is walking, dazed, or dead; only that he is no longer on the horse. When I stand up, am I unchaired?

Most home-schoolers are somewhere between these extremes, not requiring the students to hold up two fingers or sit still with their backs straight and listen, but also realizing that not all kids will learn reading, writing, arithmetic, history, geography, home economics, and penmanship just from sitting in the woods with a screwdriver and a pile of books.

Some people credit Horace Mann with starting public schooling in America. Others blame him for it. John Holt, very liberal, says public school is not a good idea gone wrong, but was a bad idea from the very start. Samuel Blumenfeld, very conservative and a fundamentalist, says we never needed schools at all. I went to school for twelve years and often tried to convince my parents I didn't need it, but some of my history lessons were about people two or three hundred years ago who surely could have used a little of it, whether they actually needed it or not.

There were books about schools before Moses left Egypt, and many more have been published since. Now, there are also many books about home-schools, and even more than a few about unschools. Books about schools and schooling are usually cataloged under the heading of Education, which considering that a government agency does the cataloging, makes unexpected sense. When they began cataloging books about home-school, they could have used the heading "Home Education," but apparently "home" was considered too homey, so they chose to call it "Domestic Education." Look on the back of the title page of any home-school book that has Cataloging in Publication Data, which is information supplied by the Library of Congress or the Library of Canada to tell librarians that *Teach Your Own* does not belong with the books on farming or plumbing.

Was the term devised as a smokescreen? Home-schools (and unschools, although authorities seldom see any difference) are not often applauded by officialdom, so perhaps the cataloging officials sought to camouflage their existence with a pedantic euphemism. If you were searching the card files in your local library for books about home-schooling, would you think (before I told you) to riffle through the D section? There might be two dozen books on the subject, and you could easily miss them all.

You will now find many homeschooling books listed under "Homeschooling." I did check with some local libraries in Canada and Maine. There are still homeschooling books listed under "Domestic Education," so be sure to check both headings.

Another possibility is that the term was invented by a public school official. School officials seldom speak English; they speak Educationese, as when the district superintendent wrote, "Please enlighten me with respect to your intentions relative to the education of your children for the approaching year." I divided both sides of the equation by the number of superintendents it takes to change a light bulb and reduced it to "Please tell me your plans for the year."

Educationese is one of the two foreign languages in which I have a little fluency, and sometimes I practice it when I correspond with school officials. Usually, however, Educationese is a lot like maple sap: It needs to be boiled down a great deal before it is of much use to human beings.

In my dictionaries, there are several definitions of "school" that don't refer to the formal institutions with which we usually associate the word. The problem, then, is not in the word, but in our associations with it. "A source of knowledge" is one of the definitions I think would be acceptable to even the most dedicated unschooler. But our conditioning is strong: When someone says school, we automatically think of report cards and corridors reeking of antiseptic. The word is lightened somewhat by the addition of "home," but some stigma remains. "Unschooling" has the disadvantage of adding a negative prefix to an already stigmatized word.

It's probably too late to coin a better term. "Home-learning" is used by some, especially those who want to make it plain that adults also can learn outside of school, but really is just as restrictive: It implies that learning takes place primarily in the home, which is little better than the conventional assumption that learning takes place only in school.

Home-schoolers and unschoolers are well aware that a great deal of learning takes place outside of both home and school — in the streets, in the woods and fields, in fact, in any situation in which we're participants or spectators. *Being alive is learning, and the extent of our learning may depend upon the extent to which we are really living.* (Italics mine. — J.R.)

John Holt's advocacy of very loose structure, and even of no structure at all, isn't new with his home-school book, *Teach Your Own*. Many similar ideas and arguments were presented in his *How Children Learn* and *How Children Fail* in the early 1960s. A few years earlier, A.S. Neill's *Summerhill* carried a similar message: If you leave kids alone, and let them study what and when they want to, they'll educate themselves. It worked for Mowgli and for Tarzan, and sometimes it has worked for us. Other times we've wondered why so few of the great educators have children of their own.

John Dewey, father of the "progressive education" movement of the first half of this century, encouraged teachers to be co-workers with their students rather than taskmasters, and to build their lessons around the students' natural interests. That was a compromise between schooling, which almost everybody had by then, and unschooling, which a lot of people had but didn't particularly want.

Before Dewey, Leo Tolstoy and Henry David Thoreau both felt that as much could be learned in the woods and fields as in the classroom. I don't think they meant that a walk in the woods would teach you the three R's, or that people didn't need the three R's; just that there's a lot to learn in the world besides the three R's, and some of it comes from doing and observing and thinking instead of listening to someone talk. Socrates and Confucius, nearly contemporaries 2,500 years ago, both used conversation as a learning aid, with the goals of discovering truth rather than teaching beliefs and of developing each pupil to his own highest potential. The approach of the modern schools differs only in that the teacher does most of the talking and then asks questions about something else, and nobody cares about silly abstractions such as truth and highest potential.

The rigid approach to teaching is repeatedly condemned by Maria Montessori, Ashley Montagu, Ivan Illich, Herbert Kohl, Paul Goodman, George Dennison, John Taylor Gatto, and many other knowledgeable educators, including John Holt. Some of them have kids of their own, and some practice on other people's kids. *Learning Magazine* frequently features articles questioning or attacking the concepts and practices of testing, grading, rigid structure, and tight curriculum. A lot of teachers read *Learning.* I don't know if any of them are allowed by their school boards to pay attention to it.

Among the growing number of books about home-schooling, the ones with a fundamentalist orientation are strongest in their recommendation of a strict curriculum. Ted Wade's *The Home School Manual* argues strongly for a planned structure, although he has written me, "Free time and exploring are important, [but] I feel it's important to work from a plan and to choose on the basis of goals rather than by what seems fun at the moment."

Most of the home-schoolers who argue against loose structure actually consider it to be synonymous with "what seems fun at the moment," and seem to rest their case primarily on a puritanical assumption that anything that is fun is automatically suspect, and is probably bad.

Advocates of loose structure repeatedly assert and sometimes demonstrate that most children are eager to learn, anything and everything, and if not stunted by educational malpractice will follow their own interests and curiosity into ever-expanding fields of knowledge and skills. No child will prefer a steady diet of comic books any more than he will choose a constant diet of candy and cookies, although a child's appetite for junk food, both intestinal and cranial, can sometimes amaze even the most imaginative adult. Before long — that's "long" by his standards — he will have a craving for real nutrition, whether in food or knowledge. Many of those who favor rigidity are basing their arguments on observations of children who have never learned in a loosely structured situation. For the sake of argument, perhaps, they "try it" for a few days or weeks, and then announce that it doesn't work. Part of the problem is that they're dealing with children who are accustomed to having some form of knowledge or opinion poured into funnels that have been stuck in their heads, and part of the problem is that sometimes that's the only way to find out if the kids are awake. Like the parents and the teachers, the kids have come to believe that this is the only way to learn, and will sit around waiting for someone to teach them something. Sometimes, it's quite a revelation to them that they can learn something by themselves.

Ironically, the proverb "Virtue is its own reward" is promoted more by the so-called secular humanists than by many fundamentalists, who make virtue synonymous with obedience, and offer material rewards for both.

Perhaps a rigid structure depends upon such rewards and punishments. The more authority is asserted, the more it will be resented and tested, and the more it must be enforced, either by coercion or by bribery. It seems axiomatic that any program needing constant enforcement — whether with subtle bribes, rewards, threats, fear, punishment, or psychological games — must have several inherent weaknesses.

"Hey, Mom, I'll be good if you give me a dime."

"Now, son, why can't you be good for nothing, like your father?"

We have never used any form of punishment with our children, and they have never given us any "discipline" problems that couldn't be resolved with discussion. They do their share of our daily work — barn chores, housework, firewood, etc. — and spend each day learning hundreds of things. We often share a bowl of popcorn, a pot of cocoa, a game of cards or Ping-Pong, but never as rewards for obedience or accomplishment. Such pleasures are ordinary parts of our daily life.

Loosely structured learning isn't necessarily "what seems fun at the moment," but usually what is fun for a child (or an adult) in a creative environment will be interesting, provocative, and broadening — in other words, educational.

Another misconception of loose structure that is firmly held by many of its opponents is that there is little or no contribution by adults. The opposite is closer to the fact. With a loose structure, children and adults interact more often without regard for artificial barriers such as age differences, school walls, and honorific formalities. The parent plays several roles, the least of which is "teacher." The parent suggests, guides, converses, questions, supports, praises, encourages, and helps to obtain material. The parent is friend, mentor, confidant, and fellow student.

Throughout *Growing Without Schooling* are scores of readers' letters recounting their experiences with loosely structured learning. The factor most common to them all is interaction between adults and children in real-life situations, in which the children learn real skills and gain real knowledge. At an age when most kids are still working on how much Sally spent for three oranges if the price is 6 for $1.00, some home-school kids are earning money, putting it into their own checking accounts, and writing their own checks.

The Holt Associates conference in Boston in 1997, celebrating 20 years of publishing *Growing Without Schooling,* was impressive not only for the organization and the speakers, but for the families themselves. It was a treat for me to be around so many happy parents and children. I heard no crying or whining, no threats or bribes for good behavior, yet the children were having a good time. The teens who spoke at the seminars were prime examples of what self-motivated learning can produce. They were young adults with great self-confidence, definitive proof that structure is not a necessary ingredient for success in learning or growing up. The writings of other unschoolers in the *GWS* magazine that followed the conference reinforced this.

It may be that not all unschoolers are as impressively accomplished learners, but then not all public school children do poorly. So far, no one has found the perfect method for educating all children. Nancy Lande's book *Homeschooling: A Patchwork of Days* provides excellent examples of the many ways learning can take place outside the public school system.

The parents whose kids are less precocious, and even dislike studying and thinking, don't often write books or articles, although they sometimes write letters asking what's wrong with them or what they are doing wrong. The answer to both questions is "nothing." Wait a while, and try again. Some kids just don't like studying and thinking — whether they're in public school, home-school, or unschool. But they can sure fix cars or build birdhouses or catch fish. I know a lot of very nice people who fix cars and couldn't tell a noun from a nun. They have expensive homes and go to Florida for two weeks every winter.

In *Better Than School* (now out of print), Nancy Wallace tells of frequently chauffeuring her children to and from music and language lessons, and of the many hours she and her husband often spent reading to their children. The Wallaces' home-school program was as far from being only "what seems fun at the moment" as it was from the rigid structure of the public schools.

The older our kids got, the longer their lunch breaks became. Jean and I compared notes and concluded that the two who had had the most contact with other kids at an early age were the quickest to lose interest in learning or creating. So much for the values of socialization.

Sometimes all four scurried through the day, learning and creating and discussing ideas, and sometimes one or two would sort of fade out and need a little jiggle, and sometimes all of them would just run down. After what we felt was a suitable break from straining their brains, we'd wind them up again.

By the time the kids were doing sixth- and seventh-grade work, we discovered a few flaws in Rousseau's, or whoever's, ideas about plunking a kid in the woods with a screwdriver and a pile of books. The biggest flaw was, then what? Once the kids have mastered the basics of language and arithmetic and nail pounding and cake making, will they go on to write and then discuss the Great Books and the History of Civilization all by themselves, or could they use a little more input from those who have gone before?

How much, if any, should an adult "interfere" with a child's natural, innate learning process? Some of the problem, I think, may be that as soon as one adopts a particular philosophy, one's effort to be consistent will be tested continually. I find it a little ironic that the unschoolers' "non-interference" with children's learning would be construed as rude condescension if applied to adults. If I interrupt my son's woodworking to show him a way to start the saw-cut without nicking a finger, then I'm interfering with his ability to learn by himself; but if I withhold the same information from an adult, and he becomes aware of it, he'll wonder why I didn't offer him this useful advice. If someone shows me a way to get more leverage on a tire iron with less effort, I don't resent him for stunting my innate ability to learn. There are ways of using axes, saws, and knives that are completely or relatively safe, and I have no intention of letting my kids explore the various ways so they can learn by themselves which ways are safe and which are not.

Part of the idea of unschooling is to treat kids like adults, but this is almost constantly negated by unschoolers who withhold useful help from children on the theory that children should be allowed to learn at their own pace and in their own way. Waiting for the child to ask for help isn't the answer, either; if a child doesn't know or suspect there's a better way, then he has no reason to ask. Letting a child struggle with a task without offering advice that would make it easier is not showing respect — and, once he realizes that you could have helped, but chose not to, will not increase his respect for you. Any philosophy, carried to its "logical," consistent extreme, can easily become ridiculous and indefensible.

Does "invited learning" mean we shouldn't occasionally try to lead them into areas of which they aren't yet aware, and therefore can't invite us to help them in? Does "invited learning" mean the same kind of choppy, incomplete, fragmented learning that's going on in the public schools?

We never really figured out exactly what "invited learning" does mean, but we decided we couldn't always wait to be invited. Sometimes we just crashed the party, and amazed ourselves with the structure and organization we could devise. "Let's hope John Holt never sees this," we'd say to each other. "He'll stop selling our books." But the kids became so interested in Alexander the Great or the Renaissance or Martin Luther and the papal bulls that they forgot all about Donald Duck. They learned psychology and economics and world history and geography and where Yellowstone National Park is. They even began inviting us to introduce more subjects, or help them with the ones they were on, and then we began feeling safe again. We always felt a little like renegades when we taught something without having been invited to do so.

When we were having unschool, the kids mostly set their own unschedules. When we were having home-school, it often went something like this:

6:45 — Jean and Donn get up with the alarm, feed fires, dress, etc. Feed dog, then let her out. Two cats in, growling at each other. Jean wakes Derek. Donn cleans and sharpens chain saw on Ping-Pong table.

7:30 — Jean wakes Cathy or Karen or Susan, who take turns daily setting the table, getting breakfast, and tending fires. Jean and Derek go to the barn; feed and water the pig, cow, calf, and 25 hens; clean the gutter; milk the cow; and collect eggs. Donn puts fuel in chain saw, then goes out to cut firewood. The one on breakfast duty calls the others, who are usually already awake and reading in bed.

8:15 — Breakfast: hot cereal, whole-wheat toast from homemade bread, homemade butter and apple jelly, honey, fresh milk, fresh eggs, peanut butter. Coffee for Jean and Donn.

9:00 — Jean and two girls clear the table, do dishes, and put them away. One girl sweeps the house and straightens odds and ends. Girls rotate these chores daily. Every fourth day, Derek sweeps. Donn goes out to split firewood.

9:30 — Derek and Susan or Cathy and Karen bring water, one dipping buckets into the brook (six feet from the corner of the house) and passing them in, the other carrying them to the kitchen and filling the 50-gallon can, stove reservoir, and large kettle on the stove. In warm weather, when the pipes aren't frozen, we have gravity-fed water from the brook directly into the house.

9:45 — Official school time, morning session, at the kitchen-dining table. Donn leading (or being led). (Jean listens, comments, sews, mends, plans meals, does laundry, plans

her afternoon schoolwork, tends fires, bakes bread, etc.) Discussion of daily offering from Word-a-Day calendar ("saprogenic") and Quote-a-Day calendar ("A sharp tongue is the only edged tool that grows keener with constant use" — Washington Irving.). We pull the legs and wings off the words, examining roots, derivations, associations, usages, sometimes using the dictionary. We discuss the quotation and its author: Do you agree? Why or why not? What is his most-famous story? Does anyone know when he lived?

10:00 (this and other times given in Official School Time are approximate; we have no schedule) — Word play, dictionary and encyclopedia assignments from yesterday. Cathy: Tass, tacit, taciturn, apocrypha, anarchy, anachronism. Karen: cosmos, cosmic, wax, wane, flat, flatulent. Susan: awesome, awful, offal, Neapolitan, obese, obeisance. Derek: auk, gross, grosbeak, eject, elect. Words for tomorrow: faker, fakir, guild, gild, microcosm, macrocosm, zenith, nadir, anathema, spike, bolt, sally, dally. Each student gives definitions, uses the words in sentences; others take notes, discuss uses and usefulness, often making puns and other bad jokes.

10:30 — Yesterday's Detective Assignment, for encyclopedia and general book shelf research. True or false? Support your answers. Cathy: The Lutheran Church was founded by Martin Luther King Jr.. Karen: George Fox was an American Indian. Susan: Betsy Ross was a famous opera singer. Derek: "Doctor Livingstone, I presume?" was said by Sherlock Holmes. Students discuss and take notes on each other's research.

10:45 — Research assignment, to be worked on individually or together, your choice. Problem: A man lost in the woods can find no food except rabbits, which are plentiful and easy to snare. He has all he wants of rabbit meat, yet a few weeks later is found dead of starvation. Why? (Students had to consult several cooking and nutrition books before finding even a hint, and then had to brainstorm their findings to arrive at the answer.)

10:50 — Poetry: Read aloud the selection you found and practiced yesterday. Cathy: Ogden Nash. Karen: Carl Sandburg. Susan: Edna St. Vincent Millay. Derek: Robert Louis Stevenson. Tomorrow, bring one of your own choosing; practice reading aloud beforehand.

11:15 — Writing assignment: Discussion of more articles for our family newsletter; who will write what. To be done on your own time and submitted for discussion and refinement tomorrow.

11:20 — Self-image: Design and draw a button or T-shirt that would express The Real You.

11:40 — Discussion of ethics. How can we know what is "right"? Do values change as society wants them to, or is there a constant right and wrong for all people and all times? How can we know? What is "conscience"?

12:00 — Donn reads excerpts from biographies, to be discussed.

12:30 — Research assignment for tomorrow: Find and read the story of the Prodigal Son. What does "prodigal" mean? What does "gospel" mean? Which are the "synoptic" gospels, and why?

12:35 — Discussion: Where do we get the common expression "I wash my hands of it." What does it mean? From last night's reading, what are some of the similarities between Christianity and Buddhism?

12:50 — History simulation. Karen, you are a prosecuting attorney at the Nuremberg Trials; your position is that anyone who contributed in any way to the persecution and murder of Jews should be punished very severely. Cathy, you are Franz Gruber; you were

17 years old, a railroad guard 60 miles from Auschwitz; you knew that Jews were in the train cars, but you had your orders; besides, you had been taught that Jews were a threat to your country. Susan and Derek, you are judges; you listen to each side as the defendant and the prosecutor argue their cases, then decide if Franz Gruber is guilty of "crimes against humanity," and, if so, what the sentence should be. Explain your decisions. (The students ad lib, with no attempt at drama or entertainment.)

1:30 — Lunch: sandwiches, milk, carrot sticks, etc. Free reading, Ping-Pong, walks.

2:15 — Official school time, afternoon session, Jean leading. (Donn works on business, orders and correspondence, or writing.) First aid, instruction and practice. Music: theory and practice; guitar, flute, clarinet, recorder, singing. Nutrition, health, anatomy. Work on individual electives, with help when wanted or needed. Cathy: Spanish, typing, history, literature, counseling, geography. Karen: French, typing, psychology. Susan: math, history, spelling, civics, French. Derek: math, handwriting, history, typing, art, Spanish, spelling.

3:30 — Official school time is over. The kids often continue working by themselves on their own electives or on morning assignments. Some go skiing or hiking. All four bring in firewood, usually five or six armloads each. The two who didn't haul water in the morning do so now. Reading. Ping-Pong. Visiting friends. Begin supper, sharing and rotating jobs.

6:00 — Donn goes to the barn for evening chores; milk cow, feed animals, etc.

6:30 — Supper. Sometimes with a history, literature, or entertaining cassette.

7:15 — Supper clean-up shared and rotated. Baking cookies, cakes, pies. Sometimes TV (powered by a car battery). Reading books and magazines. The girls sew, knit, tat, crochet, and, frequently, draw. Derek builds models of planes and spaceships. The girls have each made several articles of clothing — dresses, blouses, sweaters, etc. Small personal laundry. Letter writing, churning butter, square dancing (in town), skating, 4-H meetings, board games. Popcorn; maybe ice cream. Donn works in his office. Jean reads or plays the guitar.

10:30 — Bedtime. Cats out. Fires fed and shut down. All lights out. Goodnight!

One of my favorite dictionaries, the Oxford American, mentions several uses of the word "home" (as a noun, an adjective, a verb, and an adverb), but between "home-room" and "home-sick," where "home-school" should be, there is nothing. Even the third edition of The Random House Dictionary of the English Language, which weighs twelve pounds and is the most recent unabridged dictionary we have, with thousands of words I don't know and thousands more I don't care to know, somehow missed all references to home education, by that or any other name, when its compilers were combing the oceans of print in search of serendipitous fillers.

Nonetheless, I think "home-school" is becoming well established in the language, just as it is in society, and future lexicographers will have to make note of it.

Ironically, "unschooled" *is* offered by dictionaries, which claim it means "untrained, uneducated." Hardly accurate, of course, but I haven't time to write my own dictionary. Maybe next year.

In the meantime, we should recall the words of Shakespeare:

"What's in a name?
That which we call a home-school
By any other name would teach as well."

Not to mention the warning of Abraham Lincoln: "You can school some of the people all of the time, and all of the people some of the time, but you can't school all of the people all of the time."

OBEDIENCE TRAINING VS. "INVITED LEARNING"

or, HOME-SCHOOLING GOES TO THE DOGS

"Invited learning," as I understand it — and I'm sure some home-school theorists will be quick to say I don't — seems to mean that children intuitively know what they need to learn and when they need to learn it, and no one should presume to offer them information about anything at all until they ask for it. If they ask for it, of course, it's really invited *teaching*, but more people than you might suppose (unless you're one of them) get purple in the face over this, insisting that "teaching" is doing *something TO someone else* and is therefore a form of aggression — unless the students ask for it, and then it's okay, because then we can call it invited *learning*.

To Jean and me, the entire debate is slightly more exciting than the afternoon soaps or taking out the garbage, but "invited learning" is an intriguing concept, whether we understand it or not, and sometimes we like to play around with it and see what we can discover about it.

One of the things we've discovered about invited learning is that it often results in excessive barking, muddy paw prints on the sofa, missing or mangled shoes, and late-night festivities involving a mouthful of porcupine quills and a pair of pliers. With dogs, that is. Invited learning with children is another story, most of which can be told in polite language but isn't a part of this report.

We've had a few smart dogs over the years (usually one at a time), but we've never given much thought to leading them into any sort of Higher Education. Or even Lower Education. With our dogs, as with our children, we lean (not too firmly, I admit) toward a sort of invited learning, the biggest difference being that with the children it's usually more from conviction than laziness.

With dogs, it usually seems easier to brush mud off the sofa before sitting than to teach them to wipe their feet at the door, so we tend to excuse their poor manners by muttering, "Dogs will be dogs" (just as people used to say, "Boys will be boys" — another truism that, according to recent new magazines, is no longer the certainty we once thought it was, but that is also another story).

About a year and a half ago, Gus came to live with us, and almost immediately began challenging many of our favorite educational theories and convictions, including our smug assumption that dogs will be dogs.

Gus is about ninety percent German shepherd and ten percent something else. We found him (or vice versa) in January, at the SPCA sixty miles away, where he was being held in solitary confinement as a vagrant. He was a puppy, only eight months old, but already weighing 62 pounds, and it cost us more than a dollar a pound to spring him. When I brought him home, sitting beside me in our '84 pickup, he had the familiar dazed look of most ex-cons who have been in stir too long and didn't say much, but several times he expressed his gratitude by cleaning my right ear very thoroughly. He also made a few mechanical adjustments when my attention was elsewhere, and I finally had to explain to him — after the truck suddenly lost its oomph and nearly coasted to a stop before I found the cause of its unusual behavior — that he could move the rearview mirror all he liked but I would be in charge of the gear shift. He apologized by cleaning my ear again, and we got home with no more surprises.

Jean and I showed Gus the doors that connect Inside to Outside, and he signified his understanding by testing them all. We showed him his food and water dishes in the little nook in the hallway, and he tested them, too, giving no indication that the arrangement was less than satisfactory. We introduced him to Big Guy, our ferocious feline mouse, rat, grouse, and rabbit-killer, and said we hoped they would be friends. Gus, very pleased, offered to clean Big Guy's ears. Big Guy, who had once been chased up a very small tree by a very large dog, offered to clean Gus's clock, then ran upstairs to hide in the rafters until spring. (That turned out to be another lesson in invited learning, because for the next three months, at least once a day, we had to risk being torn to shreds by inviting Big Guy to go for a little walk outside, dog or no dog, and he soon learned to hide from us in places we couldn't reach.)

One evening about three weeks after he had come to live with us, Gus barked at the door, then at me, then again at the door. Making a natural assumption, I opened the door for him, but he stood and barked at me again. He wanted me to go outside to play toss-and-chase with his empty plastic milk jug.

"You're out of your mind," I told him. "It's ten below out there, with two feet of snow."

He still refused to go out by himself, so I shut the door and went back to my book and chair beside the woodstove, pretending to ignore the disgusted look he was giving me.

Just when I thought he had given up, Gus went to the hall closet and ran back with one of my snow boots in his teeth. He dropped it beside me, then returned to the closet for the second boot, which he dropped next to the first one.

"Gus," I managed to say, "dogs do this only in movies."

He put a paw on one of the boots and barked at me.

"Okay, okay," I said, pushing my foot into one of the boots. "You've made your point. But you should know that real dogs don't do this."

Putting the other boot on, I said to Jean, "Did you see what Gus just did? He's really smart!"

"It's a good thing one of you is," she said, as I went to the closet for my jacket and mittens.

Women tend to say things like that sometimes, so I pretended I hadn't heard her, but on the way out the door, I whispered to Gus, "See what I'm up against? You don't have to make it worse."

(It did get worse. Gus started bringing my jacket, too, and although I wouldn't have said it aloud, I didn't know how to say no to a dog that does all that, even at 15 below zero at 11:30 at night.)

A squeaky rubber football, about six inches long, became Gus's favorite indoor toy. Sometimes he just chews on it, daring it to squeak, then grabs it in his teeth and flips it into the air, then runs after it. Occasionally he loses it, and then spends twenty minutes or more searching for it — behind furniture, under pillows, down the hall, wherever a tricky rubber ball might be hiding. Usually he finds it, but sometimes he gives up and barks at Jean or me to find it for him — which eventually gave us the brilliant idea that he was inviting us to help him Learn something.

I called him to the end of the hall, then told him to sit and count to ten while I hid the ball. "Ten" is a very large number for a young dog, but I managed to get the ball behind a sofa cushion before Gus came galloping after me into the living room.

"*Find* the ball," I said, in that tricky way parents have of enlarging their children's vocabulary. "*Find* it."

Gus sniffed the air, which didn't help, then began searching, pushing chairs, poking his nose under magazines and into armpits, and flipping cushions around until he finally found the ball. He tossed it into the air, jumped and caught it, then dropped it in front of me and barked. This time, there was no doubt: He was definitely inviting me to help him learn something. (Some people might say he was inviting me to learn something, and others might say he was just inviting me to play a game, but I know better.)

We did it several times that evening, and it became a daily game. I hid the ball in different places each time, and Gus always kept searching until he found it. At the same time, his vocabulary grew. Besides *find* and *ball,* he soon learned *sit, wait, stay, come, sofa, other sofa, chair, bed, wrong way, down, higher,* and *behind the pillows.* Some of the concepts seemed pretty abstract to us, but *abstract* was one of the words Gus hadn't learned.

One day Gus took his ball into our bedroom (which is downstairs, near the kitchen), stayed a few moments, then came out without it and barked at me. It had been quite a while since I had dismissed Gus's barking as mere random noise. If he was bright enough to tell me something but I wasn't bright enough to understand him, I'd have to fake it.

Stalling for time, I asked, "Lost your ball?"

"Woof," he said, wagging his tail.

"Is it in the bedroom?" I asked.

"Woof," he said again, still wagging.

"Can you find it?" I asked.

His tail stopped wagging. Gently but firmly, he took my hand in his mouth and pulled me toward the bedroom door. Releasing my hand, he said, "Rrowrrf!" and waited expectantly. Sometimes he seems to think I'm Learning-Disabled.

Searching my mind for possibilities, I made a wild guess. "You want *me* to find the ball?" I asked him, not really believing it.

"Rowf!" Gus exclaimed, wagging his tail again.

Feeling ridiculous, I went into the bedroom to look for the ball, which I quickly found on the floor beside the bed. Gus grabbed the ball from my hand and raced excitedly down the hall, then back to the living room, then back into the bedroom. He came out — no ball — and barked at me.

"Right," I said, still not believing; "Gotcha." I found the ball in the same place beside the bed. Gus grabbed it, ran around with it to celebrate, then hid it in the bedroom again. We went through the whole thing several times, and Gus looked at me with approval each time I found the ball. I hoped he could see that I may be slow sometimes but I'm not Learning-Disabled.

"Jean," I said, "is this possible? Is Gus really hiding the ball for me to find?"

"You said he's smart," she reminded me.

"Lucky for me," I said, "he's not smart enough to put the ball in different places. He always hides it in the same place."

I shouldn't have said it when Gus was listening. The next time he told me to look for the ball, it wasn't there. I finally found it on the bed, under my pillow. "Gus," I told him, "this invited leaning is going to your head. You're forgetting you're just a dog." It's hard to tell with dogs, but I think he laughed at me.

Gus likes Flavor Snacks — crunchy, bone-shaped dog biscuits I keep on the back of my desk so I can bribe him to go away when I'm working and he wants me to play with him. As usual, he's a step ahead of me. Bounding into my office, he bumps my elbow with his nose and says, "If you give me three Flavor Snacks, I won't bother you for a while." I don't know why he wants *three*. If I give him two, he demands another. If I give him four, he accepts them, but doesn't care much about the fourth one. So I give him three, and he goes away.

"Impossible," I told myself the first few times it happened. "Numbers are too abstract for a dog. Even a smart one. I'm going to prove it."

I broke a Flavor Snack in half, held one piece up for Gus to see, and asked him, "How many?"

He woofed, once, but that didn't prove anything because in Dog Talk "woof" is a homonym; like many English words, its meaning must be deduced from its context. It can mean "Please" or "I want to go out" or "I'm hungry." I wasn't convinced that it could also mean "one."

I gave Gus the Flavor Snack, then held up two pieces, one in each hand, and asked him, "How many?"

"Woof, he said, eyeing the piece in my right hand. When I didn't give it to him he looked at the piece in my left hand and said, "Woof."

"Coincidence," I said, giving him both pieces. "Accident." Holding up one, I asked him how many.

"Woof," he said. I waited. He waited. We both waited. Finally, suspecting that his attention span might be longer than mine, I gave him the Flavor Snack, and waited for him to eat it — *crunch-glumph,* like a boa constrictor. Then I held up two pieces, one in each hand, and asked, "How many?"

He woofed at the one in my right hand, then at the one in my left hand. I gave them to him. We did it again and again that evening, and several times in the next few days, always with the same result: a woof for each hand. I still didn't know if Gus was counting them or had only decided that I wanted him to woof for each one.

About a week later, I held up two Flavor Snacks and asked Gus, "How many?" He hesitated.

He looked at one, then the other, then at the first again, and then back to the second. Back and forth, several times. Then he looked at me and very distinctly said, "Woof-woof." Two syllables; one word.

Had he finally said "two"? We did it several times, sometimes with one, sometimes with two — and he answered correctly every time. He wasn't as certain, at first, about "two" as he was about "one" — he always took time to consider very carefully before saying "two" ("woof-woof") — but he obviously knew the difference. Gus could count!

So far, he hasn't mastered "three," a quantity that often excites him to the point of saying, "Nine! Fourteen! Six!" although he is always insistent on exactly three Flavor Snacks. Apparently he knows the quantity of three, but doesn't have a word for it. I've read of an aboriginal jungle tribe, purportedly unchanged since the Stone Age, whose entire numerical system is "One, two, three, plenty," meaning that any quantity over three is too much to count separately. Gus's numerical system — "One, two, plenty" — is only one digit short of Stone Age man's.

Since then, we've continued to be impressed by Gus's intelligence, but we're seldom surprised by it. When he's hungry, he brings his food dish into the kitchen. If he wants one of us to go out with him, he brings our boots (dirty sneakers, in the summertime), and then goes back to the closet to pull a jacket (usually the right one) off the hanger. If he wants his chest scratched, he pulls someone's hand down and leans against it. If we ask him to whisper, he makes a very soft, barely audible, huff sound. When he's riding in the truck and sees a stop sign or hears the click of the turn signal, he sits down and braces his front legs.

Early one spring, a sign in town announced registration for obedience training, bringing us face-to-face with the unexpected question of formal education. We discussed it. We hadn't wanted it for any of our kids, and all four of them have done very well without it, but maybe it would be different for Gus. "Different how?" we asked ourselves. Well, socialization, for one thing; he'd get to meet other dogs, learn to interact meaningfully with his peers. Broaden his cultural horizons by showing him part of the world beyond our rural homestead. Gus said he wasn't sure what we meant by "obedience" or "socialization," but anything involving a ride in the truck was okay with him.

We still weren't sure. Having devoted so much of our lives to home-schooling, it just didn't seem right to enroll our dog in public school.

On the other hand, we home-schoolers are a strange, perverse lot. I don't mean "we" meaning us, Jean and Donn Reed, personally; I mean we home-schoolers in general, generic home-schoolers or the home-schooling masses. We reject the standards and methods and results of public schools. We say we don't want our kids to meet public school standards, because those standards are empty and false. We say the world would be better off if public school had never been invented.

And then whom do we choose as our home-school heroes? John Taylor Gatto, honored as "Teacher of the Year" three times before he quit the public school system after twenty-six years. David Colfax, described on another author's book jacket as "father of three home-schooled Harvard graduates" — not even mentioning his fourth son who was also home-schooled but hasn't gone to Harvard. Grace Llewellyn, described on the cover of her book as "a former middle school English teacher." And, of course, John Holt, who worked in public and private schools for years before "discovering" home-schooling, which some of us had been doing for years.

We're like dying atheists asking a priest for absolution — not really believing in it, but hedging our bets, not taking any chances. A stamp of approval from professional teachers who have quit the public schools after ten or twenty years seems to mean more to us than the opinions of people who got out before they got in — that is, who never got involved in public schools at all.

Perverse or not, Gus and I registered for the course. Each Tuesday evening, for eight weeks, we drove to the community recreation center and, along with about 30 other dogs and their owners, received instruction from a member of the American Kennel Club. Every day, at home, Gus and I diligently did our homework, most of which he thought was dumb and boring, but he was a good pupil, and more than willing to put up with such nonsense if it meant being outdoors with me. He even brought my boots and jacket to me two or three times a day, plainly Inviting me to help him Learn more.

We learned to Heel on Leash, which included Stopping or Starting on command, Right — and Left — Angle Turns, About Face, and promptly Sitting (Gus; not me) without command at each Stop. Gus didn't see the point of it, but he mastered it quickly and didn't argue about it.

Then came Heeling on Leash in a Figure 8, which Gus thought was one of the stupidest exercises he had ever heard of. At school, he wanted to make it a Figure 6 or 99 or 54, anything but Figure 8, and when we practiced at home during the week, he wrapped his paws around my ankle and chewed my foot.

The Long Sit (sitting and staying in place with minimal movement for at least a minute) and Long Down (lying down and staying in place for three minutes) were easy because he had already learned them at home when he was waiting for me to hide his rubber football.

Recall — sitting, staying, then coming on command — was also easy, for the same reason.

The final lesson, in preparation for exam night, was Stand for Inspection, and Gus thought it was dumber than the Figure 8. The idea was that he would sit beside me in Heel position, I would tell him to stand, and he would promptly stand; then I would walk away to the end of the leash, and he would stay, still standing, while the instructor walked up to him, ran a hand along his back, and walked away; and would remain there until I returned to his side. The whole exercise was a snap for him — all except the first part. Gus refused to stand on command. I had to nudge his belly with my toe, tug forward on his leash, and repeat the command several times, and then Gus would very reluctantly stand. Once he was standing, he did the rest of the entire exercise without a hitch, but after two weeks of practice he still refused to stand on command.

Graduation Night arrived. Gus and I discussed our test-taking strategy, and I told Jean before we left not to expect too much. Neither Gus nor I had taken the course very seriously, and I honestly expected us to score about 28th in a class of 30.

We started off with 100 points. On the Heel on Leash, we lost 3 points out of 20, for holding the leash too tight. On the Figure 8, we lost 1 point out of 10, for the same reason. On the Long Sit, no points lost, out of 20. On the Long Down, no points lost, out of 20. On Recall, 1 point was lost out of 15, for "handler error" (I tugged on the leash once when I shouldn't have). Gus was nonchalant, and I was amazed. But the worst was yet to come, and I knew it would be our downfall.

"Stand your dog for inspection," the judge said. "Stand," I commanded, knowing he wouldn't, and getting ready to sneak my toe under him. He stood immediately, without a nudge, and didn't move as I walked away from him. The judge walked up to him, ran his hand along Gus's back, then walked away, and Gus stood still as I returned to him. No points lost, out of 15.

Total points lost, 5. Final score, 95. Second place!

The next day, at home, I asked Gus to Stand. He yawned at me. I made it a command, and he chewed my foot.

There's a lesson in there somewhere, but I'm not sure what it is. Probably Gus was way ahead of us again, and just wanted to make a point about learning. Maybe about invited learning.

Gus has interrupted me several times while I've been writing this. He hid his football in the bedroom, then came to my office and told me to look for it. I knew he wouldn't leave me alone until I did, so I went to the bedroom. It wasn't beside the bed. Not under the pillows, which he had rearranged (probably just to mislead me). I finally found it under the covers, which he had pulled back, then pulled up over the ball. I told him to stay on the bed and count to 10 while I hid the ball. He's still not very good at numbers over 3, but I got the ball hidden under pile of sofa pillows before he came charging after me. He pushed pillows all over until he found the ball, then went to hide it again. Came to tell me to look for it. I went. Nowhere in the bedroom this time. I finally found it down the hall, just inside the bathroom door. Gus was laughing at me. Smart-alecky dog. My turn; I hid the ball under a folded blanket on the other sofa. Gus flipped pillows around with his nose, then checked the other sofa, lifted the blanket with his nose, and got the ball. Hid it in the bedroom again, told me to look for it. I told him I'm busy writing a serious article about education. He sighed and looked out the window and woofed.

"Not now," I said. "Maybe later."

He woofed at the box of Flavor Snacks on the back of my desk. I took two out of the box and showed them to him. He counted them, then looked at the box and growled softly. I got another. He accepted all three, one at a time, and cleaned up the crumbs on the floor.

I went back to work. Gus jumped up on one of the sofas, rearranged the pillows, then lay down and looked at Jean, who was playing de Visée's "Suite in D Minor" on her guitar. I don't even know what D minor means, but Gus does, and he doesn't like it. He always growls — a very low rumble deep in his throat — whenever Jean plays anything in D minor. He growled and muttered, so Jean switched to Bach's "Gavotte in A Minor." Gus sighed contentedly, and went to sleep.

He sure is smart.

It's a good thing one of us is.

Addendum

In the ensuing years Gus matured. He can tell time better than I can. I'm frequently absent-minded about mealtimes, but he knows exactly when it's five o'clock and time to eat. If I'm working here in the office, he'll come in and politely bump my elbow. I don't know why I ever think I can complete what I'm working on. If I ignore the gentle bump, he will do it again more firmly. If I'm talking on the phone, I have a tendency to drop it. If you call around 5 p.m., you may hear strange noises from either or both of us. The twice-yearly time changes are traumatic.

I occasionally tutor public school students. After we work for a while, we'll take a break, and one of my students' favorite break activities is playing games with Gus. One hot day I offered cookies and juice to a girl I'll call Jill. Naturally, Gus felt he should be included. Wanting to show off his talents I held up three pieces of a cookie and asked him to count. He said, "Woof-woof-woof." Very impressed, my student felt sure he could count more than three. I explained what I thought was Gus's philosophy about numbers, but my student felt I might be underrating him, so to humor my student, we tried four. Gus not only counted to four, but went on to count to five! No mistakes, no matter how I mixed up the numbers. When he got five I insisted we quit immediately, for two reasons (not that I couldn't think up five reasons!). The first was that I would have to put Gus on a diet if he learned any more. The other was that I'd soon have a dog taking my tutoring job.

I know some of you have bought this book only because you fell in love with Gus and want more Gus stories. Gus has worked hard not to disappoint you, and I'll try to tell the tales faithfully.

Gus isn't convinced that you can't teach old people new tricks, and he continues to work patiently with me. I'll admit that I'm not all that swift sometimes, but in the true spirit of invited learning and learning by doing, I try to support his efforts and not disillusion him.

All through the winter when the snow piles up in front of the house, Gus plays King of the Mountain on what accumulates from snowfall and what gets shoveled off the roof and lands in front of the patio door. Some years the mountain elevates his position only equal to the floor. Some years he can look down on the table and see what I'm eating. He uses his perch to survey his kingdom and check out the menu, and as a speaking platform. When he wants me to open the door for him he'll look me in the eye and bark. He's taught me to go down the hall and open the door, and he trots around the corner of the house and comes in. That works well for both of us. He doesn't have to wait for me, and the door isn't open long enough to let all the arctic air in. We've come to a good understanding over the years. In winter I have to open and close the door on demand. When it's warmer and weather permits I leave the door open so the menagerie can come and go as they please. It's during the in-between period when the snow recedes and Gus can no longer look me in the eye and tell me to open the door that he gets tricky. I'm not a good sport about going out to play at 20 degrees below zero, and he knows better than to ask more than once. When it warms up he wants me to come out and play more often, and I'm not always as accommodating as Donn was, even when Gus brings my boots and jacket. (If I went out to play as often as Gus wanted me to, you'd still be waiting for this book.)

After a long winter I'm well trained, and I open the door when he barks. When he wants me to play he won't come in, and he made up a game just to prove his point. It's just amusing enough that I fall for it every time. He barks, and I open the door. He doesn't come. He hides around the corner where I can't see him. I wait. He waits (he has far more patience than I do). I get impatient and take a few steps away from the door hoping I can make eye contact and decide if he really wants to come in or if I misunderstood and he was talking with the squirrels. If I still can't see him I take a few more steps away from the door. At some point I get far enough away from the door that he knows can beat me back inside, and he comes charging around the corner and through the open door and sits, waiting for me to walk back in. When I walk through the door I get this laughing look from him that says, "Ha! I win!"

If you join your children in learning and playing in freedom, you will be surprised at what you both learn.

Gus Becomes a Nanny

This story begins in 1994, when Big Guy (the cat that offered to clean Gus's clock) took a long walk one February day and didn't come back for nine months. I expected him back within a couple of days, and then in the spring, but as time went on I had to admit that maybe the mighty hunter had met his match. I went into mourning but still looked and called for him when I went out. Donn had seen how much Gus enjoyed other cats when they visited the vet, and he and Gus made plans, unbeknownst to me, for introducing a dog-friendly feline into our house.

They chose an orange and white ball of fluff so small you could hold him in the palm of your hand. We all fell in love at first sight. Donn and I didn't have a name picked out, so we decided to wait a couple of days and see what type of personality this new addition to our family possessed. (We'd been too hasty in the past with one cat, and ended up having to change the name George to Georgina.) While we dithered about names, Gus named the kitty Ruff. Well, what did you expect a dog to call his cat?

At this time Donn was sick, and his condition varied from very good to not good. When we'd agreed to get a kitty for Gus, I hadn't taken into consideration that I would have to be the one to housebreak it and keep an eye on it outside — all the things the kids had always done with new animals in the family. By day two I was not as happy about Ruff as Donn and Gus were. In fact, I would have returned Ruff with hardly a second thought. Maybe Gus is psychic, and maybe not, but that afternoon he started taking Ruff out to use the bathroom. Imagine an 85-pound dog picking up a handful of fluff in his mouth and gently carrying it outside. Gus would set Ruff down and watch while he went to the bathroom, and bring him back in and groom him. Can you imagine a tongue the same size as you giving you a bath? With the housebreaking chores off my list, I settled back with Donn and enjoyed watching Gus bring Ruff up. They went for walks together. On a nice day, we could look out the window and see Gus trotting down the road with Ruff in his mouth. They'd be gone five or ten minutes and then come back. Gus was pretty tolerant of Ruff, but he did set some limits. Ruff was not allowed under the house, and he was not to climb more than 18 inches off the ground. If Ruff went higher, Gus would pull him off the tree and take him inside. It became apparent that Gus was developing a parenting and educational philosophy. It raised the question of how much of our behavior, or a cat's, is based on nature and how much on nurture.

All in all, I'd say Gus was a good nanny. There were, and still are, a few gaps in Ruff's education. Gus likes to play. He's definitely not a hunter in the same sense that most cats are, and he never completed the job of training Ruff to be a good mouser. In a country house like ours, it's an important job, worthy of great praise when well done. Big Guy is a hunter and he never fools around when on duty. He catches his prey, kills it, puts it in his dish, and then eats it. To be honest, I should say he eats it most of the time. Sometimes he will leave leftovers in his dish for later. Once, when Susan was home for a visit, he left a quarter of a rabbit by Susan's bed as an offering for her because he felt she was special. I'm glad Big Guy was unaware of how unappreciative Susan (then vegetarian) was when she woke up the next morning and put her foot on it.

I've gotten sidetracked. My point was that Ruff never learned to be a "proper" cat. He's very good at catching things but still hasn't learned to do more than play with them. (What was the most exciting thing I did over New Year's for the new millennium? I watched Ruff's squirrel leap around my kitchen at a zillion miles an hour — but that's another story.) The first autumn after he learned to hunt, Ruff brought in enough mice to feed all the cats in the community — and he generally lost them somewhere in the house. By this time, Big Guy had reappeared, thank goodness, and we didn't have to buy food for him; he just cleaned up Ruff's escapees. Then came the day when we heard a commotion in the bathroom. Ruff had a bright idea: no more escapees! He discovered that if he put his playthings in the bathtub, they couldn't get away from him. (Well, most of them didn't leap out. The ones that did are another story.)

Donn and I understood that cats hunt, and that many of them will play with their catch before killing it. It's a cat's nature to do this, and we knew we couldn't change that predisposition, but the idea of a mouse trapped in the tub with Ruff upset us. Ruff plays rough, so Donn and I started rescuing the mice by putting a container over them to catch them. We'd take Ruff out of the tub, transport the mouse outside and away from the house, then let it go. Gus watched us each time we did this. Then came a day when we heard a BIG commotion in the bathroom. We looked at each other and went to investigate. We found Ruff in the tub with a mouse. Gus was climbing into the tub. He nudged Ruff out of the way and picked up the mouse by the tail, climbed out of the tub, took the mouse outside, and let it go. He wagged his tail, and I swear he had a big grin on his face. Now when I clean the tub (and mostly it needs cleaning even though no human has been in it), I clean up mouse tracks, cat tracks, and dog tracks. I don't know what all this has to do with homeschooling, except that someone wanted a good Gus story. Perhaps it's a lesson about the natural consequences of allowing unique talents to develop in freedom.

Ruff Is My Hero

Over the intervening years Ruff grew up happy and clean and continued to hunt like a cat and then bring his catch in for approval or something. In any case, Ruff brought things in alive whenever possible. All things — bird, mouse, mole, dragonfly, snake, ermine (very beautiful and alive and dangerous when cornered), bat, and once baby bunnies so small you could hold them in the palm of your hand. Gus and I managed to save three out of four bunnies that night. One day I watched Ruff out by our brook when he tried to catch a mink. He failed at that. Thank goodness it was a young mink, because otherwise Ruff would have been cat food in the worst sense of the word. One of Ruff's other not-so-cat-like traits — or maybe it's just that being raised by a dog he understands dog language — is that whenever Gus barks to let us know someone is coming or something wild is approaching the house, Ruff will run to the window or door to see what or who it is.

All right, you get the point. This is a cat that sometimes thinks like a dog, sort of. One lovely summer evening I was fixing supper, music cranked up on the loud side, all the doors open because the day had been hot, and I was feeling good and not thinking too much about anything when I saw an orange streak go by. The only other time I'd seen this type of behavior from Ruff was the day a bear stood up fifteen feet from the patio door to admire the flowers in a high hanging flower basket. That day Ruff was an orange streak that disappeared like the Cheshire Cat and didn't even leave a grin behind. He just vanished to I don't know where. Gone. This night he was acting like a pointer dog standing by the patio door, nose pointed in one direction and tail straight out in back. Staring. Fur up. I looked and saw nothing. I headed for the door; Ruff ran ahead but refused to go out the door. I looked around. There was nothing to be seen, but I could hear something up in the woods about fifteen feet down the driveway. I just stood there and watched as a bear came down out of the woods. I got my priorities right this time. (Last time — well, actually the time before that — I went for the camera first, leaving Gus barking up the tree right under the bear and Donn barking at me to get the dog because he wasn't physically able to do it.) I closed all the doors before going for the camera. All I saw then was the back of the bear as he went back up into the woods.

If it hadn't been for Ruff and his dog training I might have had no supper at all because of unexpected company. Originality and imitation have to be respected in animals as well as children of all ages.

DISCIPLINE

As I've said elsewhere, we have never used any form of punishment with our children, and they have never given us any "discipline" problems that couldn't be resolved with discussion. (No one's perfect; sometimes it takes a lot of discussion.)

Our children are generally honest, respectful of people and things, polite, and usually very well-behaved.

"If you don't punish your children, how do you discipline them?"

In one 1957 dictionary, "punishment" is not one of the definitions of discipline, although it's mentioned as a *colloquial synonym*. A 1973 dictionary lists "punishment" as the eighth definition, and in a 1980 dictionary it's third. The word has come a long way, baby.

"Discipline" is still used to mean "a branch of instruction or learning, such as 'an academic discipline,'" but that definition, once the first (and not really very long ago), is now fourth — coming after the meaning of "punishment given to correct a person or enforce obedience."

In verb form, "discipline" means first "to train to be obedient and orderly" and second "to punish."

When we watch other parents with their children, we think we may have many more rules of conduct than most — advice and suggestions and instructions covering nearly every situation — but our rules of conduct are more like social customs than laws, and nearly all of them could easily be expressed by the Golden Rule or a close parallel.

When our children began crawling and exploring, we placed limits only for their own protection or the protection of things that might be damaged by inexperienced handling.

In our own home, we kept fragile or dangerous items out of reach. Our house has always been arranged for the presence of the kids. When visiting in other homes, which haven't been "child-proofed," we watch our kids closely but interfere with their movements, either physically or verbally, only when really necessary. We describe and explain the limits as briefly and clearly as possible. If the kids are curious about a fragile or dangerous item, we hold the item for inspection and discussion, and then set it out of reach. We never say, "Don't touch that; you might break it." Instead, we say, "Be very careful with this, because it's very fragile, and might break if it falls," or "I'll help you hold this, to make it easier for you to see." When prescribing limits, we stick to the facts, without exaggeration or threats.

Our kids always know that we expect only good behavior from them — not because of bribes or threats, but because we know they have no natural desire to break or lie or cheat or steal. Children, like adults, want to do what is right. They want to be liked, loved, and respected. They want to respect themselves.

Whenever one of our kids does something wrong or has made a mistake in judgment, we are quick to sympathize, to understand, and to forgive. Our expectation of goodness always includes the knowledge that mistakes will be made, that they don't diminish the child's inherent goodness.

A young child understands much of what is said to him, long before he can talk. When he is big enough to hold an object, he is old enough to understand directions about handling it.

The child is always more important than the object, even if actions toward it must be limited, and he must never be made to think otherwise.

In the relatively rare instances of "bad" behavior, we do our best to make it very clear that it's the behavior which is being rejected, not the child. We know parents who put their offending child out of the room, even out of the house, saying, "You're welcome to come back in when you're ready to behave the way you should." I don't think the child will make the desired distinction; no matter what the parent says, the child will feel personally rejected. Separation from the group or situation is often very effective, but if it's used as a punishment it just fosters resentment. "I'm not punishing you," says the parent. "I'm putting you outside to think it over." The child doesn't believe it. All he will think over is that he has been rejected, he is alone, he didn't mean to misbehave — or maybe he did, and as a parent you need to find out why. In any case, he's not big enough or strong enough to put his mother and father outside to think it over when they misbehave. He shouldn't be put outside; he should be taken out, and held closely, and talked *with,* not lectured.

For a young child, even with the most loving and understanding parents, the world is very often an incomprehensible and sometimes frightening maze of people and objects and rules. A parent who really tries to understand a child's feelings from the child's own point of view will be a much more positive influence on him than will a distant judge. We try to put ourselves in our children's places, really try to understand the situation as they feel it to be. We try to remember our own childhoods, the times we misbehaved, perhaps in the same way or worse, and how we felt about the people around us, how we felt about the ways we were punished.

We don't try to exact promises from our children, such as "Now, we'll go back inside if you think you can be nice." We talk about the problem, explaining why it is a problem, not expecting to reach solutions that will cover all future problems, and then drop it, perhaps even changing the subject. The situation may come up again, and we will deal with it in the same way, but the children never feel unloved or rejected. They don't resent us or feel a need to retaliate. Willful misbehavior is very rare. We are sure our children know we love them whatever they do.

We have never punished our children, in any way, for anything. We don't withhold privileges, or spank them, or send them to bed without supper. We don't threaten them with any kind of pain or suffering or deprivation — physical or psychological. If there is a problem in action or behavior, we discuss it; we consider it *our* problem. No one is "to blame"; it isn't "your fault" or "his fault." Fault and blame are irrelevant. Nearly every conflict between people is one of misunderstanding or lack of communication or an unfulfilled need. We discuss the problem — what led to it, how it might be avoided in the future. If something different should have been done or said, we discuss it, not to assign blame, but always to seek a better relationship in the future. Assigning blame creates defensiveness, which in turn creates barriers to understanding and progress.

We don't reward our children for good behavior, or for obedience, or for doing their work. We give praise for jobs well done, conflicts dealt with creatively and positively, or problems solved intelligently, but not as a reward. Such achievements deserve honest recognition.

Our children aren't paragons of peacefulness and harmony, but there is no physical violence between them, with the exception of occasional light slaps or pokes when they're very angry. They argue, complain, bicker, and sometimes call each other names. It's interesting that the kids who have had the most contact with public school kids at early ages are the ones most prone to name-calling and petty bickering.

In working to help the kids resolve their problems and conflicts with each other or with us, Jean and I sometimes lose our tempers right along with them. They shout at us; we shout back. When it's all over, we apologize to them for our having lost our tempers, and they learn from our example that even loving parents can get angry, can lose their tempers,

and can apologize. They learn to apologize to us and to each other. They learn to accept apologies.

In examining disagreements, we search for the roots — away from issues of personality, always trying to avoid the concepts of fault and blame. The question is not who is wrong, but *what* is wrong, and what can be done to correct the present situation to avoid its recurrence.

Peaceful conflict resolution isn't easy. It takes far more time and effort, more introspection, more discussion, than would be taken by establishing blame and meting out punishment. But it works, and is well worth the effort. It also puts more responsibility on the kids for monitoring and controlling their own behavior, by not "releasing" them from past actions through having "paid" for them by receiving punishment. As the kids get older, we've seen them searching more and more for peaceful solutions.

The dual concepts of blame and punishment are rooted deeply throughout our culture — in its religions, its government, and its family life. The courts and churches insist that if you have done something wrong, you must pay for it. This belief has its roots in the pre-Mosaic code of "an eye for an eye," which may have acted as a deterrent but hardly worked as a correction, any more than such punishments do today. Jesus tried to overturn this rule but with little success, even within "his" churches. His doctrine of forgiveness is often preached but seldom practiced.

Parents who punish their children, either physically or psychologically, are using force and coercion to manipulate behavior. A child may not repeat an act for which he has been punished, but it's usually only because he fears the consequences, not because he understands the wrongness of what he has done. An ancient Hebrew said that the man who does not beat his son must hate him, and his cynical observation is taken by millions of parents to be a divine injunction to spank their children. Jesus didn't threaten children or adults with either a spanking or hellfire; he promised love and forgiveness. His lessons appeal to the conscience — realize what you have done, he said, and feel sorry about it, and don't do it anymore.

In our family, we have striven for discipline from within. We wanted our children to know and understand the difference between right and wrong, good and bad, and to choose the rightness and goodness because they want to, not because they're afraid of any external consequences or punishments.

The development of the conscience is sometimes difficult. Most of the people and institutions of our society are against it, although they often pretend otherwise.

Behavior codes are relaxing and eroding around the world, which is one of the proofs that morality cannot be enforced by laws or fear. It can come only from within each individual, from strong convictions about what is right and good, and the desire to live by those convictions. It comes from the strength and courage to go against the current — to do what is right because it is right, not because of hope of reward or fear of punishment. Those convictions and that strength constitute the only discipline, moral or social, that is lasting and real. We can't force it onto our children, or even give it to them. We can only try to help them find and develop it within themselves.

KIDDING AROUND

The practice of referring to children as kids is thought by some to have begun as a tax dodge employed by slavers in the 1700s. Rather than declare their valuable and highly dutiable cargo, the righteous captains would insist they were importing goats and their kids, which even zealous customs officers admitted to be of little value.

Our daughter Karen would certainly agree with the customs officers, if not with the slave importers. Karen is a good kid and a great kidder, but she kids you not when she suggests that goats are not overly bright.

When one of our neighbors recently liquidated much of his barnyard stock, some of the flow ended up in our barn in the forms of five goats, four of whom keep our cow company and provide healthy exercise for our children's fingers and Karen's vocabulary.

(Digressing a little: We "water the cow," meaning we give water to her, and we "milk the cow," meaning we take milk away from her, and still we think English is a language that even young children can understand. Water and milk are both liquids, at least in their most common and desirable states, so could we say in either case that we have liquidated the stock?)

(Digressing still further: Our little brook, central to our farm and our aspirations, is certainly a liquid asset, although financial reports usually reserve that term for money, as in "cash flow," as if even money might come from a spring up on the hill. Not our spring on our hill, I can assure them with satisfaction; what would our cow do with a bucket of money?)

Anyway, back to the goats. Derek cares for Shawna and Jingle, two young does who have not yet learned how to make milk. Susan milks Heidi and Karen milks Buffy, and they both care for their goats, although, playing with definitions, sometimes they say they don't very much.

The buck, we were told, was named Keyops by his parents, but a previous caretaker kept forgetting the name and decided to call him Fred. Fred went to live with a man named Fred, who called him Tyler. Then Tyler stayed with George, who continued to call him Tyler. Then Tyler moved in with us. His proud bearing, majestic horns, and strong odor reminded us of Egyptian mummies and other ancient artifacts, so we restored his earlier name, with the proper spelling Cheops.

At first, Karen and Susan and Heidi and Buffy took turns amusing each other when the former two attempted to extract milk from the latter two, and the entire operation was a splashing success. Heidi soon settled down and eventually gave Susan less trouble than milk, but Buffy continued to think milking time was circus time, and Karen developed very strong opinions about Buffy's intelligence.

Whenever Karen touched the faucets, Buffy became a rodeo queen — kicking, bucking, prancing, somersaulting, standing on her head, and sitting in the milk bucket. Karen was very impressed, and said so.

"Dumb goat," she muttered, over and over, as she tried to milk. At night, she had no need to count sheep jumping fences. "Dumb goat," we heard her mutter in her sleep.

I raided my toolbox and made a few quick installations in the goat pen.

"Observe," I instructed Karen and Susan. "This rope, with the loop in one end, attaches quickly to the goat's collar. The free end then goes through the eye-screw, down here, six inches from the floor. Notice how Buffy's head goes down as I pull the rope up. Now her collar is snug against the post, and so is her neck, and she is reluctant to practice gymnastics of any kind."

Karen and Susan nodded solemnly.

"Now," I continued, "Buffy is quite happy to wait patiently while you tie the remainder of the rope up here to this long screw. I recommend a clove hitch, which is made so — a loop, and another loop, and pull it tight. Some people call it a double half-hitch, but it's stronger if you call it a clove hitch. Any questions?"

"No," said Karen, "but you forgot two things."

"Two things?" I echoed. I looked over the entire arrangement — the taut rope, the perfect clove hitch I had learned in Boy Scouts, the waiting milk bucket, and the immobilized goat. "What did I forget?"

"A lever on the wall," Karen said grimly, "and a trapdoor under the goat."

RESOURCES FOR THE EARLY YEARS

Young children are naturally inquisitive about themselves and everything around them. Our job as parents is to provide a safe home, an environment conducive to learning, and lots of love. Even before children are able to explore many parts of the outside world, we can begin to share this world with them through books. Reading is one of the most important and pleasurable activities you can share with your child, and I don't think you can do too much. Well, you could pick a book he doesn't care for, or read longer than he wants to sit, but I think you understand my point.

I hope you will keep in mind that early learning activities should be enjoyable for your child. Don't be in a rush to "teach" him anything. With time and patience on your part, a child who is slow in starting any of these activities *will* catch up. A child's brain grows in stages, and each child develops at a different pace. If your child isn't inclined to use books when you first get them, be assured that he is busy developing other skills. Rushing your child into early reading or math before the necessary cognitive development has occurred will create only frustration, resistance, and other problems. When children get pushed into learning something they can't do yet — mind you, I didn't say won't do — we create a situation where we will get a wrong answer and they will feel they have failed.

Don't create a fear of failure; it is the antithesis of learning. Getting something wrong is not the end of the world. Skip over it lightly, and don't make a big deal out of it. For young children there is much more unknown than known, and now that I've written that I have to say the same applies to us adults too; we just have a lot more known to us because of our age.

One of the biggest obstacles to learning something new is fear of giving the wrong answer. Think back to your public school days: When the teacher asked a question and no one raised his hand to answer it, there was a BIG silence. I can remember trying to disappear so that I wouldn't be the one called on for an answer I didn't know. Not knowing the answer in a classroom full of peers is humiliating. If it happens often it creates inhibition and fear. We all make mistakes, and we learn from them best when we are open and receptive and not inhibited.

We need to create a learning atmosphere where asking questions and making mistakes are as much the norm as breathing — something so accepted that our children never think about it.

The public school system is trying to make up for its failures by starting children in school at younger and younger ages. This leaves moms free to do other things and can solve a baby-sitting problem, but I don't think sending kids to school sooner — or trying too hard to teach them at home — will cure the academic failures.

One of My Lessons in Lifelong Learning

When I went back to the community college to take a course in beginning computer skills it was my first foray into adult education. I didn't realize that I would need lessons I'd learned while homeschooling the kids. I went with fear and trembling and all my old conditioned responses from public school. I was afraid I couldn't keep up with all the younger people. As in all classrooms there were a few students who already had an understanding of the specialized vocabulary and basic keyboard skills. The teacher started out teaching to the more knowledgeable students, I think because he was enthusiastic about the subject and these students were easy to teach. I realized I didn't have a clue about what the teacher was talking about. By the mid-class break I had to take a walk and decide if I should stay in the class. How badly did I want to learn? Could I overcome my conditioned fear of asking questions or maybe giving wrong answers? I was so afraid of making a mistake or maybe looking foolish that I came very close to getting in the car and going home. Then I thought about what I had learned from our experience homeschooling the kids, and I remembered telling them that if you don't understand something and ask for help there are no foolish questions. I knew then that if I was going to learn I was going to have to ask questions. I made the second half of the class a test for myself, and the teacher. I had to dig deep for the courage, but every time the teacher said something I didn't understand I raised my hand and asked for clarity. At first he was surprised. Then he was annoyed. After a bit it got to be funny. He would say something and then look at me to see if I was going to raise my hand and ask about it. If I smiled he went on with the lesson. After class about half the young people came up to me and thanked me for asking all those questions because they had been totally lost and way too embarrassed to ask a question. That experience got me over my mountain of fear. Let's be sure we don't ever make our children uncomfortable when they ask a question.

A Place to Begin

Love them. Hug them often and tell them you love them. Make sure you separate the doer from the deed when they make mistakes or misbehave. Listen carefully and they will let you know what their needs are. Hold on to your patience and your tongue until you know what you really want to say. Lead by example. How you live every day is what they will learn from and where they will gain their lasting values.

Some of Our Favorites

***GOODNIGHT MOON,* by Margaret Wise Brown; pictures by Clement Hurd.** We began to get tired of some books after the first thousand requests, but not this one, which is still absolutely, positively one of our favorites. Warm, friendly pictures gradually darken as the little rabbit child prepares to go to sleep, saying goodnight to all the familiar things in his room. He doesn't notice the tiny mouse, but you and your child will. Whoops — where did he go? There he is, on the windowsill! Ages 2 and up. If your child is 5, it may not be too late. If he's older, have him read it with someone younger; or get it for yourself and save it for your grandchildren. The book is available in a thin paperback, which we have tried, but it didn't last. We prefer and recommend the hardcover edition, because it will surely get a lot of use.

***IF YOU WERE MY BUNNY,* by Kate McMullan.** A classic. The combination of well-written text and illustrations will make you cuddle even closer as you read this bedtime story. This is about animal mamas tucking in their little ones for the night. You can sing the included lullabies to the tune of familiar melodies. This should go on the shelf next to *Goodnight Moon*. (If you don't have that, shame on you!)

***FUN IS A FEELING,* by Chara M. Curtis.** What is "fun"? You can't see it or touch it. You can't smell it or taste it. You can't pick it off the shelf or buy it. It's not something you do, like a game, but just the same, it is something we all have inside us. Curtis's book will make it clear that it is something we feel inside us — and she includes clues for finding it. This book is bound to become a classic. It also belongs on the shelf next to *Goodnight Moon*. The good feelings you get reading this book just bubble up inside you, and you want to share them with everyone. All our grandchildren have a copy.

***WALKING WITH MAMA,* by Barbara White Stynes.** A warm, intimate tale of a mother and toddler on a nature walk — told from the child's point of view, first walking and trying to keep up with Mama, then from high up in a backpack. I wish we'd had this one when the kids were little. If we had had it, we would have had to replace it many times over. I love this book for nostalgic reasons. I carried all our children in a backpack (known in our house as a "wife saver.") Children who have been carried this way will enjoy reading this long after their backpack days are over. If you carry your child in a backpack, you will love this as much as your child will.

PRETEND SOUP: A COOKBOOK FOR PRESCHOOLERS, is joyfully illustrated and written by Mollie Katzen and Ann Henderson. To use this book successfully, you must be willing to allow a role reversal between you and your youngster. Usually you cook and your child "helps." If you use this book it will be the other way around. If you have a large ego, save your money. You are necessary, but you are not the prime mover. Recipes are wholesome (though not fanatically so) and varied. (You will find white sugar as an ingredient in some recipes. Feel free to substitute honey.) Directions for the adult helper are written, and directions for your child are clearly drawn. Great fun. I almost listed this book in "Arts and Activities," but I wanted to make sure you wouldn't miss it.

HANDS ARE NOT FOR HITTING, **by Martine Agassi, Ph.D.** A carefully crafted book with a positive message about all the wonderful things hands can do. The underlying message is that violence is never acceptable. It's designed to be read aloud, and the illustrations provide ideas for discussion. Included is a special section suggesting discussion topics and activities for parents or adults working with children.

Why do grown-ups always say, "don't hit," and then they go and start a big war? — Benjamin Rottman, letter to the *Los Angeles Times*

WORDS ARE NOT FOR HURTING, **by Elizabeth Verdick.** I disagree with the title. Of course words are used for hurting, and sometimes that is exactly what one wants to do. Aside from that, this book is a gem. It discusses the ways in which we all use words and has some important suggestions for dealing with the consequences of hurting words for the one who has said them and for the one who is hurt by them. In the back of the book are activities and discussion suggestions.

MAGNETIC LETTERS AND WORDS. Kids enjoy having magnetic letters to play with and make simple words with, but most sets have their limitations. How many sets of magnetic letters do you have to buy before it's possible to write a simple sentence? How much time does it take to use all those individual letters to make a word or a sentence? These magnetic words, numbers, and punctuation pieces are washable and color coded: green for nouns, yellow for pronouns, red for verbs, etc. There are periods, question marks, commas, exclamation marks, and even pieces with handy suffixes. You have a lot to choose from: Objects (just the picture — apple, ball, etc.), Letters With Objects, Beginner's Word Set (200+ pieces), Individual Uppercase Letters, Individual Lowercase Letters, or words within a theme (Our Planet, City and Country, Planes and Trains, Sports and Games).

We never put our kids down for naps. They slept when they were tired and regulated themselves very well most of the time, naturally adjusting to our living patterns. If you do put your kids down for naps, and they sometimes object or fuss, you could put on a quiet story for them to listen to until they fall asleep. **GOOD NIGHT,** six quiet tales of safety and love by Jim Weiss, is a good one to use.

MATHARTS: EXPLORING MATH THROUGH ART FOR 3- TO 6-YEAR-OLDS, **by MaryAnn Kohl and Cindy Gainer.** Young children naturally notice sizes, shapes, and patterns, and they enjoy sorting and counting. *MathArts* offers 200 simple, creative activities (most of which require only common household materials) that will heighten your child's conceptual awareness. Each activity begins with an explanation of the materials needed, the time involved, the optimal age, and whether or not assistance will be necessary. Teaching is neither necessary nor desirable at this age. Hours of fun are contained within these pages.

SANDBOX SCIENTIST: REAL SCIENCE ACTIVITIES FOR LITTLE KIDS, **by Michael Ross**. A great guide for early science experiences. Numerous entertaining activities. Just do it — don't "teach" it.

BEFORE YOU WERE BORN, **by Jennifer Davis.** This terrific interactive lift-the-flap book is for young children and parents to explore together. In full color, the main part of the page shows, month by month, what is happening inside Mommy's body, and lifting the flap you see how the baby is developing. Answers questions about the umbilical cord, baby's hiccups, and more. From conception through birth — "I pushed and pushed until your head showed a fraction."

TAILS ARE NOT FOR PULLING, **by Elizabeth Verdick,** comes in two editions. The book points out the good reasons for your children to respect pets. It's well done and to the point. The board book edition has tips for parents and caregivers for safe interaction between children and pets. The paperback edition goes into more detail within the book, and in the back offers tips on safety, critter care, cruelty, and fun facts.

GAMES TO PLAY WITH LITTLE ONES, **compiled by Marty Layne,** is a small treasury of poems, fingerplays, rhythm games, songs, and activities. The games Marty has collected here will give you and your child hours of enjoyment. If there were a how-to-raise-your-children manual, this booklet would be an ideal companion volume.

FOR READING OUT LOUD: WHY DO IT, HOW TO DO IT, CHOOSING BOOKS YOU AND YOUR FAMILY WILL ENJOY, **by Marty Layne.** This pamphlet has all the information you need to start your child off with a love of reading. A great guide for parents of young children and for parents dealing with a reluctant reader.

Now, take a deep breath or two and just relax. Be patient.

Please check our website for early learning resources. There are so many that I wanted to include here and couldn't, including audio books and stories, and I would hate for you to miss them. There are some funny stories there too.

READING, WRITING, AND SPELLING

A reader wrote to say that she and her husband (a math teacher) were disappointed by my comments about math. "Math literacy" — the understanding and enjoyment of all levels of math — are as important, she said, as reading literacy.

I wrote her a long letter, emphasizing that it certainly is not the study of mathematics I oppose, but the mandatory studying of math without enjoyment or purpose. I realize there are many people who really need and enjoy math, and I'm even a little envious of those who enjoy it.

Our culture — in philosophy, history, and myth — is communicated much more through literature than through math, so I can't agree that a lack of math literacy is equal to a lack of reading literacy. A person who is well-read but non-mathematical will have a greater awareness and understanding of the world than a mathematician whose reading has been confined to mathematics. That doesn't preclude the possible desirability of being well-educated in both fields, but if I have to make a choice, I'll choose literature.

All four of our kids read a great deal, but none of them seems to have a natural bent for writing, so it's as unlikely that they'll be journalists as it is that they'll be astronomers. With writing, therefore, as with math, we encourage a general, basic competency that will be of use to them in areas they probably will pursue, and in most "real-life" situations: various styles of letters, basic reports (which may or may not be useful, but are easy to master and will probably be of good use someday), simplified research notes, and so on, along with basic spelling skills, grammar, sentence structure, and a few handshakes with parts of speech. If they ever need more advanced writing (or more advanced math), they have solid foundations on which to build.

The essential purpose of language — whether it consists of animal grunts and growls, human speech, mathematical equations, or computer symbols — is the communication of information and ideas. As the subject of this chapter, I'll consider writing to be human speech on paper. Its basic purpose is still the communication of information and ideas. Spelling is little more than a standardized system of encoding sounds and their meanings to facilitate that communication.

There's an old story, which you've probably heard, about a little boy who scribbled laboriously on a piece of paper and proudly told his mother, "Look, I'm writing."

"How nice," said his mother. "What does it say?"

"I don't know," the boy replied. "I haven't learned to read yet."

Like many apocryphal stories, this one may have some basis in fact, but most of us learn to read before we learn to write.

Ideally — except in modern schools that try to teach how to read without offering reading material of any substance, and how to write without asking that the writing be about anything of substance — the two processes soon overlap, each one contributing to the other. Spelling, principal parts of speech, and basic grammar are all learned simultaneously. The reading will be about subjects that interest the kids, and they will write about things or events that interest them. Printing is also learned at the same time, as well as the extension of meanings by the use of suffixes and prefixes, by different tenses, etc.

We never taught our children to read.

When they were very young, we read to them. When they were three months old, they gurgled happily as we read nursery rhymes, poetry, and even captions of "first interest" animal books. At six months, they smiled and pointed at interesting shapes and colors. When they were a year old, we read books with them, discussing the pictures and answering millions of questions. We often asked each other, "Where is the truck?" "Can you put your finger on the nose?" "Which flower is red?" and similar questions. The kids weren't reading words yet, but even picture books with no words involved verbal communication and a growing vocabulary, including concepts of space, size, color, action, and direction.

Between eighteen months and two years, each of them spent many hours each day with books, not yet recognizing many words, but studying the pictures. Despite the kids' early interest in books, we never pushed reading. We read to them every day, but they also chose to look at books on their own every day. It was unimportant to us if they learned to read at the age of two or six or ten. When we were reading to them we made a point of moving our finger along under the words we were reading. It wasn't long before the questions were about the letters and words as often as about the pictures. The kids were fascinated by the idea that the story was not only in the pictures, and were eager to decode the words. They asked us to identify specific words, especially nouns with which they were familiar (cow, horse, car, tree) and verbs, especially of movement (run, jump, fall). They'd point at a word (sometimes at random, sometimes deliberately) and ask "Cow?" If by chance, the "choice" was correct, the child felt such pride and delight that the word might never be forgotten. When the random choice was incorrect, we moved the pointing finger to the right word, saying, "Here's 'cow.'" If the child then returned to the first choice, wanting to know what it was, then we'd tell him; otherwise, we ignored it.

Their own curiosity about the pictures and the accompanying words we read to them taught them to read. They also saw us (whenever we had a chance) reading for our own pleasure.

Frequent positive reinforcement and absolute avoidance of negative corrections encouraged the kids, and they learned rapidly. None of them ever said, "I can't get it. It's too hard," because we never asked them to "get" anything. There was never any pressure to do something they hadn't yet learned to do.

The girls could identify and read several words before they knew the sounds of individual letters. We never had a definite plan of "how to teach reading," except to be sure it was always fun and interesting, so there didn't seem much point in interrupting their reading to teach them how to read.

A Lesson in Patience

Derek learned in a different way. He had the same introduction to books, saw us and the girls reading, and asked all of us to read to him. He had a love affair with books, and it drove him (and us) nearly crazy for a couple of years. At age two he wished for a horse. At ages three and four he yearned for a horse and someone to read to him. After that he wanted a horse and he wanted to read. He would ask what a word was, but couldn't remember it a day later or even later that day. He frequently ad-libbed stories from books, some almost word for word. Sometimes he made up his own stories to go with the pictures. When he realized that the letters had individual sounds he learned the alphabet and most of the sounds, but he still couldn't read on his own.

Derek's desire to read was not lacking, but something was. It made us wonder and sometimes worry. We didn't understand why, although he yearned to read, he couldn't do it. His frustration grew, even though we reassured him that he would learn. We had his eyes checked, even though we had never seen him squint at a book or the TV. He was given glasses, which he proudly wore. He went to get a book, almost tripping on the way, and sat down to read. He looked at the letters on the page and scrunched up his eyes and face so he could see better. The glasses were obviously wrong or not the answer at all. We had his eyes rechecked by another eye specialist who advised us to throw the glasses out, so we did.

No one really understands exactly what happens when the ability to decode the written word occurs. It's still a mystery. We do know that a certain amount of brain development must take place first, just as the muscles and nervous system must develop before a child crawls or walks. Studies have shown that linguistic and mathematical skills come easily at different times to different children.

All Derek really needed was time. When he was eight, "it" finally happened. After he made the first breakthrough on his own he was an insatiable reader, and within six months was reading way beyond his grade level. Before he was able to read he would have been considered "slow," or worse, in a public school setting. I shudder to think what that would have done to this otherwise bright and happy child who went on to became a natural speed-reader with very high comprehension.

It was interesting to watch phonics and grammar grow naturally with the kids' learning to write.

We let the kids lead the way. Once the partial similarity of COW to CAR was noticed and questioned, it was very natural for us to discuss the alphabet and the different sounds of letters. Being able to "sound out" words phonetically is important, but it's just as important to be able to read entire words and even whole phrases without having to dissect them.

The conventional "sounding out" of "baby" is buh-ay-buh-ee. Once the child can point to the letters in turn and make these sounds, we are supposed to say, "Very good! Now say the sounds faster; run them together." We are supposed to demonstrate the method, slowly and ponderously saying, "BUHay-buhEE," over and over, until the child finally hears — or guesses — the word "baby." "Now you do it," we say, with the reminder "Sound out each letter, then run the sounds together — and you have the word!"

It doesn't really work that way. For most beginning readers, it still comes out as buh-ay-buh-ee, but speeded up — buhaybuhee." The sounds trip over each other, but are not "run together." The trick is to condense four syllables into two — but then it's no longer a strictly phonetic approach; it's sight reading of syllables. The transition from four separate letter sounds to two syllables is less a matter of logic than of intuition. The conclusion may be accepted, but there is no logical transition to be understood.

Later, when we began using school readers, we made the mistake of also using the tests for "comprehension and retention" that invariably followed each story. We still hadn't learned to reject the methods of the "experts." Luckily, we soon realized that our kids' lessening interest in reading was the direct result of having to answer dumb questions about their reading, but it took us longer than it should have. We should have known better without even trying it.

I was reminded of those dumb questions many years later when I read Longfellow's "The Courtship of Miles Standish" to the family. It was in a book prepared for classroom use, and the poem was followed by about fifty questions, such as "The Pilgrims came to America on the (a) Atlantic (b) Mayflower (c) Titanic (d) Damascus." Like many test questions in the public schools, some of these were not only ridiculous, but intentionally tricky. Even if the student has been asleep throughout the entire poem, he isn't likely to answer either "Titanic" or "Damascus," even if he doesn't know what they are. But a conscientious student might easily suspect a trick in the first two choices. The Pilgrims came to America on the Mayflower, but they also came on the Atlantic. The teacher has the answer key and knows that the correct answer is b, which is what most students will answer. Does that mean that a is incorrect? The student who answers "the Atlantic" will be laughed at. The teacher, smiling condescendingly, will say, "The question is about the name of the ship." "But," the student might argue, "the question didn't say 'ship.' 'Damascus' isn't a ship's name." The teacher smiles tolerantly at the student's stupidity. The other students snicker — even those who answered "Titanic."

When Derek was nine, he became interested in sharks, and quickly exhausted the small amount of material we had on the subject. He borrowed books from the public library and requested more through inter-library loans. Relatives sent him books about sharks; he searched back issues of *National Geographic*. Except for helping him find material, we left him alone. We didn't try to direct his studies, or tie them in with any other subject, or test his "comprehension and retention." We knew that if he didn't understand the books, he wouldn't have chosen to read them. Soon he scoffed at popularized images of sharks, such as the movie *Jaws,* and could point out, in detail, the errors in them — not to impress anyone with his knowledge, but because he felt that both sharks and people were being wronged by the misconceptions and misrepresentations. His "retention," apparently, was excellent.

When Derek first showed an interest in sharks, we might have thought, "A-ha! Here's our chance. We can direct his study, so that it will include history, geography, oceanography, other aquatic life forms, sociology, anthropology, and psychology. We can expand his vocabulary."

We didn't; the thought never occurred to us. Had we assigned readings, followed by tests for comprehension and retention, I'm sure he would have lost interest in the subject very quickly. Such an approach to any subject is one of the quickest ways to kill interest in it. Derek studied sharks for two years because he wanted to, and learned a great deal about history, geography, oceanography, other aquatic life forms, sociology, anthropology, and psychology. His vocabulary certainly expanded.

Books have always been a prominent part of our lives. When Jean and I aren't busy with building, gardening, barn chores, housework, or working with the kids, we read. There are books in every room of our house. In providing books for our children, from the time they could first focus their eyes on a picture, we've always treated books as sources of pleasure, adventure, information, and discovery. Reading should never be a tedious chore; it should always be exciting and rewarding — as it will be, if we don't try to harness it, control it, pen it up, or direct it for our own purposes.

Educational distributors now offer innumerable books for "the reluctant reader." Because most children spend so many hours watching movies and television, publishers and teachers offer them countless books with "TV tie-ins" — i.e., stories based on popular shows and characters — with the hope that the tie-in will lead the kids from their mania for TV to a mania for reading; then, once hooked, they'll move on to better material.

Does it work? I doubt it. Early Christians, seeking to convert the heathens, incorporated non-Christian rituals, symbols, and even dates into some of their holidays (holy days) in an attempt to make conversion more palatable. Celebration of the springtime birth of Jesus was moved to more nearly coincide with the winter solstice. Painted eggs, chicks, and baby rabbits — once parts of pre-Christian fertility rites — are now popular parts of the Easter observance of many Christians. Who was converted — the pagans or the Christians?

Meaningless trivia on a movie or TV screen is not likely to become more meaningful or less trivial in a book. Why yield to the uneducated choices of the lowest common denominator? Are the antics of television soap operas and cartoons and sitcoms really more exciting and more meaningful than the writings of Dickens, London, Stevenson, Poe, Pyle, even Shakespeare? Granted that millions of high school students are still struggling with a third-grade reading ability, they have been deprived, by an incompetent school system, of the pleasures of reading.

The concerned teacher can read to them, helping them to feel the magic of words in books such as *A Tale of Two Cities, The Three Musketeers, Lost Horizon,* and *Shane.* Such books read, not for instruction but for the mutual enjoyment of both teacher and students, and without tests afterward for comprehension and retention, might in time overshadow the TV tie-ins. Maybe not; maybe it's too late. But if the students can be helped to realize that the pleasure is worth the effort — that is, once they want to read — they will do so, just as much younger children can begin reading B-A-B-Y.

When I have taught adult illiterates, this approach was been successful in every case, as the basis for both reading and writing.

If the students will ever be led to better reading, it will be through the introduction of better literature to read, certainly not through low-vocabulary books about dirt bikes, teen romance, and the selfish cynicism of Garfield.

Teachers say, "My students will never be interested in the great authors, but at least they're reading. It's better to read about television characters than to read nothing at all."

Is it?

Is it better to write verses in restrooms than to write nothing at all? Is it better to listen to punk rock and thrash metal than to hear no music at all?

Whether the book is by an ancient great or a modern unknown, if it doesn't make at least a small positive contribution to the reader's life — his values, his knowledge, his understanding, his growth as a human being, his enjoyment of life — then it's not worth the time of reading. As an avid reader, I feel that illiteracy is a very sad handicap, but the cynicism, narcissism, and hedonism promoted by most television shows and their literary tie-ins, as well as a huge portion of other popular publications, are much greater handicaps.

It's hard for me to imagine my own life without books, but I know many people who don't read, yet are happy and successful — good neighbors, caring parents, and hard workers. Why should they clutter up their lives with books about puerile, melodramatic electronic images?

Just as Gandhi, probably the world's greatest proponent and practitioner of non-violence, said that violence is preferable to cowardice, I am sure that illiteracy is preferable to the exclusive reading of debasing or condescending trivia.

CHILDREN'S BOOK-OF-THE-MONTH CLUB, P.O. Box 6434, Camp Hill, PA 17001-9235; www.cbomc.com. Books for ages 2 to 12. They have a good introductory offer, and your commitment is to buy two more books over the following two years. I don't endorse all their choices, but in the catalog I have I saw a number of books that I know are very good.

Inexpensive classic literature (and more) is now available to you from **FOLLETT EDUCATIONAL SERVICES.** The titles change frequently, so if you don't find what you want right away go back again in a few weeks. They also have all the basic test prep and reference books like dictionaries and thesauruses (thesauri?) . Look online at www.fes.follett.com or call 800-621-4272 and request their pre-owned textbook catalog and their classroom literature catalog.

The annual ***BEST CHILDREN'S BOOKS OF THE YEAR*** volumes and ***BOOKS TO READ ALOUD WITH CHILDREN OF ALL AGES*** are compiled by the Children's Book Committee at Bank Street College of Education, 610 West 112th Street, New York, NY 10025-1898; www.bankstreet.edu/bookcom. You can purchase the books, as well as games, documentaries, and teacher resources that complement their recommendations, through the Bank Street Bookstore, 212-678-1654; www.bankstreetbooks.com.

RUINED BY READING: A LIFE IN BOOKS, **by Lynne Sharon Schwartz.** I was intrigued by the title. I fell in love with the book. Have you ever wondered why you love to read? What exactly it adds to your life, mentally and spiritually? Beyond the instant recognition you'll feel when Schwartz verbalizes your unconscious compulsion to read is the sharing of the delectable intangible love of words: their sounds, nuances, and implications; the intimate imagery that comes with reading a good book.

Indulge your addiction. If you get only one copy you'll be sorry. You'll have to share it with another addict, and I won't be surprised or sympathetic if you don't get it back — but it makes a perfect gift. I bought just one and had to order five more.

Robert E. Kay, in his article "Helping a Child Learn to Read at Home" in *Clinical Pediatrics* (August 1970, adapted from a similar article in the *Penn Home Education News*), has some very useful suggestions for helping any child learn to read well. He writes, "Most of the difficulties are, I suspect, the result of quizzing and putting kids on the spot to read out loud. Unwanted coercion, fear of judgments, struggle, inhibition, loss of pleasure, teaching before the brain is ready, happen all too often. Meanwhile, motivating them by reading aloud *TO* them, both at home and in school, may be all we need to do. *Sesame Street,* however, isn't going to do the trick. In addition, choral reading … is a marvelous supplementary technique, and is far superior to phonics, sight reading, alphabet learning, or whole-language approaches. Studies show that this can jump twelve-year-olds two grade levels for every seven hours of work put in. It's also very easy to do."

Kay's suggestions for reading together are simple. "Let the child pick out a storybook, newspaper, or a magazine of interest. Say to them: 'Let's read this together. You say the words with me or right after me. I will never ask you to figure out the words by yourself or put you on the spot to read out loud alone. You may, if you wish, try to say the word before I do, and, if it's difficult, I'll repeat the word with you.' And then one naturally speeds up with the simple stuff, slows down with the bigger words, and eventually fades out when we're pretty sure they know the word. But we're always prepared to come right back in so that there's no struggling and thus no anxiety. Use a pointer. Let the child control frequency, time, and the taking of breaks. The parent/tutor should ideally stay somewhat behind the student while almost whispering in their ear.

Some kids insist on reading on their own after a while and that's OK, of course. Above all, however, we must wait until the child is INTERESTED which may be anywhere from age three to age seven, depending on the level of brain development as regards this particular skill."

While working on this book I've been dismayed at the number of references I've made to online resources. I wish it weren't so. I'd rather kids learn from books. That said, I'm going to wax enthusiastic about this next online resource.

Here are a few excellent places to seek information about reading problems and dyslexia. I recommend them highly, with the caveat that you need to first decide if your child really has serious reading problems or just needs more time to develop. **PARENTS ACTIVE FOR VISION EDUCATION** is at www.pavevision.org, and the Davis Dyslexia Association is at www.dyslexia.com. You will find more resources at **FINDING POSITIVE SUPPORT FOR CHALLENGES:** www.hsc.org/chaos/specialchallenges.

Those without computer access can write to the The Davis Dyslexia Correction Center, 1601 Bayshore Hwy., Suite 260, Burlingame, CA 94010, and Parents Active for Vision Education (PAVE), 4135 54th Place, San Diego, CA 92105-2303; 800-PAVE988.

Don't have time to read? Use the time in the car to listen.

CBC AUDIO catalogue from Canadian Broadcasting Corporation, P.O. Box 500, Station "A", Toronto ONT M5W 1E6; 866-306-4636; TTY/Teletypewriter (Hearing impaired only): 866-220-6045 (Canada only). Impressive collection of classic literature, choice radio shows available on CD, videos, toys, and games. www.cbcradio.ca. Once you have the home page up go to the bottom and click on 'merchandise and shop', then look down the left side for CDs etc. There is also a link at the bottom of the home page for educational resources.

BTC AUDIOBOOKS, Suite 330, 500 Beaverbrook Court, Fredericton, NB E3B 5X4; 888-926-8377; info@gooselane.com; www.gooselane.com/btcaudiobooks. Catalog of uniquely Canadian literature on tape.

Writing

I think we taught our kids a little more about how to write than we did about how to read. Their writing, like their reading, seemed to grow by itself, with only a little help from us. When they asked, we showed them how to make letters, what sounds the letters represented, and so on. In the beginning, we tried to follow standard schoolbooks, but we soon found that most of them followed logical sequences as much as the beginning readers did. Very little, that is.

Although a few schoolbooks are fairly good, we were soon much happier with the various activity books sometimes sold in toy departments, drugstores, and grocery stores. Now you can find them in Wal-Mart and similar stores and in some bookstores. These books include dot-to-dot pictures (which, besides being fun, teach number recognition and sequence), math and reading readiness, writing preparation, colors, shapes, sizes, and so on. Many are very good primers in natural science. Perhaps because these books are prepared and designed to appeal to parents rather than to school boards, they are often more attractive and interesting than schoolbooks. Future sales are largely dependent on the purchasers' satisfaction, so the books are both educational, which pleases the parents, and fun, which pleases the children.

We put printed alphabet cards on the kitchen wall, where they could easily be seen and copied. Usually the first written word they wanted to learn was their name. After that we followed their lead with their favorite words, names of friends, our names, siblings, names of our pets, and the all-time favorites: YES and NO. Besides pencil or crayons and paper, we used a wall-mounted chalkboard, magnetic letters on the refrigerator, and individual letters printed on cardboard. The kids sometimes spent hours printing letters, words, names, and eventually short sentences. Jean and I printed short messages to them on the chalkboard and the kids printed answers. We arranged the magnetic letters into words; the kids rearranged them into different words.

We agree wholeheartedly with John Holt's recommendation, in *How Children Learn,* that very young children be given access to a typewriter. As John points out, the kids will be fascinated by the machine's inner workings; they'll also want to learn correct spelling, capitalization, and punctuation — perhaps because typewritten material looks so neat, so official, so permanent, and so real. (There are now simplified keyboards for young children that you can use with your computer, but the typewriter mechanism — being able to see it and touch it — is still more fascinating. Also very cheap!) Just touch a key and see how many different things move, and the letter you want is printed right beside the previous letter. Yard and garage sales and pawnshops frequently have very good typewriters for $10 to $20. You can also put an ad in the paper for little cost. Most typewriters — if you can still find them (everyone wants you to buy a computer these days) — sold in toy departments, Christmas catalogs, and even by some educational suppliers, although they look solid enough and sell for as much as $150, aren't worth shelf space. They are too flimsy for the rough handling a child will sometimes give them; the parts, including the ribbons, are often a special size or brand you can't find anywhere; and, if there happens to be a breakdown or defect covered by the very limited warranty, the only "authorized service center" is ten thousand miles away and receives mail only by Camel Express.

Crossword puzzles for children, found in book and toy stores, increase spelling and vocabulary. The girls enjoyed them; Derek didn't.

The best preparation for writing is reading — anything and everything. The child (or adult) who gets little pleasure from reading will seldom see much purpose in writing.

If you have more than one child, you may discover, as we did, that the younger ones will learn a great deal by imitating older siblings. Karen watched Cathy learn to write, and understood the process enough to want to do the same. She spent a lot of time "writing" before she could write anything we could read. Then she spent a lot of time copying actual letters, but sometimes she must have invented her own writing code. We gave her a six- by ten-inch spiral-bound notebook with about a hundred pages in it, and she filled it up. Sometimes she would ask us to write a word for her to copy and sometimes she would just "write." Her writing looked to us like squiggles and curlicues, wavy lines and loops, but to her it was writing, and we never made fun of her efforts. Sometimes she would read what she had written, so we knew she was making up stories along with her writing. Sometimes she illustrated her stories. It was great creative fun for all of us.

When Derek was nine, he began reading the Tarzan novels, by Edgar Rice Burroughs. The first of these books was written in 1929, and Burroughs' style is very formal and often pedantic, as was the style of most writers in those days; the sentences are occasionally ponderous, with several subordinate clauses. The vocabulary is sometimes just as imposing: a friendly ape may be referred to as an amiable anthropoid. Try getting all that into the local school's curriculum! I read all of the Tarzan books (more than twenty) several times when I was a kid, and I still read them occasionally, so I knew Derek was starting out in pretty deep water. He asked for help with a few words, but soon figured out most of them from their context, and was soon sailing smoothly. Within two years, he had read all the books at least once, and some of them many times.

When he was ten, Derek started writing his own stories of Tarzan and his son Korak, with enthusiastic and bloodthirsty imitation of Burroughs' own style —

KORAK, MAN OR BEAST?
By Derek Reed

He swung silently through the lower branches of the trees. He stopped now and again to sniff the air. Now he stopped, thirty feet off the ground, for he was hunting, a beast among beasts, for this is Korak, son of Tarzan, and he is in Africa, the Dark Continent. You're probably wondering what he is hunting. Well, no matter, for you shall find out. For now, he swings into a natural clearing and sees what he has been tracking for about half an hour, but he does not know this. For he carries no watch, he just knows that he is terribly hungry and he is but a scarce eight feet from Bara the deer. He but broke upon the clearing when he launched himself full upon the buck's back. He fastened his teeth in Bara's neck and sunk his knife into his heart. Bara gave a little quiver and lay still. At that moment a wounded lion came upon them. He headed straight for Korak. Korak leaped high in the air, turned around in mid-air and came down upon the lion's back.

One bronze arm encircled the throat, while the two legs locked under the belly. The free arm drew the knife and drove it home into that savage heart. Again, he drives the knife home. Three times he drives it home. He feels the giant muscles relax. The body quivers and lays still. Korak leaps up, places his foot on the lion's neck and screams forth the victory cry of the bull ape twice. Once for Bara and once for Numa. He went back to Bara and cut a hole in his neck, this is so he will bleed and not be so messy. As he cuts a juicy steak, he finds himself wondering about his friends and if they could see him now naked except for a G-string. "I'm a man" thought Korak, "but I act like a beast." And then he took his kill to a tree and finding a comfortable place, fell asleep.

THE END

Derek usually disliked assigned writing topics, but seemed to be developing adequate writing skills without them, so we gave him very few. A thank-you note for a birthday or Christmas gift might take several weeks, unless we just laid down the law. But if he was writing about a subject that interested him personally and deeply — horses, sharks, Tarzan — he could fill pages in a very short time.

Cathy, Karen, and Susan have always enjoyed writing long, newsy letters to friends and relatives. When asked, we have helped them edit their spelling and punctuation. When Cathy was elected club reporter for her 4-H club, it was her job to write about club activities for a regional 4-H newsletter and for two local newspapers. Two years later, Karen received the job of 4-H reporter. Having their articles in print, with their own bylines, was rewarding, and gave them incentive for steady improvement. Both girls developed an easy writing fluency and wrote several papers for us on research subjects such as existentialism, William Penn, and a comparison of Leonardo da Vinci and Buckminster Fuller.

About this time we started creating family newsletter publications in the form of small booklets. The kids wrote and illustrated stories about what they were doing, and sometimes we included some of their works of fiction. Donn and I also wrote short articles. The kids enjoyed seeing their work, with ours, in booklet form, and we thought it good PR for our homeschooling.

When Susan was eight, she asked to attend a public school for the entire year, mostly because she enjoyed the social life so much. Her teacher was a screaming bully and we saw several potential problems, but Susan never complained about the teacher, and we somehow convinced ourselves that any harm being done was superficial, and could be corrected easily. Early in the year, Susan lost all interest in reading to herself. When reading aloud, which she had been able to do smoothly and competently, she stuttered, coughed, covered her mouth, mumbled, mispronounced simple words, juxtaposed words, and missed words completely. Her spelling became so literally phonetic that it was almost incomprehensible: "Th tcher sed tak ot yr boke. I opnd it and b gen tu red." Her spelling hadn't been that bad since she was five. But she still seemed happy in school and did well in most other subjects. Her reading problems, we told ourselves, were superficial, and we could straighten them out next year.

We were wrong. It took us years to correct the damage, to rebuild the reading and writing skills that third-grade teacher had nearly destroyed in just a few months. Although Susan now reads avidly, for both pleasure and information, and can write and spell quite well, I'm sure that neither her reading nor her writing is as good as it would be if we had had the sense and courage to take her out of school when we saw the problems beginning. Susan's self-confidence took much longer to rebuild. "I can't do it, I just know I can't," was her standard response to any suggestion of writing. We continued to encourage her and she persevered. As a result, in April 1983, *Highlights for Children* magazine printed a prose-poem Susan had submitted when she was eleven:

The Beauty of a Tree
By Susan Reed

Can anyone see the beauty of a tree? The colors of light and dark in the summer? The leaves falling in the fall? What about the icicles hanging from the trees in the winter? Or the buds starting to grow in the spring? Some people may think a tree is just a thing to be used for firewood and building things, but it's not. A tree should be cared for, for just a square inch cut from the bark could end its life. What is the beauty of a tree? The beauty of a tree is life itself.

Her self-confidence leaped. Later that spring, she entered a 4-H club essay-writing contest, and in July 1983 two local papers, *The Woodstock Bugle* and *The Hartland Observer,* carried this story:

Knowlesville Girl Wins Kings Landing Trip

Susan Reed of Knowlesville is one of two winners in a province-wide 4-H Essay Contest, writing on the topic "Why I Would Like to Live at Kings Landing." Her prize: five days as a "Visiting Cousin" at Kings Landing.

Each year, 4-H Club members of New Brunswick are invited to submit essays about why they would like to live at Kings Landing. Only two entries are selected as winners — one in French, and one in English. The winners are each awarded five days as a Visiting Cousin at Kings Landing Historical Settlement, with all expenses paid.

Susan, twelve years old, is a member of the Glassville Co-Eds 4-H Club. She and her brother and two sisters attend school at home, taught by their parents.

"I'm very excited about the trip," Susan says. "It will be like going in a time machine to the past."

This will be the second time Susan's writing has gained public recognition. In April, "Highlights for Children Magazine" published a poem Susan had submitted last fall.

Susan will begin her visit at Kings Landing July 12, and return home July 16 — her 13th birthday.

"That's quite a plug for home-schooling," some friends told us.

Yes, we agreed, it was. But it was also much more. They would never know what a long, tedious, often frustrating journey it had been for Susan, and for Jean and me. They wouldn't know our fears and feelings of guilt about Susan's year in third grade, fears that were finally erased by Susan's achievement.

In September of that year, Susan wrote about her trip for our family newsletter:

"My trip back in time began at the Education Building, where I was fitted in a costume of 1849 and learned a little about the program I would take part in through the next week. I was assigned to the Killeen House, a square log cabin of an Irish immigrant. Besides cooking, eating, and other activities in 'my own' home, I spent time in several other homes and buildings, learning to make soap, candles, noodles, straw hats, crackers, and butter (which I already knew). I visited the blacksmith shop, spun flax, hooked a rug, learned about furniture making, and went to a quilting bee. Each day, I went to school with the other Visiting Cousins; at recess time, we played games of the 1840's. On Friday, I baked a crumb cake in the coals of the fireplace (we didn't have a stove for cooking), and on Saturday my cake and many others were served to the parents of the Visiting Cousins.

"I had a wonderful time and made many new friends."

Yes, it was definitely a plug for home-schooling. But, far more important, it was a plug for Susan, who had worked harder to reach that point than anyone outside our family would ever know.

It was also a strong lesson for us, although not a new one. It reinforced our conviction that children's learning should not be pushed. It can be encouraged, and should be, but always with care and patience and understanding.

One way to encourage a child to write is to get his work published. If you've ever seen a young writer look at his work in a "real" publication, you know what a difference it can make. You can do this for your child. **KIDS 2 KIDS BOOKS** is a nonprofit organization that publishes books of original stories, artwork, and poetry created by kids to help other kids. The books are sold as fund-raisers for other nonprofit groups. The nice thing is that for every book sold, one is donated to a needy child elsewhere in the world. Kids 2 Kids will send your child a certificate commemorating his contribution, and if his work is selected for publication he will receive a copy of the book that includes it. (And you can send a photo of your child to go along with his work.) For more information about Kids2Kids Books or about submitting your child's work, call 888-663-9283, e-mail info@kids2kidsbooks.com, or visit www.kids2kidsbooks.com.

Spelling

I before E, except after C, or when sounded as A, as in neighbor and weigh.

Silent E on the end of a word makes the preceding vowel long.

Rules such as these seem to be of some help to beginning spellers and readers, and sometimes we have tacked them up somewhere in the house. We never teach such rules, however, without a reminder that there are often exceptions to them. The first, for instance, has at least one weird exception. The second rule makes me cringe. The third rule is another form of grossness.

Try the word, we say, applying the rule; if it doesn't seem to work, then try the reverse of the rule. "When adding *ing* to a verb that ends in *e*, drop the *e*." Oddly enough, that rule works for *cringe,* but not for *singe*." "Oddly enough" is a phrase that helps the kids accept the idiosyncrasies of English. An attempt to learn spelling only by the rules will result in constant perplexity and frustration.

"That's the exception that proves the rule," some of my teachers used to say. I wondered where they had dug up such an illogical saying, and why they thought it meant anything. Years later, looking at reproductions of old English printing, I realized that some medieval monk must have forgotten his glasses when he was copying a manuscript. In some calligraphic lettering styles, the *b* still resembles a *v*. It's the exception that *probes* the rule, not *proves* it.

What makes a good speller? Why can some people spell correctly so easily, while others are forever turning to the dictionary (or should be)? I asked Jean. She is well-educated and has an above-average intelligence and a good vocabulary, but before she mails a letter to a friend or relative, she has me look it over for spelling mistakes. There won't be many, but it's seldom that I don't find at least one. Her weekly shopping lists usually have at least one word misspelled, often one that is consistently misspelled week after week. She doesn't know why, nor do I. (I love her anyway.) (That's because my mistakes made him laugh.)

When I was in school, I usually got A+ for my spelling, and I almost always won school-wide spelling bees. Why?

I used to think that the ability to spell was nurtured most by reading, but Jean reads as much as I do.

I have a theory, which you're welcome to take or leave: I think that good spellers have, to some degree, photographic memories. Not to the extent that they could Amaze Their Friends With Astounding Feats of Memory Magic; not the kind, which a gifted few actually have, that enables them to read, from memory, a page they have briefly scanned. In most things, I have as much and as little difficulty in remembering as most people have — names, dates, numbers, lists, and so on. But when I'm in doubt about the spelling of a word, I close my eyes and try to visualize it; the word, usually printed, seems to float inside my eyelids. Have I called it up from a forgotten memory? If I can't visualize it that way, I write down several possible spellings; one will just "look right" to me, and it's almost always the correct one. Neither method is infallible, but usually one or the other works for me. Both methods work for Jean, too, but not very often.

I think it's related to sight-reading. The sooner a person learns to read whole syllables and words instead of "sounding out" the words letter by letter, the better his spelling will be. Maybe. That's my theory.

If he's right, it helps to explain my inability to spell. I think that having some photographic memory helps (Donn certainly had it). I also think learning to sight-read can make a big difference. I had a very hard time learning how to read in school. I hated the process, and the teacher made me feel even worse about it. Naturally, the worse I felt about myself and reading, the less I wanted to learn how to read. Not an auspicious way for a beginning speller to feel. If I were in school now, I would probably be labeled slightly dyslexic. It was a long time before I could distinguish b's from d's, p's from q's, and the word *saw* from *was*.

But not if you are severely spelling disabled.

What's more, at home, if I asked my mother for help spelling a word, almost invariably she would tell me to look it up in the dictionary. How do you look up a word you can't spell? Not only was this an interruption to my work, but I spelled so poorly that I could rarely find the word in the dictionary. I did learn a couple of things from this experience. I learned not to ask my mother for help with spelling, and I learned that the dictionary was not my friend. Sometimes I'd get lucky, but more frequently, as time went by, I'd just make up the best spelling I could invent, and let the teacher correct it for me.

My spelling has been a source of amusement for years. I was embarrassed when the kids asked me how to spell a word and I couldn't answer them. It was even worse when I'd ask Donn about the spelling of a word, and one of the kids would butt in and tell me. Once, in a desperate attempt to save face, I quoted Emerson, saying, "A foolish consistency is the hobgoblin of little minds." I may not be able to spell but I have, I'm not sure what you'd call it, maybe music recall. It's not perfect all the time. It functions variously, from being able to repeat a simple folk song after one hearing to being able to play a symphony or Vivaldi's "Four Seasons" in my mind after hearing it several times.

I just found this note that I wrote to a troubled parent. The names have been changed. Perhaps my perception will help you help your child.

> Dear Joan,
>
> Please tell Bill that I completely understand his fear of writing caused by poor spelling. I honestly do understand. I wasn't kidding around or being funny on page 7 of *The Home School Source Book*. Donn proofed all my letters. I am just a naturally poor speller. I think good spelling has to do with photographic memory (Donn had it). English is so irregular that whatever rules work also have words that break the rules. I still can't spell, and you can explain to Bill that spelling does NOT have to have anything to do with writing well, even a 480-page book. Well, I'll modify that. You don't have to relate spelling to writing. Yes, good writing has to be spelled correctly or people can't read it or understand it. Here's the BUT, and it was a hard one for me to learn: Write even if you can't spell everything. That's what a spell check (or editor) is for. The purpose of writing is to get your ideas out on paper for yourself or for others. Just write any way you can. Go back after the ideas are down and deal with the spelling as a separate issue.
>
> Joan, you'll have to help Bill learn to separate the two issues. I know people say "use a dictionary," but it doesn't help if you can't find the word. Example: Yesterday I wanted to use the word *metaphor*. It's spelled correctly here, but I didn't know how to spell it yesterday, and when I went to the dictionary I was looking for *medafore*. Of course I couldn't find it, but it's taken years to learn all the other possible ways it MIGHT be spelled so that I can look other places in the dictionary. If Bill uses the computer there is a little trick I use that might help. I just go ahead and spell a word the best I can and then let the spell-check offer alternatives. It saves a lot of time for me. I've also found that if I consistently misspell a word then sooner or later I get disgusted with myself and learn it. I tack the word on the wall and make copies and put them in several places where I'll see them frequently. Then when I see my notes I close my eyes and try to spell the word. Sooner or later I do get it. Making my book readable meant employing a good editor. Not wasted money at all. The book

is better for it (by a long shot), and I learned from her. I think it's called continuing education.

Best of luck,
Jean

We used to have the kids study lists of words, and then we tested them, just as the public schools do. The older the kids were, and the more reading they had done, the easier the spelling was. We discarded that approach, and then discarded all approaches. It made no difference in the kids' spelling abilities. When they wrote letters or essays, they sometimes asked us how to spell a word. If the word was short, we spelled it for them; if it was long, or didn't follow a neat rule, we wrote it down for them. Sometimes we'd suggest they look in the dictionary, but this was usually such an interruption of their train of thought that we didn't do it often. We didn't want to discourage their trying unfamiliar words by making the words a tedious chore. As they got older, they consulted the dictionary more often without our suggestion. If there was a catchy rule that might help them remember the word in the future, we'd give it to them. (*Write* ends with *e;* the paper we write on is station*e*ry.)

If the word had interesting homonyms, derivatives, or second cousins, we often mentioned them, either at the time or later in general discussion. We helped the kids break words down, pull the wings off, tickle them, play with them. This builds vocabulary, spelling, perspective, and humor. Puns are excellent learning aids.

Is Sirius the only
star that doesn't
tell any jokes?
Is that because
dogs can't laugh?

Reading, writing, and spelling (and even talking) are so closely related that trying to separate them is impractical and nearly impossible.

Another device we all enjoy is Tom Swifties. Remember them? They were a small fad way back when, parodies of the writing style of the Tom Swift series of boys' books popular during the 1920s and '30s — *Tom Swift and His Electric Submarine,* etc.

"I like camping in the rain," he said intently.

"I won't eat ham," he said pigheadedly.

"I won't be there," he said absently.

"I can't find the light," he said darkly.

"There's a hole in the tire," he said flatly.

It may take the kids a while to catch on to the kind of pun involved. The adverb must be related to the statement, it must be appropriate to the implied situation, and it must be a pun. The basic statement can be almost anything; the punch is the adverb.

I was writing about spelling and got sidetracked on to reading, writing, parts of speech, and vocabulary. Or is it a sidetrack?

"Does that make you feel like a dunce?" Jean asked pointedly.

"It's my typewriter's fault," I said mechanically.

"What are you driving at?" she asked automatically.

"It's gone with the wind," I answered rhetorically.

Found sandwiched in between notes of things to write about in the future:

"I don't mind losing a few games," he said winsomely.

"I sold all my used cars," he said recklessly.

"Gilt by association," Midas said touchingly.

As you probably know, the worse the pun is (like my last one), the better it is; the proper response is a groan — unless you can top the pun with a better (worse) one. Once you get the hang of them, Tom Swifties are sort of like peanuts: you don't want to stop with just one. (I'll let you in on a secret. He got addicted. For about a week after writing about Tom Swifties he'd get up sometime in the night to make a note about a new one. Sometimes he'd make one up in his sleep and wake us both up because he was laughing.)

Back to spelling. Like all other learning, it can't be forced, but I have no doubt that a lot of reading will help it grow. Positive reinforcement definitely helps. When we're asked for the spelling of a word, we don't say, "Try to sound it out," unless the word really is phonetic and we think it can be sounded out easily. If we're not sure, either, we admit it freely, and get the dictionary.

When we spell a polysyllabic word for the kids, we do it by syllables — sometimes repeating each syllable as we go, then spelling it, then saying the whole word and spelling it all at once. Sometimes we ask to have the word spelled back to us — but only after the child has written it down. This helps to set the visual image. I think.

Trying to sound out a word that isn't fully phonetic results only in confusion, frustration, and random guessing, all of which can only reinforce incorrect spelling and a lack of confidence.

Can you sound out GHOTI?

It's "fish," of course. GH as in "tough," O as in "women," and TI as in "nation."

Probably there are some spelling books that will help, but if one doesn't read a lot and write a lot, memorization of rules won't do much good.

Here is a letter I received several years ago:

> Der Don rede
>
> how ar you gud I hop. I am fin to. I hop I getting ot frum thagt insttushn sun nd yu to. I m lrng rdng nd rtng pred gud. Thank yu fr techng me to red nd rte.
>
> Yur frend,
>
> _____ _____

The writer was twenty-two years old, serving three years in a federal prison for interstate car theft. When he joined my class for adult illiterates, six weeks before he wrote me that letter, he didn't know how to write his name.

I think he was lrng pred gud.

We can't solve problems by using the same kind of thinking we used when we created them. — Albert Einstein

I owe more to my ability to fantasize than to any knowledge I've ever acquired. — Albert Einstein

P.S. More about Tom Swifties and a few other miscellaneous notes of equal importance.

In the spring of 1992, Teri Palazzolo, a customer and occasional correspondent in Sicily, sent me a photocopied entry form for an international "adverb contest" from *Practical English Teaching,* a British teacher's magazine. Teri said she was going to enter and hoped to win an unabridged Longman Dictionary of the English Language, which was offered for both the first and second prizes. The "adverb contest" consisted of what we have always called Tom Swifties, so I revised one of my earlier favorites — "Has he gone with the wind?' Scarlett asked rhetorically" — and mailed it off to England. The following November, long after I'd forgotten the contest, I received a letter of congratulations and a large, heavy package: second prize, an unabridged Longman dictionary, sent by airmail (which cost 18 pounds sterling, or about $40). Naturally, the dictionary had British spellings and usages — kerb instead of curb, truck meaning barter, and so on (not to mention being on queer street, which in the Mother Country means being financially embarrassed) — so it wasn't of much real worth to me. Since Teri had sent me the entry form that had given me this brief moment of fame, I wrote to her, offering to give the dictionary to her if she would pay the postage (only $6 by surface mail). She accepted, and wrote me that she had been a runner-up in the competition. How's that for irony and poetic (in)justice?

I don't subscribe to *Practical English Teaching,* and Teri hasn't sent me any more entry forms, but I'm preparing for the next contest by building my stock of Tom Swifties, usually in the middle of the night when Gus wakes me up to let him out. Rather than return to bed and be almost asleep when he woofs to come back in, I exercise my mind while I wait for him. As you probably know, some of one's greatest thoughts may come when one isn't quite awake. So far, Gus's untimely excursions have helped me produce the following:

"I can't think of the letter that comes after U," the boy said vehemently.
"Thanks for loaning me your pickup, Joe," he said truculently.
"I finally went to an exorcist for help," he said dispiritedly.
"That Kelly girl was delicious," the cannibal said gracefully.
"Oy, I don't think this food is kosher," the rabbi said judiciously.
"If I were a man, I wouldn't be a queen," Elizabeth said achingly.
"I'll show you the evidence again," the lawyer said reprovingly.
"I have to go home before sunrise," Dracula said cryptically.
"A good Tom Swiftie really wakes me up," Donn said dreamily.
It's 2 a.m. and "I'm willing to belabor the point," I said effortlessly.

I cdnuolt blveiee taht I cluod aulaclty uesdnatnrd waht I was rdgnieg. The phaonmneal pweor of the hmuan mnid is aamznig. Aoccdrnig to a rscheearch at Cmabrigde Uinervtisy, it deosn't mttaer inwaht oredr the ltteers in a wrod are, the olny iprmoatnt tihng is taht the frist and lsat ltteer be in the rghit pclae. The rset can be a taotl mses and you can sitll raed it wouthit a porbelm. Tihs is bcuseae the huamn mnid deos not raed ervey lteter by istlef, but the wrod as a wlohe. Amzanig huh? yaeh and you awlyas thought slpeling was ipmorantt!

LEARNING THE ENGLISH LANGUAGE

***WORDWORKS: EXPLORING LANGUAGE PLAY,* by Bonnie von Hoff Johnson.** This book contains knowledge as well as thinking challenges, and I guarantee it will make you and your kids laugh. When it first arrived here I meant to browse through it quickly and take a serious look at it later, but I couldn't put it down. I chuckled and read until Gus insisted on being fed — and he had to growl at me twice before I paid attention. The book is divided into ten chapters. Here are some brief descriptions: Chapter 1, Names: People — eponyms (was there really a Mr. Silhouette?), first and last names, plant names, and pseudonyms. Places — do you know or can you guess what a toponym is? Where is Easy Street? Things — unusual names for familiar things, word play in business names. Chapter 2, Hink Pinks: what they are and why they are more important than you ever dreamed they should be. Chapter 3, Idioms: getting down to brass tacks — a definition of "idiom." Nothing to sneeze at — writers who introduced common idioms. Not from this neck of the woods — idioms from other cultures. Chapter 4, Established Slang (nothing offensive): Not for Goof-offs — the study of slang. Oldies but Goodies: repeating slang and rhyming slang. Chapter 5, Multiple-Meaning Words: ambiguous headlines. Chapter 6, Proverbs: They never looked like this before! Chapter 7, Alike and Different: synonyms and antonyms at play. Chapter 8, Word Formation: affixes, abbreviations, and acronyms — to name just a few discussed. Chapter 9, Etymology: word origins and borrowings from *ampersand* to *zany*. Chapter 10, A Potpourri of Language Play: euphemisms, anagrams, slogans, and more. You'll have fun reading and learning, and you'll double your fun when you share it with your kids. Each chapter contains numerous activities and ends with a listings of references and children's books for further investigation. Recommended for grades 4 to 8, but you can stretch it either way; I think this material is good for kids up to 15 or 16. If you're not familiar or comfortable with wordplay, I suggest you read it just for fun. You could also use the activities in a group setting.

***DRAW WRITE NOW,* by Marie Hablitzel and Kim Stitzer.** Rejoice! Finally, books for beginning readers, writers, and budding artists. Children love to draw, and beginning readers need encouragement and practice. Handwriting may require a bit of extra encouragement because there is a "right" way to do it, and writing neatly can seem more like work than play. Hablitzel and Stitzer have put together a series of books encouraging children to combine their writing and drawing skills.

The topic for each book is carefully chosen, and the drawing techniques are ones this age group will easily master and use. These are colorful books, with easy-to-follow instructions. There is an amazing amount of good information about the core subject of each book that your child will absorb with no apparent effort. Your children will return to these books again and again to use the drawing tips, which are based on common shapes. I do wish we had had these when our children were learning to draw and write. There aren't many books or series I would call "must-haves," but this group of books belongs in that category. These books do not teach "handwriting" per se, but will encourage neat penmanship and creativity. These books are incremental and the depth of information and scope of the drawing techniques become more complex as the series progresses. A section at the end of each book provides more information about the subject matter, lists vocabulary, and includes teaching tips. Here's what you'll find in some of the books: Book One: On the Farm, Kids and Critters, and Storybook Characters; Book Two: Christopher Columbus, Autumn Harvest, and the Weather; Book Three: North America, Native Americans, and the Pilgrims; Book Four: The Polar Regions, the Arctic, and the Antarctic; etc.

If your kids enjoy the *Draw Write Now* books they will also enjoy ***MY DRAWING AND HANDWRITING BOOK!*** by the same authors. This book includes more than 20 two-page spreads for drawing and story-writing, all neatly bound. Writing pages are lined.

LINCOLN WRITING DICTIONARY. After the early childhood picture dictionaries, most kids' dictionaries aren't worth buying. Too many words are missing, too many definitions are incomplete, and the rules of grammar are ambiguous, confusing, or nonexistent. This is one of the very few good kids' dictionaries, and is a useful bridge from early picture books to adult dictionaries. Besides being a clear and concise dictionary with more than 35,000 entries, the *Lincoln Writing Dictionary* really does have many features that will help any user — child or adult — become a better writer. There are 4,000 usage examples taken from more than 500 authors, and there are 600 short essays explaining writing techniques more fully. The 700 color illustrations include drawings and photographs. This book is out of print, but you can still get a reconditioned hardcover.

365 NEW WORDS A YEAR. This page-a-day calendar is a painless way to increase vocabulary (and improve spelling). Each page has a word and its definition, origin, and pronunciation, and sample sentence.

FOCUSING ON WORDS. If you're interested in expanding your knowledge of English and its Greek and Latin roots, you can do it easily and painlessly by visiting John Robertson's Focusing on Words website (www.wordexplorations.com) or subscribing to his online newsletter. This site is just right for curious high school students and adults.

MISS MANNERS' BASIC TRAINING: COMMUNICATION, **by Judith Martin.** It may seem stuffy to some — and unnecessary or just not important to others — to learn the proper forms of communication, but there is merit to hand-writing a personal note on some occasions rather than sending an e-mail or fax. This book explains the proper technology to use for private, professional, and public messages, and tells you when to phone, when to fax, and when a handwritten note is obligatory, a form letter forbidden, and a chain letter out of the question. There are examples of how to write a thank-you note and a letter of condolence, how to reply to various types of invitations and announcements, and a lot more. Believe it or not, this book is fun to read, and you'll notice a very subtle humor hiding in the examples.

THE ELEMENTS OF STYLE, **by William Strunk Jr. and E.B. White.** This thin book, about 90 pages (including the index), is a complete guide to rules of grammar, spelling, usage, and concise but expressive writing. Probably best for high school age and older, but you can boil down its contents for your younger students. Whether you (or they) are writing articles, stories, essays, novels, or just letters to friends, you'll be glad to have this guide to the essentials of clear, sensible writing. I've found it essential.

MERLYN'S PEN FOUNDATION is a nonprofit dedicated to encouraging young writers in grades 6 through 12 find their own voices. The organization offers a wealth of resources, including a writing course with professional one-on-one guidance (for a fee), many excellent essays searchable by topic (most with lesson plans), and ESL and EFL resources. The magazine *Merlyn's Pen* is now out of print, but past issues can be downloaded online at www.merlynspen.org. Merlyn's Pen is recommended by *Imagine,* the magazine of Johns Hopkins University's Center for Talented Youth, and by the Center for Talent Development at Northwestern University.

CAUGHT'YA! GRAMMAR WITH A GIGGLE, **by Jane Bell Kiester.** Probably lots of giggles, which may be one of the reasons this method of teaching grammar, spelling, punctuation, and vocabulary is so effective. The basic idea, put very simply, is that the teacher makes the mistakes (on purpose), and the students correct him. Add to that a few minutes each day of a humorous soap opera with Hairy Beast, Wilfred Warthog, Bertha Boa, and other residents at General Animal Hospital, and you certainly have grammar with a giggle. Don't like the plot? Make up your own! There are lots of ideas for developing your own creative approach. This book came too late for us to try it on our kids, but the general approach is similar to the approach we often used ourselves. Easily adapted by you for different grade levels, from grade 4 through high school. The second book in the series is ***CAUGHT'YA AGAIN: MORE GRAMMAR WITH A GIGGLE,*** with more stories and lots more giggles.

OK, That's All of the Serious Stuff!

MAD LIBS is the funniest grammar game around. It doesn't really look like a game, just a pad of paper with stories written out and some blank spaces. The fun comes when you fill in the blanks. Under each blank space is written a part of speech: noun, verb, adverb, etc. Only one person sees the written story. That person calls out the part of speech written under the first blank space. Everyone else thinks of a word that matches that part of speech. When words have been given for all the blanks, the person with the story reads it out loud using the provided words. Stories don't come much sillier than these, and by the time you've done a couple of them, everyone remembers the parts of speech without working at it at all. Sometimes we laughed until we cried. When the stories had been used so many times that everyone remembered them, they were still fun because the kids worked to make them as silly as possible, and then sometimes they'd make up their own stories. Fun for all ages.

***PUN AND GAMES,* by Richard Lederer, illustrated by Dave Morice.** Hours of pun for kids and adults. Sharpen your wits and prepare to giggle. A colossal collection of puns, jokes, riddles, daffynitions, tairy fales, and homographs at play. You'll find it's a "punderful life" as you read about "puns that Babylon." First you read about the multiple ways to play with words and then you are challenged to do the same.

Literature

Many titles you would expect to find in this section aren't here, because I have put them in "History and Biography" or "Politics and Government" or some other chapter I think is just as appropriate. As the author, I put historical fiction in "Literature." As my own editor, I put it with the history. As editor, after all, I have the final word. As author, I must go along with the editor's decisions, and ask you to do the same.

Some titles certainly are hard to place. I won't fault Donn's logic, but as he would be quick to agree, I have my own logic, and some titles that were in this section are now in others. Using my prerogative as author I've moved *Help Your Child Learn to Read* from this chapter to "Resources for the Early Years" (along with the beginning readers). Wearing my editor's cap, I've included many classics for young children in this section.

Over the years Donn and I have done our best to make known and available to you the best of enduring literature. I'm sure we've missed many great books. There really are too many to list, but if you feel we have committed a great (or possibly unforgivable) error or omission, please write and share your thoughts with us — after you've checked our website.

You'll soon see that all the lovely classics we had reviewed and listed in this section of *The Home School Source Book, 3rd Edition,* are not here. Prices are too volatile, and though classic books continue to be available they move from one publisher to another. I know that's not your problem, but it is mine. Again as editor and master of what does and does not go in this book, I've moved these books to our website, where I can keep the listings current and you get the right price the first time around. I do apologize for the inconvenience, especially to those who don't have a computer in the house. You can always write and tell me what you think about this policy.

Reference Tools: Good Ones You Might Miss

MACMILLAN DICTIONARY FOR CHILDREN. As kids grow away from their "first" picture dictionaries, I think this is the best step up (followed closely by a concise "adult" or college dictionary). Thousands of entries, definitions, and illustrative examples; 1,100 full-color photos; and more than 300 highlighted word histories and language notes. More illustrative sentences per main entry than any other children's dictionary. Illustrated timeline of world history. Updated atlas with maps of the world, the continents, the U.S., and Canada. Tables of weights and measures.

THE OXFORD CANADIAN DICTIONARY. Yes! Not British or Australian. Not American. Truly Canadian and extremely well researched. I'll just bet there are terms in here you've never heard or thought you'd find in a dictionary. It's great! More than 2,000 distinctly Canadian words and meanings, covering all regions of the country; 130,000 total entries with Canadian spellings and pronunciations. Your favorite doughnut may be a jambuster, a bismarck, a Burlington bun, or the more prosaic jelly doughnut, depending on where you live in Canada. Find it all in one book.

DICTIONARIES AT DISCOUNT PRICES. I had planned to offer Webster's dictionaries for sale through Brook Farm Books, but we can't beat the prices offered by Follett Educational, 1433 Internationale Parkway, Woodridge, IL 60517; 800-621-4272; www.fes.follett.com, and I doubt that anyone can. Follett Educational specializes in used, reconditioned textbooks, but these dictionaries are brand new, never used, yet at bargain prices. Ask for a catalog of their children's literature.

FIRST THESAURUS. An adult thesaurus can be intimidating to young learners. This one uses 100 key headwords that children commonly use, along with synonyms, homonyms, antonyms, and sample sentences. Easy to use. Ages 7 to 11.

THE HBJ STUDENT THESAURUS. This easy-to-use thesaurus contains 800 main entries, with a group of two to five synonyms for each entry. An example sentence for each synonym shows how the word is distinct from others in the group, and illustrations are used to demonstrate subtle differences among related words. Each main entry is the most common word in its synonym group, with the more precise or sophisticated words following. An index lists all 3,300 words discussed in the book. Full-color illustrations. This is an excellent book to use with budding and developing writers who are just learning the subtle differences between words. Ages 7 to 12 (more or less).

NEW LIFETIME READING PLAN, **by Clifton Fadiman.** This new edition includes all of the previous edition plus classic writers of the last century. It provides brief introductions to suggested readings of the best of the world's literature, from Homer to the present day. "The books here discussed," says the author, "may take you fifty years to finish. They can of course be read in a much shorter time. The point is that they are intended to occupy an important part of a whole life, no matter what your present age may be. Many of them happen to be more entertaining than the latest best-seller. Still, it is not on the entertainment level that they are most profitably read. What they offer is of larger dimensions. It is rather like what is offered by loving and marrying, having and rearing children, carving out a career, creating a home. They can be ... a source of continuous internal growth. Hence the word lifetime. These authors are life companions. Once part of you, they work in and on and with you until you die. They should not be read in a hurry, any more than friends are made in a hurry." Hardcover, to last a lifetime.

When you reread a classic you do not see more in the book than you did before; you see more in you *than there was before.* — Clifton Fadiman

The Classics — for Children Only?

It's interesting and curious that most of the books usually thought of today as "children's classics" were not written for children. Many, in fact, although enjoyable for children, are better suited to older readers, because the experience of younger readers is not yet great enough to help them understand many circumstances and situations. W.H. Auden, referring to *Alice's Adventures in Wonderland* as an example, said, "There are good books which are only for adults because comprehension presupposes adult experiences, but there are no good books which are only for children." A few years ago, I read *Alice's Adventures* aloud to the family, in daily installments, and Jean and I enjoyed it at least as much as the kids did. Not long ago, I reread *The Three Musketeers* and enjoyed it more than I did when I was 12; perhaps not "more," but in a different way, and on many more levels. I can read *A Tale of Two Cities* every five or six years, and browse in it occasionally, each time with a little more enjoyment, as if each reading earns compound interest. Classics are those books that endure, sometimes for centuries, not only because they tell exciting stories, or acquaint us with times and people of the past — but, more especially, because they tell us something of ourselves. At the age of 12, I enjoyed the excitement and intrigue of *The Three Musketeers;* a decade later, I could better appreciate the more subtle verbal exchanges; after another decade, I could also admire the writer's artistry and wit. Each time I read the book, I am able to receive more from it because I'm able to take more to it. Each time I read it, I bounce myself against it and come back amplified, like an echo rebounding in a canyon. Children will enjoy the classics, but their parents may enjoy them even more.

***TENDING THE HEART OF VIRTUE: HOW CLASSIC STORIES AWAKEN A CHILD'S MORAL IMAGINATION,* by Vigen Guroian.** An outstanding guide to and discussion of excellent children's books for those of us with the desire to inspire, as opposed to instill, a set of moral values to guide our children through life's dilemmas. Our children learn their values from us and others around them. They also can learn from what they read and what we read with them.

Guroian speaks about the need children have for guidance and moral road maps from adults: "Our society is finding it difficult to meet these needs. ... Some well-meaning educators and parents seem to want to drive the passion for moral clarity out of children rather than use it to the advantage of shaping their character. We want our children to be tolerant, and we sometimes seem to think that a too-sure sense of right and wrong only produces fanatics. ... Mostly we fall back on the excuse that we are respecting our children's freedom by permitting them to determine right from wrong and to choose for themselves clear goals of moral living. But this is the paean of a false freedom that pays misdirected tribute to a deeply flawed notion of individual autonomy. We end up forfeiting our parental authority and failing to be mentors to our children in the moral life." He has strong opinions.

We can tell our children that fire is hot, and some will learn from the telling. Many have to feel the heat before learning the lesson for life. We cannot expose our children to all of life's lessons, but through good literature they can steep themselves in another world, another character, and learn some of the lessons.

We tell our children it is always better to tell the truth, yet each must learn through trial and error that this is so. If we confront our children with a lie they have told, they generally become defensive. It is difficult to work with them when they feel this way. Yet through sharing a story about lying we can create an opportunity to discuss the value of telling the truth in a non-threatening atmosphere; for instance, children instinctively identify with Pinocchio's struggles and learn not only about telling the truth, but about the struggle to do so.

From the table of contents: 1) Awakening the Moral Imagination. 2) On Becoming a Real Human Child: Pinocchio. 3) Love and Immortality in *The Velveteen Rabbit* and *The Little Mermaid.* 4) Friends and Mentors in *The Wind in the Willows, Charlotte's Web,* and *Bambi.* 5) Evil and Redemption in *The Snow Queen* and *The Lion, the Witch and the Wardrobe.* 6) Heroines of Faith and Courage: Princess Irene in *The Princess* and the Goblin and Lucy in *Prince Caspian.*

Guroian's book is a refresher course in using imagination as a teacher. This book is a pleasure to read.

***INTRODUCING LITERARY GENRES: A TAPESTRY OF READING,* by Terry Zahniser McDermid.** This book presents an excellent concept. It's too bad it was written for teachers. If you ignore the educational jargon and references to motivation and class work you can have a ball with this book. Beginning with the section about different types of media, this book has unit studies on biography, mystery, drama, fairy tales, romance, mythology, science fiction, and research. Clearly outlined goals, specialized vocabulary section, information about each genre, projects for individuals and groups, and suggested reading lists all make this resource easy to use.

***THE DARK IS RISING,* by Susan Cooper.** A classic series on par with the Chronicles of Narnia. Like C.S. Lewis, Susan Cooper writes about the age-old struggle between good and evil, the light and the dark forces of human nature. Cooper is a bit more open and obvious about the struggle, but it doesn't spoil this series even a little bit; it just makes its message easier to understand for early teens reading this on their own, and younger children being read to will need less coaxing to get the message and symbolism. A good introduction to reading for symbols and meaning. This series takes place in the British Isles and makes good use of English and Celtic myth, legend, and tradition. A pleasure for the whole family if you read it aloud. Suitable for the whole family but best for around 12 and up on their own. (I just reread the whole series this year and loved it. Somehow I missed reading it when the children were all home. Cathy remembers loving the whole series.) Set includes six books: *Over Sea, Under Stone; The Dark Is Rising; Greenwitch; The Grey King; Dawn of Fear;* and *Silver on the Tree.*

***TO KILL A MOCKINGBIRD,* by Harper Lee.** A classic study of personalities, prejudice, and good and evil in a small Southern town in the mid-1930s, as seen through the eyes of a young girl. A book to grow with. I've read it three times and enjoy it more with each reading.

***MORE THAN HUMAN,* by Theodore Sturgeon.** We recommended this novel to our kids as they reached the age of 16 or 17 — not just as a great story (which it is), but also for its moral and ethical implications. *Homo gestalt* seems to be the next step in human evolution, but is still in its infancy: a small group of social misfits, each with a certain psychic ability or power, including orphaned twins who can't talk but can disappear at will; the village idiot, whose strength seems to be in his eyes; a young girl who can move things with her mind; and a "mongoloid" baby, whose computer-like brain holds them together. Together they are more powerful than any other being on earth — but, so far, *Homo gestalt* lacks the most human attribute — a conscience.

Zenna Henderson wrote ***THE ANYTHING BOX*** years ago, and it is out of print. If you can find a copy you'll have a treasure chest of good science fiction reading. These short stories — on a great variety of themes — are delightful mind stretchers for everyone from 10 to 110. Our whole family loved this book, and our copy is falling apart. I've since found copies for everyone. Computers are good for something! You can now get this on Amazon.com.

***SHAKESPEARE FOR KIDS: HIS LIFE AND TIMES,* by Colleen Aagesen and Margie Blumberg.** This book has 21 interesting activities that help make Shakespeare's life and times come alive. The text is well written. Photos, drawings, and original artwork of the time make it easy to see what life was like. Activities include making a quill pen, learning to juggle, making a hornbook, playing Elizabethan games, making a sword and staging a fight, producing a scene from *Julius Caesar,* and more. Glossary and related websites included.

BULFINCH'S GREEK AND ROMAN MYTHOLOGY. An unabridged republication of the original in a paperback edition. Everything you need for an exciting time — adventure, gods and goddesses, heroes, warriors, scoundrels, and romance. A great book to read aloud.

***A WONDER BOOK FOR GIRLS AND BOYS,* by Nathaniel Hawthorne, illustrated by Walter Crane, with an introduction by Ola D'Aulaire.** Mythology at its best for young and old, with classic color illustrations. A treasury of old Greek myths and early American stories. A book to be treasured through the years and reread with much pleasure. This makes a beautiful gift. A great read-aloud.

I owe more to my ability to fantasize than to any knowledge I've ever acquired. — Albert Einstein

Poetry

There is no money in poetry, but then there is no poetry in money, either. — Robert Graves

Do you feel you don't understand poetry? Can't wring the hidden meanings out of the words? Help is at hand. These tapes bring sense and meaning to an often overlooked source of enjoyment. Sometimes just listening to someone who understands the poetry reading it aloud can make it clear to you. Maybe you want to decode new poetry. These tapes will give you the tools to open a different form of communication.

***SOUND AND SENSE IN POETRY,* by G.B. Harrison.** The great importance of sound in understanding poetry is illustrated through the reading of well-known poems by William Shakespeare, John Donne, John Milton, Robert Browning, and others. Harrison adds commentary about each poet.

OBSCURITY IN POETRY and ***COULD IT BE VERSE?*** are two lectures so comprehensive that they are worth listening to several times (at least). Learn why some important and memorable poems are difficult to understand. Find out how to get the most out of funny poems and punning verses.

***THE OXFORD BOOK OF STORY POEMS,* compiled by Michael Harrison and Christopher Stuart-Clark.** A perfect introduction to poetry. Children love stories, dragons, castles, knights, mermaids, witches, and magicians. 66 stories to ignite the imagination, enhanced with color and black-and-white illustrations. Perfect to share aloud or read in a cozy chair.

Audio Literature

Jim Weiss, a vivacious, captivating storyteller, brings these tales to life with great expression and excitement. Guaranteed: hours of happy listening, all the while enhancing your imagination and bringing some of our cultural legacy to life. If CD players had been around when our kids were still at home we'd have bought all our stories in that format. We wore out a lot of cassette tapes with our repeated listening! Here's a partial listing of what's on the web: ***ANIMAL TALES*** — nine classics from Aesop, Grimm, Chaucer, and others; ***ARABIAN NIGHTS*** — Scheherazade and three more tales; ***A CHRISTMAS CAROL*** — "Gift of the Magi" and others; ***FAIRYTALE FAVORITES IN SONG AND STORY*** — "Stone Soup," "Puss in Boots," "Rapunzel," and other favorites; ***THE JUNGLE BOOK*** — three Kipling tales; ***KING ARTHUR AND HIS KNIGHTS; RASCAL;*** and many more.

LISTEN-AND-READ AUDIO THRIFT CLASSICS FOR CHILDREN. One 60-minute cassette with illustrated paperback book. Stories on tape stimulate each listener to re-create the story in his own mind, so imagination flourishes and the importance of literature and reading develop without effort. Here are a few: *Adventures of Peter Cottontail, Aladdin and Other Favorite Arabian Nights, A Child's Garden Of Verses, A Christmas Carol, Favorite Poems of Childhood, The Little Mermaid, North American Indian Legends, Uncle Wiggily Bedtime Stories.*

PESKY PRONOUNS, GENDER BLENDING, AND THE NON-SEXIST NAMES OF GOD

In 1850, the British Parliament — perhaps afloat on a sea of verbiage, as is often the fate of such bodies — enacted "An act for shortening the language used in acts of parliament," decreeing that "in all acts, words importing the masculine gender shall be deemed and taken to include females."

This is an example of "theoretical English," which tacitly stipulates that which is not explicitly stated, as in "Each student should open his book."

A few years earlier, when the Boston patriots symbolically dumped King George overboard and coffee suddenly became the national drink, those colonists who still preferred tea either escaped to Canada or were hanged. (To this day, the only Americans who drink tea are secret Loyalists. Britons and even Canadians have periodic tea-times, but real Americans never observe anything but a coffee break, even if it's only to nibble a Kit-Kat or sip a diet cola.) It's the nature of Americans, however, to be forgiving (with the exception of certain high executives, who are merely forgetful), and by 1850 sufficient détente had been regained to allow a few English words and speech conventions into the American language. One of the most significant conventions acquired — the generic pronoun, as it's called these days — although steeped in common English usage and further strengthened by Parliamentary edict, was prohibited by the belated First Amendment from a similar Congressional edict.

That Parliamentary edict is still upheld today by major dictionaries (although their editors are beginning to look warily over their shoulders). One dictionary says: "he, pronoun. 1. The male person or animal mentioned. 2. A person of unspecified sex, [as in] 'He who hesitates is lost.'" Another dictionary agrees: "2. Used in a generic sense or when the sex of the person is unspecified, [as in] 'He that hath ears to hear, let him hear.'"

Feminists don't want women to be included in words that sometimes refer exclusively to males. They say it's discriminatory, because they're not receiving specific recognition; demeaning, because it still relegates them to a subordinate position; and confusing, because when someone says, "Look at that man," the reference is obviously to an adult human male, but when someone says, "Man will go to the stars someday," they don't know if women will be invited. (People, men or women, who are so easily confused must have a hard time with homonyms. If they hear of someone telling a bare-faced lie, they'll expect to see an animal costume.)

I heartily approve of equal opportunity, equal liability, equal rights, equal everything, including equal pay for equal work, and if Jean seriously wants to shovel out the barn while I sweep the kitchen floor, I won't argue very hard. I realize there's still a long way to go before this fair and logical equality is fully achieved, but let's not get wound up in such a strictly literal interpretation of words and phrases that we lose sight of the real problems.

Many words and phrases in English certainly are "sexist" — that is, discriminatory against either men or women. Feminists claim that women are the targets more often than men, which may be true. They also claim that it's part of an age-old male conspiracy to demean and subjugate women, which is sexist hogwash. It's simply the way the language evolved. They claim that the changes they want in the language — right now — are just further steps in its evolution. More hogwash. It isn't evolution; it's erosion.

Attitudes, especially of multitudes, change slowly, and the changed attitudes will be reflected in a slowly changing language. But the feminists want to reverse the process; they want to change the attitudes by changing the language.

George Orwell's *1984* vividly illustrates how the feminists' strategy could easily succeed. The best way to control people's thoughts, he points out, is to control their vocabulary. If all the ways of expressing a certain concept are removed from people's knowledge, then it will be impossible for them to entertain the concept, except perhaps in vague circumlocution. Even that possibility can be eliminated by letting the words remain, but with all meaning removed, as in the slogan, "War is peace." Once people have been fully taught that war is peace and peace is war, how can they express a thought about the state of non-war?

(On the other hand, erasing words to express emotions — love, hate, fear — will not erase the emotions.)

Marie Shear, in an article about "Solving the Great Pronoun Problem," ho ho, complains that she heard a radio announcer refer to a wire-chewing squirrel as "he." "Had a reporter been to the morgue," she asks, "to check the corpse's sex?" Pausing only to start another paragraph, she answers her own question: "Of course not. Like lots of other organizations and individuals, the radio station had simply assumed that anything worth mentioning is male, until proved otherwise. That assumption creates The Great Pronoun Problem."

Turning a squirrel into The Great Pronoun Problem is giving him quite a big responsibility, and seems close to making a mountain out of a molehill. It even skirts pretty close to exactly the same sort of assumption Ms. Shear objects to. Did she check to see if the writer of the announcement was male or female, or did she simply assume that only a male would be guilty of such a sexist offense? Would her antennae have twitched any less if the reporter had referred to the squirrel as "she," or would Ms. Shear then have complained about the assumption that any mischief-making worth mentioning is female, until proved otherwise?

Male and female, man and woman, and boy and girl, say the feminists, refer to biological sex — the function of reproduction and (if the weather doesn't change) its attendant duties, such as breastfeeding. Period. The words should not be used in conjunction with any person or activity in which this specific function is not relevant. "Woman police officer" or "male nurse" are offensive because being a police officer or a nurse has nothing to do with being male or female. That's true, of course, and rightly so. But try to explain to the feminists that it has not always been so, and that those expressions are used not to reinforce stereotypes but to dispel them, and you'll get your lip buttoned. The next time you hear the word "nurse," feminists want you to picture a generic human being, neither male nor female, because that human being's reproductive functions have nothing to do with his/her/its ability to be a nurse.

This sort of discussion can easily engender — whoops — confusion, but I'm trying to make it as clear as I can.

When I was little, my grandmother told me that a dragonfly would sew up my lips if I told a fib. I don't think I fibbed any more than most little boys, possibly a little less, but whenever I saw a dragonfly I'd cover my mouth and go the other way, not knowing how fair the dragonfly's judgment might be. I tried to avoid fibbing, but I also avoided dragonflies, in case I'd slipped up without knowing it. When I say now that I try in the same way to avoid active confrontation with feminists, I don't mean to imply that feminists are like dragonflies. The problem is, the minute you let slip what you think is an innocent phrase such as "hired man" or "woman's work is never done," some Feminist Thought Police Person is ready to threaten you with something worse than dragonflies. You should say "hired person" or "worker," unless that person's biological sex is specifically involved in the work being done, in which case you're in a whole different kettle of fish, about which feminists are also very sensitive. I have always thought the old saying "A man works from sun to sun, but woman's work is never done" was either a woman's complaint or a man's tribute, or a little of both, or just a statement of unfortunate fact, but the feminists claim it shouldn't be said even if it's true, because it shouldn't be true. Sort of like hearing a noise at night; if you ignore it, maybe it will go away.

I don't know if all states have a position known as Revisor of Statutes, but there is one in Minnesota, and in 1984 that Revisor was ordered by the state legislature to remove "gender-specific language" from the state statutes. Without changing the meaning of the law, of course.

It was an excellent example of Your Tax Dollars At Work. The whole process took two years, and the Revisor and his staff must have been as happy as pigs in a mud puddle. They removed 20,000 "nonsubstantive gender-specific" pronouns. "His" was changed more than 10,000 times. "He" was eliminated 6,000 times. One hundred gender-specific nouns and adjectives (such as "chairman," "foreman," and "fisherman") were eliminated about 1,400 times. The Revisor reported to the legislature that a few gender-specific words, such as "manhole," were allowed to remain "because every proposed substitute has drawn so much bad press." (Well, yes, I can imagine a few editorial comments that might have been made, hee hee.) The Revisor's report ends with the humble opinion: "We are confident that the revised statutes are no worse than the originals. In many cases they are improved."

One down; forty-nine to go.

But feminists aren't happy attacking only generic pronouns and gender-specific work descriptions. They want to eliminate from the language all gender-specific references. Trying to keep abreast of feminist thought ("Forewarned, forearmed," Don Quixote advised), I've invested a few dollars in a couple of non-sexist dictionaries. I can entertain Jean for hours, without reading a single word aloud. She is not a feminist, and wouldn't dream of asking why I read the book and laugh and then read the book and cry and then read the book and bang my head on the wall and then read the book and throw it across the room.

— Let's rewrite Shakespeare: "The evil people do" instead of "the evil men do."

— Avoid "hysteria," which not only comes from the Greek word meaning "womb" (a female organ), but is almost always used (say the feminists) in referring to women.

— "Jack of all trades" uses a man's name. Sexist. Don't use.

— "Hit the jackpot." Another man's name. Substitute "strike it rich."

— "Hobson's choice." Ignore the historical basis for this phrase; it uses a man's name, so substitute a non-sexist phrase such as "No choice at all."

— "Jekyll and Hyde personality." Two masculine names! Substitute "split personality."

— "The patience of Job." You guessed it, Job was a man. Say instead "long-suffering," "very patient," or "uncomplaining."

— What about sexism in the barnyard? Feminists object to "Mad as a wet hen" (although many of them are), and want to substitute "Mad as a hornet." I've known several wet hens over the years, and have had a passing acquaintance once or twice with several mad hornets. Given a choice, I'll take the wet hens.

— "Man overboard!" is obviously sexist, unless you're sure it's a man, and even then, it wasn't his maleness that made him go over, so substitute "Person overboard!" and hope he or she or it doesn't drown while you get it right.

— Don't call a dog "man's best friend" because the only similar phrase referring to women is in the popular song of a few years back "Diamonds Are a Girl's Best Friend," which makes women seem greedy and materialistic, which isn't fair, so don't call a dog man's best friend. (Honest. I'm not making this up.)

— "Motherly," "fatherly," "sisterly," and "brotherly" are gender-specific, which makes them sexist, and should be replaced by more precise adjectives, such as "loving," "kind," "supportive," etc., which can be applied to anyone regardless of gender.

Those are probably enough examples to help you understand why Jean is so entertained by my reactions.

Wait. Let's not forget our Father in Heaven. Why not Mother in Heaven, the feminists indignantly want to know? In fact, since gender is an attitude learned from one's culture, God probably doesn't have gender, and is neither masculine nor feminine. God can't be male or female, either, because those words refer to biological function, and let's not get absurd. Therefore, the proper personal pronoun for God is "it." But calling God "It," even with a capital I, somehow doesn't sound right, so let's not give God a personal pronoun. Instead, let's search our little heads for other gender-fair, non-sexist, divine nouns and pronouns for God, such as Author, Being, Good Parent, Guide, God of Abraham and Sarah (we need Sarah, for non-sexist balance), Heavenly Parent, and so on. The Coordinating Center for Women in Church and Society (1400 N. 7th Street, St. Louis, MO 63106) has a report called "Inclusive Language Guidelines for Use and Study in the United Church of Christ," which explains the whole problem and lists 196 gender-free, non-sexist names, titles, and phrases referring to God. You can order a copy for a mere $2, postpaid.

"He or she who hesitates is lost" and "He or she that hath ears to hear, let him or her hear" are grammatically correct, and are acceptable to feminists, but they're awkward verbosities, as well as mangled corruptions of the originals.

"He or she," "him or her," "his or hers," and similar constructions always have at least three words for gender clarity where previously there was no doubt or confusion; hence, no need for clarification. The advantage, as with Russia's missiles in Cuba, is merely political, not strategic.

At first, some writers attempted compromise by putting "her" in parenthesis after "his," but feminists objected right away that this still included women only as an afterthought. Next came the slash, or diagonal, mark separating (or joining?) the two words, thus creating compound bisexual pronouns such as "his/her," "he/she," and so on. Sometimes the slash is called a stroke; sometimes it almost causes one. I'll return in a moment to the slash/stroke/diagonal.

Some hurried writers have harried us with another gelded pronoun, created by juxtaposing "he/she" and omitting the duplicated letters, thus arriving at "s/he," which can be pronounced aloud only as a sibilant hiccough; and can be read silently only with a slight mental back-flip, as one tries to define it: A split personality? A bearded lady? A gender-blender?

Many writers alternate the masculine and feminine pronouns from paragraph to paragraph, or even sentence to sentence, so they always have a fifty percent chance of being right, and the reader always has a fifty percent chance of being satisfied. Also a fifty percent tendency to skip every other paragraph. A book on parenting, for instance, is very disconcerting when the sex of your child keeps changing from male to female and back again.

I sometimes receive letters addressed to "Dear Sir or Madam," which is understandable and appropriate, since the writer doesn't know which I am, but many letters, third-class in particular, address me as "Sir/Madam," as if I might be half-and-half. That may be appropriate these days for some people, but it is definitely not for me.

In reading sentences such as "Each student must bring his/her book," some readers skip over the punctuation, reading it as "his her book," but with a slight pause between the pronouns to indicate an awareness that something isn't quite right; some supply the supplanted conjunction, as if the diagonal line were a grammalogue representing "or" — "his or her book"; and some others name the oblique punctuation as if it were a synonym for "or," thus: "Each student should bring his slash her book."

Apparently, not many people know that the tipsy line's real name is "virgule," which is just as well. Things are bad enough already. We don't need people saying, "bring his virgule her book." It sounds like a tropical fish. Why not stick to "or"?

Better yet, let's go back to one of the most intelligent enactments of the British Parliament. If men are gracious enough to allow the temporary emasculation of masculine pronouns, women should be gracious enough to accept their chivalry with dignity and even a slight smile of appreciation.

Please, before we all become he/shes and sir/madams.

Some readers write to me, "Dear Person," which solves the problem neatly and has little chance of being wrong.

Phantom conjunctions, bisexual pronouns, and conjunctive virgules are not the only language slashers lurking behind the bushes. Enter the plural singulars, rapidly increasing in popular usage. "Everyone should bring their book," "Each person should get their share," and "Everyone should watch their language." New math or not, "one" is singular and "their" refers to more than one — "of or belonging to them," which is also more than one — and never the twain should meet. Feminists say it's better to be wrong in quantity than confused in gender, but we could be correct in both if feminists didn't insist on redefining words to suit themselves.

The speech of radio and television announcers abounds with singular forms that suddenly become plural in the middle of the verbal stream. English teachers, without blushing, use this abrupt shift of number not only in their speaking, but also in their writing. They know it's grammatically incorrect, but, because it's in common usage, they say it's "permissible."

It shouldn't be. There are many speech and writing habits that are "in common usage," but shouldn't be. Sloppy English from a teacher makes us think he/she doesn't know their business.

In our home-school teaching, and in my book, I follow the edict of the British Parliament, although I'm not a loyalist, and I don't drink tea.

If anyone wants to write me about this, he/she is welcome to send their letter.

***A SHORT BUT VERY AUTHORITATIVE HISTORY OF WOMEN'S LIB (by a man*) (*with his wife's permission),* by Donn Reed,** is available from us. $5 postpaid.

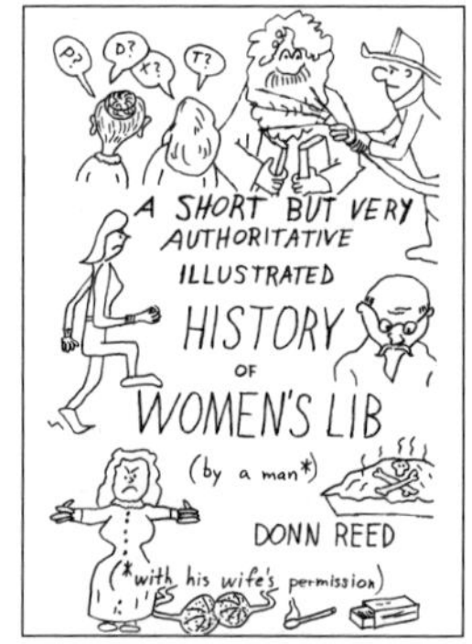

***GENDER BLENDING: CONFRONTING THE LIMITS OF DUALITY,* by Holly Devor.** I haven't read this book and don't intend to. The publisher's description of it is enough to make me wander about muttering and bumping into things. A recent "Help Wanted" ad in our local newspaper said, with italic emphasis, that applicants "*must be either male or female.*" At the time, I didn't think that would be too difficult, although I realize some people seem to be a little confused on the matter. Then along came this book, whose author, says the publisher, "interprets gender as a social distinction related to, but different from, biological sex. … Gender is … learned by displaying the culturally defined insignia of the gender category with which one identifies." The book is also about "fifteen women who have … rejected traditional femininity, but not their femaleness … [are] sometimes mistaken for men … [and] minimize their female vulnerability in a patriarchal world by minimizing their femininity. … Their gender identity does not fit either of the two roles socially and culturally defined as feminine and masculine." Hmmm. Let me see if I've got this, now. If you're dissatisfied with your gender but can't get a refund, you should homogenize yourself? Bob Hope once said the Old West was where men were men and women were women "— and I like it that way!" Me, too. You can buy this study of neutered neutrality from Indiana University Press. It's illustrated for the curious.

GEOGRAPHY

It's nice to be able to travel and learn about places firsthand, but it's not always feasible. When you study geography you can plan a trip anywhere you might like to go. You can begin by researching the route and places you want to investigate along the way to your destination. How will you get there? How far can or do you want to go in a day? What will you do when you get there? What's of interest in Chicago or Houston, Paris or Calcutta? Would it be more fun to fly around Europe or take the train, drive a car, or ride a bicycle? Are there hiking trails? What will you see? What languages will you need? Are there local customs you will need or want to observe? Take this trip across the curriculum and have the kids figure out how much it will cost to take the family. Find out about currency exchange. Read stories from your chosen destination spot. Ask your local travel agency for old travel posters and brochures.

THE BOOK OF WHERE: HOW TO BE NATURALLY GEOGRAPHIC, by Neill Bell. Where in the world are you, anyway? You may think you know the answer, but don't be too sure. "Sitting on the floor at the foot of my bed next to my sneakers," is only part of the answer. The world is a pretty big place, and if you don't know where most of its parts are, you can't possibly be sure of your own location. If you think the Philippines is a rock group or the name of an all-you-can-eat vegetarian restaurant, then you need to look inside this book. If you aren't sure where the Andes are (or even what they are), look inside this book. And if you don't know that most of us live on big hunks of earth that move around like dinner plates, look in this book. It's a trip around the world in 199 pages. This book is out of print but well worth getting online at Amazon.com or one of the other used-book sites.

WHERE IN THE WORLD? Yes, it's back and completely updated. This is a multi-faceted game, which can be played on six levels of varying challenge. Crazy Countries Card Game, played like Crazy Eights, introduces players to the countries of each continent. Statesman, Diplomat, and Ambassador board games acquaint players with the geographical locations as well as cultural and economic information about all the countries of the world. Several variations, from easy to difficult, may be chosen. Experts and novices can play the same game at levels of individual challenge. Age 8 and up, with 2 to 6 players.

***DISCOVERING GEOGRAPHY OF NORTH AMERICA WITH BOOKS KIDS LOVE,* by Carol J. Fuhler.** This book has enough content to keep you and your kids busy for well over a year if you take advantage of all the suggestions, and Carol's program crosses over into other parts of the curriculum. Studies are organized by region of the U.S., plus sections to cover Canada and Mexico. The literature suggested is good, but I'd search the library to broaden it. Each section begins with an overview of the region. Lessons proceed to look at the region through themes of location and human/environmental interactions. Objectives are clearly stated, along with needed materials. All geographic map skills are covered and meet the National Geography Standards. Carol's activity lists are extensive and specific, and yet allow latitude to follow personal interests. Good bibliography, reference, and glossary section.

***DISCOVERING WORLD GEOGRAPHY WITH BOOKS KIDS LOVE,* by Nancy A. Chicola and Eleanor B. English.** This book has the same approach as the one above. The world is divided into twelve realms, each studied through fiction and non-fiction. You'll find the same abundance of well-organized reading and activities, plus bibliography, reference, and glossary sections. Recommended for ages 6 to 12. I think it's better for ages 8 to 12.

On our website you'll find where to order *National Geographic* and *National Geographic for Kids*, maps, great globes, and more.

Why Don't We Fall Off?

The roundness of the world is a difficult concept for young children, and is a fascinating subject to consider and explore in many ways. We compare the land mass with the immensity of the waters. Using a flashlight and a baseball, we demonstrate the relationship of the sun, moon, and earth: sunrise, sunset, eclipses, quarters of the moon, earth's orbit around the sun, and the moon's orbit around the earth. When we begin working with maps, which are also fascinating, we show the relationship of the two-dimensional plane to the three-dimensional ball. What is "down"? Why don't we fall off? The earth is spinning rapidly, and the law of centrifugal force says we should be thrown off by the spin, yet we're not. Gravity? What is gravity? Scientists tell us it's the force that pulls objects toward the center of the earth — but that doesn't explain what it is, or how it works, or why; just that it does. Certainly there is not enough "magnetic attraction" between earth, wood, flesh, and water to counter the force and speed of our earth's movement through space. We introduce the mystery, and we never pretend it isn't a mystery.

A WORLD OF FUN

"Right here is where your Grandma Betty lives," I told the kids as my finger dropped half-way to the equator on our world globe. "This is called Florida."

"Why is it green?" asked Karen, who was six years old.

"Because it's carpeted with money," I told her, firmly believing in telling children the truth. "This is Canada, where we live." I pointed. "And over here is Vermont, where we used to live."

"Wow," exclaimed Cathy, who was eight. "It sure took us a long time to drive just from here to here!"

"It's a lot farther than it looks on this globe, Cathy. You know the earth is like a ball. This globe is a little map of the world. Even a big city wouldn't —"

Derek, two years old, interrupted me. "Daddy, can I turn this ball?"

"Uh … just a little, Derek. A big city, Cathy, would be smaller than a tiny dot on this globe. Even a city with millions of —"

"Can I turn it more, Daddy?"

"Not now, Derek, please. Even a city with millions of people would be —"

"Daddy, I want to turn the ball!"

"Where was I? Oh, yes. Even a city with —"

"Do people live on the earth, Daddy?" asked four-year-old Susan.

"Sure they do. We live on the earth, and everybody —"

"But, Daddy, I don't see any people!"

"There aren't any people on this globe. This is a —"

"But, Daddy, you just said —"

"Daddy! I want to turn this ball!"

"Dad, where's our house on this globe?"

"Remember, Karen, Dad just said a million people —"

"Member-shmember! Dad said we live here, so our house must be here. But I don't see it! Dad, how come —"

"Whoa, kids, back up! Wait a minute! The real earth is much larger than this. This is just a … a toy. No, I don't mean a toy, not a toy to play with. I mean this is a pretend earth. Not real. Look, these big blue spaces are the oceans. This is Russia, here's Africa, here's Australia —"

"Dad," asked Cathy, "is this the place Columbus was looking for?"

"You mean India? Yes, you're right. He was looking for India. And China. But he found America instead. That's why the people he found were called Indians."

"You mean because they were in America?"

"No, I mean because Columbus thought he'd gotten to India."

"Too bad he doesn't have a globe like this," Karen said scornfully. "Then he wouldn't get losted like that if he did. Right, Dad?"

"Ah … right."

Cathy put her finger on India and asked, "You mean Columbus wanted to get here, Dad?"

"Right," I said again. "He was looking for a new way to the East."

Cathy nodded solemnly. "So he took his boat west. Isn't that a little strange, Dad?"

"He didn't know there was a big island in the way," I explained.

"Even so," Cathy said, "that would sure be a new way, all right, going west to get east. Are the people in America really called Indians?"

"Well, no, not most of them. Just the ones Columbus found when he first got there."

Karen's eyes got big. "You mean they're still alive?"

"No, no," I said quickly. "Not the same ones. I mean —"

"I know, Dad!" Susan said excitedly. "This is where we used to live, right?"

"Uh … right."

"And this is where Grandma Mary lives?"

"Right, Susan! Very good! You're really catching on."

Susan's eyes twinkled. She put her finger on Mexico and said, "I bet I know what this is!"

"Sure you do," I said proudly. "Tell us, then. What is it?"

She grinned, with pride matching mine, and said happily, "Our driveway!"

"Uh …"

"Daddy, can I please play with this ball now?"

HISTORY AND BIOGRAPHY

Yesterday, we played the cassette tape of an old radio program called "Battle Hymn of the Republic" that tells the dramatic story of Julia Ward Howe writing the words to go with the popular tune of "John Brown's Body." This morning, we started another tape, with a script written by Stephen Vincent Benét. We didn't get past the introduction. (We'll try again tomorrow.)

"That name sounds familiar," one of the kids said. "Don't we have some books by him?"

I stopped the tape and waited, as the kids looked at each other, searching their memories.

Seeing that they were all drawing blanks, I prompted. "It was mentioned briefly in the tape we heard yesterday," I said. "That is, something of the same name. A long poem, book-length."

"Hiawatha?" someone suggested, knowing better.

"What was the song in the story?" I asked.

"Battle Hymn! Of the Republic!"

"Right," I said. "Where did the tune come from?"

"Someone wrote it." (Always a wise guy.)

"Who?"

"Stephen Vincent Benét?" "Longfellow?" "John Brown?"

"'John Brown's Body'? Nobody knows who wrote it!"

"You win again. Perhaps it just grew, as people repeated the song. Who was John Brown? Did people really sing about his body?"

And so on. Sometimes the kids know the answers, or can brainstorm the answers. Sometimes we jog their memories with hints, riddles, puns, jokes, and related tidbits of information. Sometimes the subject or concept is new to them, and we tell them of our own ideas and experiences, books we've read, places we've seen. We bring out maps, posters, magazine articles, and more books.

We help them collect miscellaneous pieces of information and ideas and tie them together — to relate the facts and ideas to each other, to the world, and to themselves.

This morning, John Brown led to states' rights, the Declaration of Independence, the Constitution, the Gettysburg Address, slavery, the Fugitive Slave Act, Thoreau, the Boston Tea Party, the Mexican War, democracy, *Uncle Tom's Cabin,* and several versions and usages of the word "yankee." The discussion that was interwoven with all these subjects was lively, with quick exchanges of ideas and opinions, and spiced with several puns, jokes, and wisecracks.

We like history, but there are very few history books we like. Browse through a public school's history books; notice how much they are concerned with wars. Not big wars, fought for principle, good against evil, but petty wars, fought for greed, money, power, and territory. See how little attention is given to the great thinkers, to inventions and discoveries, to works of art, music, philosophy, and medicine.

I received passing grades when I was in school, so I suppose I must have learned the answers to at least half the questions, such as Who fought the battle of Kickme? On what date did the commanding general lose his suspenders, and why? How did anteaters affect the outcome? Why was this battle important to the development of the fur trade in colonial Chicago? I have long since forgotten most of the answers, and I doubt that remembering them would contribute very greatly to my happiness or my worth as a person.

We learn more from historical novels than from textbooks. We listen to dramatized historical events on cassette tapes; we put up facsimiles of historical posters; we assemble models of historical buildings and castles and towns; we color pictures of great events and great people; we cut out and arrange paper dolls of great people and read their biographies; and we talk, talk, talk. We use history books, but seldom as intended by the authors and editors. Sometimes we immerse ourselves in an event or a period, collecting information about it from as many different sources as possible. Other times, we skip and bounce, skim and dive, reading aloud, discussing what we find, and relating it to other times and other events. We show the kids how to search out the highlights and the hidden undercurrents. We look for truly significant happenings in the development of humanity and human society. We look for "human interest" — unusual or humorous facts that demonstrate that the people of the past were real people, like us, who ate, slept, loved, feared, and hoped just as we do, not just shadows or silhouettes. We use maps — regional, national, historical, and world — and a globe. We point; we let our fingers do the walking over continents and over centuries.

Some scientists say humanity began here … Biblical scholars say it began here … Here is where agriculture is believed to have started … Here, glaciers swept the continent … How did people survive? Here was the first man to proclaim there is only one God … Here, a new thought in philosophy … government … science … medicine … architecture …

We look for the forerunners of democracy. We trace the evolution of human government

— family patriarchs or matriarchs, tribal chiefs, religious leaders, monarchies, oligarchies. We discuss "good" kings and "bad" kings — what made them so, and what influence did they have on society's growth? We often brush over the names and usually settle for an approximate time, such as "about a thousand years ago." For our purposes, it seldom matters if an event occurred in the year 1169 or 1269. As the gap narrows, as the event is closer to us in time, we make finer distinctions.

Many facts of history stand by themselves; they have significance regardless of the time in which they occurred. Taking the history of mankind as a whole, very few individual names, dates, or happenings have any great significance. There is no reason to memorize most of them just for the sake of "knowing" them. For centuries, the little kingdoms and countries of western Europe were embroiled in countless wars, with heads of state shifting as fast as boundaries. Stevenson's *The Black Arrow* gives us a vivid picture of shifting alliances in medieval Britain. We can read about one or two "representative" wars and imagine the rest; there's no need to memorize all the dates and principals.

Other facts seem meaningless until they are put into perspective by relating them to their own time, their own place, and their own circumstances. Pivotal points and key figures in society's growth deserve a closer look. We have old radio programs on cassettes that take us back to Alexander's conquest of Asia, to Julius Caesar's victories and defeats, and to the signing of the Magna Carta, giving us front-row seats at some of the most significant events in history.

Besides knowing that Alexander the Great conquered a vast part of the world known to him, it's interesting and probably significant to know that he was taught by Aristotle, who was taught by Plato, whose teacher was Socrates. Was Alexander only seeking territory and power, or did he intend to promote a better form of government? What's the evidence? What would our society be like today if Caesar had not crossed the Rubicon? If Constantine, after pledging to spread Christianity if he won the next day's battle, had lost?

We feel it's important to have an understanding of the broad sweep of history — the long journey people have made from the caves and swamps to the moon. We believe it's important to know that we of today are not the first real people; that a hundred years ago, and a thousand, ten thousand, people got dressed and ate breakfast and worked for a living, and taught their children; they laughed and cried; when a boy of ancient Rome skinned his knee, it hurt and bled just as it would today.

We are not so greatly removed from our ancestors as we often think. Despite today's great advantages (and many disadvantages) in technology, industry, and medicine, we have changed very little over the centuries. That which makes us human — whether it's the size of our brain, the opposable thumb, or a share of divinity — is unchanged.

We marvel at the scientific discoveries and advances of the last hundred years. Technologically, why did mankind crawl for so long, and then suddenly walk, run, and fly? We marvel at our humanity, our self-healing bodies, our hopes and fears. The men who have walked on the moon have the same flesh as did the students of Socrates.

As we draw our fingers over the globe or map, and scan the centuries with our talk and our hands, we can back off into space for a broad overview or zoom in closely for a detailed picture. This big ball has been spinning through space for a long time, warmed and lighted by one of the dimmest stars. Down here a woman is preparing breakfast for her family. Is it charred mammoth, or corn flakes and toast? Here is a man digging a hole. A pitfall for a tiger? A hiding place for pirates' treasure? A city sewage line?

Men and women have always been concerned with good and bad, right and wrong. They have always striven for truth, for a good life, and for good government. Most of the best ideas in today's governments had their roots in very ancient times. Our social growth has not kept pace with our technological growth, but we are still advancing, moving from various forms of tyranny toward total emancipation.

A very few, here and there, such as the Hopi Indians of Arizona and the traditional Society of Friends, are models of what all humanity may one day achieve. Democracy, as visualized by Paine, Washington, Jefferson, and other architects of the U.S. government and by Lincoln — "government of the people, by the people, and for the people" — is the highest form of government yet achieved by any large society, but it's just a stepping-stone. Majority rule is better than dictatorship, but the majority is not always right, and the minority may still be misused and wronged. We wait, and strive, for the next development.

The next step in social government will be consensus and general agreement. Each member will seek what is right and good for all members, not only what is right for himself, or what is desirable for the majority or for those with the most influence and power. There will be no lobbying or filibustering or voting, only calm consideration and discussion until unanimity of opinion is reached.

"But that would take too long," many object. "People can never agree that much. Nothing would ever get done."

That's true, of course. As most of us are now, democracy is the best we can hope for. A thousand years ago, democracy was considered an impractical dream, when it was considered at all. A thousand years from now — who knows?

Our descendants will be living then, and we like to think that their society's conscience and spirit will have begun to catch up to the spaceships and computers. We hope the study of our yesterdays will help them have better tomorrows.

Some children learn best when there is action involved, and others can read a biography of another's life and enjoy it. Some children seem to have no interest in history. If your child is reluctant to read biographies, I suggest you read them aloud and make what you learn a shared experience. A biography isn't just an isolated story of one life. It encompasses historical background and social values, and puts it all into perspective.

There are many creative ways to approach this subject. We particularly enjoyed using dramatized history (old radio cassettes and movies) and biographies to expand our knowledge of history. Sometimes we listened to tapes during our school time, sometimes during a meal. We found the kids enjoyed them as bedtime stories after we put speakers in their bedrooms.

Don't just read a book; discuss events and the people who created them. Every major event in history has at least two sides. It's important to discuss both (or all). Investigate the people involved. Find pictures. They can be invaluable; without conscious awareness we learn a multitude of details from a picture. The action may be obvious, but the style of dress, furniture, architecture, and background action or scenery tell more. Many old movies are worth watching. Although many were fictional or historical (sometimes romanticized) fiction and fanciful, Donn and I grew up with vivid images of swashbuckling pirates and heroic knights in armor, and mental pictures of medieval times that made those parts of history alive and interesting.

Some people think you can't pass college entrance tests if you've taken this approach to learning history. If this concerns you, I suggest you first create an approach to history that makes it come alive. If a child is interested he will learn. Then as your child reaches high school age and expresses a desire to attend college, you can use other types of books to fill in facts related to passing college entrance tests. A good GED or SAT book will help you determine the areas you haven't covered. Before that time, make history as alive as it was for those who lived it.

Here are a few of our favorite resources.

***LIES MY TEACHER TOLD ME,* by James Loewen.** This may be the most important book about history that you've read in a long time — maybe ever. Most of the books reviewed here are for children. This book is for you. High school students may be interested too. This book will change the way you think about and teach history, even to your youngest child.

Loewen has studied and taught history on many different levels. He made an exhaustive study of history textbooks because he found his students bored, crammed with facts (many of which were untrue), and unable to separate the trivial details from the major events. His study revealed that conventional texts are based not on primary sources, but on other texts that have been adjusted to meet publishers' standards, which fluctuate according to current ideas of political correctness and what publishers think will sell. In other words, publishers instruct writers to write books that will sell, not books based on objective facts. The main issues that have influenced these decisions are race and religion. Many current history books leave out the influences of religion on migration to North America and have modified facts surrounding racial issues. This book explores and explodes the Columbus myth and gives a truer picture of Helen Keller, Woodrow Wilson, and other historical figures. Unlike many other books, this one does not have a hidden agenda advocating separate ethnic studies; it strives to promote integrated studies. Toward the end of the book you will find guidelines for investigating and evaluating the history material you encounter in standard texts.

Loewen has practical suggestions for making history a living subject for teachers and students. He suggests you approach history as you do current news reports. Modern communication can show us in vivid colors the living detail of tomorrow's history. Human history is full of conflict. Scrutinize your history material as you should the daily news.

***THE FUTURE OF HISTORY,* by Howard Zinn,** contains very provocative material. In a series of interviews with David Barsamian, Zinn offers a reflection on history, a critical look at why history is written the way it is, and an examination of how social change happens. Included is material from Zinn's book *You Can't Be Neutral on a Moving Train*. Zinn, always an advocate of the people, speaks with humor and foresight. This stimulating critique will leave you with much to consider, and thoughtful readers will come away with critical tools for evaluating written histories. An excellent tool for those of us helping our kids develop critical thinking skills.

***THE WORLD'S GREAT SPEECHES,* edited by Lewis Copeland and Lawrence W. Lamm.** This wide-ranging collection of 278 speeches from the early Greeks to 1970 presents a powerful, unique look at history.

THE READER'S DIGEST CHILDREN'S ATLAS OF WORLD HISTORY. The rise of the Roman Empire, great dynasties of China, Viking invasions, kingdoms of Africa, the age of exploration — every key period in the history of the world is vividly portrayed in this beautifully illustrated atlas. Young readers are taken inside all the great moments of the past — from the very first civilization in Mesopotamia through the Middle Ages, the world's great empires, and the age of industry and revolution — all the way up to the wars and scientific advances of the 20th century. Each important historic period is given its own two-page spread, with an easy-to-read introduction providing an overview of the time and putting it into context. A complete world map for each section shows major empires, centers of civilization, and nations of that time, and also includes such important information as trade routes, invasion paths, and voyages. A time chart puts major events into context; boxed features cover key people, places, and events; everyday life throughout history is shown in photographs of art and other illustrations. Special "Who's Who in History" and "The World Today" sections and a comprehensive glossary enhance the value of the atlas. This has been our favorite.

***CLASSICAL KIDS: AN ACTIVITY GUIDE TO LIFE IN ANCIENT GREECE AND ROME,* by Laurie Carlson.** Great hands-on creative activities guaranteed to be fun. Make a star gazer, chisel a clay tablet, weave Roman sandals, create a Greek mosaic, and much more, while learning about life in Greek and Roman times.

***A HISTORY OF US,* a set of 11 volumes, by Joy Hakim.** These very readable books don't even resemble "schoolbooks" despite having been written by a former teacher. Hakim presents history as the story of people, which is as it should be. You meet ordinary people, not just the presidents and well-known figures, and discover how they lived. These engaging books, with excellent color illustrations, ask the reader to think and form opinions. Hakim makes good use of original sources, newspaper excerpts, cartoons, diaries, drawings, maps, and the original artwork of the time. You'll find yourself spending more time thinking about the people and the issues than memorizing meaningless names, battles, and dates. While this series of books is not cheap, it will be all that you will need from about third grade through junior high. If you have young children, I suggest that you can take your time going through the books, concentrating on one historical period at a time, or you can go through the books more quickly, returning for a more in-depth study when the children are older. Hakim's inclusion of an extensive list of related reading material in the back of each book is a real boon to those who like to explore in depth. While the original set was 10 volumes, the newly revised set is 11 volumes. This most recent addition to the set contains a complete index for the series, a good glossary of terms, essential documents and speeches that have shaped the country, and commentary about why each is important. This series has extensive reading lists.

***CIVIL RIGHTS FOR KIDS,* by Mary C. Turck.** Most history we present or share with our kids seems ancient to them even if we go back only to the 1920s or 1940s, 1960s, or 1970s — times when our parents were young or we were young. Most kids feel that anything before their birth is ancient history. I'm not bothered that they feel this way about much of history, but in the last century there were major civil rights issues, ones still present today, that have nothing to do with the usual historic battles — fighting for territory or political gain. These issues are important not only because they are still unresolved, but also because the fight for civil rights reintroduced non-violent confrontation — active non-violence as a means to bringing about needed changes to our modern society. We all want our children to grow up in a world that is safe and just. If we want to make this a reality, we must help our children understand what is important, how to achieve that goal, and, hopefully, how to use methods that do not create more violence and hatred. Working to end segregation and prejudice can be done non-violently. This book is the story of courageous men, women, and children who believed in equality for all and lived their lives accordingly, nonviolently in the face of violence — some at the cost of their lives. It's not a pretty story, but it's real. These people changed our nation. All of us, young and old, can learn from them. Interspersed with illustrations, true stories, and a chronology of events are activities your kids will find challenging and enjoy.

Chapter one, "Let the Children Lead," describes segregation in the U.S. before the civil rights movement. Chapter two, "Tired of Being Mistreated," introduces Rosa Parks, Martin Luther King Jr., and the bus boycotts. Chapter three is "Non-violent Resistance: Student Sit-ins 1960." Chapter four, "If Not Us, Then Who?" discusses the Freedom Riders. Chapter five, "Standing Up for Freedom," covers Birmingham, with its fire hoses, police dogs, murder, and police involvement — and non-involvement. Chapter six is "The March on Washington and the 'I Have a Dream' Speech." There's a lot more, too.

Note to Canadians: This isn't about your history, but there are discrimination problems within Canada that need resolution. Learning about the non-violent methods used in the civil rights movement would be useful.

***THE SPIRIT THAT MOVES US: A LITERATURE-BASED RESOURCE GUIDE, TEACHING ABOUT THE HOLOCAUST AND HUMAN RIGHTS,* Volume 1, by Laura R. Petovello, J.D., and Volume 2, by Rachel Quenk, both in association with the Holocaust Human Rights Center of Maine.** Two very important books that can be used for exploring and learning about the Holocaust through literature. Why make a study of the Holocaust and human rights? *The Spirit That Moves Us* provides a framework with many suggestions for studying not only the Holocaust, but our society, culture, and civic responsibilities. While it includes lesson plans, you are free to pick and choose what suits you and your children. Many books are recommended, with age guidelines enabling you to choose those appropriate to your reader. These books look deeply into the nature of culture, immigration, immigrants and refugees, and injustice and discrimination, and how we can react and choose our own path through the moral and ethical issues. You'll find chapters on the rise of Hitler, Jewish families living in Hitler's Germany, courageous acts of resistance, and how we can make a difference in the lives of others. Appendices at the end provide numerous resources for students and teachers looking for more material about the Holocaust and human rights. Excellent suggestions are given for using the material in these books in creative ways for many age levels. Take your time with these books. I suggest spreading out the reading over an extended period, allowing lots of breaks so that the horror is understood but isn't overwhelming. Although the main focus is on the Holocaust, there is also an ongoing theme: that prejudice and discrimination are still a problem in many places today. The books suggest actions we can take individually and as part of a community to tackle this issue. Volume 1 is for grades K to 4, Volume 2 for grades 5 to 8.

Dramatized History and Biography From "Old-Time Radio"

I was astonished at Donn's excitement when he discovered some old-time radio tapes for sale — and somewhat dismayed at the amount of money he sent off in the mail to get them — but then he went on to tell me about listening to the radio when he was growing up, and I realized that the difference in our attitudes was generational.

I grew up just as radio was being replaced by television in middle-class homes. I remember watching *Howdy Doody, Captain Video, The Roy Rogers Show, Melody Ranch with Gene Autry,* and *The Lone Ranger* on our new seven-inch black-and-white set. My entertainment was presented to me. I didn't have to do anything more than sit passively and watch.

Donn's youth was strongly influenced by the end of the Depression and by living part time on his grandparents' farm. He vividly remembered his grandfather leaning against one of the cows he was milking and listening to a favorite show. He remembered sitting spellbound in the farmhouse kitchen with his parents and grandparents listening to the radio, his grandfather leaning his head on the polished wooden casing to ensure that he didn't miss a word of a favorite show. They listened to many of the shows listed below, as well as to mysteries, Westerns, science fiction, dramatized literature, and comedy shows. To enjoy a radio or a taped broadcast requires audience participation, because it engages the imagination. You have to create your own pictures. The body may remain still, but the mind is active.

I thought we would listen to these tapes once and then they'd gather dust, become part of the general clutter, and eventually be packed away in a box. Was I ever mistaken! Like favorite books, to be read and then reread, the tapes became a part of our way of life. We rewired the house so the kids could listen in their bedrooms. Although we continued to read to the kids every night, after a certain point (when we were starting to fall asleep) we asked for requests for tapes; the kids trundled off to bed, snuggled down under the covers with the lights off, and let their imaginations fly with stories from faraway places and different eras.

Old radio programs became one of our favorite learning tools. Besides being very entertaining, they give us a feeling of "being there" that is almost as good as actually being able to go back in time. Our kids frequently enjoyed coloring some of the related historical coloring books while listening.

I just discovered I can put all the old radio programs on CD! I'm not sure yet how many programs with fit on a CD, but it will be the best deal yet. Here is a partial listing of what's available; check the website for a complete list and prices: *The Last Day of Pompeii, The Fall of Troy, Alexander: The Battle for Asia, Alexander: Mutiny in India, Joan of Arc, Caesar Crosses the Rubicon, Assassination of Caesar, The Signing of the Magna Carta, Sailing of the Mayflower, The Count of Monte Cristo, Philadelphia, July 4, 1776, Ratification of the Constitution, A Tale of Two Cities, Les Misérables ...*

DRAMATIZED AMERICAN HISTORY brings it all alive. Narrated by Kenneth Bruce, a master storyteller and historian, with sound effects, music, and multiple voices. You will hear the excitement of the times — the problems, obstacles, and victories. You'll play these over and over because they'd be exciting to listen to even if you weren't learning something. These stories make complex issues understandable. The following is a partial listing: *Pathway to Independence, The American Revolution, John Adams and the Undeclared War With France, The Louisiana Purchase, The Lone Star Republic, The Lewis and Clark Expedition, The Era of Mountain Men, Manifest Destiny, The Oregon Trail, The Rise of Sectionalism and the Monroe Doctrine, The Civil War, The San Francisco Earthquake and Fire, The Titanic Disaster, The Flight of The Spirit of St. Louis,* and many more.

GREAT IDEAS THAT SHAPED OUR WORLD. The works of classic thinkers throughout history are sometimes referred to as the "Great Conversation," because the authors respond to each other's ideas, although they may have lived thousands of miles or hundreds of years apart, and because, in various ways, they all address the most important and enduring questions and problems of humanity: What is truth? What is happiness? What is human nature? What principles should guide our actions? What authorities deserve our allegiance? These questions are as new — and as old — for us today as they were for Plato. The Great Conversation (or the Great Ideas) is not the useless ponderings of ancient, abstract philosophers. If we consider them in their historical contexts, we gain a better understanding of the past; if we apply them to our own time, they become powerful tools to help us better understand these times, our real nature, and our rights and responsibilities as human beings. Most of the Great Ideas were developed within the context of particular events of the past, and studying them will give us not only a better understanding of those events, but a higher value: that the basic principles are applicable to any period and circumstance, including our own.

When I first saw this cassette program advertised, I was very skeptical, expecting it to be no more than readings of condensed classics, which would be interesting and valuable, but of limited use. I requested a sample ("Civil Disobedience," by Henry David Thoreau, because I am especially interested in Thoreau's life and philosophy). I was very agreeably surprised and impressed.

The cassette tapes of Great Ideas That Shaped Our World are dramatized, with multiple voices portraying the author, contemporary observers, and critics, drawing on actual writings and quotations of the time, with an overview presented by a narrator. Each tape is about 90 minutes long, divided into shorter segments (about 20 minutes each) for more convenient study. The social and historical background of each work is presented, as well as the effects, both immediate and long-term, that the work had on contemporary and future society. There are numerous references to other works and historical events, demonstrating the continuing influence of the author's ideas.

The knowledge and understanding to be gained from each cassette program is easily equivalent to several hours of reading or high school- and college-level lecturing. These tapes won't take the place of the books presented, but they are very comprehensive introductions, and will definitely increase one's enjoyment and understanding of those works. For those who don't have the time or inclination to read the original works, these programs will make a very adequate substitute. After our complete satisfaction with our first tape, we bought several more, and are steadily adding titles to our library. We have listened to them several times, not only for "study" but for repeated enjoyment, just as we often browse through the Great Ideas in books. A partial listing:

COMMON SENSE, by Thomas Paine
THE DECLARATION OF INDEPENDENCE
CIVIL DISOBEDIENCE, by Henry David Thoreau
THE LIBERATOR, edited by William Lloyd Garrison
WEALTH OF NATIONS, by Adam Smith, Part 1
ON LIBERTY, by John Stuart Mill
VINDICATION OF THE RIGHTS OF WOMEN, by Mary Wollstonecraft

HISTORYCENTRAL.COM is one of the largest history sites online (www.historycentral.com). Drawing on materials from the 21 History CD ROMs developed by MultiEducator, Inc., over the last decade, HistoryCentral.com "brings history alive." A key component of HistoryCentral.com is the timeline of major world history events beginning in 10,000 B.C. and ending with 1999. Links are provided to related websites and to additional information. Another link on this site is www.NationbyNation, providing historical, economic, demographic, and geographic information on all countries of the world. Four hundred primary source documents are available on the site.

Reasons to Avoid Standard History Textbooks

Religion in History: Some things don't seem to change. Learning magazine reported in November 1987 that the Association for Supervision and Curriculum Development encourages teachers to return to the inclusion of religion in their courses about history and society. Learning said the ASCD report, "Religion in the Curriculum," complained that "public school children aren't learning enough about the importance of religion in American history and society because educators and textbook publishers fear controversy."

Omission of Religion From Textbooks: U.S. District Court Judge W. Brevard Hand ruled on March 4, 1987, that 39 nationally distributed history and social studies texts and six home economics texts used in Alabama's 129 school systems "discriminate against the very concept of religion and theistic religions in particular, by omissions so serious that a student learning history from them would not be apprised of relevant facts about America's history. ... References to religion are isolated and the integration of religion in the history of American society is ignored."

And Then: On August 26, 1987, the U.S. Court of Appeals for the Eleventh Circuit unanimously overturned Judge Hand's decision by ruling that the information in the books was "essentially neutral in its religious content." The fact that the texts omitted references to religion was "not an advancement of secular humanism or an active hostility toward theistic religion." Superior courts refused to hear further appeals.

Freedom of the Press? This information is from the American Library Association's *Banned Books Week '89: A Resource Book,* published for the use of booksellers in promoting the freedom to read. The American Library Association, the American Booksellers Association, and other sponsors of Banned Books Week considered Judge Hand's ruling against the books to be an act of censorship, in that the charge of "promoting secular humanism" had been brought by fundamentalists, but the ruling that overturned Judge Hand's ruling was regarded as a righteous blow struck for freedom of the press.

The members of that Court of Appeals should be reminded that fictional history is not the same as historical fiction. Whether or not the omission of references to religion constitutes "active hostility toward religion," it certainly seems to indicate a disdain for truth and accuracy in history. Religion, Christianity in particular, was of unimpeachable importance in the founding and growth of the United States; the deliberate omission of the fact from school textbooks, along with supporting references throughout, is hardly "neutral." Such "neutrality" constitutes a censorship far more real and more malignant than Judge Hand's ruling against it.

Mark Twain said that God made a fool for practice, and then made school boards. I'd say that was for further practice; then God made the U.S. Court of Appeals that overturned Judge Hand's efforts to remove fictional history from the schools of Alabama.

The details have changed over the years, but most textbook publishers today are still sanitizing what they publish so as not to "offend" anyone for any reason. I find that offensive. Why can't they let us read the facts and let us make up our own minds? Even biased reports are better than totally deleted content. Maybe they just don't give us credit for having any brains. What do you think? For up-to-date information on banned books and authors, go to www.ala.org.

POLITICS AND GOVERNMENT; CURRENT EVENTS

Censorship and Conspiracies

Which came first, the right-wing censorship or the left-wing conspiracies? The extreme right complains that the schools are teaching secular humanism, and the extreme left complains that its First Amendment rights are being violated if children are told anything at all about religion. The right-wing arguments are based primarily on a strict, literal interpretation of the Bible; the left-wing arguments are based on a strict, literal interpretation of the U.S. Constitution. Education, caught in the middle and pulled by both groups in a tug-of-war, has stretched and snapped and gotten lost in the shuffle.

It's sadly true that public schools don't include much about religion, even in history courses. It's also sadly true that they don't include much about anything. Sometimes both sides seem to have some very valid, reasonable arguments and examples, and sometimes they both just bounce off the walls. The complaints and threats of both sides have scared textbook publishers, whose main desire (second to making money, of course) is to avoid offending anyone. Since someone, somewhere, either left or right, will be offended by anything at all, the publishers have thought it prudent to publish books that don't say anything, and find it very discouraging that some people are offended even by that. At present, despite the Bush administration and a growth spurt of fundamentalism, the left-wingers seem to be gaining ground in the schools and in the courts. Perhaps the irresponsible "rights" demanded by the far left will eventually result in an even greater reaction from the far right, which might result, for a while at least, in a more reasonable balance between the two. Probably neither side will be satisfied with a balance, but will continue to fight for increasing control, so the scales will continue to teeter-totter. Both extremes, the far-right fundamentalists and the far-left "secular humanists," are loud minorities. The "Moral Majority" was nothing more than a splinter of the right-wing minority, but there is a real moral majority — the great number of people who are not fundamentalists but disapprove of flag-burning and pornography; who don't believe the universe was created in six days but do believe hate-music is wrong. This real majority, out-shouted by the left-right extremists, is too intimidated by both groups to speak up in favor of a return to sound, "old-fashioned" moral values, academic competence, and common-sense education.

Let the far both extremes return to being consenting adults in the privacy of their own homes, and let the far right teach Scientific Creationism in the privacy of their own homes and churches.

Don't expect great intellectual feats from either side. Left-wingers take the Bible from school, claiming that exposure to a religious book is an infringement of their First Amendment rights. Right-wingers remove *Charlotte's Web* and *Peter Rabbit* from many schools because animals can't really talk, and *The Adventures of Huckleberry Finn* because Huck would rather go to Hell than betray an escaped slave. Joseph Scheidler, director of the ultra-right Pro-Life Action League, says "contraception is disgusting — people using each other for pleasure." Planned Parenthood, determined to match Scheidler's ignorance and stupidity, quotes his pious complaint to support its claim that making abortion illegal will "return women to a position of subservience." Both sides act as if their brains had been aborted.

I'm not a fundamentalist, as you've probably inferred by now, and I don't usually consider myself a right-winger in much of anything, but it seems to me that many of the arguments of the right wing are more valid than those of the left wing. I don't think "Bible science" should be taught in schools, but neither do I think that the recognition of Thanksgiving and Christmas as religious holidays will threaten anyone's liberty.

My brother says the older we get, the more conservative we get. I think I'm still as "liberal" as I've ever been, but the far left keeps moving so much further left that my liberalism seems increasingly conservative.

Kahlil Gibran tells of four frogs on a floating log, arguing about whether the log is moving, or the river is moving, or their movement is only in their thoughts. A fourth frog, who has stayed out of the argument, finally says, "All three of you are right. The river is moving, the log is moving, and we move in our thoughts." The first three frogs stare at the fourth for a moment; then all together, they rush at him and push him off the log.

Splash.

You can only protect your liberties in this world by protecting the other man's freedom. You can only be free if I am free. — Clarence Darrow

***INTRODUCTION TO POLITICS AND GOVERNMENT,* by Janet Cook, Stephen Kirby, Judy Tatchell, and Cheryl Evans,** is an Usborne book with very clear, detailed, unbiased descriptions of various forms of government, how they compare, and how they relate to each other, with historic and modern examples, including dictatorships, fascism, republics, democracy, autocracy, Marxism, electoral systems, diplomacy, and summit meetings. Accurate information about Britain's parliamentary system, a presidential system, and a one-party system. A well-illustrated hardcover with detailed, colorful drawings. This book is out of print but you can still find it on Amazon.com.

HAIL TO THE CHIEF: THE PRESIDENTIAL ELECTION GAME. Thank goodness they've brought this game back! Players compete to become elected president of the United States. First, they must achieve candidacy by answering historical and constitutional questions about the presidency. Then, on the campaign trail, they travel from state to state to win electoral votes by answering questions on the history and geography of the 50 states. (No mention is made of political promises, party fund-raising or TV advertising, but players will learn a lot about U.S. history and geography anyway, as well as the theory of how presidents are elected.)

Special features: Each president is pictured on the board, the game can be updated, four levels of play allow parents and children to play together, and there are more than 600 questions to challenge you. Awards: Parent's Choice Awards and Media & Methods Excellence in Education.

Perils of Democracy: Who should know better than an elected public servant what dangers there are in a democracy? In July 1989, the *Los Angeles Times* noted that California State Sen. Bill Craven was worried about "the rise in citizens' initiatives, in which people sign petitions to enact changes in laws," and quoted Craven as saying, "[If we legislators] don't watch our respective tails, the people are going to be running the government."

A politician thinks of the next election; a statesman, of the next generation.
— James Freeman Clarke

Quoted in *Newsweek:* Robert Carroll, spokesman for Pratt and Whitney, explaining why his company charged the Air Force $999 for a single pair of pliers, said, "They're multipurpose; not only do they put the clips on but they take them off."

Current Events and the News?

I don't think there are any really objective news magazines being published today. The news articles are riddled with opinions, pontifical analyses, and biased writing. I've almost learned to tolerate it with radio weather forecasts, so I don't mutter too loudly when the "meteorologist" says, "Well, folks, it's going to be another miserable day tomorrow, with lots of rain all day." Why should it be assumed that rain will make the day miserable for me? Perhaps my garden needs water, or maybe I like to walk in the rain. It's worse when the "reporting" is of national or international events. Just tell me what's going on, without what you and your team of experts *think* it "means." We'd like to boycott all the news magazines, but, for all their fluff and biases, they do tell us a little of current events, so we grit our teeth and try to read between the lines. We assume that half of the truth isn't being told and that half of what is being told isn't true or is being told in a slanted, misleading manner. If a magazine has a four-page car advertisement, costing thousands of dollars per inch, we don't expect the magazine to say much about the safety hazards of automobiles. If the magazine receives support from major oil companies, we don't expect it to dig very deeply into the causes of oil spills or the failures of oil companies to clean up their messes. If the magazine's demographic surveys show that 76 percent of its readers are suspicious of what the Russians, Cubans, Chinese, etc., are up to now, we don't expect it to risk six million cancelled subscriptions by telling the truth when the Russians, Cubans, Chinese, etc., actually do something good and right. We try to balance our understanding of the news by reading publications such as the Nation and the Washington Spectator, which don't depend on big corporations for their revenue. Since most of them tend to be somewhat or very left-wing, we don't believe all they say either, but at least their biases are more open and honest. We read both viewpoints, divide by the number of starving children in the world, multiply by the number of politicians it takes to change a light bulb, and hope thereby to arrive at some measure of the truth.

We tried *Time, Newsweek,* and *U.S. News & World Report,* all at one time, comparing them for a full year. *U.S. News* claims to have a higher percentage of "hard" news than the other two, but I think its extra margin is concerned primarily with the stock market. *Time* and *Newsweek* were neck and neck, but *Time* kept billing us for our subscription long after we had paid for it, so for several years we've subscribed only to *Newsweek,* and don't feel any great loss. You can't judge any of the magazines by their cover stories, which will be about real news one week (politics, wars, elections) and popular culture the next week (the latest movie craze or why Americans like to go to the beach). Inside, the magazine will always be the same mishmash of news and garbage and expert analyses of both. Lumping all such publications under one representative name, Thoreau said, "Read not the *Times;* read the eternities." *Reader's Digest* recently printed an anecdote about a vacationer in the woods of Wisconsin who told his guide, "It'll be interesting when I get back home to read the papers and see what's been happening in the real world." The guide replied, "I thought that was why you came out here."

It's now 2009 and I find that *Newsweek* has more pop culture than I can stand. I'm about to switch to the *Christian Science Monitor.* I would truly like to be able to stick my head in the sand and forget about politics and foreign wars, droughts, and starving children. I don't enjoy reading about them. But something inside compels me to attempt to make a contribution toward making the world a better place, or at least to help it hold its own for my children and the children of the future. As PBS has said, "If we don't do it, who will?" Oh! That reminds me about PBS here in Maine. I can now get the BBC news on the radio a couple times a day and in the evening. It helps to have a different point of view.

News in the Classroom

As always, PBS offers high-quality resources for all ages, addressing emergency services, terrorism, tolerance, and human rights: www.pbs.org. Every weekday, *The New York Times* produces daily lesson plans based on current events: www.nytimes.com/learning/index.html.

WEEKLY READER. Student newspapers, with a different edition for each level from pre-K to 6. Varied subject matter, appropriate to the grade level: news, science, global issues, etc. Our kids always looked forward to receiving this newspaper, and Donn and I remembered enjoying it when we were in school. Inquire for current rates: 3001 Cindel Drive, Delran, NJ 08370; 800-446-3355; www.weeklyreader.com.

CURRENT EVENTS. Student newspaper, 26 issues per school year. It does a competent job of reporting key issues, although from a very standard perspective. Includes photographs, helpful graphs, tables, and maps. Good variety of information, puzzles, vocabulary lists, and more based on current news. Grades 6 and up (the level of most adult publications). For subscription information: Weekly Reader Corp., 3001 Cindel Drive, Delran, NJ 08370; 800-446-3355; www.weeklyreader.com.

"Be the change you want to see." — Gandhi

MAKING A DIFFERENCE

GLOBAL AWARENESS — MULTICULTURALISM

The world is shrinking.

Figuratively, because of the speed of modern transportation and communication, and literally, because some of the earth's substance is dissipating into space in the form of gas and some of the earth's substance is settling and becoming compacted. Global warming is also a major factor in our lives.

Although codes of behavior vary from culture to culture, there are some standards that have always existed in nearly all of them. Among these is the law that it's wrong to hurt another member of one's own group, whether the group is a family, a tribe, or a nation. Murder or theft within one's own group is a punishable offense everywhere, even among those people whose highest awards and honor are for such actions if the victims are from another group.

As the world shrinks, the boundaries of our groups blend and overlap. We can no longer pretend, as we have for centuries, that humanity is not all one family, regardless of color or religion or place of birth.

"Am I my brother's keeper?" Cain asked God, but God knew Cain was being sarcastic, and didn't answer. The shrinking of our world is his answer now.

Most of the materials in this book relate, in one way or another, to global awareness — i.e., awareness that we occupy this planet with billions of other beings and life-forms, with whom we share the responsibility of preserving the health of the earth and its creatures. To do so, we need at least basic information about our fellow beings, and about both the good and the bad directions in which our species seems to be going. Entries in this section are those that most specifically address the subject.

In North America we are spoiled. With the notable exception of the 9/11 attacks, this continent is isolated from the violence we see on TV or read about. We don't worry, and we can't possibly imagine what it would be like to worry, about IEDs or bombs falling on us or on our kids. If you can afford this book, you live in a world of wealth compared to much of the world. We are innocent in many ways. When our children, or grandchildren in my case, grow up, the world will be very different. The need for coming generations to understand other cultures becomes more apparent every day.

Traveling or living abroad is the best way to understand another culture. Most of us can't afford to travel extensively. That's no excuse for remaining ignorant of other peoples or other ways of living and thinking. With the information in this chapter you can create an understanding of other cultures and meet people from around the world. The world is more accessible daily. Using a computer can help.

I may be an optimist (I've been called worse), but I believe that some day it will be possible for every citizen of planet earth to have adequate health care; meaningful work; enough to eat; a warm, dry place to sleep; a chance to dream; and the opportunity to grow in peace. It's not happening now, or very fast. Very few of us have, or will have, the chance to change our world with a world-shaking inspiration, but we can change it one person at a time, and if we work together we *can* make a difference. We have to start somewhere. This is my place to start, with this book, with the following resources. Please join me.

The greatest evil today is indifference. To know and not to act is a way of consenting to these injustices. The planet has become a very small place. What happens in other countries affects us. — Elie Wiesel

When I go into my office in the morning and start up the computer, I always start with a visit to **THE HUNGER SITE** (www.thehungersite.com). It's part of a U.N. program to feed people in need. The money comes from corporate sponsors (such as Sprint), and the amount of food donated daily is based on the number of people who visit the site that day. Please bookmark this site. It takes less than a minute every day to click on the button at the top of the home page and ensure that one more hungry person will receive something to eat. This evening I looked and saw that 152,754 cups of food were donated today. It's not a great thing that I do, but I feel better knowing I've helped to feed someone else. Since the Hunger Site began in 1999, more than 500,000,000 cups of food have been donated and given to someone in need. It makes a difference. There are also links so you can help breast cancer research, literacy efforts, and animal shelters.

I couldn't decide where to put this information for a long time — maybe with information about ecology or science. The reason I decided to put it here is that it has to do with each of us making an effort to improve our world in whatever way we can. Last May, on National Public Radio, Robert Watson, speaking about agriculture, population, conservation, and ecology and the great need for good instruction and materials for children, commented that the United States is the laughingstock of the world because of the credibility given to the idea of intelligent design. Me, I'm not going to add to that. If our children are going to deal intelligently with the problems facing their generation they need good basic facts. At the moment the United States has about 5% of the world population and it consumes 25% of just about everything available. From my perspective it seems to me that there will eventually have to be a great shift in the wealth to eliminate the massive poverty.

If we all ate very simply one day a week and put the money saved into helping others, we could make a difference. It brings to mind what author Farley Mowat said when asked about defending wildlife: "Think globally. Act locally." What are you doing to set an example for your children?

***THE KID'S GUIDE TO SOCIAL ACTION: HOW TO SOLVE THE SOCIAL PROBLEMS YOU CHOOSE — AND TURN CREATIVE THINKING INTO POSITIVE ACTION,* by Barbara A. Lewis.** Here's everything kids need to take social action: step-by-step directions for letter-writing, interviewing, speech-making, fund-raising, media coverage, and more; petitions, proclamations, and news releases; addresses and phone numbers for government offices, other social action groups, and awards programs; and inspiring true stories about real kids accomplishing great things. This is the most comprehensive guide available for kids who want to make a difference in the world, written by a teacher whose own students' efforts have resulted in the cleanup of a hazardous waste site and the passage of two new laws.

***THE KID'S GUIDE TO SERVICE PROJECTS,* by Barbara A. Lewis.** This book has a slightly different emphasis than her book above. This book is focused on service projects that can be carried out within your community, county, or city that will make a difference in people's lives. Endorsed by Youth Service America.

Youth activism? You bet. Two Canadians have created a way to get young people involved in making the world a better place. The organization is called **TakingITGlobal**, and it works with UNICEF, the Lifebridge Foundation, Oxfam, Global Youth Action Network, Earth Charter Youth Initiative, Peace Child International, and many grassroots organizations. Join them with your kids and make a difference. Check out www.takingitglobal.org.

Host an exchange student — it will enrich your life. **ASSE**, a nonprofit group, can help you do it. When you do this you become a force for change in our global society. For information call 800-677-2773. Website: www.asse.com.

AMNESTY INTERNATIONAL, founded in 1961, is a worldwide nonpartisan organization supported in more than 150 countries and territories. It is independent of any government, political faction, ideology, economic interest, or religious creed. It is also a winner of the 1977 Nobel Peace Prize for its efforts to promote global observance of the U.N. Universal Declaration of Human Rights.

Amnesty International's Freedom Writers network makes it easy to make a real and practical difference in the world. By subscribing, you can actively help prisoners of conscience who have not advocated violence and are being held unjustly. Periodically you will receive information about these prisoners and instructions on how to write a letter (examples given) to protest the injustice being perpetrated. Amnesty International, 322 8th Ave., 10th Floor, New York, NY 10117-0398, or Amnesty International, 294 Albert St., Suite 204, Ottawa, ON K1P 6E6.

Heard on *Cambridge Forum* on the Maine Public Broadcasting Network: The U.S. exports two-thirds of all weapons worldwide, a huge number of them sold by the government. Think about the taxes you pay and the consequences of this. If it bothers you, write your representatives and let them know.

Please, Don't Color My World

Fools rush in where angels fear to tread. — Alexander Pope

I've taken the liberty as editor of making a few changes I believe help to bring Donn's essay up to date. This has been a much misunderstood part of this book. Donn was color-blind — not literally, but figuratively when it came to his relationship with people. His intention here was not to hurt or make anyone feel defensive. His main point, which is maybe even more relevant today than when he wrote it in 1991, is that each of us has a unique cultural background; that our own unique histories are important, but that we must keep our perspectives and priorities clear. While acknowledging our differences we must remember that we are one people and that our common goals are greater than our differences.

I find it interesting, but not alarming, that a Jewish home-school group and a Muslim home-school group are included in a published list of groups that excludes all "exclusivist" Christian groups — that is, those that accept as members only those who profess certain religious tenets. There are also Catholic and Mormon groups, presumably (although I don't know why) not so exclusivist as Protestants.

Interesting, because it seems inconsistent, but I'm frequently inconsistent, too, so I don't mind allowing others the same privilege. Not alarming, because the fundamentalist Christians have their own national network, and are in no danger of being unnoticed by anyone who is qualified to join. It seems to be true that birds of feather flock together, but I think it's a narrow way of thinking when the "feather" is a particular religious belief; however, I don't think these groups pose any threat to other home-schoolers — certainly not to me — so I don't find their existence any more alarming than their presence on a list that excludes other exclusivist groups.

I am very alarmed, however, by a different kind of exclusivist thinking that is growing, not only in general society, but also within the home-school movement: racism.

I would be among the very first to denounce any "all-white" home-school group or publication, and I don't see any difference between that and an "all–non-white" group or publication.

Some newsletters are for "Homeschoolers of Color," and invite as subscribers "both Latina/o and Black home-schoolers … and anyone else out there who identifies themselves as a person/family of color, regardless of nationality, percentage of color, language, religion, or any of the other factors that sometimes keep us apart." Unless you're white, that is, with "no percentage of color."

To the best of my knowledge, I have no "percentage of color" — but I have known blacks, some of whom were very close friends, and I have lived in the Hopi village of Hotevilla in Arizona, and I have taught blacks and Indians (along with whites, Asians, and Latinos) to read and write English, and Mexicans to read and write Spanish, and was once a librarian with an Indian assistant. I have known people of many races and ethnic backgrounds, in a variety of circumstances, and have gotten to know them all fairly well. We were not "colored" and "white" to each other, but just people. We all laughed and cried and bled in the same color, and I absolutely do not believe that their children "are not like everybody else's children."

Some of these special-interest homeschooling groups say their "children of color" have special needs as distinguished from children who are white. In other words, the needs and concerns of children "of color" are different from the needs and concerns of white children. Turn it around, and you have the bigoted argument with which white supremacists have justified their actions for centuries — that "colored" people don't have the same needs and concerns that white people have.

Have you seen Crayola's "multicultural" crayons, pencils, modeling clay, and washable paints and markers? Apricot, burnt sienna, mahogany, peach, sepia, tan, plus black and white for blending — "to help build skills and self-esteem," say the ads.

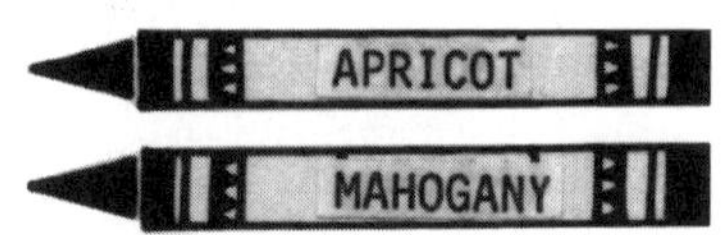

Of course, it's nicer to talk about "culture" than "race," but you won't convince me that those colors refer to culture. They refer to skin color, which is one of the factors often differentiating races. There is no such thing as a "black culture" or "red culture" — or "apricot" or "mahogany culture" — any more than there is a "white culture." All races have had as many differences among themselves as with each other. Some people of each race have built castles or pyramids while others of the same race were building mud huts.

I'm not against the skin-colored crayons. In fact, I think they're a good idea. I remember the frustration of trying to find a good skin-colored crayon — my skin, that is, or so-called "white" — when I was a kid. Light pink didn't work, and white was anemic. The larger crayon sets had "flesh," which was closest and worked the best.

Maybe the people "of color" want to think their needs are different because it was the white Europeans who enslaved or slaughtered their ancestors (and to some extent are still doing so, either literally or symbolically), but the Europeans were not alone in their guilt. Quite often they didn't even have to leave their ships to kidnap a cargo of Africans — because the people of some tribes were quite happy to sell the people of other tribes once they realized it was more profitable than killing them, enslaving them, or eating them. Africans had been enslaving each other long before the whites came along to buy slaves, just as earlier Europeans had enslaved each other, and just as many American Indians enslaved those of other tribes. The sins and crimes of white Europeans have been truly terrible, but they are not unique. With the possible exception of the Hopis and the Kalahari Bushmen, there has probably been no society in human history that hasn't practiced its own full quota of atrocities on someone.

The Chinese invented gunpowder, but the Europeans discovered how effective it was in killing people — just other Europeans, at first, but eventually it proved to be just as effective when used on blacks, reds, browns, and other non-whites. I don't think history would have been much different if the power of gunpowder had been discovered first by people of some other race; only the names (and colors) would be changed.

While we're remembering unpleasant facts, let's not forget that some of the rich and powerful plantation owners in the antebellum Southern states were free blacks, who bought and sold other blacks at the same auctions attended by the whites. The bad guys haven't always been white.

White Europeans and their descendants have certainly wreaked havoc around the world, but they have also produced some of the world's greatest philosophies, scientific advances, and humanitarian impulses — including the American ideals of "life, liberty, and the pursuit of happiness" for all people, and the premise that "all men are created equal."

Because those ideals have been only partially realized is certainly no reason to discard them and revert to ethnic tribalism. We have made greater advances toward achieving them in the past three decades than in the previous three centuries. Some newsletters threaten to undermine all the advances begun by Rosa Parks and Martin Luther King Jr. just as surely as a "whites-only" policy would. They are not "celebrating diversity," as they claim, but merely emphasizing racial differences and turning their backs on the greater similarities of people, regardless of race.

This is not multiculturalism, but racial tribalism, which has been around since before people climbed out of trees to live in caves. It probably began when Og and his mate Ooga discovered that a single mastodon wasn't enough to feed their entire village and all the people from the next valley, too. Homo wasn't very sapiens then, so Og said, "I know, let's just feed the people who look like us." Ooga said, "That's logical," and they began throwing rocks at the people with different hair, eyes, clothing, and skin color.

Only recently, at least ten thousand years later, have we begun to find ways of living without throwing rocks at each other, and now some of those who have been stoned the most want to revive the attitudes that led to the rock-throwing in the first place.

We don't have to be identical to communicate with each other, nor do we need to have the same skin color to understand each other. Just because North American society doesn't revolve around the cultures of ancient Africa or China or pre-Columbian America doesn't mean that people whose ancestors lived there are being denied the right to identify with any ethnicity they choose. Not many have had the advantage of an Alex Haley to trace their roots for them, so it really is a choice, and the choices must often be fairly general and made at random. Africa is a very large continent, and the people who lived there before the whites arrived were just as diversified in their cultures — not to mention many aspects of stature and physiognomy — as European whites were. After so many centuries, so much intermingling of various tribes, so much interracial mixing, how does one decide which ancestors to claim?

I think M.B. Tolson had at least part of the best answer: "I, as a black poet, have absorbed the Great Ideas of the Great White World, and interpreted them in the melting-pot idiom of my people. My roots are in Africa, Europe, and America."

Having grown up in the United States, but living now in Canada, Jean and I still prefer to celebrate the American Thanksgiving in November rather than the Canadian Thanksgiving in mid-October. We still "feel" American, and continue to identify more with American history and heritage than Canadian. Our Canadian neighbors don't share our preferences, or several other family and cultural traditions we have, but that doesn't mean they are trying in any way to deny our ethnicity, nor do they think we are interfering with theirs. We accept each other and get along well. Occasionally, we compare some of the differences in our backgrounds, but our similarities — working for a living, raising a family, trying to stay sane and healthy in an increasingly complex world — are far more important than our differences.

Some special-interest groups seem to be saying, as are people "of color" throughout society, that if the prevalent histories and popular culture don't reflect their roots and viewpoints, then their ethnicity is being denied. To a large extent, this has certainly been true in the past, but modern society had begun rectifying the injustice even before the current fad of decrying the absence in history books (and in literature in general) of blacks, Indians, Native Americans, Hispanics, women, and other minority groups. (I've always assumed that women comprise about half of the world's population, give or take a few thousand, but lately many of them seem to feel they're in a minority, a large percentage of whom are black belts in karate, so who am I to argue? You open a door for one of them and get a thumb in the eye for your trouble.)

The victors usually write the histories, along with their own rationalizations and self-justifications, which certainly promotes a certain degree of inaccuracy, but I doubt that the history books would be any more objective or accurate if they were written by the vanquished.

Most North American history in the last four hundred years has involved descendants of Western Europeans more than people from other places around the world, so it seems natural, even if not "right," for history to have been written from their viewpoint.

The treatment by the whites of the blacks, browns, reds, and yellows has certainly been despicable, but it's still a fact, whether "right" or "wrong," that the whites have usually been pretty much in charge of things. Scores of minorities, religious and philosophical as well as racial and cultural (and even including many with various sexual differences), want the history books rewritten from their viewpoints, and insist that books not written from their viewpoints are discriminatory and racist. The societies of Canada and the United States have become much more diverse, racially and ethnically, but their legal and cultural backgrounds are mostly derived from Western Europe, so most of the histories will probably continue to be written from that viewpoint, although many recent publications have made a serious effort to include experiences and viewpoints of the minorities.

Some changes aren't being made fast enough to suit some minorities, however, so they're writing their own history books — but instead of writing new histories with a more balanced picture of life as it really was, with a sincere attempt at objectivity, they're writing specialized black, red, Hispanic, and women's histories, to be studied separately, or even exclusively. Black students may now choose to study black history only — which may help them know and appreciate their own ancestral heritage, but will hardly give them a realistic picture of their actual roles in world history.

Women study women; Indians study Indians; and so on. Each special-interest group thinks it is studying the hub of history, rather than an important but smaller spoke.

Our history books should include the many achievements — in the arts, politics, science, sports, music, education, etc. — of minority peoples who have been skipped in most history books of the past, but without emphasis, or even undue mention, of the color or race of the achiever unless it was a significant factor in the achievement. It's significant that Jackie Robinson was the first black player in major-league baseball, but the race or color of players since then has been much less significant. To concentrate exclusively on the achievements of any special-interest group — as in Black History Month — is even more false and deceptive than the abridged histories that have been in use. Studying any subject out of context greatly reduces its meaning. Such "studies" are often intended to increase the "self-esteem" of the minority peoples who have been too much ignored — but anyone whose self-esteem is dependent on being submerged in a larger entity, whether it's a race, a nation, a religion, or a place of birth, needs a different kind of therapy than fictional history will give.

I don't need to wear my hair as my ancestors did, or worship the same gods or dance around the same fires, to know that I have a place in the universe. It pleases me to know that I had two ancestors who fought in the Civil War and five ancestors on the Mayflower, but that knowledge isn't a matter of "pride" for me anymore than the hanging of another ancestor as a horse thief is a matter of shame. My ancestors came from Europe, but I don't consider myself a "European-American"; I'm simply "American."

If the term "Afro-American" is used to identify blacks, what do we call a white person whose ancestors lived in Africa? Some American Indians — Native Americans — referred to blacks as "black white men," because they seemed so much alike except in skin color.

If students study only fragments of history, based on their own race, nationality, religion, or gender, society will become like scattered pieces of several jigsaw puzzles, growing steadily away from the American ideal of a cultural "melting pot" or the Canadian ideal of a cultural "mosaic." It will take more than all the king's horses and all the king's men to put the pieces together again. Separating into groups based on race or religion won't put the pieces together again, either.

I fully realize that racial minorities have problems with poverty, education, and health that much of the white population doesn't have — but those problems will never be solved by a renewed emphasis on racial and cultural differences. It was exactly that kind of paranoia and exclusionary thinking — on the part of many races and cultures — that led to the problems in the first place.

If "people of color" really want to be included in the larger home-school community, they certainly won't achieve it by withdrawing into self-conscious shells, or by wearing placards proclaiming, "We're different" and "Nobody understands us." They'll achieve it, and be warmly welcomed, when they realize that we are all different in many ways, but the goals and values that we, as parents and as home-schoolers, have in common — happy, well-educated children — are far more important than superficial differences such as skin color or racial origins.

You may not agree with Donn; that's all right. We all come into adulthood with problems and differences; with possible disabilities related to color, religion, race, poverty, or even wealth; or physical, mental, or emotional challenges. To me, it's how we deal with them, the choices we make as we grow up and out of them, as we strive to make ourselves better people, that counts. The only people we can change are ourselves. If the goal is equality, we must live it.

I recently watched the old musical *South Pacific*. It made a very strong point in the song "You've Got to Be Carefully Taught." For those of you who haven't seen this production, the song points out that prejudice is something that is absorbed when we are very young. If we want our children to grow up with an understanding of other peoples and cultures we need to start when they are very young. According to 2006 statistics the states of Maine and Vermont have the least racial and cultural diversity. This is also true of many regions in Canada. Good books can set the stage for tolerance and understanding. It is only when we are able to embrace views that differ from our own that we can begin to grow.

Books and Resources That Help Break Barriers

From *When All You've Ever Wanted Isn't Enough,* by Harold Kushner: "Jean Piaget was a Swiss psychologist who was fascinated by the question of how children grow mentally. At what age do they start to understand concepts of "mine" and "yours"? What do they understand about time and space, about truth and make-believe at various ages? ... *The Moral Judgment of the Child* deals with a child's concept of right and wrong, permitted and forbidden."

Piaget found that children go through stages in discovering just how and why rules work. Very young children accept rules as coming from a "higher" authority that is not questioned. As adolescents they realize that not only do the rules come from people but that they have a choice to follow the rules or to break them; they can make these choices for themselves. They strive to understand the reasons for the rules and make their own decisions.

An extension of this is our attitude toward rules and all authority. As youngsters we feel weak and unable to question rules that are given to us. Kushner goes on to say: "A 'good' child is not necessarily a generous or morally sensitive child but a docile and obedient one. At this stage, we have difficulty accepting the idea that other people, other cultures, other religions have different rules than we do. If we are right and they are different, they must be wrong." I think this a very astute observation and one we must be aware of as parents if we are to help our children grown into the ever-changing multicultural world.

TEACHING TOLERANCE is an organization devoted to the abolition of prejudice remaining in our society. They follow Gandhi's idea that "if we are to reach real peace in the world, we shall have to begin with children." For materials, write to Teaching Tolerance, c/o Southern Poverty Law Center, 400 Washington Ave., Montgomery, AL 36104, or visit them on the web at www.tolerance.org. The site offers discussion ideas and many useful and thoughtful materials you can download.

***PEOPLES OF THE WORLD,* by Roma Trundle.** Colorful introduction to the customs, traditions, languages, and beliefs of different cultures around the world. Topics include foods, crafts, folk dances, and celebrations. Detailed illustrations throughout, with many specific examples of customs, such as the Japanese bow of greeting, the body paint of the Nuba tribe, Indonesian batik, and how to wrap a sari. The major religions of the world are described in simple terms. Discover what makes our various cultures different and what we have in common.

***THE ATLAS OF WORLD CULTURES,* by Brunetto Chiarelli, illustrated by Paola Ravaglia.** Open this oversized book and you'll find the flags of the world in bright color on the endpapers. The contents are much like any other atlas of cultures, with maps, charts, pictures, and information. What sets this one apart from the rest are the special-interest sections on language and writing, religions, food and costumes, art, dance and song, and cultures in conflict. It's more than a reference book to be pulled off the shelf occasionally; there are so many illustrations of people actively engaged in daily life that it's fun to just open it randomly and browse. I like the fact that the book was originally published in Italy. And guess what? There isn't a picture of a white North American male on the front cover!

***LET'S CELEBRATE! CANADA'S SPECIAL DAYS,* by Caroline Parry.** Parry, a well-known folklorist, has packed 250 pages with information, cartoons, pictures, jokes, games, crafts, science experiments, poems, special activities, and the history of more than 250 special days of celebration. As diverse as Canada, with something for everyone to celebrate. This book is so culturally diverse that I really didn't want to put in the subtitle for fear only Canadians would be interested. You don't have to be Canadian to enjoy this book. It will be just as useful and fun in the U.S. or anywhere. Learn about Chinese birthdays, two-season calendars, the winter solstice, Boxing Day, Black History Month, Lent, Turkish Children's Day, Coptic New Year, Oktoberfest, and more. For all ages. From the book: "Knock, knock! Who's there? Snow. Snow who? Snow idea, have you?"

"OH, IT'S NOT SEGREGATION"

Can an all-white student group at the University of Pennsylvania keep black students out? Oh, yes. A black woman was barred from a meeting of White Women Against Racism because the presence of a black woman would make whites uncomfortable as they examined their racist ways.
— *U.S. News & World Report,* February 12, 1996

***FREEDOM CHALLENGE: AFRICAN AMERICAN HOMESCHOOLERS,* edited by Grace Llewellyn.** If you're African American and having doubts that homeschooling will work for you because you're black, this is the book to help you see that it will — and very well. True stories written by those who have lived them.

What Do I Call Myself?

A while ago I read a short article in *Reader's Digest* by Keith B. Richburg, author of *Out of America*. It was about his time as a journalist posted in Africa, a time when he confronted some truths about the birthplace of his ancestors — and about himself. He wrote: "I do not hate Africa or the Africans. What I hate is the senseless brutality, the way repressive systems strip decent people of their dignity.

"I am an American, a black American, and I feel no connection to this strange and violent place.

"You see? I just wrote 'black American.' I couldn't even bring myself to write 'African-American.' Is there anything really 'African' left in the descendents of slaves who made that torturous journey across the Atlantic? Are white Americans whose ancestors sailed across the same ocean 'English-Americans' or 'Dutch-Americans'? Haven't the centuries erased these ancient connections, so that we are now simply 'Americans'?"

SKIPPING STONES. This is the best multicultural magazine for kids that I've ever seen. It is full of excellent and exciting prose and poetry by and about children from every imaginable background. There are book and video reviews; contributions from city and country kids telling of their hopes and dreams, their living conditions, and the problems they cope with on a daily basis; pen pals from around the world; bilingual pages; photos by and about kids; and more. Exciting! Low-income subscription allowance and multiple copy discount; write for information. Sample copy $5 (and there's a free one on the website); subscription $25 (and worth it). Skipping Stones, P.O. Box 3939, Eugene, OR 97403-0939; www.skippingstones.org.

A quote from a reader: "I'm so glad you are a non-Christian group. I have nothing against Christianity, but I dislike exclusive special-interest groups. The special-interest groups would make more sense if they didn't filter their learning through a narrow point of view and those that were interested in learning about them could be included. I feel that home-schoolers have many more ideas and ideals in common to share than differences. The world is too small to wear blinders."

In the end, we will conserve only what we love,
we will love only what we understand,
we will understand only what we are taught.
— From *The Diversity of Life,* by Edward O. Wilson

A couple of years ago I watched a TV special on PBS about a program called Seeds of Peace, founded by John Wallach, in Androscoggin, Maine. This camp has many activities common to summer camps as we know them, but with a difference. The young people (teens) who come are from countries around the world where there is long-standing violent conflict: Bosnia and Herzegovina, Egypt, Israel, Palestine, Jordan, etc. By agreement, and with the endorsement of the heads of these troubled governments, these children come to look for ways to help themselves and their countries find and build peaceful solutions. The purpose of Seeds of Peace is to help these young people move past their prejudices, to see their "enemies" as people, to see that as people they have much in common, including the dream of living in a peaceful society where death and destruction are not a daily fact of life. Seeds of Peace reaches for this goal through activities and discussions facilitated by highly trained personnel.

These young people come to Seeds of Peace with all the hatred and prejudice their societies have conditioned them to feel. They are armed with all the political, racial, or religious propaganda they have acquired since birth to support their point of view. I was going to say the propaganda inherent in their culture, but that is not true. It is not the cultures that hate. It is individuals, and it is conditioning fed by misinformation that breeds hatred and prejudice.

At first the participants begin with very strong feelings of cultural identity. They don't want to be separated from their countrymen. As "enemies" they don't know how to play together with those from other groups. They are suspicious. As the program progresses they begin to talk in small groups that are carefully monitored by the staff. The talk quickly becomes an argument. Everyone has a chance to voice his thoughts and opinions. You can see that at first it is very hard for these kids to sit and listen to someone else say why he and his country are right and the other wrong. The discussion gets heated, they yell at each other, some cry, and after a while they begin to really listen to each other. I was stunned by the emotion that finally drew these kids together in their first common bond. It wasn't love or caring about each other or a desire for peace or political solutions. It was the sharing of personal pain and fear. These are old young faces and they do not love each other at this point, but they all share the pain that comes with the loss of loved ones and the fear they have lived with all their lives. I am humbled. We are so innocent living here in North America.

Once the participants have established a common bond in spite of their differences, activities continue in a carefully planned progression. The campers begin to understand each other. They learn to play games together, they talk a lot, and they begin to make friends with those outside their own group.

The PBS program showed the last evening at Seeds of Peace. Along with a talent show and awards, the kids talked about what they had learned and what they wanted to achieve when they returned home. It was clear they had learned it is not the difference in cultures that creates and breeds violence and prejudice; it is the difference in the "facts" given by the media, it is the self-serving motives of the politicians, and it is never being allowed to see the "enemy" as an individual. Through the time spent at camp they found that as people, not cultures or countries, they had common dreams. These young people, maybe the leaders of the future, left with a determination to heal the differences wherever they could, to find ways to seek peace, with a place for all, because behind all the differences, they were finally able to see each other as human beings, each unique, each with something special to share. These young people found that after all was said and argued, they did have a common goal. They would all like to live in a peaceful place, without fear, and to create understanding, because fear and hatred cannot coexist with understanding.

In Germany they came first for the Communists, and I didn't speak up
because I wasn't a Communist.
Then they came for the Jews, and I didn't speak up
because I wasn't a Jew.
Then they came for the trade unionists, and I didn't speak up
because I wasn't a trade unionist.
Then they came for the Catholics, and I didn't speak up
because I was a Protestant.
Then they came for me, and by that time no one was left to speak up.
— Pastor Martin Niemöller

The Media

***THE LORDS OF THE GLOBAL VILLAGE,* by Ben H. Bagdikian.** This lead article in a special issue of *The Nation* assesses the alarming growth of the communications corporations; the shrinking of the media universe; and the consequent threat to freedom and diversity in global news, information, and culture. Meet a gallery of media barons such as Rupert Murdoch and Reinhard Mohn, who amass, homogenize, dominate, and devour media corporations around the world. "A handful of mammoth private organizations have begun to dominate the world's mass media," says the article. "Most of them confidently announce that … they — five to ten corporate giants — will control most of the world's important newspapers, magazines, books, broadcast stations, movies, recordings, and videocassettes. Moreover, each of these planetary corporations plans to gather under its control every step in the information process, from creation of 'the product' to all the various means by which modern technology delivers media messages to the public — news, information, ideas, entertainment, and public culture." Very scary and thought-provoking. Essential reading if you're concerned about freedom of communication and ideas. Inquire about the current price and order by title from The Nation — Reprints, 33 Irving Place, New York, NY 10003.

Donn wrote that fifteen years ago, and it is becoming more of a reality every day. The growth of the Internet has helped with the dissemination of information, but it is not nearly enough of a breakthrough to have much effect.

I've watched the book publishing industry over the last five years. You still see a wide variety of publishing houses listed, but if you look a bit further you quickly notice that they are not all independently owned. Many — way too many — are owned by very large national or international corporations. It is limiting what you will find in your local bookstore and the quality of the mass-market books available. The current trend in publishing seems to be to publish what the public will consume — and discard (e.g., romance novels and adventure thrillers) — rather than books of enduring value. I think many publishers choose new books to publish that are about on the level of the majority of TV programs — and most of those are not worth watching.

I urge you to support your small, local, independent bookseller. They will carry titles you will not find in Wal-Mart, Barnes and Noble, or Borders, booksellers that base their businesses on mass-market sales rather on the quality of content.

FOREIGN LANGUAGES

Learn to Talk Your Way Around the World —or to Your Neighbor

The best way to learn a language is to grow up with it. The next-best way, we're often told, is to live in the country in which the desired language is spoken. I think the next-best way is to live in the country and use some good books, tapes, or other study guides. I became fairly fluent in Spanish while living in Mexico, but if I hadn't studied the grammar and vocabulary at the same time, my Spanish would have been limited to that of the uneducated poor people with whom I spent most of my time. The same is usually true even in learning one's native language: If one's family and everyday associates speak ungrammatically, one's own speech will be the same unless an effort is made to improve it through study and practice. If you want to learn a language but don't expect to be living where it's spoken, or you want to learn some of it before you go, there are many different ways of learning: tapes, phrase books, classroom studies, and so on. Finding someone in your community to act as a mentor is an excellent way to learn a language and make new friends. We've investigated and tried several methods, and we believe the selections we've made are among the best language-learning aids available.

I've considered some of the new computer software programs for learning languages and found that although you can hear native-born speakers, the sound isn't as clear as on an audiocassette, CD, videotape or DVD. Although some of the software came highly recommended, I found myself getting numb after the novelty wore off, and my eyes didn't like staring at the monitor. I wouldn't want my children using software for learning a language, even though the multimedia effects are quite good.

Cathy traveled and lived in Mexico for several months after high school. She started studying Spanish at home with the book *Madrigal's Magic Key to Spanish* and used an advanced cassette course. She didn't finish either the book or the course before she left, but these resources gave her a basic working vocabulary and an idea of the grammar. She learned enough to have a great time and make some very good friends.

Donn, on his first trip to Mexico, assumed that there would be English speakers on the bus between Texas and Mexico City to ease his language transition — but there weren't. There are many words in Spanish that are similar to English, requiring just a change in accent. He found that the little bus-stop stores offered drinks for sale — Coca-Cola, various beers, and coffee — all easy to say and all easy to drink. It was a bumpy road, and it wasn't very long before he realized that his phrase book lacked something very important. You can pantomime many things, but have you ever had to pantomime, in public, "Where is the bathroom?" There is no substitute for a good bilingual dictionary. Don't leave home without it!

If you are beginning language study with young children you will find that all the beginning programs are incomplete. Your kids will want words that are not on the tapes or in the books. You'll want a good bilingual dictionary: one that goes from English to your target language and from the target language to English. You will also be better prepared to help your kids if you study along with them or use a more advanced course at the same time. It will give you a better understanding of the pronunciation and grammatical construction. I think everyone will benefit from using more than one program for young learners. The variety will increase vocabulary and decrease the chance of boredom stemming from listening to the same thing repeatedly. The more exposure you get to the sound of the language the better your ears will hear it, and your pronunciation will improve.

On the very large North American continent, we happen to live in relative isolation, with the exception of Mexico to our south. Europeans have a better chance of exposure to other languages because of their geography. In our quickly shrinking and changing world a second language is a real advantage. I've watched Derek's daughter become bilingual. She was a little slower learning to talk, but she grew from infancy hearing two languages because her babysitter spoke mostly in Spanish. She now switches languages easily depending on whom she is talking to. I expect Susan's son will grow up with two, if not three, languages. If you already speak a second language I encourage you to speak it to your children from the time they are born. Statistics show that those who speak two languages can learn a third or fourth language more easily.

A mama cat was playing with her kittens in the back yard. A dog came along and started to bark, scaring the kittens. The mama cat barked right back and the dog ran away. The kittens were surprised to hear their mama barking. The mama cat said, "I always told you it was important to learn a second language."

— My Uncle Al, who travels a lot!

Most of our recommended resources are up on the website, but there are a few I don't want anyone to miss.

BABYLON (www.babylon.com) is downloadable software that works as an instant language translator and dictionary. The program works by loading a large dictionary onto your hard drive. Add-ons make the translation/dictionary program work in more languages than you'll ever need to know. Babylon also offers special programs for kids. Very reasonably priced too.

Just a quick note about the most widely advertised children's language programs:

Having looked at many, I much prefer the BBC's **MUZZY** program to Rosetta Stone. Muzzy was fun to watch, and somehow they managed to get in enough repetition — *without being boring* — to make the vocabulary stick in my mind. This was a remarkable experience. I tried this with their French program because I can't spell well in English and French spelling boggles my mind so I have a built in resistance to it, and I still learned French from their program.

If you want extensive language materials or literature in a foreign language, I recommend writing to **CALLIOPE BOOKS,** Route 3, Box 3395, Saylorsburg, PA 18353. Their extensive catalog has learning materials and foreign-language books at all levels.

I've seen a lot of attractive ads for the **LEARNABLES**. Check www.learnables.com, 800-237-1830. They offer Bible stories, readable after level 2, but they are extra and not part of the curriculum.

Check out the website **WWW.SPANISHWORKBOOKS.COM** for Spanish workbooks, puzzles, and vocabulary building once you've gotten started with your own materials.

***LATIN FOR CHILDREN,* Primers A,B,C,** with a book about logic and a workbook. You may have seen the ads for these. They seem to be working hard to market these primers. You'll find these books fairly well organized and sometimes entertaining. These primers have a useful pronunciation key in the front of each book. There are regular spaces for practice and opportunity for reviewing material covered at the end of each section and at the end of the book. I find it nice that the English derivatives are regularly linked to their Latin roots. A high point for me was the glossary of useful famous Latin sayings in the appendix of Primer C. There is a website students can use if they are interested.

I think you may find the pages cramped at times, with too much information. Sometimes the illustrations don't make any sense to me. You may not find this so. There are more military references than I like. A friend who knows Latin better than I do found some confusion in the translation in spots and a few misspellings. She also felt these books best for self-motivated mid-teens.

Now that I've written all that I'm not sure if I'm recommending this or not. Mostly I am, but with caveats.

CONCORDIA LANGUAGE VILLAGES is a unique camp designed for youngsters ages 7 to 18 who would enjoy living in a camp atmosphere and learning a foreign language. It's all done "immersion" style. They offer 13 languages. Contact: 901 8th St. S., Moorhead, MN 56562; 800-222-4750 or 218-299-3807; clvweb.cord.edu.

Here's a plug for learning a second language and the scoop on the call from the ambulance (see the "High School" chapter, page 252). The call came from Derek, who was working in Quebec. He called to say that he had finished up a training ride and was sitting on a horse talking to its owner, and something spooked the horse. It reared, Derek came off, and the horse fell on his leg. He heard his leg break. I'm not sure how he managed to think enough to call me, but I'm grateful he did — and it was from the ambulance. He was in enough pain that after telling me he had a broken leg and trying to assure me it was going to be all right he gave the phone to a friend, who gave me the name and phone number of the hospital. Thoughtful.

While I waited what I considered a reasonable amount of time for him to get processed through the ER and have a leg set, I spent the intervening time practicing my limited French and decided I'd best just ask, in French, to speak to someone who spoke English. I'm not kidding when I say my French is limited. You have to keep in mind that this was at a time when Quebec was determined that everyone there must speak only French. (Once Derek rode the bus home to bilingual New Brunswick, and on the ride back to Quebec the driver pulled the bus off to the side of the road before entering Quebec to ask if anyone had any questions to be asked in English, because once he crossed into Quebec he was allowed to speak only French. Another time when we were driving through Quebec and stopped for gas and directions we encountered a different attitude toward the English-French debate. The customer at the counter ahead of us, who was speaking English, got progressively louder and louder because the man waiting on him didn't seem to understand what he was saying. Finally the man gave up and left. Donn, who knew about six words in French, stepped up to the counter and said, "Bonsoir. Parlez-vous anglais?" The man behind the counter put on a really big grin, shrugged his shoulders, and said, "But of course!" He, like so many other Quebecers, just wanted his language preference acknowledged.)

Where was I? Oh — I'm not kidding when I say my French is limited. I dialed the number I had been given for the hospital, and a woman answered with a spate of French I couldn't understand, so I tried to interrupt her. That didn't work. When she ran down I asked, in French, if anyone spoke English. More French. I was trying very hard not to get upset. I tried again, and she interrupted me with more unintelligible French, and we did that dance several times. All the while I'm getting more and more upset and afraid she is trying to tell me very bad news. Finally the woman gave in with some English and told me I was connected to the Canadian Tire hardware store. Wrong number. Yes, I did finally get the hospital and found someone who kindly spoke English to me. Horses aren't all glamour, and second languages really are advantageous.

A note from one of our readers had this story: A linguistics professor was lecturing his class one day. "In English," he said, "a double negative forms a positive. In some languages, though, such as Russian, a double negative is still a negative. However, there is no language wherein a double positive can form a negative. "

A voice from the back of the room piped up: "Yeah, right."

MORE EXPENSIVE BY THE DOZEN

Rural New Brunswick is very similar to the Vermont of my boyhood (in the '40s and early '50s), and Canada is pretty much what the United States would have become without the Boston Tea Party. The majority in both countries speak some form of English, and tabloids in both countries entertain us weekly with the latest adventures of British royalty. (It puzzles us sometimes that the longer we live in Canada the more American we feel, but we have a nice home and good neighbors, and we live just a few miles from the United States border, so we exercise our Americanism mostly on the frequent visits to our post office box in Maine.)

One of the more significant differences we've found between the two countries is that Americans still believe (or so they claim) in free enterprise, while Canada has "marketing agencies," which establish quotas and set prices and in many other ways regulate the production and sale of milk, eggs, lumber, and countless other consumer goods, all of which may be enterprising but is certainly not free. You don't cut costs by increasing the number of middlemen.

Government agencies often do funny things, but that doesn't mean their actions are humorous, and sometimes the public is severely taxed to find a single smile in a shovelful of government edicts. ("Shovelful," of course, isn't a metric term, and is therefore probably illegal in Canada now, but at present I can't think of a polite metric form of measurement to use for political excretions.)

Take for example, the Canadian Egg Marketing Agency. We all know that Saudi Arabia is one of the poorest nations in the world, so no sensible person would have protested a few years ago when the Egg Marketing Agency sold that country millions of Canadian eggs for half the price Canadians had to pay. It was only fair, of course. After all, don't we always get their oil for half price?

When one of the Agency's shipments to Saudi Arabia of four million eggs (or 333,333 dozen, with four left over) got sucked into the twilight zone by high-seas hijinks, who could blame the Saudi Arabians for being reluctant to pay the bill? After all, the CEMA was charging them five cents per egg, or 60 cents a dozen. That was $200,000 for the whole kit and cockadoodle, which must be nearly half a week's wages for some of those middle-class oil dealers.

The Marketing Agency lost the eggs, and the Saudis refused to pay for them, so the Agency charged the Canadian public by raising the price of eggs sold at home. A neat solution to a problem that might have left the Agency with egg on its collective face.

According to one of its humorous — I mean, funny — press releases at the time, the purpose of the Egg Marketing Agency is the "orderly marketing of egg production at a fair price to both producer and consumer." In line with that purpose, the Agency offered farmers a price increase of one to three cents per dozen to help meet rising costs of feed and labor. (This was one of the points in the bill I sent to the Agency, which I'll explain in greater detail later on.)

Next, faced with more eggs than they could lose at sea, and fearing that the price per dozen on a glutted market might drop as low for Canadians as they had set it for the Saudi Arabians, the Agency's managers played with their pocket calculators and found another logical solution. They offered poultry farmers $2.07 per hen to kill off one and a half million laying hens, and to refrain from raising more hens for sixteen weeks.

My own calculator, which I wear under my hat, ran that through twice and came up with the news that the Agency was sticking taxpayers for $3,105,000 for eggs they would never eat, in order to make them pay more than 10 cents for each egg they did eat.

Naturally, I could see great possibilities in this for myself, and I went to discuss it with the Brook Farm Ladies Aid and Missionary Society, which lives in our barn and gives us an average of 20 eggs a day. The society has one rooster, named Hamlet, but he doesn't get out much, so I do most of the missionary work. Just to make it proper, I sent away $3 and received a card in the mail announcing that I am now fully ordained and should be addressed as "Reverend," and I have full authority to preside over marriages, baptisms, and funerals. So far, I have exercised that authority over 18 marriages (all bigamous, I'm afraid) and three funerals, all in my henhouse. I have yet to conduct a baptism, although I was surprised one day by a hen sticking her head into my boot, and I accidentally poured a bucket of water over two others.

When I told the ladies about the Marketing Agency's patriotic offer, they laughed so hard that one of them nearly turned inside out. Apparently it's difficult to live with a prolapsed intestine, which accounted for the first $2.07 I thought the Agency should pay me, and I went back to the house right away to prepare a bill, along with a letter to explain, itemize, and justify the total amount of $7.21 for which I finally billed the Agency.

I showed another hen, I wrote, what happens when the ax meets the chopping block, making another $2.07 the Agency owed me.

Matilda, with white flecks on her red feathers and beady black eyes, was a cute little thing, and Hamlet had had his gimlet eyes on her for some time. Whenever he tried to show his affection, however, she would glance shyly at the nest of eggs and say, "Please, dear, not in front of the children." So Hamlet took cold showers (not under my baptismal authority) and waited for us to collect the eggs.

One day, Hamlet fluttered up to the top roost for a midday nap and was perched there, like King Kong on the Empire State Building, when Matilda wandered in from the yard. Matilda perceived a delicious bug crawling on the floor, and Hamlet perceived an opportunity.

Hamlet has responded to countless magazine ads that promised to enlarge his biceps, triceps, forceps, and brain capacity. The courses have done wonders for him — all but the last. Nearly two feet tall at the shoulders and built like a ham, Hamlet is a 97-pound idiot.

He leaped off the roost, travelling eight feet out and six feet down, and landed squarely on Matilda's back. She surrendered meekly, and Hamlet bragged for weeks about his brilliant strategy.

What he didn't realize was that Matilda's neck was broken, making it a total of $6.21 the Agency owed me.

With an average of 20 eggs a day, our hens give us about 600 eggs a month. That's 50 dozen, believe it or not, with which we could help to glut the market if we didn't use them to glut ourselves. (I hasten to tell you that this was before our kids grew up and flew the coop.) By eating all our eggs — fried; scrambled; boiled; and in bread, cookies, and doughnuts — instead of selling them, we were doing our part to help the Agency inflate the market. This was a hardship we would gladly endure if it would help the national economy.

However, we still had to provide feed and labor, and here I called the Agency's attention to its offer of one to three cents per dozen.

My third-grade teacher used to insist that we can't multiply apples by oranges, but the government frequently proves that much of our education is worthless, so I cheerfully followed the Agency's example, as follows: The average of one and three is two, and two cents multiplied by 50 dozen equals 100 cents, which I rounded off to an even dollar.

"There you have it," I wrote. "My bill for this month: $6.21 for the demise of three hens, and $1.00 for grain fed to the remaining hens to help them produce eggs, which I promise not to sell — total, $7.21."

"Please remit promptly," I said, "as additional billing will increase my operating expenses, making me an even greater burden on the taxpayers."

You think the U.S. mail is slow sometimes? You should try Canada Post. I sent my bill to Ottawa six years ago, and I'm still waiting for a reply.

P.S. This story was written in 1991. It's now 2000 and still there has been no response. It seems Canada Post gets slower every year. Should I now bill the Agency for interest?

P.P.S. As of January 2009, I think that by the time I get a check in the mail I can use the money and accumulated interest to retire.

MATHEMATICS

ATTITUDES — NEEDS
A CONFESSION — RESOURCES

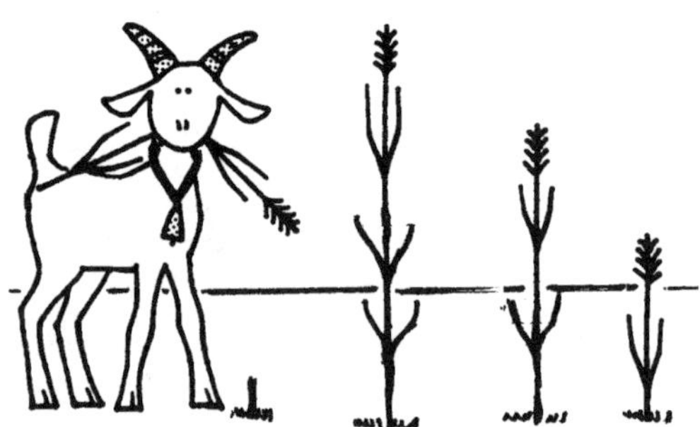

I planted a tree that was 8 inches tall. At the end of the first year it was 12 inches tall; at the end of the second year it was 18 inches tall; and at the end of the third year it was 27 inches tall. How tall was it at the end of the fourth year?

When I was a high school junior, in Brattleboro, Vermont, I wanted to take a course in auto mechanics.

"You can't," the guidance director told me. "That isn't part of the college prep course."

"But I don't plan to go to college," I said. "I plan to travel and work and study."

He chuckled. We argued. The guidance director had the final word, of course: "Your IQ and your aptitude tests indicate that you belong in the college prep program. I'm sure you'll come to your senses about college when the time comes."

Although I think college is fine for those who want or need it, I didn't change my mind. I traveled and I worked, and I have never attended college (except for a brief summer workshop at the University of Denver). When another institution asked for my high school transcript, the same guidance director wrote in the margin, "Too much a nonconformist to ever be happy." The split infinitive was his. I concluded that he knew as much about English as I knew about auto mechanics. The difference was that he was employed as an English teacher as well as a guidance director, and I have never been employed as an auto mechanic. I can change a tire, but I didn't learn how to in high school.

I did learn in school that a quadrilateral is a parallelogram if the diagonals bisect each other. I also learned how to find FH and DF if AB, CD, EF, and GH are parallel and AC and CE and EG and BD each equal 3. I've read that everything we ever learn or experience is tucked away somewhere in a dusty corner of the mind, and I don't doubt it, but you may be surprised to learn that since I graduated from high school I have had neither reason nor desire to find FH and DF. Most of the quadrilaterals I've encountered since then have been school officials, and their purposes are usually perpendicular to mine.

So much for at least half of the math I learned in twelve years of schooling. Hypnosis might revive my memory of it, just as it could help me remember the first time I fell off a bike, but I'm content to leave both memories buried in cobwebs.

If you like math, or expect to have a good use for it, then study it. We all use math in our daily lives, directly and personally; without it, our lives would be very different and probably difficult. We need math to bake a cake, plan a shopping list, or balance a checkbook. Jean and the kids and I built our own house, doing all the work ourselves, and we did a lot of measuring and calculating, both in building the house and in buying materials for it.

Most of the math we used, however, and most of that which I use daily, is no more advanced than simple long division, which is usually mastered by the fifth grade. I use a little plane geometry and, occasionally, some very elementary solid geometry (how big a hayloft do I need to hold three tons of hay?).

If I were suddenly confronted with a need to find FH and DF, I'm sure I could learn quickly how to do so, even if I had never once learned it. The desire to learn is the greatest incentive.

Most school students, if asked why they study math (or most other subjects), will answer, "It's required" or "So I can pass the exams." Neither reason is enough. Over a twelve-year period, first grade through high school, most students will spend an hour a day, not including homework, for about 200 days of the year, trying to learn various forms of arithmetic and mathematics. That's over 2,400 hours out of a lifetime. (See how easily I figured that out?) Will the information studied be used half that many hours after school? It's not a bad exchange if the information and skill are of real interest or use. Some people enjoy math, just as others enjoy word puzzles; others may not enjoy it, but know or expect that it will be of practical use to them in a chosen career, such as chemistry, astronomy, or architecture. I have no argument against studying advanced math for those who like it or need it, but to spend over a hundred twenty-four-hour days studying something only to pass a series of tests is a ridiculous waste of time and energy.

A common argument in favor of math, with or without practical application, is that "it develops skills of reasoning" — that is, a logical approach to problem-solving. That's undoubtedly true, but is it the only exercise — or even the best — that develops reasoning? Mathematicians have no monopoly on the ability to perceive, consider, compare, evaluate, extrapolate, hypothesize, and reach conclusions. These processes are frequently related to math, but never limited to it.

Author Henry Miller once wrote, "Anyone can write; a writer can't do anything else." The same might be said of math and mathematicians. For those of us who need and use math only occasionally, just a few basics are necessary. If I need to calculate the stress of a certain weight on a ten-foot 2x4, I can easily find the appropriate formula, or even a chart or graph with the answer already given. An understanding of elementary mathematics is very desirable, perhaps necessary, in daily life, but tedious memorization of principles and facts that I'll probably never use, and in which I have no interest, is neither reasonable nor logical.

For many years, we tried several standard math textbooks, at all grade levels, and found partial satisfaction only after two of our children had grown up and left home. Most math books seem to have been written by people who know a great deal about mathematics but very little about children or about the learning process. Before we found a few existing books that make math enjoyable, understandable, and useful, we tortured our kids and ourselves with the same textbooks used in the public schools. Like most parents (and teachers), we believed that math was a necessary evil; that, no matter how unpleasant it might be, it must be mastered — "because someday you'll need it." The standard

textbooks — being unpleasant, illogical, and monotonous — reinforced that belief. For more years than I want to admit, we didn't stop to realize that the only use Jean and I had for most of the math we had learned in school was to try to teach it to our kids. In the normal scheme of things, they would someday pass it on to their own kids, and so on. The sins of the fathers are visited upon the children.

I don't know why it took us so much longer to break away from conventional study of math than from most other forms of conventional study. Like many other home-schoolers, we believed the public system was wrong or inadequate, but we lacked enough confidence in ourselves to reject it; we were afraid that if our kids didn't measure up to the standards of the public schools, they would be at a disadvantage in later life. Gradually, we realized that just the opposite is true. By adhering to public school standards (not only in math), we were holding our kids back. We directed so much of their energy into the study of ordinary math — "to develop skills of reasoning" — that real reasoning skills were being stunted or warped.

"Laziness in doing a stupid thing," said the High Lama of Shangri-La in James Hilton's *Lost Horizon,* "can be a virtue."

Sometimes, the study of math became so frustrating and unpleasant, for all of us, that we just dropped it for a few days, or even weeks, and spent the time with other studies. We noticed that the kids were still using math frequently — in cooking, drawing spaceships, feeding the hens and cow, making dresses, calculating their babysitting earnings, or buying material for a new blouse. We stopped worrying.

Still, we thought, they had learned the basics of the math they were using very painfully, by being beaten over the head daily with standard textbooks. There must be a better way. Once we were open to better approaches, we found several — the best of which is the use of tools and materials of ordinary daily life.

The first step to a better approach was a change of attitude. We had to realize that a child's age has no bearing on the level or degree of math (or reading, or writing) he can or should master. If it doesn't come easily, there is no need to push and no need to worry; it will come sometime.

At age nine, Derek was bored and angered by his fourth-grade arithmetic book. We gave him a math kit — protractor, compass, and ruler — and turned him loose with a high school plane geometry book. He asked a few questions and we helped him sort out a few beginning principles. He drew spaceships, inside and out, with wonderful complexity and precision. Although he continued to bristle at the thought of the fourth-grade math, he could measure angles, bisect lines, and correctly construct complex geometric designs. He could also read and follow a cooking recipe, measure the pig's grain, and draw accurate plans of his room. We didn't push him, and we didn't worry. We knew that Derek might not go back to simple multiplication and division for many years, or he might return to them a week later. When he felt in need of them, he would study them, and learning them would be like learning to fry an egg after mastering soufflé. It was a number of years before he went back to the "beginning" and filled in the gaps. What was lost?

Suppose walking or talking were taught in the same way math and reading are usually taught: "Dear Parent, Your son/daughter is not achieving the level of Walking Competency that is expected for his/her age. He/she is now 13.8 months old and should have completed Level 7.9, but still crawls on Level 5.4. I am sorry to report that he/she may be Walking Disabled. I will place him/her in the Bluebird Section for Slow Walkers, but I think he/she may need Special Assistance. Sincerely, His/Her Teacher."

Children begin counting very early. They like to count — fingers, toes, cars, leaves, spoons, stones, steps, anything. By the age of three or four, most children will have gained several mathematical skills, and will enjoy using them. By the age of six, if they go to public schools, or if they are pushed too much at home, they will have lost much of their skill and all of their interest.

At sixteen, Cathy was taking a high school correspondence course, besides working with our own materials. She worked at her own speed, sending in completed lessons for grading. When she began algebra, it was clear sailing at first, but less than halfway through the course, it became increasingly difficult. Dad to the rescue, confident that he could recall enough from years ago to smooth out the wrinkles. Looking through her textbook, I quickly realized that this was an entirely different animal from the one I had struggled with for two years before going on to struggle for another two years with plane and solid geometry. I passed all four courses, and that was back in the days when students didn't pass unless they actually earned passing grades, but it was more through the patience and hard work of my teachers than through any great understanding on my part. Cathy's dislike of math was not acquired; it was in my genes, and she inherited it from me. (I studied biology, too!) It didn't help me that her book was titled Modern Algebra. What was wrong with the old algebra? I put myself through a quick refresher course, from the beginning, skimming and sorting until I felt I could handle it — with a lot of luck. Cathy and I worked together on the lessons and problems. It was still very difficult, for both of us. We weren't enjoying it, and were doing it only because it was a required subject in the college prep course. Cathy and I were both frustrated and bored by this modern algebra. One of the simpler problems ran something like this:

$$\frac{3a^3b^2 + 15a^3b^2}{2ab^2} + \frac{4a^6b^3 - 10a^6b^3}{2a^4b^3} = ?$$

I'm sure it's easy for some, and I'm even willing to admit that some people might enjoy playing with it. I'd rather split wood or shovel manure. If Cathy or we could anticipate any need for such math in her future, we would have continued struggling with it, but we knew she was very unlikely to pursue a career or way of life requiring the use of a subject that was so distasteful to her. Why waste so much time and energy? The only reason seemed to be that it was required as part of the college prep course; it was required because many colleges required it, and many colleges required it because they had always required it — or just because, that's why.

Math stretches the brain and gives you new reasoning skills. With the new reasoning skills I gained from this course, I came up with a brilliant solution: ask the school to change Cathy's course from College Prep to General High School. It was done, and with no arguments from the guidance director. In place of algebra, to obtain the necessary credits Cathy chose general math, more of the physical and social sciences, and more literature. She enjoyed them all. We both kept our sanity. It was an excellent exchange.

My mathematical aptitudes and attitudes embarrass me a little (but not very much). I think it's obvious that the universe and nearly all things in it (the exceptions include most math books) are constructed and governed by very precise principles, all of which can be or someday will be expressed in mathematical terms — which is, perhaps, a step toward understanding. However, I think it is just as true that mathematics is only one of many ways to view and understand the universe. A poet or mystic may understand as much as a mathematician; the biggest difference may be that it's easier for the mathematician to communicate what he has learned — but with the significant drawback that only other mathematicians can understand what he's saying.

There are a few fortunate exceptions.

Stephen Hawking, perhaps the most brilliant physicist and mathematician in the world's history, insists that even the most profound discoveries and theories about the universe can be expressed in non-mathematical terms. His book *A Brief History of Time* (see "Science") seems to be evidence of this.

We have found several basic arithmetic and math books that not only develop necessary skills and knowledge, but are actually fun to read and use, thus removing most of the drudgery. Unfortunately, a few things — e.g., basic multiplication tables, and deciding which procedures to use in solving word problems — may still need to be learned through boring repetition, but once they are learned, most of the rest will be clear and easy sailing, at least for all that's really necessary. Approaching math through a side door, the *I Hate Mathematics!* book and *Math for Smarty Pants* fool you into thinking math is fun, ha ha.

Fun or not, math seems to be here to stay. Waiting patiently while the cashier tries to figure the cost of half a dozen doughnuts if the price of a dozen is $1.99 has led me to realize that a little math won't hurt anyone, so we have come full circle to the point of telling our kids that they have to learn some of it whether it hurts or not. The important thing is to know when to stop. Let's consider carefully before we spend too much of our time or our children's time trying to learn facts and gain skills that will probably have little or no use in life. If the study is easy or fun or has a probable use, then carry on. If running headfirst into a brick wall would be more fun, force yourselves through *Essential Math,* then go for a walk or read a book or shovel manure.

My Confession

My dictionary defines phobia as "a long-lasting abnormal fear or great dislike of something."

This embarrasses me, but you need to know that I am math-phobic. If I don't fight it, thinking about algebra produces narcolepsy.

There! I've said it. In theory — not a mathematical one, I assure you — confession is good for the soul and healing can begin. Do I feel better now? Not particularly, but now you have no illusions.

It doesn't mean I can't do arithmetic. I can. I just don't actively enjoy it.

I've heard from many of you that we share this problem in varying degrees. So how do we help our children find at least a comfortable competence in learning mathematical skills, preferably without inheriting our disability? First we need to understand why we have a problem with math. I believe it began because our teachers didn't understand the difference between mathematics and arithmetic.

I had never separated the two concepts until I started looking at the resources for the third edition of *The Home School Source Book*. *Arithmetic* is the science of numbers and operations performed with numbers. It's what most of us had in school. This is the skill required for passing most tests. *Mathematics* is about patterns in numbers, shapes, and relationships. There are patterns in our daily life, such as the seasons, the symmetry in a flower or snowflake, and the ticking of a clock or the rhythm of our favorite piece of music. Most of us don't consider these things as part of mathematics, but they are the heart and soul of the field. If our children are to find enjoyment in math, those of us who grew up with only arithmetic must broaden our horizons.

About now, if I were reading this book instead of writing it, I would have to wonder how a math-phobe could produce a reasonable set of suggestions for learning math. It may not be an entirely fair test of the many materials I looked at, but I immediately dismissed anything that induced narcolepsy, made me want to take a walk, upset my stomach, or caused me to decide I'd rather clean the bathroom or see the dentist.

I think math games, hands-on exploration, and practical applications are among the best ways to give our children an enjoyment of numbers and math. I'm not saying there isn't a time and place for workbooks, or even textbooks, but first there should be an appreciation and enjoyment of the fundamentals. Sometimes it's useful to have a variety of small, inexpensive workbooks. A change of scenery can perk up your child's interest and outlook. If you're working with an older child who does not enjoy math I suggest using games that are at a level that will build confidence.

Whatever works is right. Also keep in mind that not all your kids will be strong in math, so after a certain point there's no point in banging anyone's head (yours included) against the wall. You'll find other talents to develop. Something that many of us don't keep in mind enough is that there are no grades or tests for being an honest, hard-working, good person for one's self, family, or community. Some things that count aren't counted but are above common values.

***YES YOU CAN! HELP YOUR KID SUCCEED IN MATH EVEN IF YOU THINK YOU CAN'T,* by Jean Bullard and Louise Oborne.** This book is for you, not your kids. Although written for parents of publicly schooled kids, this is a great resource for all math coaches. It's a confidence builder. If your child has been in public school and has developed a poor attitude toward math and his ability to do it, this book contains strategies that will enable you to help your child, including numerous suggestions for overcoming a child's resentment, embarrassment, and resistance. You'll find good advice about recognizing your child's best learning style. There's honest talk about most math curricula and textbooks; e.g., too much too soon is often expected from most children, and most math texts lack basic explanations on how to do the problems. There's a section about test-taking you can skip if it's not relevant to your situation. I don't agree with the reward strategies suggested, but I won't argue with their demonstration of the complexity of a division problem. They have a sensible attitude about the appropriate use of calculators. Illustrated with cartoons, tables, and charts. Resource list included. $18 including shipping from Bufflehead Publishing, 2400 N.W. 80th St., Suite 173, Seattle, WA 98117. Credit card orders call 888-937-7737, toll free in the U.S. and Canada. You can also request their free catalog and curriculum index. The index has a distillation of the standard math curriculum used throughout the U.S. and Canada. A good tool for helping you plan your studies.

***PLAY AND FIND OUT ABOUT MATH: EASY ACTIVITIES FOR YOUNG CHILDREN,* by Janice VanCleave.** How long is five seconds? How can I draw a star? How much is one-half of something? Is my foot a foot long? I wonder ... How can I do a math trick? These are just a few of the questions to be explored and learned about in this book. Your children may not know the words *fraction* and *symmetry*, but they will discover the concepts from these easy-to-do projects — and they'll have fun doing it. Concepts covered are counting, numbers, addition and subtraction from 1 to 10, fractions (the concept of one-half), time, shapes, patterns, measurements, and quantities. All measurements are in given in standard and metric. (Why not learn both and be mathematically bilingual?) The projects use household materials and are designed for parent participation, but many activities can be just started by you. Easy, clear directions. Great illustrations. 50 simple activities. This book is part of an early-learning series that includes similar learning activities about science, nature, and the human body.

***PATTERNS IN ARITHMETIC,* by Suki Glenn,** is the best introduction to mathematics and arithmetic I've seen. I like the Usborne math books and they are very good for children to work with, but I would start with this one first and use the Usborne books for practice and reinforcement if it's needed. This book was developed at the Farm School, a development and research school affiliated with the University of California at Irvine. The book is about the exploration of mathematical concepts. Its approach is to encourage the child to do the discovering, as opposed to the normal approach of "teaching" concepts. Glenn's method is very hands-on, and her excellent understanding of child development makes each lesson, game, or concept a process that happens very naturally. Her excellent ideas for exploring concepts with your child will make it fun for you too. You already have many of the materials needed, but you will need to purchase Cuisenaire rods and a set of base-ten blocks. Pattern Press, P.O. Box 2737, Fallbrook, CA 92088; members.aol.com/patternpr.

***HOW MUCH, HOW MANY, HOW FAR, HOW HEAVY, HOW LONG, HOW TALL IS 1,000?,* by Helen Nolan.** Nolan has made great fun out of exploring the concepts of big, small, short, tall, distance, and more. Emphasis is on estimation rather than counting. Fun!

SAXON MATH. John Saxon's now-famous math books may be the only ones making full use of an "incremental" approach to learning — the introduction of topics in bits and pieces, which permits complete assimilation of one facet of a concept before the next is introduced, along with continuous review of all material learned previously.

We first learned of "the Saxon method" in 1985 from an article in *Reader's Digest*. We bought a copy of *Algebra ½,* tried it, and were very favorably impressed. Since then, we have used most of the other Saxon math books, with fairly remarkable results. Two of our four children, who had seemed to have almost no mathematical aptitudes, gained a basic understanding (and even a little interest) in a very short time. On the other hand, the only "advanced" math studied by our daughter Karen, the only one of our children ever to be officially tested, was in an outdated, out-of-print copy of High School Subjects Self-Taught, and later she scored very high in the national SSAT (and was accepted by a college with only our high school diploma and no other official credentials).

For mastering advanced math, especially if it will have application in sciences such as chemistry (which is emphasized in some Saxon books), or if you're going to need a lot of math to get into college, Saxon's method may be the best — but many people are mastering math without ever seeing a Saxon book. A $15 book that covers all the basic math principles, with enough drill and practice to know whether or not you're going to be a nuclear physicist, may be sufficient; it's a lot easier on the wallet, and may be a lot easier on the student.

In his last edition of *The Home School Source Book,* Donn said we were no longer recommending or selling the Saxon math books. I've had second thoughts spawned by the tutoring I've done.

You can't explain math clearly to anyone if you don't understand it yourself. In an effort to educate myself enough to tutor, I looked at a number of textbooks. I talked with math teachers and had to accord them a lot of respect; it seems that some of them, too, are victims of the system. In search of the perfect textbook, schools frequently change textbooks from year to year. The methods of explaining math, if any, vary from text to text. As one teacher told me, many teachers have their own way of teaching various math concepts and prefer that math books be written without any specific methods. Publishers, being well aware of the large profit margin in producing textbooks, are all too happy to accommodate these teachers.

I ordered some used Saxon books, and not only did I find them helpful, but they worked miracles for my students. Yes, we had to work at the basic tables. Boring? Yes, but within a short time my students were seeing progress as well as the reasoning behind learning the tables. The explanations and examples in the books were clear to me as well as to my students. Unfortunately, they were so good that I no longer have students paying to provide me with extra goodies for Gus.

Saxon's K-3 program, originally developed "especially for classroom use," was very difficult to adapt to individual use, but don't let that frighten you. The special "home study kit" for individual use in kindergarten comes with the hefty price of $55. Now add $85 for first grade, $87.50 for second grade, and $90 for third grade, and although you didn't grow up using Saxon math, you don't need a calculator, a degree in mathematics, or a special course in financial management to know that the Saxon folks must think homeschoolers have bottomless pockets! (Those prices do not include the recommended manipulatives.) Fortunately, the prices drop with the more advanced books.

I won't sell the Saxon K-3 courses because I object to the pricing, and because you can find cheap workbooks and make your own manipulatives. For the remaining grades I do suggest the Saxon books if you are trying to follow a prescribed school curriculum or if your own math skills are weak.

Used Saxon books are readily available on many homeschooling websites. Make sure the textbook and answer books are for the same editions.

High School and Up

The Question Is, Which Half?: An official in the Department of Education told me one day that a certain school district was retiring 1.3 teachers. Another district would have no change in staff, but was hiring two new teachers. In another district, there would be 3.5 new teachers.

I scratched my head and murmured, "Pardon me?"

He said it all again, which didn't help, and I tried to visualize 3.5 teachers coming to work in the morning, but that didn't help, either.

It reminded me of the stage magician who asked another magician, "Who was that lady I sawed with you last night?"

"Oh, that was no lady," the second magician replied. "That was my half-sister."

I asked the official if he meant an average of 3.5 teachers. Say, two in one district and five in another. The average would be...

"No," he said, "not an average." He spoke slowly, to help me understand. "Three point five teachers."

In plain English, spelled out, that's three and a half teachers. Isn't it?

I'm still working on it. Just give me a little more time.

My cousin, who was a great editor, had two doctorate degrees, and taught at a college in North Carolina, once explained this to me, too. The explanation didn't help me either, so I think this must be some kind of new math or a symptom of a new cognitive disease that's highly contagious, and hopefully confined to the educational system.

ESSENTIAL MATH (formerly titled *Survival Mathematics*). All the practical math skills and basic concepts most people will ever find useful or essential in everyday life, with a minimum of "abstract" math; with emphasis on skills and knowledge needed in bank transactions, stores, restaurants, tax forms, etc., and a full introduction to fractions, percentages, simple graphs, and elementary algebra. An excellent alternative to standard textbooks and more useful in daily applications even if you plan to study advanced math, too. Also covers the metric system.

From "It Matters," by Lynne Warren in the August 2003 *National Geographic:*

> How far apart are those two planets? Scientists measure length in meters. Kilometers and centimeters are just multiples and fractions (respectively) of the basic unit. But exactly how long is a meter? Since 1983 the International Bureau of Weights and Measures in Sèvres, France (keepers by treaty of the world's standard units of measurement), has decreed that a meter is precisely the distance light travels through a vacuum in 1/299,792,458 of a second. (How do you measure a hundred-millionth of a second?) That degree of precision matters. If astronomers measure a meter the way most Americans do ("Y'know, about a yard") imprecision would multiply prodigiously. Just between Earth and Mars you'd get a measurement mistake four million miles long.

***MAKING CENTS: EVERY KID'S GUIDE TO MAKING MONEY,* by Elizabeth Wilkinson.** A Brown Paper School Book. How can kids have fun making money in their spare time? By starting with this book, which gives a kid's-eye view of money, where it started, what it represents, how it's spent, and (best of all) how to earn it — all in a book the kids will enjoy reading.

In a Nutshell

"Omit needless words" is one of the rules for clear writing in Strunk and White's *The Elements of Style*. The Lord's Prayer has 56 words. The Gettysburg Address has 266 words. The Ten Commandments have 297 words. The Declaration of Independence has 300 words. A U.S. government directive on setting the price of cabbage has 29,611 words.

WHY WE CLOSED ONE OF OUR BANK ACCOUNTS

AND DISCONTINUED BUSINESS AS OUR OWN AD AGENCY

BROOK FARM BOOKS
GLASSVILLE, NB E0J 1L0

Assistant Manager
Bank of Nova Scotia
Florenceville, N.B. E0J 1K0

Sir:

In reply to your letter stating that my other business account, J-D Advertising Associates, is currently overdrawn 86¢, please find enclosed herewith a check from myself as a client of J-D Advertising Associates to myself as a partner in J-D Advertising Associates, in the amount of $1.00, which should restore said account to a state of solvency.

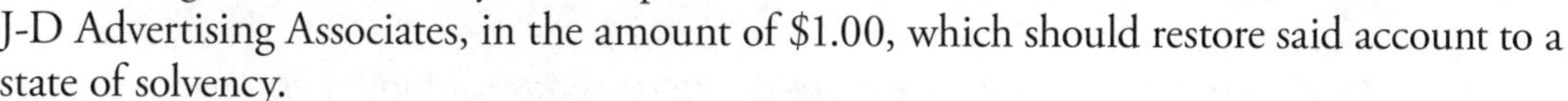

As I explained to the teller when setting up the account, it is not really a business. It is my left pocket, into which I put money I have taken from my right pocket. In the course of trying to make a living without robbing banks, I sometimes place advertisements in various publications, some of which allow discounts to advertising agencies. I therefore hired the printing of ad agency order forms, transforming myself into what the media call “a house agency” — meaning that I function as an ad agency in placing my own ads. These forms entitle me to a discount. So far, I have paid myself one commission of $6.00, the amount of discount allowed on a certain ad. That $6.00 was the deposit with which I opened an account in the name of myself as an ad agency, and was paid out of my regular account, which I maintain in my other guise as myself. Within a few days, I received a bank statement, noting that $1.50 has been deducted as a service charge, making my balance $4.50.

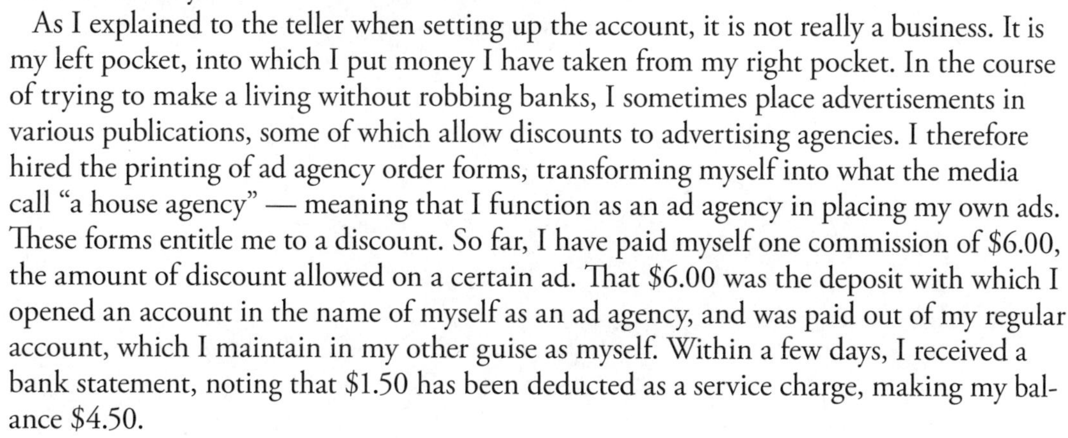

A few days later, I received some personalized checks that had been printed incorrectly. I returned them promptly to the bank, explaining the error. I assumed I would not be charged for these checks, which should indicate how naïve I am when it comes to matters of high finance. As I have written no checks on this account, and have not withdrawn any money from it in any other way, I am now assuming that I have already been charged for the incorrectly printed checks. Since my previous balance was $4.50, and you say the account is now in the red to the tune of 86¢, I compute the cost of the checks to be $5.36.

Is that a penalty imposed on me for not accepting the checks? How much more will it cost me to have some checks printed correctly? Let me know quickly, before my account becomes overdrawn again, so that I can mail myself a check to cover the amount.

Incidentally, there is no use trying to get money from me as a partner in J-D Advertising Associates. The only money ever owned, even fleetingly, by me as an ad agency is in the account. The next time the ad agency's account slips down out of the black, you should write to me as myself and not to me as the ad agency. If your accounts say the ad agency is bankrupt, then it is really so. Write to me and I'll have a word with myself, and loan myself a little money to get over the hump. Which I am now doing, with the enclosed check for $1.00. That is not a commission for anything, so I have to regard it as a loan, which I will have to pay back to myself as soon as I pay myself enough commissions to do so. That may take quite a while, because so far I have put money into the account and have taken none out, but you have been taking money out of it faster than I can put it in.

I wonder if you have any little pamphlets explaining to me the benefits of a business account. So far, the only benefits I have noticed seem to be to the bank. How much more must I invest in the bank before some of the benefits come to me?

I hope some of my questions will be answered soon, unless such attention will result in more service charges, in which case I'll be better off if you leave me wondering.

Sincerely yours,
Donn Reed

P.S. Dear Canadian customers: The above letter, written some years ago, demonstrates the principles involved in maintaining a business account. This is why we now ask for payment in U.S. funds. We apologize for the inconvenience, but the bank doesn't.

Banking establishments are more dangerous than standing armies.
— Thomas Jefferson

SCIENCE

HOW AND WHY; QUESTIONS AND ANSWERS AND MORE QUESTIONS

Science has not been one of the most popular fields of study in the last few decades. This is evident in popular polls and is reflected in test scores from high schools and universities around the country. I don't understand this lack of interest. The exploration of ourselves and the world around us preoccupies youngsters. I could spend a lot of time and waste space discussing what has happened to bring this about, but it's more to the point to give you a variety of exciting resources to stimulate and satisfy curiosity.

***LAST CHILD IN THE WOODS: SAVING OUR CHILDREN FROM NATURE-DEFICIT DISORDER,* by Richard Louv.** Here's a new set of initials for an increasing problem: NDD. Have you heard of this one? I'm not being facetious; it's Nature Deficit Disorder, meaning the lack of enough contact with nature. I think Louv is right. Most of today's kids spend too much time either with technology or just inside the house. Louv and I both believe that kids need to be out and in contact with natural surroundings, even if it's just a wild patch in the back yard or a park if you can't do better. I know, that shows a bit of an attitude, but you won't get an apology from me on this one. Well worth reading. Louv's studies have shown that children with high energy or school-diagnosed learning disorders settle down and function much better when exposed to natural surroundings. You don't have to make a big project out of this or "teach" anything. Just get your kids outside. Go on a hike. Play in the grass. Put this book down and do it now. The book will be here when you come back, and you'll feel refreshed.

Gy=c — If you agree with Albert Einstein's opinion that God does not play dice with the universe, you may be interested in this equation, which I found in *The Godwhale,* a science fiction novel by T.J. Bass. (It's now out of print. You might be able to find it with an Internet search or in the library.) The letters stand for "gravity times a year equals the speed of light." The kids and I spent several hours one morning playing with it, trying to prove or disprove it. Sure enough: The acceleration of gravity (32 feet per second per second) times the number of seconds in a year equals the speed of light (expressed in feet per second). Try it. The speed of light is the one absolute constant fact throughout the universe. Does this have any real significance — or is it just the roll of the dice? A "coincidence" — or God's signature?

That the universe was formed by a fortuitous concourse of atoms, I will no more believe than that the accidental jumbling of the alphabet would fall into a most ingenious treatise of philosophy. — Jonathan Swift

Here are some of our favorite resources; the rest are on the website.

***POWERS OF TEN: ABOUT THE RELATIVE SIZE OF THINGS IN THE UNIVERSE,* by Philip and Phylis Morrison.** A fascinating, mind-boggling excursion through the universe, from the very smallest subatomic particles known to the farthest limits of space yet discovered, moving in 42 orders of magnitude, taking us one jump at a time to give us a breathtaking sense of the relative sizes within us and around us. A book to browse in, over and over, very slowly, with awe and wonder.

***A BRIEF HISTORY OF TIME,* by Stephen W. Hawking.** "[When] I decided to ... write a popular book about space and time ... there were already a considerable number of books about the early universe and black holes. ... I felt that none of them really addressed the questions that had led me to do research in cosmology and quantum theory: Where did the universe come from? How and why did it begin? Will it come to an end, and if so, how? These are questions that are of interest to us all. Modern science has become so technical that only a very small number of specialists are able to master the mathematics used to describe them. Yet the basic ideas about the origin and fate of the universe can be stated without mathematics in a form that people without a scientific education can understand. This is what I have attempted to do." If you've read my comments about math, you may be surprised that I'd read a book by the man who is considered by many to be the most brilliant physicist in the history of the world, and even more surprised that I understand it enough to enjoy it. I'll admit I've taken some of it in very small doses and I do a lot of ruminating, but it hasn't been as tedious for me as you might think. *Time* said of Hawking, "Even as he sits helpless in his wheelchair, his mind seems to soar ever more brilliantly across the vastness of space and time to unlock the secrets of the universe." *Astronomy* wrote, "The work of Stephen Hawking will be writ large in the annals of science." *Vanity Fair:* "Stephen Hawking has overcome a crippling disease to become the supernova of world physics. ... He is leaping beyond quantum mechanics, beyond the big bang, to the 'dance of geometry' that created the universe." Listening to this clear reading of Hawking's book is even better than reading it myself; I can close my eyes and imagine that Hawking is leading me through veils of human knowledge, a little closer to the nature of the universe.

***FROM BUTTERFLIES TO THUNDERBOLTS: DISCOVERING SCIENCE WITH BOOKS KIDS LOVE,* by Anthony D. Fredericks.** A unique book. Fredericks recommends books for ages 5 to 12 that use award-winning books and other sources to teach science (e.g., biology, botany, and paleontology) in a cross-curriculum approach as integrated as our lives. Fredericks recommends books, poses questions about the books for kids to think about, and shares ideas to explore with lots of hands-on projects and activities, all based on the recommended books. You will have to get the books he recommends. If you can't find one of his recommendations please let us know and we will try to get it for you. Most should be readily available through any library or bookstore. There is a helpful list of recommended science periodicals and science supply companies listed in the appendix.

***OH, YUCK! THE ENCYCLOPEDIA OF EVERYTHING NASTY,* by Joy Masoff.** "Exhaustively researched and impeccably scientific, yet written with a lively lack of earnestness. ... An ants-to-zits encyclopedic compendium covering people, animals, insects, plants, foods, and more" is just part of the publisher's description. Here are all the things your kids are interested in that never appear in textbooks and usually not even in most creatively written books. Filled with hundreds of cartoons and real-life photographs, the book helps your kids learn about vampire bats, which sip blood and pee at the same time so they'll always be light enough to fly away; where dandruff comes from; why vomit smells; why maggots adore rotting meat; and a lot more you probably don't want to know. The book also features gross recipes, putrid projects, ten foods that make you airborne, and more. Publishers always list a book as hardcover or paperback. This one is listed as "Paper over slime cover. A full-size, non-toxic slime-filled, plastic pouch is affixed to the front cover."

***THE EVOLUTION BOOK,* by Sara Stein.** Books such as this (one of the best) should be read, and perhaps discussed, with at least a little skepticism now and then, tempered with reason. Evolution within a species is obvious, even in the limited time and space of a barnyard. Evolution of one species to another is still without evidence of any kind. The missing link is still missing. This book offers scores of projects from preserving sea stars to making seaweed pudding, has hundreds of drawings and photos, and attempts to answer several important questions, such as How did life begin? What makes the continents move? The answers to such questions, says the author, can be discovered by reading the ancient messages left on the earth.

Like Voltaire, I can't believe "the watch has no watchmaker," so I don't swallow the entire evolutionary theory, but neither do I believe "the watchmaker" is a white-bearded egomaniac playing with mudpies. Movement of continents is a measurable phenomenon. The beginning of life, supposedly from a chance collision of cosmic debris, is only a "scientific" doctrine, with no more to support it than corresponding religious doctrines. Most of this book deals with demonstrable facts, presenting them in very informative and interesting ways. The attempts to describe and define the greater mysteries, such as the beginning of life and consciousness, should be recognized as no more than current theory, with as little foundation as the divine creation theory. Lots to think about, observe, and discuss.

GREEN THUMBS: A KID'S ACTIVITY GUIDE TO INDOOR AND OUTDOOR GARDENING. Author Laurie Carlson created this activity book to encourage kids to acquire one of life's most satisfying skills. Whether your interest is flowers or vegetables, the well-written text, clear directions, and line drawings weave facts and fun together so kids can successfully create a garden indoors or outside.

YOUR BIG BACKYARD. The National Wildlife Federation publishes this magazine full of eye-pleasing, kid-pleasing photos and illustrations with articles about our natural world. There are crafts and activities along with notes for parents offering suggestions for using the magazine with kids. Write for subscription information: 11100 Wildlife Center Dr., Reston, VA 20190; www.nwf.org/yourbigbackyard is designed with nice children's activities and learning opportunities.

***LIFETIMES,* by Michael Maydak.** This book has a unique and special message. Maydak demonstrates that each life on this earth is different and has an important place within our ecosystem. Did you know that the life span of a mayfly is about one day? Do you know what it does with its day? How long does a whale live? An earthworm? A Venus flytrap? Bacteria? What does each do? Some of the values presented are cooperation among species, saving for the future, and the need to play. Many books have teaching guides that seem unnecessary. The guide that comes with *Lifetimes* is an extension of the main book, with activities, lesson plans (if you want to use them), things to think about, a list of more resources, and a thoughtful list of "skills for living" that is used by the Education for Life Foundation. Teaching guide available separately.

***EVERYBODY'S SOMEBODY'S LUNCH,* by Cherie Mason.** Finally! A sensible and sensitively written book about the food chain, and how everything fits into it with an intricate and perfect order. Many people, children in particular, think of animals as either good or bad, when in fact each animal does only what is natural. This is the story of a young girl shocked, saddened, and confused by the death of her cat. The girl gradually comes to understand the relationship between predator and prey, and finally makes her peace with natural law. Hardcover, with wonderful illustrations!

The teacher's guide for this book is actually larger than the book it accompanies. A wonderful tool for teaching and learning about life cycles and the food chain, predators, and prey. Much to think about and many fun projects.

***BLOOD AND GUTS: A WORKING GUIDE TO YOUR OWN INSIDES,* by Linda Allison** (a Brown Paper School Book). You are many things — miles of blood vessels, hundreds of muscles, many thousands of hairs. You are a furnace, filters, and a fancy computer with a huge memory bank. You are a finely tuned organism with more parts than there are people in New York. This book will help you explore the amazing territory inside the bag you call your skin. It will show you experiments to try, tests to take, and tools to make that will help you see and feel and hear what is going on inside. You'll amaze yourself.

***THE BONES BOOK AND SKELETON,* by Stephen Cumbaa, illustrated by Kim La Fave.** Shake those bones and become an anatomist! Then put them all together to get a good look at how your amazing bones form one of nature's most successful inventions — the skeleton. From maxilla and mandible to pelvis and patella, *The Bones Book* is a lively and informative head-to-toe account of how bones grow, fit, flex, and sometimes break. Learn how bones make blood, why people shrink during the day and grow again at night, and what the shape of bones may be in the future. The book also describes all the vital parts bones protect in the body, including the brain, digestive tract, and circulatory system. The accompanying plastic skeleton is the most accurate model available for children on the market today, sculpted by a professional prosthetist to the standards set by *Gray's Anatomy*. The skeleton's joints simulate the connections of real bones and move like an actual skeleton. The 21-piece skeleton comes unassembled in a clear plastic cylinder, which may be used to display the assembled 12-inch skeleton. There is also a games book to go with this.

***THE NEW WAY THINGS WORK,* by David Macaulay.** From levers to lasers, cars to computers — a visual guide to the world of machines. Intricate, full-color illustrations and clear, explanatory text give a fascinating depiction of how machines do what they do, from the simplest lever to the space shuttle, including the building of the pyramids and many "simple" gadgets we use daily without thinking of them as machines, such as zippers. Difficult concepts are made easy, and common bits of technology we usually take for granted are shown to have greater significance. If this were no more than a textbook, to be skimmed or studied and then forgotten, I'd balk at the price; but it's a book that will draw readers of all ages back for frequent browsing, each time giving added knowledge and understanding of many key inventions that shape our lives. Children and adults — all ages. It will fascinate everyone. Absolutely worth the price. Now available on CD-ROM with a great kit for creating your own sail-powered land yacht, pneumatic earth mover, winch, hoist, and other materials to create 12 working models. Good instructions. All in a toolbox-shaped carrying case.

***THE NIGHT SKY BOOK: AN EVERYDAY GUIDE TO EVERY NIGHT,* by Jamie Jobb** (a Brown Paper School Book). Learn the wonders of the night sky! You will get to know Pegasus, Andromeda, Hercules, and many other fascinating constellations. Stories from long ago will show you how people used the signposts in the sky to lead them home through the darkest nights. Have you ever wanted to make a cross-staff or nadir-zenith finder? (Do you know what they are?) Do you know your longitude and latitude? Meteors, auroras, zodiacal light, and counterglow are just a few of the night-sky events that will top any fireworks show. This book will keep you up all night!

***THE WIND AT WORK: AN ACTIVITY GUIDE TO WINDMILLS,* by Gretchen Woelfle.** Includes an interesting history of design and function, and how windmills have evolved. More than 12 wind-related projects.

SOUND SCIENCE. Etta Kaner's activity book is full of easy-to-do experiments about sound. More than 40 fun-filled experiments, and Kaner gives us some challenging questions to ponder. The directions are clear, and the illustrations are fun to look at.

***THIS BOOK IS ABOUT TIME,* by Marilyn Burns** (a Brown Paper School Book). Time to read, time to think, time to do, time to wonder about time and you. When did people start measuring time? Why did they do it at all? What did they use to measure time? What does time have to with flowers, birds, bees, and the fiddler crab? Besides telling you the whole story, this book's activities will help you perk up your time sense, make a timepiece or two, understand time zones, and look at your own biological clock. When you learn about time, you learn about history, biology, biorhythms, and more — the Mayas, the ancient Egyptians, jet lag, and the Roman calendar. And you'll have the time of your life.

Every school-room needs an "old-fashioned" face clock! With a face clock, it's easy to convey the divisions of the day into hours, hours into minutes, and minutes into seconds. If you must have a digital clock or watch, show how the numbers relate to the positions of the hands on a face clock. A digital clock may tell what time it is, but it won't give any sense of time.

You might want two face clocks — one to learn about time and the other for hands-on fun. If it lands on the floor and breaks, it will provide another type of investigation! The internal works are fascinating.

"Mommy, where does lightning come from? Mommy, why do stars twinkle? Mommy, what are hiccups?" "Hey Daddy, why are bubbles round? Daddy, why are you yawning, and why does it make me yawn too?" "Mommy, why is the sky blue?" "Mommy!" "Daddy!!" Sound familiar? ***HOW COME?,* by Kathy Wollard,** is for every kid who wants to know — and for every parent who almost knows, but isn't sure how to explain it all. More than 100 frequently asked questions with the answers.

***GEE, WIZ! HOW TO MIX ART AND SCIENCE, OR THE ART OF THINKING SCIENTIFICALLY,* by Linda Allison and David Katz** (a Brown Paper School Book). This book is about science. It's also about art. Inside you'll find the Wizard (also known as Professor Bumble) and the Lizard (who is the Wizard's reptilian sidekick). You'll learn that science is more than test tubes, lab coats, and microscopes. Science is a way of thinking about the world. It's a way of finding out what you don't know by figuring out what you do know. This book will show you that scientists and artists share one very important trait: imagination. The absentminded scientist Wiz and his efficient, curious assistant, Art, will lead you to new answers to some old questions. One of the best things about science is that you don't need experts or books or magical hocus-pocus to get answers. All you need is a question and enough curiosity to find an answer.

***SCIENCE IS ...,* by Susan Bosak,** working with the Youth Science Foundation of Canada. Here, in one book, are enough exciting and informative activities to help your child (and you) learn the basics in nearly all areas of earth science, under headings such as "Science Olympics," "Matter and Energy," "Humans," "Environmental Awareness," "Rocks," "Plants," "Weather," "The Heavens," and a lot more. This book will satisfy all learning styles, and I particularly recommend it for children who learn best when they are actively involved with their hands as well as their minds. Learn how to do a bee dance and how animals do yoga. Learn about the impossible-to-straighten cord, cookie concerns, soap bubble derby, shadow creatures, and the "plane" truth. Suitable for children around 6 to 14 working by themselves; also enjoyable for older kids, and for kids and adults working together. More than 500 pages, including a long list of other exciting and related resources. The book is divided into three major sections: "Quickies," short activities requiring few or no materials; "Make Time," activities requiring a little planning and using a few inexpensive materials; and "One Leads to Another," a series of activities related to each other. Interesting tidbits of information are scattered throughout the book in "Fact and Fun Circles" (e.g., "Are clouds really light? A mid-sized cloud can have the mass of five elephants!") *Science Is ...* is absolutely one of the best science books you'll find.

Why Did They Do It!

I just read ***RECYCLE! A HANDBOOK FOR KIDS,*** written **by Gail Gibbons** and published by Little, Brown. Recycling is important and I don't intend to preach to the choir, but this book made me think that we need to give recycling a bigger spot in educating our kids. Children learn what they live. We know that. Just listen to them use that word they weren't supposed to hear! I suggest that everyone have a book on recycling in the house even if it doesn't get reread, because just having one on your child's bookshelf reinforces the idea.

I liked the idea of this book but felt that some of it was too simplistic, with way too much repetition to hold a child's interest, and it was a bit condescending. I think the author added a few big words like *biodegradable* to compensate. *Biodegradable* is a good word to understand, but I didn't like some of the definitions, e.g., "An object biodegrades when it is eaten away by the sun, the rain, and the wind, and by microorganisms (very tiny animals and plants)." I tried to picture the sun, and the rain, and the wind "eating away" bits of trash. Try it and see if it makes sense to you.

I really liked the last three pages. Two of them gave concrete facts about trash and recycling, and the last page gave good suggestions about what each individual can do to use less and recycle more.

The bottom line was that I felt the need to include something specifically on this subject for young kids, but that there had to be something better.

Then I read (with little hope for the future) ***DINOSAURS TO THE RESCUE!; A GUIDE TO PROTECTING OUR PLANET,*** written **by Laurie Krasny Brown and Marc Brown,** and like the book above, published by Little, Brown. I recognized the name Marc Brown. He writes the Arthur series that I like. Still, I was not prepared to like this book either. Why the combination of dinosaurs and recycling? Yes, most kids like dinosaurs, but there wasn't a trash problem when they ruled the earth. I was so nicely surprised as I read through this book. There are illustrations kids will enjoy. It's not overly simplistic, and all the ideas are there. The main points of recycling are discussed among the characters (no lectures here), and yet there is plenty of room to discuss the ideas presented by the illustrations. Why did this normally sensible publisher put out two books on the same subject when one good one would do — and save resources? This is the book to buy.

SHADOW MOUNTAIN: A MEMOIR OF WOLVES, A WOMAN, AND THE WILD, **by Renée Askins.** Astute, deep, complex, and lyrical are just a few words to describe my reaction to this book. I went looking for a book about wolves for purely personal reasons and found myself in the midst of a dissection of our culture and its relationship to all things wild, and a detailed exposure to how, if we are to make progress in being stewards of this earth, we must learn to work with and understand those who hold opposing ideas.

I discovered something interesting going through the **PATAGONIA** clothing catalog: There were interesting articles about sustainable living and green energy with the suggestion that the reader check out the following websites: www.usgbc.org/leed/leed_Main.asp for information about water savings, energy efficiency, and more; www.GreenHomeGuide.com for advice about environmentally sound home remodeling; www.thegreenguide.com for advice about environmentally friendly living.

The Sierra Club leads weeklong training programs for high school and college students who want to become environmental leaders. For more information, visit www.ssc.org/trainings, or call 888-564-6772 and wait for the recording to give you the direct number of the training director.

ENVIRONMENTAL PROJECTS: Project Learning Tree (www.plt.org) sponsored by the American Forest Council, Project WILD and Project WILD Aquatic, sponsored by the Council for Environment Education, (both at www.projectwild.org) integrate environmental/forestry information into a curriculum. Although designed for classrooms, they are ideal for small groups and can be adapted for individual use. A good opportunity for support groups to create a project that can involve everyone. All materials are free to facilitators; if you attend a workshop, you may or may not be charged a minimal sum. American Forest Council, 1250 Connecticut Ave. NW, Suite 320, Washington, DC 20036; www.plt.org.

PHILOSOPHY AND RELIGION

Experience

The battery-powered phonograph shuts itself off and I step out into the crunchy morning with the quiet joy of Mozart's thirty-fourth symphony still stirring through my veins. Wispy gray clouds fade away from the dawning sky, and sudden sunlight streaks through the frosty lace of the icy woods around me.

The moment is timeless. I lose myself in the simple magnificence of sparkling crystals, the shadows. Saplings and branches and towering trees are bent together under the weight of their jewels, curving together to form countless circles and arches, surrounding me in a cathedral of awe and wonder. Am I inside, looking out? Or outside, looking in?

A chickadee flies above me; a bashful rabbit pauses nearby; a phoebe calls; a hawk circles and soars away. Under the snow and ice over our little foot-bridge, the brook murmurs contentedly. They all have the answer.

Then I have it, too. There is no "inside" and "outside." Those are illusions I create when I separate myself from the reality around me.

Many Paths

Whatever we believe or teach our children about God and our relationship to Him, it becomes increasingly important each day that we know, respect, and understand what others believe and teach. Whether we believe that ours is the one and only true religion or that there are many different paths to God and truth (or even if we don't believe in God at all), we need to understand at least the basic beliefs and teachings of others in the human family.

Some of the oldest legends and artifacts of human civilization indicate that people have always searched for truth and goodness; that they have always sought to understand the mystery of life, of being.

Religion did not begin two thousand years ago, nor four, nor five. Jesus was not the first to preach the return of good for evil, although others who have taught the same thing have been ignored and disobeyed just as much.

We teach our children that the universe and everything in it are basically good; that

often what we call bad is only goodness distorted, or goodness frustrated, or goodness undeveloped. From a God's-eye view, even the most horrible criminals are never beyond redemption. They're just not ripe — but God has plenty of time. I don't believe that God gambles or experiments or makes mistakes. He won't punish parts of his creation for being slower to develop than others. A parent may say to a child, "I'm punishing you because I love you," but the Creator of billions of stars and flowers and grains of sand is never so foolish. Kindness, understanding, forgiveness, and patient guidance are facets of love; punishments are not.

What loving parent would sentence his child to eternal fear and suffering, no matter what the transgression? Yet there are still some who suggest that the Being whose love and goodness fill the void between the stars will do so for the crime of mistaken belief. Was Jesus lying when he told the parable of the prodigal son?

No doubt we are all prodigal — at times. We waste life, we waste time, still arguing — as did some medieval monks — about how many angels can dance on the head of a pin. "As if you can kill time," wrote Thoreau, "without injuring eternity."

We teach our children that people everywhere want to know God; that the followers of Buddha do not worship his statue, but that they believe in the Eightfold Path of Right Thought and Right Action as devoutly as Christians believe in the Ten Commandments.

In our home, we don't teach denominational dogma, but we often study about it. Our studies include ancient myths and legends as well as the various holy books that have grown from them. In comparing different religions of the world, our purpose is never to proclaim one better or more true than another, but to find what each has to offer for the betterment of humanity. We're curious about the various beliefs regarding creation and the afterlife, but we're more concerned with the moral and ethical teachings — as Jesus was. We're far more interested in the many similarities among various religions than in their differences.

All four of our children have attended various church services with their friends, and have made several interesting observations. The preachers all talk about Jesus quite a bit, but seldom say anything about Jesus's own teachings. The non-fundamentalist churches, of course, are not so concerned with damnation and redemption, but even these say little about applying Jesus's teachings to our own everyday lives. Far more is said about joy in eternity than about meaningful relationships here and now. In general, our kids have found that unbelievers are neither more nor less friendly and considerate than devout believers.

Conversion

When Susan was in her early teens, she decided to attend Sunday school at the local Baptist church — initially just to be with her friends, so we saw no reason not to allow it.

We had underestimated the church's techniques of persuasion. Susan was given homework — searching for specified Bible verses (almost always dealing with sin and redemption), competing for prizes in Bible-verse memorization contests, and writing short paragraphs about how her "life of lasciviousness and wickedness" could be changed by accepting Jesus as her savior. The church's literature, bought from a Midwestern publishing company, used adolescent psychology as a strong lever, insisting that Susan's awakening body and "confused thoughts" were under the control of Satan, and repeatedly telling her that she was sinful by nature and unworthy of God's love, which would be given to her only if she accepted God's sacrifice of his son. Recognizing the need of many adolescents to rebel and at the same time to belong to a group, the church distributed stories and articles about "Living With Un-Christian Parents" and "How to Convince Your Parents That They Are Wrong." Susan was encouraged to attend many extracurricular church activities. She stayed up late at night, studying the Bible, copying and memorizing passages — particularly from the Book of Revelations. In the morning, she was tired and antagonistic.

We told Susan we certainly had no objection to her being a Christian, if that was her choice, but that she should examine the church's teachings, investigate other churches, and learn more about Christianity before accepting the teachings of one particular church. Especially, we said, read the four Gospels. They are supposedly the basis of all Christianity; read them carefully, giving particular attention to the message of Jesus himself. She said there was no need to, because she had already found the truth. She accused us of being against the church only because she had chosen it, and then cried because God was going to throw us into a lake of fire and she would be the only one of our family to go to Heaven. She thought she would lose us. We thought we had lost her.

There are many, of course, who would feel that Susan was the only one of our family who had seen the Light. To us, any light that produces blindness is worse than darkness. After so many years of helping our children gain intellectual freedom, we were frightened by the ease with which others could inject intolerance and bigotry into one of them. We reminded ourselves that we should have known; we should have realized the emotional appeal, especially for a young teenager, of being one of God's Chosen.

Our other children were repulsed by the concept of a God who would throw people into a lake of fire, or simply snuff them out like candles.

One Sunday, Susan told us the church's preacher had told the congregation that Pete Seeger and Jane Fonda were communists, and he advised anyone who owned Jane Fonda's workout book to throw it away immediately, and to be careful not to listen to any of Pete Seeger's recordings. She was puzzled and apprehensive, having enjoyed our Pete Seeger records for years, and having looked through Jane Fonda's book in the public library. The principle of the issue wasn't new to our kids, but we were all a little surprised to see it pop up — ironically, in 1984 — in our small rural community in New Brunswick.

In the following week, our speculations about the preacher's concept of communism led into a lively discussion of Senator Joseph McCarthy's witch hunt of the '50s; the subsequent media blacklist of Pete Seeger, the Weavers, Paul Robeson, and many other entertainers because of their refusal to cooperate with the House Un-American Activities Committee (HUAC); and Jane Fonda's opposition to the Vietnam War.

We discussed the nature and dangers of stereotypes, prejudice, and false or incomplete information, and the humorous possibilities of political contamination from contact with an exercise book or a record of folk songs.

After Susan had been a militant born-again fundamentalist for about two years, her friends began drifting away from the church, and she slowly drifted with them.

We know now that Susan did learn from that experience — from the people she knew, from history, from the daily news, and from her own experiences — that there are many ways to find God.

As adults the children have all learned that those who have the most faith, hope, and charity are not always Christians or Jews or Buddhists, and that an atheist is not necessarily lacking in love and sympathy and generosity.

In this week's news magazine, how many reports are there of wars between religious factions — Arabs and Jews, Catholics and Protestants, Christians and atheists, even Christians against Christians?

Credo

I sometimes teach about God. Should I say "preach"? My text comes from dozens of holy books; from the many evenings I have lain in my sleeping bag, looking up at the stars; from the smell of new-mown grass; from the births of our children; from Strauss's *Also Sprach Zarathustra*; from the sparkle of ice crystals on the tree branches; from the drowning sloth who puts her baby on her head to save its life from the flood rising around her shoulders; from the cut on my finger that knits and heals; from my eye, a small mass of fluid and membrane and blood and nerves, which transmits the image of a star or a flower or a sunset or a loved one to my inner self.

What I teach about God is too much for some, not enough for some, all wrong for some.

"Why, who makes much of miracles?" asked Walt Whitman. "To me every hour of the light and dark is a miracle, every cubic inch of space is a miracle."

When we hear or read of miracles, we look for something out of the ordinary, as if everything ordinary were not a miracle enough. There is no separation between the natural and the supernatural. God is not a remote being to whom we telegraph our requests, dabbling when he pleases in human lives, granting his favors as arbitrary rewards for obeisance or flattery. God is far more natural and more supernatural than that. God IS. All that is, is God. God is the I Am, the Word, the Way, Tao, the Great Spirit, the Over-Soul, the Force, all matter and non-matter, everything seen and unseen, all power and glory forever. Not a star or person or microbe is separate or distinct from God.

The early Greeks personified the earth as Gaia — Mother Earth — and saw all things earthly as being essentially one being, totally interrelated in a global ecology of earth and mind and body and spirit. British scientist James Havelock very seriously proposes the "Gaia Hypothesis" — that the entire earth functions as a single self-regulating organism. Lyall Watson, in *Supernature,* writes, "There is life on earth — one life, which embraces every animal and plant on the planet. Time has divided it up into several million parts, but each is an integral part of the whole. A rose is a rose, but it is also a robin and a rabbit. We are all of one flesh, drawn from the same crucible."

The God of which I teach is that same all-encompassing ecology — not only of the earth, but of the entire universe. Each of us is a droplet of water in the vast and unending Ocean of God. There is nothing that is not God. Our belief or unbelief, doctrine or doubt, searching or scoffing are also parts of what is, which is God. "No man is an island, entire of itself," wrote John Donne. "Every man is a piece of the continent, a part of the main; if a clod be washed away by the sea, Europe is the less, as well as if a promontory were, as well as if a manor of thy friends of thine own were. Any man's death diminishes me, because I am involved in mankind; and therefore never send to know for whom the bell tolls; it tolls for thee."

Those words, for me, are literally true, not only in a global sense, or only human, but referring to all things that exist, everywhere.

And how do we "pray"? The ancient psalmist told us: Be still —

"Be still, and know that I am God."

Not with words of supplication, or even of praise, but with surrender and quietness, with openness to let peace and love flow through us and become us.

Lesson

When Karen was twelve, she stayed overnight with a friend and went to church with her the next morning.

"The preacher asked how many were praying and their prayers weren't being answered," Karen told us. "A lot of people raised their hands. So the preacher told them their mistake was in saying, 'If it be Thy will.' Instead, he told them, they should praise God, tell him how much they love him, and then he'll give them what they want."

"Do you agree?" we asked her.

"That's just trying to butter God up," Karen said firmly, "and make him feel good, so he'll give us what we want. God is too smart for that."

In the Light

Officer Archie O'Henry, on a routine patrol one evening, spotted a potted gentleman crawling on hands and knees under the streetlight.

"Can I help you, sir?" he called through his rolled-down window.

The man looked up and finally managed to focus on Officer O'Henry. "Lost my car keys," he explained.

The officer sighed, shut off his motor, and went to help. "Are you sure you lost them here?" he asked.

"Nope," said the man, "lost 'em over there, under that tree. Or maybe that one over there."

The officer scratched his chin. "I hope you won't think I'm being too critical, sir," he said, "but if you lost them over there, wouldn't it make more sense to look for them over there?"

The man hiccoughed and took a deep breath and said indignantly, "'Course not. There's no light over there."

Sermon

Calvin Coolidge, the Vermonter who became the thirtieth American president, was asked one day what the preacher had talked about in church that morning.

"Hell," Coolidge replied.

"Oh? What did he say about it?"

"He's agin it," Coolidge replied.

Last Words

Preacher Jones, the traveling pastor, had decided to retire, and had finally found a buyer for his horse.

"Joe," he said, "I'm disappointed that you've never come around to be saved, but if you've got the money, the horse is yours."

Joe handed over the money, and Preacher handed Joe the reins.

"By the way, Joe, there are two things I should tell you about this horse. First, when you want him to go, you'll have to say, 'Praise the Lord.' Nothing else will make him move."

Joe frowned, but nodded his understanding.

"The second thing," Preacher said, "is when you want him to stop, you've got to say, 'Amen.' Nothing else will make him even slow down."

Joe frowned again, then nodded and swung into the saddle. He jabbed his heels into the horse's sides and said, "Giddap!"

The horse lazily turned its head to look at Joe, then stretched its neck down to nibble at some grass.

"Remember what I told you, Joe," Preacher said.

"Oh, all right," Joe said disgustedly. "Praise the Lord!"

The horse took off like a shot, neck stretched in front of him, tail flying behind. Joe grabbed the pommel and barely managed to stay in the saddle as the horse galloped away.

Just as Joe finally got himself settled comfortably in the saddle and was beginning to enjoy the ride, he noticed that the horse was going about forty miles an hour straight toward a cliff and his speed was increasing. Joe pulled back on the reins as hard as he could, shouting, "Whoa! Stop! Whoa!" but the horse galloped on.

Just yards from the cliff's edge, Joe remembered. "Amen!" he screamed frantically. "Amen!" The horse stiffened its legs, leaned back on its haunches, and slid to a stop, coming to rest two inches from the edge of the cliff, then stood trembling, anxiously waiting for Joe's command.

Joe looked down — three miles down — over the sheer cliff.

He sighed, wiped the sweat from his forehead with his sleeve, and said, "Praise the Lord."

Divine Comedy

God, on a routine patrol one day, stalked me as I walked through the winter woods.

"Can I help you, sir?" he called through a curious chickadee.

I looked up. "I've lost the secret of the universe," I explained.

God sighed in a breeze, circled in a hawk, and came to help in a little flurry of snowflakes. "Are you sure you lost it here?" he asked.

"No," I said. "I think it was in one of those philosophies over there. Or maybe in one of those religions."

God chuckled in the brook. "I hope you won't think I'm being too critical, sir," he said, "but if you lost it in a thought, why are you searching for it in the woods?"

"The light is better here," I answered.

"Trying to butter me up?" God asked.

"No," I answered. "When Adam asked for creatures, you thought he said preachers, so you gave him a lot."

God chuckled in the brook. "Not bad," he said.

"Thank you," I said.

"Not very bad," God amended. "Have you heard the story about Calvin Coolidge?"

Pilgrimage

Our children must form their own relationships with the universe. Knowledge of God can't be taught; it must come from within. Trying to describe God with words is like dipping a bucket into the rushing brook beside our house: The water in the bucket, captured and held, is no longer the same as it was; it no longer bubbles and breathes and gurgles. We can hint and point a general direction, commensurate with our own understanding, but our children must find their own ways by themselves, when they're ready.

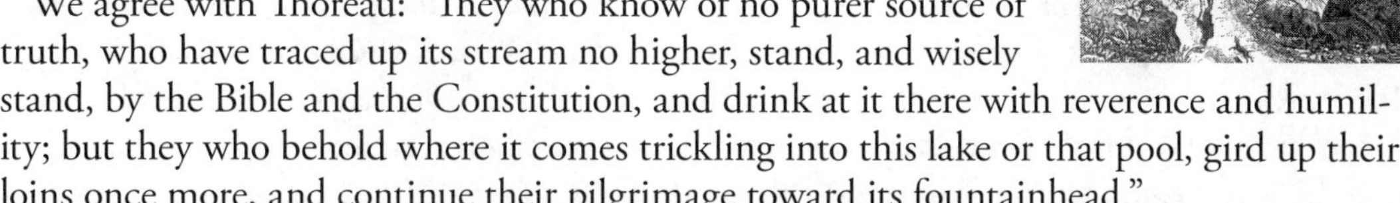

We agree with Thoreau: "They who know of no purer source of truth, who have traced up its stream no higher, stand, and wisely stand, by the Bible and the Constitution, and drink at it there with reverence and humility; but they who behold where it comes trickling into this lake or that pool, gird up their loins once more, and continue their pilgrimage toward its fountainhead."

We hope to give our children the strength and desire to continue that pilgrimage.

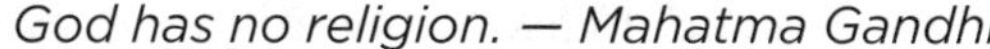

God has no religion. — Mahatma Gandhi

***ALL I SEE IS PART OF ME,* by Chara M. Curtis and expressively illustrated in full color by Cynthia Aldrich.** A book of wonder and delight, suitable to use regardless of your religion (or non-religion). This is a child's journey of discovery, of learning that he is a part of, and connected in many ways to, the whole universe; a journey in which he understands that he has an inner life as well as a physical one. The exceptional author and artist combination makes this a treasure. Ages 2 and up, and if you think 8, or 18, or 88 is too old, you need it! This is one I will give my children for their children.

***IN THE BEGINNING: CREATION STORIES FROM AROUND THE WORLD,* compiled and edited by Virginia Hamilton.** Twenty-five intriguing stories from cultures around the world about the creation of the world and mankind. Illustrated with beautiful watercolors by Barry Moser.

***THE HERO WITH A THOUSAND FACES,* by Joseph Campbell.** This two-hour audiocassette adaptation of Joseph Campbell's best-selling book and popular PBS television show brings to life his insightful, poetic interpretation of mythology. Drawing on myths and legends from around the world, Campbell describes "the universal hero," asserting that myths are not merely enchanting fairy tales filled with demons, rituals, and romance, but are allegories that can help us make sense of the timeless mysteries of humankind's physical and spiritual worlds. Weaving traditional wisdom of the past with the modern struggle for identity and spiritual growth, Campbell demonstrates that folklore and mystic literature are potent sources of universal meaning that can serve as spiritual metaphors for modern man.

***WISDOM TALES FROM AROUND THE WORLD,* by Heather Forest.** A book filled with folk-tales, proverbs, and parables that impart lessons for living in a very readable, some-times funny, and thought-provoking manner.

CONCISE DICTIONARY OF WORLD RELIGIONS. A more affordable pocket edition: 700 pages, with 8,200 entries; topic index; and introductory essays about basics of each religion, movements, sects, cults, sacred texts, individuals, sacred sites, customs, eth-ics, and more. Cross-referenced and easy to use.

Try This on Your Computer — Important Correction!! In the first edition of the *Home School Source Book* (1991), I said that in the mid-1800s Bishop James Ussher calculated that God finished the creation of everything on October 22, 4004 B.C., at exactly 6:30 a.m. I was wrong, on two counts, and I hope my faulty reporting didn't make you late for any appointments. Ussher (1581-1656), while Archbishop of Armagh, calculated that God finished the creation on October 22, 4004 B.C., not at 6:30 a.m., but at exactly 6:00 p.m. However, in 1859, more than 200 years later, Dr. John Lightfoot, vice chancellor of the University of Cambridge, said Ussher was wrong anyway. "Heaven and earth and man," he said, "was created by the Trinity on twenty-third October, 4004 B.C., at nine o'clock in the morning." (Now that that's settled, let's work on our grammar.)

gy=c. Look for this item in "Science" to learn why this might be God's signature.

RELIGION, SCRIPTURES, AND SPIRITUALITY. Since the dawn of civilization, religions have expressed the concerns at the core of human existence: life's meaning and purpose, the significance of birth and death, moral commitments, and the proper conduct of life. Religion transcends *making a living* to guide us in *how we should live*. It involves us with what some theologians call "an other" — an inexpressible, non-rational part of existence that may be an emotional refuge or a source of spiritual nourishment and enlightenment. The history of the world is intertwined with religion, and can never be fully understood without a basic knowledge of the beliefs that have shaped it.

Each of these programs consists of two 90-minute cassette tapes, narrated by actor Ben

Kingsley and featuring dozens of dramatizations and characterizations of great religious leaders, theologians, historians, and readers of the various scriptures.

SET 1: ORTHODOX AND ROMAN CATHOLIC CHRISTIANITY
SET 2: PROTESTANT CHRISTIANITY
SET 3: JUDAISM
SET 4: ISLAM
SET 5: HINDUISM
SET 6: BUDDHISM
SET 7: SHINTO AND JAPANESE NEW RELIGIONS
SET 8: CONFUCIANISM AND TAOISM
SET 9: NON-LITERATE RELIGIONS
SET 10: CLASSICAL MEDITERRANEAN RELIGIONS AND MYTHS
SET 11: AFRICAN AND AFRICAN-AMERICAN RELIGION
SET 12: NATIVE RELIGIONS OF THE AMERICAS
SET 13: SKEPTICISM AND RELIGIOUS RELATIVISM

***WALDEN, OR LIFE IN THE WOODS,* by Henry David Thoreau.** I spent many of my childhood and teenage weekends and summers hiking and camping in the woods of southern Vermont, sometimes with one or two friends but more often by myself. One day, my sophomore English teacher, Walter Cohen, had written the title of this book on the chalkboard, and the subtitle made me wait eagerly for his explanation — which never came. At the end of the day, the note was erased. I realized much later that he had been sowing a random seed, and I may have been the most fertile ground in that particular class.

About that time, the early '50s, some of the world's best literature was being published in inexpensive paperbacks for the first time. Browsing in a bookstore one afternoon (a favorite pastime), I recognized that title and bought it — for 35 cents — and soon entered into one of the most important revolutions of my life. The first pages told me the book wasn't about camping at all, and not very much about life in the woods. It was about life in society, life in the world, life in the universe, life within oneself. How should I live my life? To whom or to what do I owe allegiance? How should I relate to other people, to society, to government, to my own existence?

"Why should we be in such desperate haste to succeed," Thoreau asked, "and in such desperate enterprises? If a man does not keep pace with his companions, perhaps it is because he hears a different drummer. Let him step to the music which he hears, however measured or far away" — not meaning, as many would have it today, that one should act capriciously or merely for self-gratification, but that one should listen for, and be guided by, the inner voice of conscience, of principle, of higher laws than those devised by governments. "I think that we should be men first, and subjects afterward. It is not desirable to cultivate a respect for the law, so much as for the right."

I devoured the book; it devoured me. What I felt was not so much agreement as recognition, as if many of Thoreau's thoughts were already in my mind and soul, hidden, waiting only to be called forth by an expression of them far greater than I would ever achieve.

Thoreau refused to pay his poll tax to Massachusetts, because that state supported the Fugitive Slave Act and the Mexican War, both of which he believed were wrong. For a while he was a schoolmaster, but was fired for taking his students on nature walks, and for refusing to whip them periodically to keep them in line.

Thoreau's essay "Civil Disobedience" has encouraged thousands, perhaps millions, to resist injustice, not through bloodshed and violence, but by personal withdrawal from the injustice. You can't stop the machinery of government, he said, but your deliberate opposition to its tyranny may throw a little sand in the gears. Gandhi, Tolstoy, and Martin Luther King Jr. credit their reading of "Civil Disobedience" as a turning point in their own educations and careers. No one, before or since, has so eloquently and accurately summed up the ideal relation of a person to society, to government, and to oneself.

Thoreau used words carefully and exactly, never settling for an approximation of what he meant, always choosing the word that precisely conveyed his meaning. He was a classical scholar, and likened the tending of his bean field to ancient battles — "Daily the beans saw me come to their rescue armed with a hoe, and thin the ranks of their enemies, filling up the trenches with weedy dead. Many a lusty crest-waving Hector, that towered a whole foot above his crowding comrades, fell before my weapon and rolled in the dust." He enjoyed puns — "If you are chosen town clerk, you cannot go to Tierra del Fuego this summer; but you may go to the land of infernal fire nevertheless."

Walden and "Civil Disobedience" shouldn't be required reading, because the person who isn't ready for them will get little from them, but every thinking person should have a copy, and browse in it occasionally, ready for the moment when Thoreau's words suddenly open the shutter and let the sunlight in.

I've read *Walden* many times, and reread bits of it — a sentence here, a paragraph there, often becoming absorbed and finishing the chapter — scores of times. I always discover something new in myself.

There are many editions of Walden and Thoreau's other works. I recommend the Modern Library edition, *Walden And Other Writings By Henry David Thoreau,* which includes his two other books — A Week on the Concord and Merrimack Rivers and Cape Cod — and six of his most important essays — "The Allegash and East Branch," "Walking," "Civil Disobedience," "Slavery in Massachusetts, "A Plea for Captain John Brown," and "Life Without Principle." This is a durable hardcover with clear text and a reasonable price.

***A MAN NAMED THOREAU,* by Robert Burleigh.** An excellent introduction to Henry David Thoreau for all ages. Quotations from *Walden* have been woven with biographical facts and bits of Thoreau's philosophy to give an intriguing picture of an unusual man and his examination of conventional society. Many difficult concepts have been simplified without loss or distortion of meaning, making this a very good introduction to many questions of ethics and morality as well as a portrait of Thoreau.

If you've never read Thoreau this is a good introduction. If you've read Thoreau and found his style difficult, this little volume will unlock the secret of reading him with joy. Perhaps you can find it at your library.

Do not be too moral. You may cheat yourself out of much life so.
Aim above morality. Be not simply good; be good for something.
— Henry David Thoreau

***WHAT DO YOU STAND FOR?,* by Barbara A. Lewis.** Written for adults working with children in volunteer situations, this unique book is much more. It is a tool to help you and your kids explore your values and place in the community. It discusses courage, friendship, honesty, responsibility, empathy, forgiveness, loyalty, and more. It's thought-provoking and inspirational, with challenging activities to explore and develop individual values. Highly recommended.

***THE BOOK OF THINK, OR HOW TO SOLVE A PROBLEM TWICE YOUR SIZE,* by Marilyn Burns** (a Brown Paper School Book). Did you ever have a traffic jam in your head? Did you ever feel as if on some days you just won't do anything right? Did you ever get yourself into a corner and know that whichever way you tried to get out was going to be the wrong way? If the answer to any of those questions is yes, then this book is for you. This book is about what to do when you are puzzled, or perplexed, or stumped, or can't get there from here. It's about using your noggin. It's about being smart even when you feel dumb. This book is about how to think even when you know you're fresh out of ideas. If you are a person who never has a problem, then don't read this book.

Exercise for people of all ages: Think about the things you want to do before you die. Make a list of at least 30, then decide which are the most important and reorganize your list. Think about what you are doing to accomplish what you would like to do. Do this every year and keep your lists.

Physical bravery is an animal instinct; moral bravery is a much higher and truer courage. — Wendell Phillips

***PSYCHOLOGY FOR KIDS #1 — DISCOVER YOURSELF,* by Jonni Kincher.** Are you an extrovert or an introvert, an optimist or a pessimist? Forty fun (and fascinating) quizzes, based on sound psychological concepts, will help you discover who you are and how you think about yourself.

***PSYCHOLOGY FOR KIDS #2 — LEARN ABOUT OTHERS,* by Jonni Kincher.** A companion to the book above. Lots to ponder and discuss. Are people more logical or emotional? Is there really a difference between the way males and females think? Do you think competition improves performance? Sharpen your observation skills. Learning about others helps us learn about ourselves.

***THE FIRST HONEST BOOK ABOUT LIES,* by Jonni Kincher.** This exceptional book is one of the most important you and your children will read and discuss — ideally, together. Serious and thought-provoking, yet also funny and full of experiments, examples, and games to help you explore truth, the nature of lies, and how they are used by you, on you, and around you. This book probes for the reasons for lying and promotes active questioning: Do lies serve a purpose? What purpose? The book won't tell you what to think, but it will help you establish good thinking habits about truth and lies. A good book to share and discuss — if you can get it away from your kids long enough to get a look at it.

***COMMENTARIES ON LIVING: SERIES I, II, AND III,* by J. Krishnamurti.** "Without first knowing yourself, how can you know what is true?" Not for the faint of heart yet very easy to read, this series will take you within yourself and our society, and you will come out with a clearer view of both. These books are written without religious dogma and delve into the psychological problems that beset all human beings. I don't know why Donn didn't put these in his editions of *The Home School Source Book*. These books opened my eyes to many facets of living I had not thought about very deeply and helped me examine myself and my beliefs. Highly recommended reading for a quiet evening.

THE GIANTS OF PHILOSOPHY. "Moderation in all things." "I think, therefore I am." "The unexamined life is not worth living." "And it is this that everyone understands to be

God." These are the men whose thoughts have formed much of our Western civilization: Plato, Aristotle, St. Augustine, Immanuel Kant, and nine others. These are the men who have contributed greatly to the ideas we now have about happiness, love, art, God, morality, reason, justice, goodness, and evil.

The format of these presentations is the same as that of the Great Ideas That Have Shaped Our World (see "History and Biography"). The cassette tapes of the Giants of Philosophy are dramatized, with multiple voices portraying the author, contemporary observers, and critics, drawing on actual writings and quotations of the time and later history, with an overview narrated by actor Charlton Heston. Each tape is about 90 minutes long, divided into shorter segments — about 20 minutes each — for more convenient study. The social and historical background of each work is presented, as well as the effects, both immediate and long-term, that the work had on other thinkers and on society. There are numerous references to other works and historical events, demonstrating the continuing influence of the author's ideas.

Listening to these tapes is much better than simply reading the works discussed. The full background of the works and their influences on contemporary and future society are fully explored, giving a much deeper understanding than could be gained from the works by themselves.

SET 1: PLATO (CA. 430-350 B.C.), GREECE
SET 2: ARISTOTLE (384-322 B.C.), GREECE
SET 3: ST. AUGUSTINE (A.D. 354-430), ROME
SET 4: ST. THOMAS AQUINAS (1224-1274), ITALY
SET 5: BARUCH SPINOZA (1632-1677), THE NETHERLANDS
SET 6: DAVID HUME (1711-1776), SCOTLAND
SET 7: IMMANUEL KANT (1724-1804), GERMANY
SET 8: GEORG WILHELM FRIEDRICH HEGEL (1770-1831), GERMANY
SET 9: ARTHUR SCHOPENHAUER (1788-1860), GERMANY

Every man takes the limits of his own field of vision for the limits of the world. — Schopenhauer

SET 10: SOREN KIERKEGAARD (1813-1855), DENMARK

Life can only be understood backwards; but it must be lived forwards. — Kierkegaard

SET 11: FRIEDRICH NIETZSCHE (1844-1900), GERMANY
SET 12: JOHN DEWEY (1859-1952), UNITED STATES
SET 13: JEAN-PAUL SARTRE (1905-1980), FRANCE

When angry, count ten before you speak; if very angry, a hundred.
— Thomas Jefferson

When angry, count four; when very angry, swear. — Mark Twain

... ministers who spoke of God as if they enjoyed a monopoly of the subject.
— Henry David Thoreau

I hate people who are intolerant. — Laurence J. Peter

Humanity is the Son of God. — Theodore Parker

The test of a preacher is that his congregation goes away saying, not "What a lovely sermon," but, "I will do something!" — St. Francis de Sales

Man is not the sum of what he has but the totality of what he does not yet have, of what he might have. — Sartre

COMPUTERS

Our option message has changed. Please listen carefully.
For quality service your call may be monitored.
Please press 1 for service in English.
Press 2 for routine services.
Press 3 for non-routine services.
Press 4 if you know your party's extension.
Press 5 if you would like to access a directory.
Press 6 if you detest this menu and would like to speak to a person.
Please hold and enjoy this junk music while your call is connected.

DONN AND I ACTUALLY HAVE SOME DISAGREEMENT!

"If you think computers will make you smart, then you'll believe having a library card will make you well-read." This was a smart remark — and you may take that any way you'd like to — that I overheard on National Public Radio. I apologize for not remembering the name of the speaker.

Donn wrote his part of this chapter in 1991. After I took computer classes we had some interesting discussions and ongoing disagreement about computers. At that time computers were just moving into our lives, mostly through big business. They were expensive and more difficult to use than the ones available now. Today they are a part of nearly everyone's daily lives, either directly or indirectly, whether we like it or not. This book comes to you compliments of a computer. Times have changed, and I know his perspective would be different now, but I believe many of his objections, observations, and reservations are still important to consider. I know it is highly unjust to take advantage of his inability to respond, but I now have the last word, and I intend to make the most of the situation!

"Computers are man's most beautiful creation," said U.S. Navy Captain Grace M. Hopper, who set the standards of computer language for the Pentagon (in 1991). "All children older than four should have their own computers. We may even get a generation that can spell."

That's like saying anyone who owns a gun will know how to make bullets.

Or using a calculator means you can do basic math or make change.

Or owning a TV and VCR implies you can program your remote control.

Or owning a car means you can fix it.

Or reading this nonsense means you can't add on at least ten more examples.

Captain Hopper must mean that all previous generations, those unlucky enough to have grown up computerless, can't spell. She may be right. A little while ago, I was looking through the diary my grandmother kept during her first year as a schoolteacher. That was more than ninety years ago, and my grandmother was sixteen. Not once in the diary did she spell "computer" correctly. In fact, she avoided the word completely.

Although excessive love of gadgets and gimmicks is the root of much evil in the world, it's good to be familiar with the basic usage of some of those gadgets. Books are tools of communication and learning; cars and planes take us to interesting places; telephones help us to reach out and touch someone. We try to help our children become book-literate, telephone-literate, and even airplane-literate.

(See what happens when a word is suddenly uprooted and transplanted into foreign soil? "Literacy" used to be related only to the ability to read and write. Then computer folk tacked it on to the word "computer," with the guilt-trip implication that if you're not able to operate one of the new-fangled gadgets, it's tantamount to the other kind of illiteracy. In other words, "literacy" came to mean "competency," which gave it an added dimension, but also robbed its original meaning of much of its potency. E.D. Hirsch Jr. compounded the felony by tacking the word to "cultural," with the implied parallel suggestion that a lack of cultural knowledge and awareness is as serious as the inability to read and write. Okay, then, why can't I say "telephone-literate" and "airplane-literate"?)

I have little interest in computer literacy. Computers are undoubtedly very useful tools, but I am unconvinced that they're essential to a happy life or a creative career. An apple a day may keep the doctor away, but an Apple a day may increase society's need for psychiatrists.

Donn, I don't disagree with your conviction that a happy life or fulfilling career can be had without ever using a computer, but there is much to be said in favor of being able to use one. I wrote that more than five years ago, and I'd now say that being able to use a computer, even if you never own one, is even more important. The computer has become more than a casual tool. Just about everything that can be computerized has been or will be soon. The access to information is both amazing and a bit frightening. You can get up-to-the minute news online and follow an archaeological dig in real time. You can also Google your neighbor and maybe find out more than he wants you to know about him. I worry about personal privacy.

Also, if the power goes out way too many businesses and things, like Bill Gates' house (although I'd bet he has his own backup power supply), won't work. On the home front it's not too bad yet. Just wait until your home appliances, lights, and heating are completely computerized and the power goes out. That thought is enough to keep me back here in the woods with my wood heat and gravity-fed water for a long time. As things stand now, when the power goes out, I consider it a vacation at home. I can light my propane lights and read or play my guitar. I can still cook on my propane stove, and I can put another chunk of wood in the woodstove and never miss the outside world.

I am one of the "computer literate." (Pardon the terminology, Donn.) No, I don't know how they work, but I can use one with ease. No, it hasn't taught me to spell; however, I am freer to use my reading vocabulary because I know the spelling will be corrected (if I remember to use the spell-checker). I am no longer chained to the dictionary, a time-consuming activity when I have no idea how a word is spelled. I readily admit that Microsoft Word doesn't know how to spell pteranodon; the spell-check function can't tell a typo from a typewriter, and the dictionary and thesaurus in this software are not as extensive as our old-fashioned bound volumes, but I am less inhibited and freer to concentrate on what I want to say because I no longer have to disrupt my work to look up many words.

The computer is faster and more accurate with the math I need to use in the business. I can even keep the checkbook up-to-date and make it balance. I like the ease with which the computer can generate reports that instantly tell me into which hole all the money has disappeared.

The computer keeps my work more organized. It insists I file each piece of work when I finish it. Even better, if I can't remember where I filed it, the computer knows and can retrieve it for me. I certainly can't say the same for myself and the unfiled paperwork lying in piles around the office.

To address your comment about computers improving the standard of living for psychiatrists: If computer use leads to the need for psychiatric help, then a rapidly increasing segment of the world is already in deep trouble. Computer use is multiplying even faster than bitey-bugs on a camping trip or in the garden. When my first computer crashed, I needed a box of tissues and a regular backup program, not a psychiatrist. I felt I'd lost half my memory. I wondered if my experience was similar to knowing that your Alzheimer's disease is progressing. I knew I'd lost things, but I couldn't remember just what. Looking back on that event, maybe I should have had my head examined for not having a regular backup program.

I do agree with you on the most important point. The computer is a useful tool, but like all tools, it does not make for a happier life. Shane (in the book by the same name) said, "A gun is a tool. It is only as good or as bad as the man using it." Satisfactory living comes only from within yourself and your relationship to the people and the world around you. If you think you need a computer to be happy, you do need a psychiatrist.

On a larger scale, computerized society becomes increasingly impersonal, and the value of life becomes reduced each day by a few more decimal points. On a smaller scale, people who use computers a great deal tend to think in computer-like patterns, in which life becomes a series of problems to be dealt with in a systematic, orderly manner, with a logical solution to each problem at the end of each operation. Life is seldom that orderly and logical. Solutions are reached by feelings, hunches, and intuitive empathy as often as by orderly examination.

Yes and no, Donn. I think you would have changed some of your thinking by now if you had a computer to use. Yes, computerized society is becoming more and more impersonal in many ways. I detest some of the more common computerized services. A phone menu is enough to frustrate a saint. Mabel at the local exchange would be faster and friendlier. When a computer makes a mistake, it takes forever to straighten the problem out, and you definitely need a *person* to help you and to correct the computer. Computers do have their limitations. However, I love the ATM at the bank. It's always much faster than the tellers (and sometimes friendlier), and the waiting line is never as long. Being able to do research on the Internet at any hour of the day on any subject is a boon, and I know you'd appreciate it. Taken altogether, I think today's computers are as good or as bad as the people programming them and the manner in which they are used.

Donn, if you could watch me use the computer, I'm sure you would quickly realize that it hasn't improved my logic, or made my work habits much more systematic. It's better at filing and spelling, and many other logical and consistent tasks, than I am, but it doesn't offer "solutions" to my problems.

I agree that real-life solutions are often reached through feelings, hunches, and intuitive empathy. A computer can extrapolate, but only within the limitations of data supplied by a person. The day computers make imaginative, intuitive leaps to reach conclusions, we had better hope the science fiction buffs have figured out what to do about it. There is already quite enough trouble with computer use when we can more or less control what they do.

To give the devil his due (to use one of those strange phrases that seem to make sense until you examine them), Mario Pagnoni almost convinces me, in *The Complete Home Educator* (now sadly out of print), that computers are not the bad guys I think they are. His explanation of the uses and values of a computer, especially as a learning tool, is the clearest and most convincing I've found. I'm just as suspicious of computers, and as concerned about their detrimental influences on human ways of thinking, but Mario's book has shown me that computers can be controlled and can have a proper place in the home or home-school. Maybe.

I think there is definitely a place for computers in education. Actually, it doesn't matter what any of us thinks about the place of computers in education. They are in the schools and in toys for young children, and for better or for worse, just like wedding vows when you marry, they are now a part of modern society and life on most of the planet. One thing I regret that you've never seen, Donn, is the growth of the Internet. Access to an overwhelming amount of knowledge is easy. The Internet provides information on any subject you might care to investigate and a lot you wouldn't ever care about, and you don't have to go farther than your computer to find it — and you can check out numerous sources around the world. Computers make it possible for students to participate in high school and college classes that are actually taking place miles away. Donn, you would love being able to sit here in our quiet woodsy home, in the comfort of your own chair, with a cup of coffee in hand, and follow a NASA mission, or look over the shoulder of a scientist working on an archaeological site halfway around the world. I think you would concede, without quibbling, that the computer *can* (can being the operative word here) be a valuable learning tool.

Computers have also changed our means of communication forever. I correspond freely with our kids, now scattered across the continent, and I hear from them far more often than I would without my computer e-mail. Communication is so fast and easy that we frequently carry on conversations through the course of a day or an evening. I can just as easily and quickly correspond with people on the other side of the world.

I know you would be concerned that computers tend to separate people from "living." I don't think computers isolate people from one another. People isolate themselves, with or without a computer. It is a matter of use and misuse. I believe our mental, spiritual, and emotional growth comes from interacting with other people and the world around us.

The greatest advances in art, music, literature, philosophy, and science have been made by men and women who were open to inspiration, hunches, and wild guesses. Computers often do away with the need for creative thinking: Just feed the problem into the keyboard and wait for the computer to find the solution. This approach may produce rapid and astonishing advances in the already existing arts and sciences, but it is incapable of producing new arts and sciences. The computer's "reasoning" can be based only on information and procedures that are fed or built into it; a human being — genius, mystic, or you or I — unfettered by controls and programs, with circuits and synapses of flesh and spirit infinitely greater than anything of silicon and magnetic impulses will ever be, can leap light-years while the computer is still singing "Daisy, Daisy."

The possibilities of extrapolation open to a computer may be nearly infinite, but that extrapolation must still be based upon existing data. Any situation or problem of life processed from a computer's view is reduced to a paint-by-number picture. No matter how the combinations or choices of colors are varied, the end result is still no more, and usually less, than the original.

Again, yes and no, Donn. Computers will probably never be capable of the truly creative thought process, although they are working on it as I write. Is anyone surprised? There is experimentation with computers and the creative thought process. There are computerized robotic vacuums, and they are working on robots that will wash dishes and, and ... who knows what next? Yes, Donn, I'm hedging my bets with the word "probably," because computers and programming are changing rapidly. We have computer-generated music, but to me it will never equal the genius of Beethoven or Mozart, and synthetic music will never equal a live performance. A computer can make a picture, but for me it will never rival Monet. Computers have changed, and software programming is changing so rapidly most of us can't keep up with it. I think that as servants of creative and inquisitive people, computers can work out complex problems faster, eliminating hours of computation with a pencil, paper, and calculator.

I do agree with you that computers can give us knowledge but not "living." I think it's possible to lead a very satisfactory life without ever learning how to use a computer. The benefits from this new technology are many, yet I know in my heart that in many ways the joy of discovery will never be as great when gained through a computer as it is through active hands-on experience or through interaction with people. A joyful life is created through interacting with your family, friends, and the people in your community, and being at peace with your surroundings. A computer picture of a desert sunset or a recording of wolves howling will not instill peace in your soul or raise the hair on the back of your neck. The audiovisual experience translated through a machine doesn't engage the spirit in the same way. A picture may be worth a thousand words; a hug and a laugh with someone you love is beyond price.

Our job as parents must include finding a sane balance between use and misuse of computers. Computers, like televisions, can be overused "baby-sitters." Flashy software programs are relatively cheap and will distract a child (and some adults) for a long time. There are Internet sites that are not suitable for children (or most adults). As with the television, remember that there is an "off" button.

As more educational computer opportunities become available, we need to evaluate not only the programs, but our children's human needs. There are complete home education courses available in computer format, from Baby Einstein to college degrees. The information in some is excellent, but I don't think it's a healthy way to learn. I think it's essential, if you are using a computer as a learning tool, to balance its use with books, physical activities, and hands-on learning. Calvert School has put out a King Arthur CD-ROM. It's packed with information: a marvelous collection of classic artwork in vivid color, a variety of myths to compare with actual history, an audio guide to pronunciation, and an interactive game. With the exception of the game (which I think would be much better if played as a board game) and the pronunciation guide, the rest would be better in book form.

Before you consider using computer resources, consider your child as well as the educational possibilities. A computer user spends most of his time sitting, using the keyboard, and staring at the monitor. Anyone sitting for hours at a computer risks injury to his eyesight, carpal tunnel syndrome, back problems, circulatory problems, and more. Our human bodies, young and old, are not designed to sit still for long periods of time. How long do you want your child to sit in one position, staring at one spot? Consider how much you want your child to learn by himself at the computer and how much you want to be an active part of his learning and his life. I consider moderation and vigilance the key to making constructive use of this relatively new tool. I can hardly wait to finish this book and put more activity back into my life. I know it hasn't been good for me.

When I started this chapter I wanted the last word in this conversation. I've changed my mind, Donn. It's all yours. I'm just going to add a bit about being careful because the Internet is a brave new world.

We don't want paint-by-number lives, for ourselves or for our children. We're willing to accept the benefits and beneficial possibilities of computers, but I am not convinced that they will make any significant contributions to the world in any terms of real human progress. The art of living, if reduced to lines and numbers, would no longer be art and hardly living.

Online Safety and Other Bits of Useful Information

I've never found any objectionable material on the web, but I haven't the time or the inclination to look for it. I have had objectionable unsolicited e-mail delivered to my desktop by spammers, and I certainly wouldn't want children exposed to it. I have heard many people complain about material found on the web, and I agree that the material they said they found was not suitable for children. Using a computer for study or just for fun is great, but I think the bottom line is whether or not you trust your kids to stay with constructive material. If you're not sure, or want to be sure, use one of the filtering programs below.

Net Nanny: www.netnanny.com/home.html

Safesurf: www.safesurf.com

Web Wise Kids (www.webwisekids.com) has an interactive website that your kids can use to learn how to be safe when they are online.

If you or your children have favorite magazines remember to look for their websites. You'll often find interesting activities that can be done online or downloaded.

Since I began writing I've bought several new computers; some of them have been big-name brands and some not. I can't speak for the resources in your area, but I've been the most satisfied when I've gone into a local computer store and had them build one to my specifications. You don't have to be a computer whiz to do this. You only need to know what you want to do with your computer, and they will figure out what you need. The advantage I find in getting my computer put together locally is that when I have a problem help is only a local call away, and because we do business face to face I think they feel more responsible for keeping me happy and keeping my computer running smoothly.

EDVENTURES (discover.edventures.com) has some great projects that a lot of kids will learn from and enjoy. You get a free trial, and then you have to pay for it. Well worth it if your kids enjoy computers, don't already spend too much time with them, and have fun doing the projects.

THE SMITHSONIAN CENTER FOR EDUCATION AND MUSEUM STUDIES has launched a new education-based website (www.smithsonianeducation.org) that targets educators, families, and students. It includes content from 16 Smithsonian museums, the National Zoo, and the Smithsonian's research centers. Smithsonian Education offers nearly 1,000 educational resources searchable by grade, subject, and museum. Lessons, activities, and teaching tools are aligned with national education standards and include interactive activities that engage students through rich graphics and animation. The site also lists special events for teachers, and a step by-step guide to planning field trips to the Smithsonian and other museums.

PBS (the Public Broadcasting System) has revamped its website (www.pbs.org/teachers), making it more inviting than ever. Aside from the nifty new look, it offers some helpful new features that enhance educators' use of the site, which includes more than 4,500 free lesson plans.

ARTS AND ACTIVITIES

CRAFTS — GAMES — HOBBIES — SPORTS — MUSIC
ACTIVITIES FOR GIFTS AND HOLIDAYS

Arts and crafts aren't just time fillers or exercises in manual dexterity. These activities help fulfill a human need to create something unique, to express ourselves, and to learn in a totally different medium. Making good use of the materials in this section will help your children learn skills beyond what a strictly academic program provides. Most of the academic subjects that are normally part of a homeschool program require left-brain thinking. The arts develop the right side of the brain, promoting creativity, intuition, and a different type of personal satisfaction. Research shows that listening to music — classical music in particular — can affect the mind and the body, releasing tension and reducing stress. (Many of the best animal kennels play classical music, and there are dairy barns that have found that playing quiet music increases milk production. Quiet music is used in stores to make you feel calm so that you will take your time shopping — in hopes that you'll buy more.) Music and the other creative arts are being used very successfully in healing and rehabilitation programs.

Your efforts to create enjoyment for your children from these activities can build a foundation for future interests that will carry over into adulthood and become a lifelong pleasure — or perhaps a passion — or a way to make a living. I've never considered the arts to be "extracurricular."

Necessary Items to Have on Hand

Paper, pencils, crayons, watercolors, poster paints, finger-paints, scissors, ruler, glue, paste, glue sticks, colored construction paper. Our kids never liked the oversized pencils and crayons supposedly meant for "little fingers." For older kids, ballpoint pens, colored pencils, and felt-tip markers.

Supplies and Items of Interest You Might Not Find Elsewhere

On the Internet you can take a tour of the Louvre from the comfort of your own home at www.louvre.fr.

THE JERRY'S CATALOG, 5325 Departure Drive, Raleigh, NC 27616; www.jerryscatalog.com.

DICK BLICK, P.O. Box 1267, Galesburg, IL 61402-1267; www.dickblick.com. Ask about their School Sale Flyer, published twice annually (a supplemental catalog).

Full-color reproductions of the world's art masterpieces are available from **ART EXTENSION PRESS,** P.O. Box 389, Westport, CT 06881; www.artextensionpress.com.

The **NATIONAL GALLERY OF ART** has free-loan educational resources — slides, teaching packets, videos, etc. Also online lessons! To learn more go to www.nga.gov and click on Education.

On our website you'll find all manner of creative activities for all seasons of the year, inside the house and out. You'll find non-competitive games, cooperative sports and games, hobby ideas, books that have instructions for making simple toys, sticker books, and dot-to-dot books. There are some really fabulous learn-to-draw books, books of native crafts you can do at home, books about acting and theater, books about how to work with clay, and beginning cookbooks — even for those who can't read yet. There are a number of good books about the great artists, and many holiday crafts. Here is a small sampling from the resources on our website.

***DRAWING WITH CHILDREN: A CREATIVE TEACHING AND LEARNING METHOD THAT WORKS FOR ADULTS, TOO,* by Mona Brookes.** Hundreds of very helpful tips on techniques and art materials, used with great success even with very young children. This is a wonderful book!

***DRAWING ON THE RIGHT SIDE OF THE BRAIN: A COURSE IN ENHANCING CREATIVITY AND ARTISTIC CONFIDENCE,* by Betty Edwards.** I seldom think about which side of my brain I'm using, but a few years ago when Karen was feeling frustrated by the elusiveness of a tricky subject she was trying to draw, we got out this book and tried its techniques. Hooray! Karen captured the subject she was after with little trouble, and went on to use the book's ideas to improve her artwork immensely. We both give it our wholehearted endorsement.

Children who like to draw and need some encouragement with writing will enjoy the **DRAW-WRITE-NOW** series in the English Language and Literature chapter. The authors have made it very easy to learn how to draw a great variety of people, animals, and objects using very simple lines. Children are encouraged to write captions and stories with their drawings.

***STEVEN CANEY'S TOY BOOK,* by Steven Caney.** My dad used to make racing spools for me, and a little while ago I tried to remember how he did it. They're simple gadgets — a spool, a rubber band, a thumbtack, and a wooden match — but the secret kept eluding me. This book came to the rescue. Racing spools, clothespin wrestlers, a water lens, a pocket parachute, a tube telephone, a bull roarer, and much more. Fifty very simple, inexpensive (or free, from household throwaways) games, pretending toys, building toys, action toys, discovery toys. Ages 2 to 12, and older kids will enjoy making these things for younger ones, or even for themselves on a rainy day.

***LEONARDO DA VINCI FOR KIDS,* by Janis Herbert.** A great blend of art and science with lots of activities, a good glossary, a bibliography, a listing of museums and websites, and a timeline. Wonderful full-color illustrations.

***LOAVES OF FUN,* by Elizabeth M. Harbison,** is just what it sounds like — and more. Even if you've never baked before, you'll enjoy baking these breads from around the world. Exploring these recipes will keep you well fed in body and soul, and teach you history and geography as you travel the globe. There's even a timeline history of bread! There is a good glossary that explains the ingredients and how they interact. Nice illustrations and clear directions make this book suitable for children under 6 with adult help in the kitchen; ages 6 to 12 can use it on their own, or if you're older and like to bake bread, you can ignore the age recommendations just like I did. More than 50 recipes and activities, a multicultural journey with pita bread, pretzels, and plain and fancy breads for all seasons, all from ingredients you probably already have in your kitchen.

ARTISTS' WORKSHOP SERIES: *ANIMALS, PAPER, AND PORTRAITS.* Each of these books is especially designed for ages 7 to 13. These unusually creative projects, drawn from arts and crafts around the world, will enhance your children's creativity and give them the tools necessary to satisfy their creative desires. Well-illustrated, with easy-to-follow instructions. All techniques are demonstrated using famous artists' creations. Techniques to duplicate special effects are demonstrated. These books are terrific. I wish we had had these when the kids were home!

Games: Cooperative! Challenging! No Referee Necessary!!

Yes, it is possible to play games without a referee. Playing games is — or should be — a friendly social act. How strange that in most games players work to eliminate others, to outsmart them, to take advantage of another's oversight, age, or weakness. The games below call for cooperation, not competition. Some are mostly a matter of luck; others call for thinking skills. Some are for one age group, and others allow players of different ages to work together. A few games can be played solo if no one else wants to play. A number of them come with suggestions for variations so you actually get more than one game in a package. I'm limited in space so I'm going to list just a few for each age group. If you're interested in a full-color catalog, send us $1 and ask for the Cooperative Games Catalog.

BEAUTIFUL PLACE. An ecology game for children! Environmental concepts are presented in a simple way. The object is to restore the planet before the pollution clouds take over. You can do it if you work together. 2 to 4 players (more if you play with partners), ages 4 to 7.

THE SECRET DOOR. One of the most popular with young children. Definitely a cooperative mystery game. Besides needing a bit of luck, you'll need your memory and thinking skills. 1 to 8 players, ages 5 to 8.

NEW AMERICA. Be part of a team redesigning the socioeconomic system before it's too late. The focus is on energy and resources, but many other fields are explored. Designed to provoke discussion. 2 to 4 players, ages 12 to adult.

Books You Should Positively, Absolutely Have, No Matter What

GAMES MANUAL. Many times when we didn't have a birthday to celebrate and the kids wanted a party, we would have an "unbirthday party" and invite everyone's friends. Each person brought a small gift costing less than $5 that would do for a girl or a boy. We played games and had ice cream and cake — complete with lots and lots of candles. Everyone helped to blow out the candles (picture it!). I wish we'd had this collection of games to use. This book has 170 co-op games and activities for ages 3 to 12. Little or no equipment needed; good for small or large groups. Most games can be played indoors or out. You'll never do better than this for price or value.

***EVERYBODY WINS!* by Jody Blosser.** This book lists 45 non-competitive party games and activities for children. You don't need to have a party to have fun with these games and activities — just several children, or you and your child can do these together. Almost every activity in this book comes with a bonus — it teaches skills such as counting and coordination. I particularly like the introduction, in which Blosser gives you a very clear idea of the difference between activities that produce real self-esteem and ones that just make your child feel good at the moment. Materials needed are around the house or not expensive. Each activity listed comes with information about preparation time, a list of materials, age level, what procedures to follow, and some helpful hints for success.

Beauty in things exists in the mind that contemplates them.
— David Hume

I shut my eyes in order to see. — Paul Gauguin

MUSIC

Enjoyment of music is common to the human experience. It strikes a common chord in all of us, and we respond to it in conscious and subconscious ways. Music is a poetic expression of our innermost feelings painted in sound. It can express our anger, love, frustrations, dreams, loss, and joy, and reflects our soul. It is a gift to be enjoyed in every way possible. Some of us can create it, some can play it, and some of us can barely hum a tune, but we can all enjoy it.

I was lucky to enjoy music in many forms while I was growing up. I studied dance for years; sang in several choruses; played piano moderately well, but without great talent; played clarinet, not as well; played the violin with promise (I was told); and found playing the drums in the orchestra absolutely boring because there were long pauses between the times they were played. It wasn't until I reached my mid-teens that I found the right instrument for me (the guitar), one I felt could help me express what I couldn't put into words, one that vibrated with my inner being and gave it expression. I think every child should have the opportunity to learn at least one instrument. Speaking from my own experience I would not, as a parent, be discouraged if a child starts and stops music lessons or changes instruments over a period of years. Many people try various instruments before they find the one that's right for them, and many adults who had music lessons as children and stopped playing start again later in life.

Children love music. They feel it and move to it; they love lullabies and story songs. (They even respond to music in utero.) There's lots of great children's music available to listen to, and there are thousands of good songs to sing and learn. Don't let the language of music — the notes, the musical alphabet — discourage you. It's very simple in its basic form, much simpler than learning English or French. It is a gift you can give your children that will last long after the lessons are forgotten.

If you've never played an instrument, I suggest you start with a recorder. It's inexpensive and not complicated to play. A piano is also a good beginning instrument, because the keyboard is very logical and it is easy to relate to the written notes. If a piano is beyond your means, don't give up! Get an electronic keyboard, which is much cheaper. They usually come with instructions for beginners.

Warning: Your dog may howl. Gus had definite musical preferences. He groaned and muttered when I played in the key of D minor on the guitar, but only with some pieces. It always puzzled me. He was completely intolerant (as in howling mad) of the recorder and the flute when I played them, but not at all bothered by a recording of these instruments. I tried not to take this personally. If you love classical music and/or the recorder, listen to Souvenir, an RCA CD recording of Michala Petri on recorder with Lars Hannibal on lute and guitar, and if I had only one CD to listen to for the rest of my life it would be Paul Galbraith playing Bach on his eight-string guitar.

Without music life would be a mistake. — Friedrich Nietzsche

Beginning Music Studies

***SOUND CHOICES: GUIDING YOUR CHILD'S MUSICAL EXPERIENCES,* by Wilma Machover and Marienne Uszler.** I love it! It's for everyone who would like to provide some musical experience for his children. If you just want to give your children a casual acquaintance with music, this book has a lot more than you will need, yet it offers the best ideas for even the most basic experiences. The scope of this book goes far beyond choosing an instrument and providing lessons. There are extensive sections of other music resources that address the needs of various age groups, with suggestions for parents. You'll find chapters on practical issues: singing lessons, electronic instruments, very detailed suggestions for choosing a teacher, practicing, different learning systems (Suzuki, Orff, etc.), and much more. There's well-researched information about recognizing the musically gifted. Even more important is the chapter devoted to children with special needs, covering music as therapy; help for the physically limited, the learning disabled, and those with varying degrees of hearing or sight loss; and information about adapting instruments and other ways of making it possible for these children to make music. Each section of the book is followed by a list of resources: books, CDs, videos, camps, and organizations. Sprinkled in with all this information about music is a lot of commonsense psychology about listening to your children and how and when to encourage them.

***PRACTICING FOR YOUNG MUSICIANS: YOU ARE YOUR OWN TEACHER,* by Harvey Snitkin, Ph.D.** This is the best book I've ever seen concerning the motivation for practicing and effective practice strategies. It will give you and your child strategies that take the nightmare out of practice time. This book puts the student in charge. After all, learning to play mostly takes place between lessons during practice time, not during the lessons themselves. Fun to read. Highly recommended for all adults, teens, and parents of younger musicians — and all music teachers.

***THE I CAN'T SING BOOK: FOR GROWNUPS WHO CAN'T CARRY A TUNE IN A PAPER BAG ... BUT WANT TO DO MUSIC WITH YOUNG CHILDREN,* by Jackie Silberg.** What a title! What a book! And not just for those who feel they can't sing. Great ideas for musical enjoyment without any technical terms. Silberg makes it all so easy that anyone can make music by putting together high and low sounds, simple rhythms, cheek popping, and body sounds. Also included: games, activities, simple homemade instruments, answers to frequently asked questions, and more. I've always had music as a part of my life and shared it with the family, and I still wish we'd had this when the kids were home. For adults with children birth through 10, but you're never too old to learn.

SING OUT is a nonprofit organization formed to preserve the cultural diversity and heritage of traditional folk music from all countries and cultures, and to encourage the practice of folk music as a living phenomenon. If you love to sing, order *Rise Up Singing* from them. It has a huge number of songs you'll know or would like to learn, and they all have guitar chords. You can even order CDs with the songs on them, making it easier to learn new tunes. For more information about membership and receiving their quarterly magazine, write to Sing Out, P.O. Box 5460, Bethlehem, PA 18015-0460; 1-888-SINGOUT; www.singout.org.

***STORIES AND SONGS FOR LITTLE CHILDREN,* told and sung by Pete Seeger** with many of his best songs for kids (and playful adults), including "Abiyoyo," "Froggie Went a-Courting," and more. One of my favorites.

Of all noises I think music is the least disagreeable. — Samuel Johnson

I used **Frederick Noad**'s books ***SOLO GUITAR PLAYING,* Books 1 and 2,** when I started to learn classical guitar. These books are excellent, but I recommend working with a teacher because there are specific techniques that should be acquired when you begin this type of playing. I started out on my own, and it wasn't until I met another classical guitarist that I learned I was playing all the right notes — but I wasn't using the correct techniques to bring out the melody properly. I didn't have to start over from scratch, but I paid a price for my ignorance and independence.

***THE GIFT OF MUSIC,* by Jane Stuart Smith and Betty Carlson.** If you'd like to enrich your listening pleasure by learning about classical music composers, I recommend this very accessible book with interesting biographical information about composers and music from the age of the Psalms to modern times. Each chapter has further reading and listening suggestions. There's a good glossary and a chart showing the progression of music and a few of the other arts through the ages. Mainly about the composers' lives rather than about music of specific periods.

If it sounds good, it is good. — Duke Ellington

Wow! **PHILHARMONIC FOR KIDS:** www.nyphilkids.org. I haven't enjoyed a site like this in a long time. Many philharmonics offer special educational programs to home-schoolers as well as the public schools. If you investigate you may find times they give special performances or will allow you to attend a rehearsal during the day or on weekends. If you're planning a visit to the philharmonic near you, check out this site and help your kids become familiar with what they may see and hear there. This site offers a composers gallery, news, an instrument storage room, a section to make your own instrument, a composer's workshop, and more. Remember to turn on the sound on your computer.

***TAKE ME HOME, COUNTRY ROADS,* words and music by John Denver, lovingly illustrated by Christopher Canyon.** You already know the song, or you should learn it. Each page illustrates a line of the song. This is an excellent way to reinforce reading skills. Lots to look at and enjoy, and you'll find the words and music, with guitar chords, at the back of the book. The hardcover edition comes with a CD.

Don't let the term "classical music" fool you into thinking it's inaccessible. This kind of music expresses every possible human emotion. Just listen, feel, and enjoy.

CLASSICAL KIDS. This series (which deserves all the awards it's gotten) is a wonderful and gentle introduction to classical music, the most famous composers, and their work. Each selection comprises a dramatic story, a bit of history, and the featured composer's music — all blended for imaginative listening. Like other recorded works, these will be listened to many times. Someone on National Public Radio said the other day that listening to radio (or recorded) music and stories is "the finest visual medium." I agree and would add that it's all in your head. Ages 5 to 12 (except for Daydreams and Lullabies).

MOZART'S MAGNIFICENT VOYAGE

HALLELUJAH HANDEL

TCHAIKOVSKY DISCOVERS AMERICA

VIVALDI'S RING OF MYSTERY

MOZART'S MAGIC FANTASY

BEETHOVEN LIVES UPSTAIRS

DAYDREAMS AND LULLABIES (ages newborn to 6)

MR. BACH COMES TO CALL

CLASSICAL KIDS TEACHING NOTES. These notes provide additional background information, discussion topics, and activities divided by age group, with suggestions for exploring the music across the curriculum.

May 5, 2005

Dear Mom,

I want to say thank you for exposing me throughout my childhood to many kinds of music: classical, folk, big band, jazz, soft rock, gospel, blues. ... I even had childish daydreams of becoming a musician. Although I dabbled with a few instruments I didn't develop the focus or drive to pursue any of them long term, but my appreciation has grown. I have continued to listen to and collect a variety of music. I realize that it was you who, almost without trying, fostered my love and appreciation for music. I want to say thank you for encouraging my interest in trying different instruments, but mostly for fostering a love of music. I find music soothing, energizing, intriguing. ... The two kinds of music that give me the most are classical and folk. They make me feel and think and smile and laugh and cry ... they feed my mind and heart and soul. ...

Thank you.

Happy Mother's Day.

Love,
Catherine

First, master your instrument.
Then forget all that #$&%&
and play! — Charlie Parker

Bach
gave us God's Word

Mozart
gave us God's laughter

Beethoven
gave us God's fire

God
gave us music that we
might pray without words

TRANSITIONING INTO ADOLESCENCE

Experimentation throughout the grade school years enabled us to discover the various ways each of our children learned best. Our philosophy about learning didn't change when our children reached the high school years, but we did find ourselves doubting and questioning ourselves again, challenged by different types of problems, and investigating new learning options. It was a time of trials and errors. Here are some of our observations and the lessons we learned.

From the time they could move about freely, the kids played at many roles — father, mother, dog, lion, cowboy, nurse, clown, superhero — testing each one, experimenting with their own possible roles in society. Throughout, they have felt secure in their knowledge of belonging to the family. Actually leaving the family someday was not a reality. Academically we found that basic skills and a general knowledge of the world — reading, writing, arithmetic, history, geography, government, science, and beginning literature — fit well into the ages from six or seven to thirteen or fourteen, roughly equivalent to the ages spent in the first eight grades of public school.

At puberty, as the body begins rapid changes and emotions become stronger, the mind also grows suddenly and rapidly. Our children began to realize that they really would leave home someday, and the world was still a huge, intimidating mass of uncertainties. They looked forward to being on their own as adults, but at the same time were apprehensive about it. They wanted more time, more preparation, and more practice.

Once again they tried on different roles, this time outside the home, testing themselves in community functions and clubs and traveling alone — fitting into groups larger than the family and separate from it. Some of them experimented with popular teen fashions — dress, makeup, slang, music, and opinions. We noted that because there were rarely other home-schoolers in our area, our kids related to their friends and tended to think in terms of grade levels, with a definite division between elementary school and high school, based on their ages more than on their actual studies and achievements. We observed that our children's own desire and capacity for a deeper and broader educational base — which we may call "high school" — was roughly concurrent with adolescence.

Did you know that there is now a name for this period of moving into adolescence? Kids going through this stage are called "tweeners," and I like it that this time of life has its own label even though I'm opposed to labels. You can call me oxymoronic if you'd like, but this stage of growth has its own complications and rewards, and is deserving of recognition. You and your tweener can read all about it in ***I AM NOT A SHORT ADULT!***, by **Marilyn Burns.** It's out of print but is frequently available on Amazon.com for anywhere between one cent and $15.

Adolescent Problems and Transitions

Adolescence is a time of rapid changes and can cause a variety of difficulties. Homeschoolers are not necessarily exempt. One minute adolescent kids think and feel they know it all, and the next they doubt and challenge themselves and everybody and everything around them. Sometimes they feel they know themselves well, other times not at all. We sometimes felt we knew our kids well, other times not at all.

Adolescence can be a roller-coaster ride for parents as well as kids. All of a sudden the time spent with diapers, runny noses, and "he hit me first" can look easy in retrospect. This is the time when all the years of homeschooling and working together can provide a secure base for everyone.

When under stress, we can, without thought, fall into unconscious patterns of behavior stemming from our own childhood. In other words, we do as our parents did with us. Sometimes this is a good thing; other times, if we thought about it consciously, we would be horrified.

Cathy and I went through a period when we seemed to be having frequent arguments. We were surprised, hurt, and confused by this. As soon as Donn realized that these disputes were basically a power struggle between Cathy and me we were able to deal with the problem. I realized that my knee-jerk reaction was a part of my built-in conditioning — from my past relationship with my mother — coming back to haunt me. Cathy and I started discussing issues as they came up and found ways to resolve our problems. Sometimes I had to take a "time out" to think before answering so I could really consider my answers.

Everyone has problems. No child is perfect. No parent is perfect. Each of us does the best we can at the time. Sometimes our best is not what's needed, or is not good enough. We've had our share of problems over the years. Sometimes Donn and I could see we'd made a mistake in handling problems with the kids. We spent time thinking and talking to find a resolution to the problem. In retrospect, there are things we could have done differently. We had power struggles with the kids, were too strict, were too lenient, said yes when we shouldn't have, said no when we shouldn't have. At times Donn had serious doubts and fears and wondered if he had the right to create a homeschooling book when we, or the kids, had problems. We have dealt with lying, stealing, drugs, alcohol, and personality conflicts. Homeschooling didn't exempt our family from dealing with problems that occur with children in public schools. Homeschooling did create strong family bonds that gave us a better understanding of each other and the strength to deal with these problems and resolve them creatively and constructively. It's a case of on-the-job training and learning. Kids don't come with a training manual.

Other Challenges That Come With Adolescence

We learned that we needed to reexamine our goals and continue to focus on the kids' interests as we worked to impart lifelong learning skills.

Much of our education was introspective; that is, we frequently examined what we were doing as we did it, continually looking for ways to improve our learning, abandoning methods or materials that weren't working well and searching for others that were better. We had read and discussed John Holt's *How Children Learn,* applying it to ourselves, testing it against our own experience. Despite the title, many of John's observations can be applied to how *anyone* learns, at any age.

Our approach to many of the subjects, as you have seen, was often different, sometimes oblique — as with Derek's study of sharks. We often introduced new subjects, or new facets, and we led, guided, instructed, and questioned, but we let the kids' own interests determine the scope and direction of our leadership. Sooner or later, their interests usually led them not only to all the fields and subjects prescribed by law or convention, but to many others as well, and often beyond the levels expected in public schools. We tried to lead the kids in the directions where their interest was low, feeling some general knowledge was necessary for a liberal arts education. We made an effort to not force higher math or higher levels of some skills on the kids who seemed to have little inclination for the subject. **Our aim was to see they had the skills to learn whatever might be useful to them in the future.**

This has proved itself to be a reasonable approach for our kids. To the best of my knowledge none of the kids has felt handicapped because of the education he did or did not get at home. Since leaving home, all of them have learned higher math or other skills when they have had use for them. Along with whatever knowledge they had when they left home, they have taken the all-important skill of knowing how to learn with them.

Several years after Derek left home we had an interesting conversation about his studies. When I asked him if he felt he had learned what he needed to know before leaving home, he said no. I raised my eyebrows. He went on to explain that he wished he had had more math, so I asked him if he felt we should have pushed him to do more. He chuckled and said, "No. I resisted. You and Dad did all you could do for me. It's my fault I didn't learn more." I asked if he'd had any trouble learning the math he needed after he left home, and he assured me that he hadn't. I've heard similar stories from other parents. In comparing stories we all felt reassured.

Beyond the psychological and emotional challenges that come with adolescence there is a tendency by some parents to prematurely encourage the kids into early career choices. We felt it was important not to do this.

Some public schools encourage children as young as eleven or twelve to choose their academic and vocational futures. Twice that age would be a much better time for such choices, if they must be made. We encouraged our kids not to make choices and decisions, but to watch and explore their own feelings and desires — to watch their general inclinations, and follow them, but without committing themselves beyond their present interests.

Our kids saw many of their friends move steadily, or so it seemed, toward definite goals, but they rarely envied them, whether the goals were college, careers, the military, or working in the local frozen food plant. They knew that many of their friends had been programmed by parents, teachers, aptitude tests, guidance counselors, or even economic necessity to make early decisions, often based on narrow or incomplete data, and that many would probably be frustrated and unhappy adults.

With high school, as with earlier learning, the children's own interests and preferences were the best indications of the direction their studies should take. Working with them, we helped them to discover and develop fields of study that would give them solid foundations for nearly any career or lifestyle, as well as the knowledge, skills, and self-confidence to develop other foundations if their interests changed.

We tried to show our children the broadest fields of possibilities, always emphasizing that there's no need to make an immediate choice — that following one's own interests and instincts, not as a goal but as an exciting journey, would lead naturally to a happy, creative life. If a child of ten or fifteen (or any age) has a particular talent or interest, and is determined to follow it, that's good — provided that determination doesn't become a dutiful consistency without a continuing interest. How many adults would like to change careers or lifestyles when they're thirty or forty or fifty, but don't dare to, or don't feel capable of doing so? Any early choices made should allow for the possibility that a more desirable alternative might suddenly pop up at any time, and for the freedom of thought and circumstance to accept that alternative.

HIGH SCHOOL (AND GETTING TO THE NEXT STEP, WHATEVER THAT IS)

STUDY OPTIONS BY THE TRIAL-AND-ERROR METHOD
DEVELOPING STUDIES — GRADUATION AND DIPLOMAS
AVOIDING THE EMPTY-NEST SYNDROME

Trials and Errors

We learned the pros and cons of correspondence schools. We concluded that they covered only the basics, and we and our children wanted more depth in our learning experiences.

Many of the conventional high school subjects are part of a good beginning. Cathy enrolled in the American School of Chicago, possibly the best known of the many correspondence high schools. At that time, the entire four-year course cost about five hundred dollars, which we were allowed to pay in small monthly installments. Each of this school's courses consisted of a basic textbook and examination booklet, sometimes including a brief study guide. Cathy read a chapter, wrote out a test, and mailed it in; the test was graded by the school and returned, usually with brief comments. Cathy had three or four courses at one time; when one was completed, she began another. The textbooks were average; i.e., not outstanding, but adequate. Her algebra text was based on "new math," which none of us liked, and her general science book seemed to be poorly written and confusing.

After we had seen half a dozen of Cathy's courses, Jean and I realized we could provide a much better education ourselves, choosing our own textbooks, and, not so incidentally, save at least two hundred dollars. We sent for, and studied, the catalogs from several correspondence high schools and found most of them to be like the American School. They offered little more than fifteen or sixteen textbooks, a few brief study guides, a series of short tests (most of which could be completed quite easily by reading the questions and then searching the text for the answers), and a diploma. A conscientious student can learn a great deal from them; a lazy student could receive high marks and a diploma almost as easily. Most of the schools offered some individual attention if the student had problems or specific questions.

Extension courses offered by universities and state departments of education usually have a much wider range of subjects, sometimes with laboratory materials (when appropriate), and more personalized tutoring, by mail or telephone. A supervisor approved by a local official often is required for courses taken for credit. Non-credit courses require no supervision, and usually cost much less. (Many universities and community colleges will now allow high school students to make use of their correspondence or online courses.)

At least half the correspondence high schools whose catalogs we received were not accredited, which means that they had not yet been "certified" by an independent examining board. The majority of these schools had curricula identical, or at least very similar, to those that were accredited. Diplomas from these non-accredited schools are genuine and represent at least as much study and learning as most accredited correspondence schools or public schools.

None of the high school programs we examined seemed to meet our needs. We felt that the education itself was far more important than the diploma, and all the correspondence courses lacked many of the subjects we felt were most desirable or necessary. As thousands of functional illiterates receive fully accredited diplomas from public schools, more and more colleges and employers realize that the decorated parchment may mean nothing at all except that the student has met minimal attendance requirements.

How We Developed Our High School Studies

We decided that our own curriculum was superior to that of almost any public or correspondence school. We broadened our literature base considerably by adding books from many different genres and many cultures. We read much of the literature together and discussed it. We talked about the ideas and characters, the authors and the time in which they lived, how they were influenced by the people and events around them, and how they in turn influenced their times and the world. We found biographies to supplement and deepen our understanding of history and literature and incorporated geography. We spent more time talking about the development of philosophy and religion throughout history and in our own time. We read about nature and ecology. We used several scientific magazines as well as textbooks and discussed developments and possibilities for the future. We talked about world news, world conflicts, and conflict resolution. We used public television, *Smithsonian* magazine, *Newsweek,* and many audio and videocassettes as well as numerous books to investigate and learn about the arts. We read and discussed psychology and personal ideals. We studied languages (French and Spanish as well as English). We talked about the meaning of life, in both the totally abstract and the intensely personal. Jean and the girls all played musical instruments — guitars, recorders, flute, clarinet, keyboard — and sang together. All the kids stuck mostly with basic practical math and geometry except for Karen, who studied more advanced math because she wanted to do it.

Other activities, many of which are discussed elsewhere in this book, were just as much a part of the education we provided: youth groups, 4-H, ball games, skiing, skating, sliding, carrying firewood, churning butter, building our barn, building our house, square dancing, gardening, cooking, washing dishes, caring for our farm animals, gathering maple sap, traveling, and on and on. The kids had jobs at times — working in a grocery store, the library, a secondhand bookstore; cleaning a stable; picking potatoes; picking rocks; baby-sitting. They learned how to save money and how to spend it, how to study catalogs and decide what to buy, and how to evaluate their purchases afterwards.

We always sought ways to expand the children's knowledge and experience far beyond that of our rural home. Cathy and Karen participated in national 4-H exchange programs, Cathy traveling to Alberta and Karen to Manitoba. Cathy worked once a week as a volunteer helper in a public library, and the following summer was hired as a full-time assistant. The next year she was a counselor in a girls' camp in Vermont. Karen visited relatives in Vermont and New York, went to Virginia and New Hampshire for two-week visits with families we had "met" by correspondence, and worked for a few hours in John Holt's office in Boston. Susan won a trip into the past at New Brunswick's Kings Landing Historical Settlement (see "Reading, Writing, and Spelling") and went on month-long Outward Bound trips in Maine and Texas. She, too, worked at a summer camp. If you can't afford

to send your kids as a camper, help them get jobs as counselors or assistant counselors! Derek worked in a sporting goods store and later cleaned horse stalls to pay for riding lessons and the opportunity to be near horses. He later worked at a riding camp in Virginia as a counselor-in-training. It wasn't long before he was training horses and riders at stables near home.

But back to the academics: Cathy continued her American School studies until she had finished the few courses that were left on hand, augmenting them substantially with our own materials, then shifted to our own curriculum. We had learned an important lesson. We sat down with Karen and worked out her high school courses, and then sent away for books and other materials. The skeleton of her academic work was *High School Subjects Self-Taught,* edited by Lewis Copeland, a comprehensive distillation of 28 subjects. (This book is out of print. Amazon.com does have used copies for sale.) A few subjects, such as history and science, needed supplementation, for which we used several of the "Made Simple" series and various other books especially pertinent to Karen's interests. Karen finished all 28 courses in *High School Subjects Self-Taught* in two very intense years of study (her idea) and went on to expand her studies in literature, psychology, art, and miscellaneous reading. With a few books from the public library, Karen had a complete high school education for less than three hundred dollars (not including all the books and other materials we already had on hand).

Susan used our own high school program for two years and then wanted to enroll in the local high school for the remaining two years. We rejected this idea because we didn't like the curriculum or the presence of drugs and alcohol in the school. We compromised on The Meeting School, a small private school in New Hampshire from which she graduated.

Derek also followed our high school curriculum for a couple of years. When he was 16 he began working part time, saving his money for a car, and began supporting himself. He still read voraciously, but drifted away from academic studies to pursue his longtime ambition to work with horses by obtaining a job teaching riding and training horses in a stable. This was a good choice for him. He now rides, trains, and shows horses for a living.

Conundrum

If you have a teenager who decides he would like to go to public school and you aren't in favor of it, know you are not the only one. It's hard to be in this position. It's hard to homeschool a teenager who doesn't want to be learning at home. On top of dealing with this problem within your family, you may feel pressure from other homeschoolers to keep your teen at home. It can feel embarrassing; they may make you feel like a traitor. Teens want and need to develop independence. This is one way to express this desire. You'll have to make up your own mind, preferably through a lot of discussion with your teen. My advice is to bring up all the pros and cons, and then let him go with the stipulation that if he runs into big problems you will bring him home again. Even if you know you can give him a better academic education, he will still be learning other lessons. Know that you have given him good foundations. It's time to trust him.

Graduation Time

As the children gained knowledge and the necessary skills for living independent lives, Donn and I pondered the meaning of a graduation ceremony. We recognized its importance, not for the diploma — a mere piece of paper — but as a rite of passage into the world at large.

We felt that a diploma from Brook Farm School would have at least as much moral validity as any public or correspondence school diploma. We wrote a rough draft and had the local print shop set it in type and print it on a standard diploma form. It cost about twenty dollars, and to us was much more valuable than others that might have cost us several hundred dollars but would have represented much less work and learning. Those of you with computers can create and print your own diploma for just pennies.

This is how the local newspaper reported Cathy's graduation ceremony:

Unique Graduation Ceremony
THE OBSERVER, Hartland, New Brunswick,
Wednesday, June 20, 1984

Brook Farm School celebrated its first high school graduate, Catherine Barbara Reed, 17, at a unique graduation ceremony held at the Women's Institute Hall in

Knowlesville, Saturday, June 16. A family enterprise, Brook Farm School is operated by Donn and Jean Reed.

Donn Reed opened the Commencement and Awards Ceremony, and welcomed the 35 guests present. He then presented certificates to Catherine and Karen for maintaining exceptional standards of study, workmanship, perseverance, and independent endeavor, and to Susan and Derek for outstanding work and progress in specific areas of investigation, study, and accomplishment. Notes of appreciation were given by the four children to their parents.

Rev. Maynard Rector offered the Baccalaureate, after which Mr. Reed presented Catherine with her diploma. In his address, Mr. Reed said, in part, "Basic academic skills … are all parts of the education in our school. Several other subjects are just as much a part of our education — the study of other countries, and their people, other ways of thinking, other beliefs about humanity and God and the universe. Activities such as daily chores, ball games, participation in 4-H and youth groups, jobs away from home, are invaluable parts of education."

Presenting the Class History, Mr. Reed said, "Through the modern miracles of airplanes, buses, satellite television, and first-class mail, Brook Farm School has drawn freely upon resources and instructors from around the world."

In the Valedictory Address, Catherine said, "I think my education has given me imagination, a sense of truth, and a feeling of responsibility, which I hope to share with people wherever I go."

Following the reading of the Class History, the Last Will and Testament, and the Class Prophecy, the ceremony ended, and guests sat down to a potluck supper. A copy of Catherine's yearbook was presented to each guest.

Catherine is leaving shortly to work as a camp counselor at a private girls' camp in the States, after which she plans to continue her education.

Just How Important Is an "Official" Diploma?

I've checked with all four of our kids, and none has ever been asked to physically present a high school diploma. When applying to a college or for a job, the question is usually "Did you finish high school?" or "What is the highest level of education completed?"

Cathy found that mentioning that she had been homeschooled had unintended consequences during job interviews. On the plus side, she felt that it made her more memorable and stand out among job applicants. On the minus side, it sometimes sidetracked the interview to the point where she had to bring the interviewer back on the interview track.

Graduation: A Time of Dread or Celebration?
Parental Transitions • An Empty Nest!!!

Homeschooling is a way of life. I hear from many parents that they dread the time when their children will be gone and this lifestyle will disappear, too. Some parents fear they will no longer be needed, that there will never again be anything as meaningful in their lives. Some parents are afraid because they don't know what they will do with their own lives. For some parents these thoughts create anxiety, for others panic. Some parents see this time as a doorway to the future, offering new adventures in living and learning for themselves. I know how easy it is to get caught up in the daily routines and activities of homeschooling. As homeschooling parents we work very hard to help our children look ahead to their future. It is vitally and equally important to remember that we too have a future. Through exploring what lies ahead for ourselves we become an ongoing model for our children.

If you're afraid you will no longer be needed, that the meaning of your life will diminish, you are mistaken. Think about your ongoing relationship with your parents. You will always be a parent, and your children will need you at all stages of their lives. However, your role will change over time. Children are born to become increasingly independent. You may stunt them, but you can't entirely stop them. Remember how easy it was to adjust to the myriad changes that occurred over the first few years of your children's lives. It was a natural progression from having a totally dependent baby to having a more independent toddler. At some point you will stop being the chauffeur and hand over the car keys. You can guide and lead by example, and then at some point you must trust your children and trust the life process itself. As your kids become adults they will look to you more as a longtime trusted friend. Although it is rarely said, when your children leave home — for short periods of time or forever — they do so trusting that you will be there for them if they need you. The love and shared memories remain, but your job description changes, and your own developmental challenges change.

When you think about your life after the children are on their own, imagine all the things you haven't had time for while you were involved in the complex daily routine centered around your children. Just as you have worked to make your children aware of the many possibilities for their lives, you too should envision a future filled with possibilities, whether continuing your education, creating or finding a job, developing your artistic talents, finding satisfaction in volunteer work, gardening, reading, or working with other children. There is a future for you to dream about, to work toward, and to bring into reality. This is a time to renew yourself and a time to celebrate a job well done. *Celebrate it!*

For Donn and me, the end of our homeschooling journey had much in common with the beginning stages of our adventure — it was a time of questioning and doubt, a time for reflection and anticipation and new joys. Our children are now scattered across the country, and we've found that the bonds of love, companionship, and understanding formed over the years of living, working, growing, playing, laughing, and crying together overcome the distances between us. As our children became increasingly independent, we found a new maturity, a deepening of respect, and a new feeling of equality developing between us. These intangible rewards of the homeschooling years are lifetime treasures, a living legacy binding our family together through the years.

I used to wonder what an empty nest would be like: Would I find it traumatic when the last child left home? When the time came, Donn and I were surprised at how naturally our lives filled with a variety of interesting and challenging options. Unlike children, these interests didn't require us to be on call 24 hours a day. I went back to college part time, to study computers, sign language, and emergency medicine, and began a serious and engrossing study of classical guitar. Donn worked more intensely on his writing. Both of us enjoyed the time we had to refresh our relationship, to work and play together, just the two of us. We treasured the times when the kids came home, filling the house with their love and laughter. When they left again, we felt immense satisfaction that they were happy establishing their own lives. (Warning! You may still get those late-night calls. So far we've had: 1. "Guess what? We're getting married!" 2. "We just had a baby!" 3. One that started with "Everything's all right, but ... I'm calling from the ambulance." Once a parent, always a parent!)

Options for Continuing Education

Today, you and your children have more options to explore than we did. One recent development is the increased number of community and private colleges, as well as some universities, allowing homeschooled students to take higher-level courses for credit while still in high school. Community college courses are relatively inexpensive. If you have been a resident of the area for at least six months, there are usually scholarships or reduced rates available.

Another option is to use a computer to participate in the rapidly expanding possibilities offered by high school and college distance-learning courses on the Internet. I get excited when I think that a student can take a class that may originate across the country (and be able to interact with the class as it takes place), monitor an archaeological dig in Egypt, or follow a space mission — all from a home computer. Distance-learning classes can provide stimulating and challenging opportunities for your children — and you. It's possible to get full credit for your distance learning, which can help with college admissions. If you don't have a computer, your child may be able to use one at the library or a community resource center. If the course taken is a non-credit course, be sure to document the work done and create a portfolio.

Here is a short list of correspondence schools that will take you through high school:

AMERICAN SCHOOL, 2200 E. 170th St., Dept. #105, Lansing, IL 60438-1002; 800-531-9268; www.americanschoolofcorr.com. Offers a general high school course and a college prep course.

CLONLARA HOME-BASED EDUCATION PROGRAM, 1289 Jewett St., Ann Arbor, MI 48104; www.clonlara.org. Helps homeschoolers design a customized high school education.

THE SYCAMORE TREE, 2179 Meyer Place, Costa Mesa, CA 92627; www.sycamoretree.com.

UNIVERSITY OF NEBRASKA AT LINCOLN, P.O. Box 888400, Lincoln, NE 68588-8400; nebraskahs.unl.edu.

CANADIAN BRANCH OF ICS (INTERNATIONAL CORRESPONDENCE SCHOOLS), 888-427-2400; www.icslearn.ca.

INTERNATIONAL STUDY. Free information from the Council on International Education Exchange: www.ciee.org/hsabroad.

For independent study, see ***PETERSON'S INDEPENDENT STUDY CATALOG*** on page 260.

BEARS' GUIDE TO EARNING HIGH SCHOOL DIPLOMAS NONTRADITIONALLY: A GUIDE TO MORE THAN 500 DIPLOMA PROGRAMS AND SCHOOLS **by Thomas Nixon.**

You can also write to the **DISTANCE EDUCATION AND TRAINING COUNCIL,** 1601 18th St. NW, Washington, DC 20009-2529, and request their Directory of Accredited Institutions. It's free. It's also available online at www.detc.org.

THE TEENAGER'S GUIDE TO SCHOOL OUTSIDE THE BOX, **by Rebecca Greene.** The book to use to put real spice into the high school years. It's full of real accounts by teens about their experiences with internships, mentorships, volunteering, study abroad, community service, apprenticeships, and numerous other exciting learning experiences. Many of these opportunities can be done from home; others involve travel. Details in the book explain how to scout out opportunities and evaluate them so you know if they will be right for you, how to prepare, what to expect, how to make the most of your experience, and how to overcome obstacles such as cost and distance. Greene has good listings of where to go to find out more about hundreds of programs. Good for teens and other young adults.

I don't think it matters if you are not sure your child will go on to college; create a portfolio of what is studied, and be sure to document those non-traditional activities too. If you need it for college admission you'll have it. If your child isn't going to college it will give you a good sense of what has been accomplished — and it may be that after a year or two your child will change his mind and apply to college.

AFTER HIGH SCHOOL, NOW WHAT?

TO COLLEGE OR NOT — ALTERNATIVES

Parents and young adults begin to have renewed doubts about homeschooling and feel more pressure during the high school years, for several reasons. For parents the obvious discomfort is caused by thoughts about whether or not they have prepared their child adequately for the future — including college, if that is the goal. Many students wonder what they would like to do after graduating and feel they must face the traditional choice between college and work. Many homeschoolers are challenging that choice, and I feel this is healthy.

If you are having doubts about getting into college, relax! Getting into college is no longer the "BIG QUESTION" it used to be. I know of no college or university that has turned down a homeschooled student's application just because he was homeschooled. Increasingly, colleges and universities are coming to appreciate homeschooled students because they are more self-motivated, because they know what they want to get from their continuing educational experience, and because they know how to direct their own studies far better than many of their traditionally educated peers. Colleges actively seek out students with these abilities. Pat Farenga, the former publisher of *Growing Without Schooling,* says some colleges are now sending recruiters to homeschooling conferences!

These are the important questions to consider when thinking about college: Is college attendance necessary or desirable to reach the long-term goals of the student? Is it necessary or desirable to attend college in the traditional manner? Would an internship or working with a mentor be more productive? If more formal education is the right way to reach the end goals, what is the best manner to prepare for it?

The answer to the first question should be answered by your young adult. If you feel your child should attend college just because it feels like the best option to you, but your child is opposed to the idea, you should read Herbert Kohl's book *The Question Is College* (see below). It will help you sort out this problem. If you have been homeschooling, I hope you are aware that there is no point in anyone's pursuing a college education without inner motivation.

If you're still reading, you probably need to seriously consider the second question: Is it necessary or desirable to attend college in the traditional manner? There are many pursuits in life that will necessitate attendance, on campus, at a college. If this is the course your young person has decided to pursue, you will need to search for the appropriate institution. Your local library should have books listing colleges and universities along with notes about their specialties, if any. The Peterson's guides (see pages 257 and 260) will help, too.

For those wishing to pursue more education in a non-traditional manner, there are many opportunities available, and it is no longer as difficult to find them as it used to be. Although there are jobs and careers that require college attendance, there are many that require only the necessary knowledge, in which case an apprenticeship or learning through work experience may be more satisfactory.

Fortunately, one of the blessings that come with non-traditional education at all levels is the ability to pick and choose the best possible resource or resources for each individual circumstance. Community colleges are lower in cost and available to everyone. Your young adult can attend as many or as few classes as he wishes, making it possible to work part time and take classes. An option to consider for your college-bound high school student is taking one or more college courses while still doing most of high school at home. This can be done through local colleges or community colleges, through correspondence, or over the Internet. One of the benefits of the increasing number of high-school-age homeschoolers is that more and more traditional learning institutions are becoming responsive to requests for part-time attendance and participation in their programs.

To Consider

Warning! If you want and expect your kids to go to college, do not let them read this book, unless you are willing to consider other options. If you'd like to help your child find a way to live a fulfilling life doing work he loves whether it involves college or not, then all of you will benefit from the following book: ***THE QUESTION IS COLLEGE: ON FINDING AND DOING WORK YOU LOVE,*** **by Herbert Kohl.** Yes, if you've read through "Homeschooling and Education" earlier in this book, you've seen this listed before. It brings us full circle, back to evaluating the true needs of educational goals. I hope you've reread this book. If not, this is the time to do it again — and for your young adult to read it, too. In spite of the warning, which may make you feel this book is anti-college, you should know it is not against college. Kohl questions the need for college, and that need will vary according to your long-term goals.

In the first section of the book Kohl challenges you to think deeply about lifetime goals — what constitutes satisfactory living — and you may find yourself evaluating your needs as well as those of your children. Kohl will help you see how important it is to support your child in whatever decision he makes about college, and help you consider whether or not taking time off before or during college would be advantageous. The second and third sections have specific tools to help your young adult determine what will be the best course of action after high school — and how to achieve it. There are charts to set up a career profile and a thorough explanation of how to use this information. The appendices have useful information about further resources you or your young adult can use to find other opportunities for the future.

HOMESCHOOLERS' COLLEGE ADMISSIONS HANDBOOK: PREPARING YOUR 12- TO 18-YEAR-OLD FOR A SMOOTH TRANSITION, **by Cafi Cohen.** All I can say is, "read it." I also suggest you read her excellent book *And What About College?*

FROM HOMESCHOOL TO COLLEGE AND WORK: TURNING YOUR HOMESCHOOLED EXPERIENCES INTO COLLEGE AND JOB PORTFOLIOS, **by Alison McKee.** This clearly written book is an excellent guide for all parents and students learning at home, no matter what your particular "brand" of learning. It will help you learn how to take advantage of your unique experiences to apply for college or work. McKee outlines when and how to begin your documentation, how to compile your data, and how to put it together in a final form — all with examples. There is also a good list of resources if you feel you need more information. Highly recommended. There may be flashier books, but this one has all the basics you'll need.

And don't forget to check the **NATIONAL HOME EDUCATION NETWORK**'s huge collection of information and resources on high school and beyond: www.nhen.org/nhen/pov/teens.

Ideas

Here are a few hints for using the web as a resource for finding and applying to college. Use the College Board at www.collegeboard.org, Kaplan at www.kaplan.com, or the Princeton Review at www.review.com to help you plan when to take various exams, file applications, and a lot more. One of the features you'll find on some online sites that may be particularly useful is a series of multiple-choice questions along with SAT scores to help you match your young person's interests to a suitable college. Many college applications can be filled out online, but I think particularly for homeschoolers, because our kids offer so much more than the typical public school students, it's best to send in a regular application and take advantage of the opportunity to write about special abilities and experiences.

College by Correspondence

For those who prefer to continue their studies at home or while working, there are hundreds of institutions that offer college credits and even grant fully accredited degrees mostly or entirely by correspondence. The cost is far below that of an on-campus education. Usually, the correspondence program can be completed in a shorter time than an on-campus program would take, if you're in a hurry. Another advantage is being able to work at the same time if you find it necessary or desirable. The credits and degrees thus earned are completely legal and are recognized throughout the world as being just as good as if they were obtained on campus. One can earn a bachelor of arts, a bachelor of science, a master's in several fields, even a law degree and several doctorates — all without ever attending a school except through a post office. It is often possible to earn a full degree without taking any courses, by having one's work, hobbies, previous training and study, military service, and travel experiences evaluated.

Contact the **NATIONAL ASSOCIATION FOR COLLEGE ADMISSION COUNSELING,** 1631 Prince St., Alexandria, VA 22301; 800-822-6285; www.nacacnet.org/memberportal/Events/CollegeFairs for information about college fairs in your area where you can talk directly with representatives about courses, financing, and your other concerns.

Some of the best college-by-correspondence programs are offered by:

STATE UNIVERSITY OF NEW YORK, ALBANY, NY 12230; SLN.suny.edu/SLN.

UNIVERSITY OF NEBRASKA AT LINCOLN, College Counselor, Division of Continuing Studies, 511 Nebraska Hall, Lincoln, NE 68588; extended.unl.edu. The College Independent Study program offers the opportunity for high school juniors and seniors to earn college credits while still in high school; for students who are attending on-campus college classes to make up academic deficiencies; and for students who are off campus (at home or elsewhere) to expand their academic background without attending classes. More than 100 courses are offered. Non-credit college-level courses are also offered in specific professional and personal interest areas. Counseling for students is available.

UNIVERSITY OF PHOENIX, P.O. Box 52031, Phoenix, AZ 85072-9352; 877-879-4723; www.phoenix.edu. B.S. and M.A. degrees through distance learning.

UNIVERSITY OF WISCONSIN EXTENSION SERVICE believes in making high school and college courses available to those who want them. Very supportive. Check out their website, www.uwex.edu, to find out more.

Other Resources

PETERSON'S UNDERGRADUATE GUIDE TO FOUR-YEAR COLLEGES. Incredible guide to four-year degree programs — or just exciting study. Created in cooperation with the University Continuing Education Association, this is the only comprehensive guide providing details on thousands of degree and certificate distance-learning opportunities in almost 800 accredited institutions in the U.S. and Canada. Wow! If you want to study at home, this is for you.

In Canada

ATHABASCA UNIVERSITY, 1 University Dr., Athabasca, AB T9S 3A3; www.athabascau.ca. Very comprehensive and inexpensive. Full degree programs entirely by mail and open to residents of the U.S. and Canada for very reasonable fees. Write for current catalog.

UNIVERSITY OF GUELPH, Independent Study, Guelph, ON N1G 2W1; www.open.uoguelph.ca. Offers a variety of courses.

Test Preparation

Let's start by putting testing into perspective. Passing a test isn't necessarily the measure of anything meaningful, or is it? In Chicago a 2001 investigation by the *Sun-Times* showed that more than 800 Illinois teachers failed the state's basic skills test over a period of thirteen years. In Pennsylvania nearly a quarter of the state's public school teachers struck out on their certification tests in 2003. In 2005 the *Sarasota Herald-Tribune* reported that "a third of [Florida's] teachers, teacher's aides, and substitutes had failed certification tests at least once."

When I was in school I froze up when tested. Papers would come back with many items marked as incorrect. I'd look at the questions and wonder how I could have made a mistake, because I knew the material. Some of us just don't respond well to pressure. Each of us learns skills at a different pace. We do not learn to walk or talk at the same time. Testing leaves no room for individualization in learning styles or needs. Why should school kids have to be held to a strict standard that makes no allowance for different learning abilities?

There is more mandatory testing in schools now. A study by the Great Lakes Center for Education Research and Practice (www.greatlakescenter.org/research.htm), using data from twenty-eight states, found that high-stakes tests may "ultimately hinder student achievement rather than improve it." According to researchers at the Center for Mental Health in Schools at the University of California at Los Angeles, a heavy emphasis on tests can be damaging to vulnerable students' mental health and self-esteem. Respected educational thinker Alfie Kohn says, "Tests measure what matters least, reinforcing compliance and standardized thinking rather than creativity and innovation. In addition, tests offer little insight into the quality of instruction in a school. They tend to reinforce pedagogy that is not supported by research."

Studies have shown that there is a low correlation between good grades in school and what is accepted as "success" in life. It is also known that many who have done poorly in school have attained great success in life. The testing associated with the No Child Left Behind (NCLB) Act does not, and cannot, assess personal characteristics that I feel are more important than the ability to regurgitate facts. I think the NCLB act has narrowed the curriculum, leaving less time for creative teaching, and I expect we've all read the newspaper articles about the cheating done by students and teachers in order to attain higher scores.

I think we can all agree that schools need to be held accountable for a student's education and that no child should be passed through the system unable to read or without a broad base of knowledge, but there has to be a better way. I applaud those of you who have taken your kids out of schools so that your children have the freedom to grow at their own pace.

If you would like to protest testing you can investigate the following, which I learned about on the listserv of the Alternative Education Resource Organization (AERO; www.educationrevolution.org): "Students Against Testing is sending out anti-standardized testing action packs to organizations, schools, and individuals around the country. They include: 2 visual flyers for copying and distributing, a "10 Ways to Fight the Tests" flyer, a couple of fact sheets, and a bumper sticker. If you or anyone you know would be interested in receiving this, please send your snail mail address to: mail@nomoretests.com. On the web at: www.NoMoreTests.com. More information: info@NoMoreTests.com."

As you face college admissions you have a choice to make: You can go the more traditional route and have your child take one of the standardized tests, or you can create a portfolio. Here are some thoughts about each that I hope will help.

What Does SAT Stand For?

Nothing. Initially titled the Scholastic Aptitude Test and then the Scholastic Assessment Test, it is now officially named just SAT because of uneasiness about defining just what the test measures.

I recently heard Dr. Ruth Simmons, president of Smith College from 1995 to 2001, on National Public Radio speaking to the Commonwealth Club of California. Simmons grew up in poverty and went on to become the first black woman to achieve the title of college president, and she has filled her life with rich accomplishments. When she spoke of college admissions tests, her opinion was that sometimes the students who do the poorest actually have the greatest potential. She did not mean you shouldn't study and work hard if college is your goal. She meant that many students of great potential will not have great test scores, which is why Smith College (like many others) asks for an essay. This is the place to show off your homeschooling work; your original thinking; and your ideas, ideals, and goals. By the way, Smith also invites parents to write something for them.

Not all colleges and universities require SAT or other College Board testing. Plan ahead. If you're faced with official testing, read about it. Your child can achieve higher scores if he understands more about the testing procedure, and there are ways to increase scores without "knowing more."

Now, having mentioned the SAT and College Board testing I want to move on the ACT test. It is rapidly becoming the most acceptable test for college entrance. It seems to be easier on students, and an increasing number of colleges will accept it in place of the SAT. One advantage to the ACT is that you can retake it and then use the best score. According to a recent article in Newsweek, the recently revised SAT is losing support,. The same article says FairTest, "a Cambridge, Massachusetts, nonprofit organization that opposes over-reliance on testing, has a list of 700 four-year colleges and universities it says do not use the SAT or the ACT to make decisions about a significant number of applicants." You can get a free updated list by sending a #10 SASE to "Tests Optional," Fair Test; www.fairtest.org/optional.htm.

We used a number of "test preparation" guides over the years, not with any intention of preparing anyone for a test, but as comprehensive curriculum guides and basic reference works. The guides for the SAT, the SSAT, and the GED (there is a Canadian GED), especially, include full review and instruction in the basic subjects that are generally considered part of a good high school education. We usually ignored the tests, unless the kids wanted to do them to discover "weak" points, but we gained much useful information from the instructional sections.

There are a number of websites devoted to SAT preparation. Some of these charge up to $500 for unlimited use of their service, and some are free. In September 2006, *Consumer Reports* WebWatch tested ten of these sites. They found that Number2.com was as helpful as Kaplan and Princeton Review (not affiliated with the university), which charge a goodly sum for limited access. CR suggests that your student choose the opt-out boxes to avoid college-related promotional e-mail. Testers found that there were fewer glitches when using Internet Explorer. The best options for using the web for SAT prep are using Number2.com or downloading free practice tests at www.collegeboard.com.

Me, I still think the investment in a good prep book is the best way to study. With a book you will have all the pertinent information at hand, and you can review and use it in the most useful way for your student.

LEARN IN FREEDOM (learninfreedom.org/colleges_4_hmsc.html) is an excellent website with a long list of colleges that have accepted homeschoolers. If you don't have a computer, it's worth a trip to a community access center or the library to use theirs.

Guides for Independent Study

PETERSON'S INDEPENDENT STUDY CATALOG. Lists hundreds of onsite as well as reputable correspondence and distance-learning opportunities (for high school, college, and lifelong learners) and what each offers. Helpful information answering common questions (e.g., who should consider independent study, why consider it, what it offers, questions you should ask before registering with a college, how it really works, and how to finance your studies). U.S. and Canadian listings.

BEAR'S GUIDE TO EARNING COLLEGE DEGREES NONTRADITIONALLY, **by John Bear, Ph.D.** This book has been revised to such an extent they've changed the title! It's now called ***BEAR'S GUIDE TO EARNING DEGREES BY DISTANCE LEARNING.*** It's still the best resource for earning a bachelor's, master's, doctorate, law, or medical degree through a wide range of unconventional methods. Discusses more than 2,500 schools and programs. 400 brand-new listings.

COLLEGE DEGREES BY MAIL & INTERNET, **by John Bear, Ph.D.** The best guide to the 100 best accredited non-traditional institutions that grant degrees at undergraduate or graduate levels without requiring attendance on campus.

FROM HOMESCHOOL TO COLLEGE AND WORK: TURNING YOUR HOMESCHOOLED EXPERIENCES INTO COLLEGE AND JOB PORTFOLIOS, **by Alison McKee.** This clearly written book is an excellent guide for all parents and students learning at home, no matter what your particular "brand" of learning. It will help you learn how to take advantage of your unique experiences to apply for college or work. McKee outlines when and how to begin your documentation, how to compile your data, and how to put it together in a final form — all with examples. There is also a good list of resources if you feel you need more information. Highly recommended. There may be flashier books, but this one has all the basics you'll need.

Training is everything. The peach was once a bitter almond; cauliflower is nothing but a cabbage with a college education. — Mark Twain

Financing That College Degree

Keep in mind that public universities may not be the cheapest schools. Public institutions rely on government money. It is only a limited amount, and they are not at liberty or likely to give complete scholarships. A private university may have an endowment fund and be able to afford anything from a partial to a full scholarship.

Fill out the Free Application for Federal Student Aid. This will determine how much your family is expected to contribute to your child's tuition. Make sure you check with the admissions officer about all the scholarship possibilities. The advice from Peterson's (the people who put out the great college and career guides) is that the less-selective schools tend to be the most generous with scholarship money. Look for schools where your student will be in the top 25 percent of all applicants. Look for schools with good regional reputations but little national visibility, such as Lewis and Clark College in Portland, Oregon. Their names may not be well known, but they are academically sound, and you are more likely to find smaller classes. With high grades from a smaller college it is always possible to move to a bigger institution with more scholarship money.

The library is a good place to start looking for scholarship money, either in books or online. Check out the College Board's online scholarship search at apps.collegeboard.com/cbsearch_ss/welcome.jsp, which will help you match interests and talents with available scholarships. There is a wide selection of books about finding scholarships on Amazon.com. Look for private grants. Many civic groups, private foundations, professional organizations, and corporations award grants. Westinghouse gives out from $1,000 to $40,000 in science awards. Coca-Cola also gives out awards.

Before filling out an application for college or financial aid, look in the library for the following books. They will help you make the most of your financial situation, whether you are in dire need of financial help or have enough income so you don't think you qualify for help. Look in the Princeton Review's ***STUDENT ACCESS GUIDE TO PAYING FOR COLLEGE,*** by Kalman Chany, and the College Board's ***COLLEGE COSTS AND FINANCIAL AID HANDBOOK.***

Finding Scholarship $$$$$$

The free online service **FASTWEB.COM** will match your student with appropriate scholarships. There is a fairly lengthy registration process, but you can't expect good results without completing all the possibly pertinent information. FastWeb will deposit search results from its database of 180,000 scholarships and future updates to your personal mailbox. With help like this, there is every reason to believe you will find some financial help.

HOMESCHOOLER'S SCHOLARSHIP FUND. The Quaqua Society, Inc. (www.quaqua.org), was formed by former homeschool student Dan Witte to provide scholarships to outstanding home-educated graduates of diverse backgrounds who are headed to college or some other institution of advanced learning, as an attempt to give back to home education what home education had given to him. In a FAQ blurb Dan describes Quaqua. "Quaqua Society, Inc., is a tax-exempt, non-profit, charitable, pro-bono, all-volunteer foundation. Quaqua provides financial assistance, recognition, and information to outstanding home-education graduates pursuing advanced studies in college or vocational school, regardless of race, religion, worldview, gender, age, geographic residence, citizenship, pedagogy, curriculum, organizational affiliation, income level, or related criteria."

The federal **Department of Education** has a "student gateway to the U.S. government," www.students.gov, where you can find information about planning and preparing for two- and four-year programs; applying for student aid, including federal, state, and private sources of grants, scholarships, and loans; how to repay those loans; and testing.

Is a Career Desirable?

Common opinion these days — or "conventional wisdom," as it's sometimes called, although it's seldom very wise — is that it's important to decide upon a career as early in life as possible, and to work diligently to achieve that career and to advance in it. In the United States and Canada, the question "What do you do?" usually means "What do you do for a living?" In most other parts of the world, although the earning of money is considered a necessary part of one's life, "What do you do?" refers to one's hobbies, avocations, or personal interests — "What do you do for enjoyment?" Not everyone is fortunate enough to have his strongest interests coincide with means of earning money; many people resign themselves to working for money at jobs they don't care for, but are able to fill their other hours with more interesting activities, and don't feel their lives are wasted. Many people are content to have a variety of jobs during their lifetimes, although much of society sees this as being unsettled and indecisive, if not downright shiftless. "Jack of all trades, master of none" used to be the common pejorative applied to someone who didn't stay settled in one line of work.

I have never had a desire for any one career. Since I left high school, I've worked at many things — road construction worker, newspaper editor, psychiatric aide, migrant farm worker, freelance columnist, sawmill edgerman, etc. Usually, I stayed with the jobs for as long as I enjoyed them; when my enjoyment began to wane, I moved on to something else. Many times I have had the opportunity of staying with a job and advancing in it — "making a career" of it — but I knew I'd soon become bored and wish I were doing something else. "A foolish consistency," said Emerson, "is the hobgoblin of little minds." Not consistency, but a "foolish consistency" — being consistent just for the sake of being consistent.

Even now, although most of my monetary income is derived from my books and our mail-order book service, not all of our living comes from them. We have a cow and chickens and pigs and a garden, and a great deal of our living comes from a sort of part-time farming, although it doesn't bring us any money. The monetary value of the food we produce through our own efforts could be expressed as the amount of money we would have to spend to buy it, but that doesn't say anything about our enjoyment and satisfaction in raising it. We'd rather put the time and labor into milking the cow and collecting eggs than half the time into earning money with which to buy milk and eggs produced by someone else.

There is nothing dishonorable in having a variety of work, either concurrently or consecutively; a peripatetic career can be as remunerative and often more satisfying than the single-minded pursuit of only one kind of work.

Choosing a career should be done only if one wants a career.

TELEVISION

I disagree with the fairly common belief that many kids of today can't read because they watch too much television. I think they watch too much television because they can't read, which is not the same thing. (I think it's safe to lump video and computer games in with TV in this instance.)

The great public furor over "why Johnny can't read" began before TV became a common household appliance. Public school teachers, not realizing that the teaching methods they had learned were different from those of the previous generation, and feeling perplexed and frustrated by their students' reading failures, thought they had finally discovered the reason for those failures.

Like many other things, television can be a useful tool of learning (as well as a source of good entertainment), or it can be an escape from life. There are times when I resent its intrusion into our lives, even with good programs, and I can understand and sympathize with those who choose not to have a television. On the other hand, I'm just as impatient with those who preach against it as I am with those who watch it for ten or twelve hours a day. If your kids' minds are being turned into soggy oatmeal by too much television, there's no need to throw away the television, as many critics suggest; just cut down on the viewing time. If you can't control your kids' television use, how will you control anything else in their lives?

The number of hours we spend, as a family, in watching television varies from year to year, depending somewhat on our other activities and somewhat on the programs available. Our choices are limited to the programs available in our area, through one Canadian network, one American network, and the American Public Broadcasting Service. We check the TV guide in the local newspaper for National Geographic specials, wildlife and science shows, vintage movies, and occasional music or movie specials. Jean and I choose about a fourth of the programs, although the kids might have chosen the same ones. Our average, over the years, has been about ten or twelve hours a week, although not everyone watched all the shows. A "special," such as *The Ten Commandments,* would add to our time.

Some of the kids wanted to watch some of the soap operas, but we discussed them all democratically and then Jean and I democratically ruled them out.

Some people say that kids will eventually tire of too much television, and shut it off without adult direction. We experimented with that approach a few times, but neither Jean nor I had the stamina to follow through. Many of our kids' friends were hooked on soap operas, and talked of the characters as if they were real acquaintances. If there was a saturation point for them, they hadn't reached it.

Our kids have always spent at least three hours reading for every hour spent watching television. They read before TV, after TV, and even during commercials. They also knit, crochet, and draw during both the programs and the commercials.

One evening, after an episode of *Hill Street Blues* in which a character mentioned casually that a certain situation was "like something out of Kafka," Cathy said she had recently read one of Kafka's stories that didn't seem to fit the allusion. Our discussion of the subject added new dimensions to her studies as well as to the television program.

Sometimes we have discussed the shows, especially if we thought the kids might need help in putting them into useful or healthy perspectives. Some of the situations and people in many of the big-city settings would have been confusing or even incomprehensible to kids whose only contact with cities had been brief visits to relatives in New York, Chicago, and Boston.

Sesame Street was a favorite when the kids were younger. We assumed, like millions of other parents, that it was Good For Them, but after a while we no longer thought so, and we were glad when the kids finally tired of it. John Holt has criticized the show's flashy bombardment of letters and numbers, and we agree with him, but we became more concerned with the relationships of the characters. Most of them are selfish, sarcastic, and inconsiderate. They criticize each other constantly, usually in a bossy, nagging way, or whine about their own misfortunes. (I think *Sesame Street* does nothing constructive toward developing a child's attention span.) Our kids always needed at least an hour of active physical play to counteract each hour of *Sesame Street*.

The only children's show that never disappointed us was *Mister Rogers' Neighborhood*. Mr. Rogers' cheerfulness is never artificial, and he really believes that you — you, to whom he is speaking — are a very special person, just as you are. We were sorry when the kids eventually outgrew it and wished there might be a similar show for older kids.

Even on the programs we enjoy and think are "worthwhile," we are often jolted by the subjects of drugs, violence (both physical and psychological), sexual promiscuity, prostitution, and rape, but we never reject shows just because of them (although we used more "parental discretion" when the kids were younger). Such subjects, unfortunately, are part of everyday conversation throughout society, and our kids need to know how to deal with them. Playing ostrich won't help. So we judge each show by its treatment of such subjects: Is it realistic and accurate? What is the attitude of the show's main protagonist? We accepted the early *Dallas* shows because the "good" characters tried to lead moral lives. We reject *Three's Company* because promiscuity and homosexuality are treated lightly, with double-meaning jokes and naughty winks. Our children's friends who attend public school and watch television for forty hours a week won't keep their "knowledge" secret, so we have the choice of helping our kids understand the subjects or moving to a remote island.

We never tried to develop a formal philosophy about television, but we soon reached several informal rules.

Television, like most other tools, is neither good nor bad in itself. For us, the weekly average of ten to twelve hours has never seemed harmful, and at least half that time has been either directly or indirectly informative and educational, as well as entertaining. We always try not to be arbitrary in our decisions about which shows will be allowed. We're always willing to try a new show if the kids want it, and then we discuss it, although Jean and I retain final veto authority. In limiting viewing time or choosing programs, we always discuss it with the kids; they may disagree with us, but they understand our viewpoint, and usually accept our decisions graciously. We don't grant viewing as a reward, or withhold it as a punishment. We don't use television as a babysitter.

There are many good shows on television — art, nature, science, history, sociology, music, theater — and throwing away the TV in spite of them would be like throwing away all our books because there are so many bad books being published.

We live in a small rural community, fairly isolated both geographically and culturally, which makes television especially valuable for us; but in any situation, the judicious use of television can be very broadening, showing us other countries and ways of life, the deep-sea adventures of Jacques Cousteau, and the exploration of outer space.

Television is certainly not a substitute for books, but neither are books a substitute for television.

One evening, through the combined miracles of intrauterine filming and television, we watched the hazardous journey of a sperm, its union with an ovum, and the magical growth of the resulting single cell into a human being — transparent, without eyes or ears, rapidly developing features and losing its atavistic tail, floating weightlessly inside every mother who has ever lived.

We've watched births and deaths, and thousands of lives, both animal and human. We've attended concerts, not sitting somewhere back in the balcony, but wandering freely through the orchestra, savoring each instrument's voice, then standing with the conductor to hear the blended sounds. Sometimes we spend a few minutes with Grand Prix racing or a prize fight or Billy Graham — not because they have particular meaning in our own lives, but because seeing them increases our knowledge and understanding of those who consider them to be of great importance. We've seen presidents, dictators, winos, junkies, and saints.

Through that little black window, we travel in time and space, and our little home in the woods is everywhere in the world and the universe.

P.S. My observation of today's TV programming is that there are more channels to watch and fewer programs worth watching. It used to be that the TV was a place the family could share entertainment without worrying that it might be offensive. Now it seems to me that it is too frequently used as a baby-sitter, or at least a place to park the kids while you do whatever. Why? I don't know. It has always seemed to me that kids are better off doing something active — and I consider reading an activity — or playing a game with another person, or playing outside; most anything is better most of the time. Now with the computer entering more and more homes there is another place to just sit. The mind may be busy and even doing something that is good for it, but the body is just sitting and staring. Take the time to figure out how much of the day should be spent sitting and staring.

PBS HOME VIDEO, 1320 Braddock Place, Alexandria, VA 22314-1698; www.shoppbs.com. Select videos from Public Broadcasting.

PBS has revamped its website (www.pbs.org), making it more inviting than ever. It offers some helpful new features that enhance educators' use of the site, which includes more than 4,500 free lesson plans, broadcasting schedules, and a lot more good stuff.

A study published in 2004 in *Pediatrics,* the journal of the American Academy of Pediatrics, found that preschoolers watching TV run a more than 10 percent risk developing attention-deficit problems later in life, and of course the percentage goes up when more than an hour of TV a day is watched — and that includes "educational" programming. The study suggests that even with the "educational" programs the quick action, rapid scene changes, and high noise levels might overstimulate the developing brain. If you add that to previous studies that have linked early television viewing with obesity and aggression, there really isn't any valid reason I can see to have a young child sit in front of a TV for any amount of time.

Children are inclined to learn from television [because] ... it is never too busy to talk to them, and it never has to brush them aside while it does household chores. Unlike their preoccupied parents, television seems to want their attention at any time, and goes to considerable lengths to attract it. — National Commission on the Causes and Prevention of Violence, *New York Times,* September 25, 1969

Television Stations and Advertisers Are Targeting Your Babies

Did you know that Direct TV is now airing shows just for your babies? No, kidding, they are, and you pay for the privilege. Only $9.99 a month to introduce your innocent, wonderful, naturally developing babies to shows and advertisements specially designed to turn them into passive, unthinking, conditioned consumers. Isn't the world of business amazing? Did you know that in a survey in 2005 they found that 60 percent of children under the age of two watch television everyday? Save your child! Pull the plug. Let them grow up in the real world around them. It's even more amazing than TV shows and ads.

My TV didn't work for a period of about three months, and during that time I heard more about the bad effects of watching TV than ever before. The consensus among all those who have researched the subject seems to be that children under the age of two should not be watching television or videos at all, because the content, or lack thereof, leads to shortened attention span, lack of or delay in developing physical and mental skills, passivity, and even obesity. Why? Because a young child's mind and body are growing and making connections that are the basis for all future learning and living. Do you want your child to think passivity is the way to live? I challenge you to turn off your TV for a month and then observe the changes in your lives. Write and tell me what you've learned.

FAMILY LIVING — SIMPLE LIVING?

CONFLICT RESOLUTION — HOMESTEADING AND GARDENING SUMMER AND TRAVEL OPPORTUNITIES

Notes and Resources That I Hope Will Make Your Life Better

There is nothing simple about family living. Homeschooling — being both parent and teacher — is not always easy. Each of us is unique. It's all right to be human, to be mad or sad or frightened, to be happy and joyful and full of laughter. To be fully alive we must all laugh and cry, and it is through our example as parents that our children learn how to live — so don't be afraid to show your feelings. Joy and laughter are easy to share. Sorrow and hurt are harder. We tend to want to shelter our children from the hard things in life, but they will learn to cope with their own inner lives and feelings better if they begin to understand these feelings through our experiences and examples. A child who is afraid of the dark or of getting an injection will not think less of you if you tell him you used to feel the same way too. The path to learning courage is to know that it is all right to be afraid and yet do what needs to be done.

***VOLUNTARY SIMPLICITY,* by Duane Elgin,** is not about living in poverty. It is a book about living within the context of balance with our daily needs (as opposed to wants), developing global awareness and personal growth, and seeking the richness within our lives. Elgin is very aware that lasting changes in our society will come from individuals making changes in their own lives and not from government, although these changes will eventually be reflected there.

MEMORY SKILLS, an Usborne book, will give your kids an advantage when they study. It's a boon for parents and teachers, too. Tips and techniques to improve your memory, then some tests you can give yourself to gauge how well you've done. This will help you get names and faces together correctly, and help with studies and Trivial Pursuit. I won't guarantee that the kids will remember to pick up after themselves, but they should at least remember that you told them to do so.

SURVIVAL SKILLS. This Usborne book provides basic knowledge for survival in a variety of circumstances. (For people like me it should begin with the directive to read *Memory Skills* first, so I'll remember to take my bee-sting kit when I pick berries.) Excellent ideas for putting together your own first-aid kit and knowing what you can do in emergencies.

***KIDS TO THE RESCUE! FIRST AID TECHNIQUES FOR KIDS,* by Maribeth and Darwin Boelts.** This book is designed to be used by parents and prereaders together or older children learning the basics of first aid. This is not a complicated book. Very practical, down-to-earth information every child should know so he will not be too frightened to help. They recommend, and I agree, that each section be read, discussed, and then acted out. This book will help your child help others and himself. After assimilating the information, your child will know what to do in certain situations as well as when and how to get help from an adult. Topics covered: bleeding, broken bones, chemical burns in the eye, choking, clothing on fire, dog bite, electric shock, burn, insect sting, nose bleed, poisoning, snake bite, something in the eye, and unconsciousness. This is not an alarming book, and it does not go into gory consequences.

If you really care about survival at home, in town, or in the wilds, enroll everyone in your family, 14 and older, in a CPR course. It doesn't cost much, and that small investment in time can save a life — yours or someone else's. *Survival Skills* won't teach you CPR, but it will be a good beginning.

If you'd rather not learn CPR that way and don't care about certification, you can do it at home and learn just as much. Get your own CPR kit for $36.90, including shipping, by going to www.americanheart.org. On the left, click the tab that says "CPR & ECC," then click on "CPR Anytime" to order. I'm certified in CPR through the National Ski Patrol, but I live in a rural community with an aging population, and I've been concerned for a number of years that we will lose someone because the nearest CPR skills are miles away. I've finally talked our community women's group into ordering this kit, and we will all learn together. I hope we never have to use it, but I will feel better knowing that there are many around with the basic life-saving skills.

***I AM NOT A SHORT ADULT!,* by Marilyn Burns.** A Brown Paper School Book about how to make the best of being a kid. Often much of growing up is spent getting ready for what comes next (kindergarten is preparation for first grade and so on). This is a lighthearted book about the serious business of being a kid right now, about relationships within the family, money, work, TV, and legal rights. A book for creative thinking about what you can and can't control and how to make the best choices for yourself.

***KIDS AND GRANDPARENTS: AN ACTIVITY BOOK,* by Ann Love and Jane Drake.** You can use this book even if the grandparents in your family live across the country — or on the other side of the world. Packed with ideas for things to do and share across the generations by creating together or swapping crafts, recipes, cassette tapes, and more. Ages 6 to 106.

We found that conflict resolution works much better if "blame" is not the issue discussed. We felt that blame was counterproductive, because what is past can't be changed. The current need was a solution. We discussed individual points of view so that all parties involved could see the other perspectives. This did not necessarily mean agreement, just understanding. We put our emphasis on finding solutions and compromises, and finding ways to avoid similar problems in the future. Children of all ages look to their parents for guidance not only in finding an immediate answer, but to learn how we go about finding solutions. It can require a great deal of time and patience, but these lessons are ones that last a lifetime and are worthy of our time and effort. The immediate issue will disappear, but the ways in which we help our children learn to deal with conflict in a peaceable manner will last. It is an example we can set. It is a gift we can give.

Now, many years later, I see that the time we took to help our kids work through their conflicts through discussion were well worth the time and effort. All our kids now have children of their own, and although I've never said anything to them about it I can see them using and passing on the same skills to their children. There's no spanking and no spoiling either.

***THE DISCIPLINE BOOK,* by William Sears, M.D., and Martha Sears, R.N.** I like this book. Based on the theory of attachment parenting, its philosophy is one of observation and appropriate response without physical or psychological violence. The Searses do not believe there is ever a need to spank (I really want to say "hit") a child; however, they recognize that some very loving and committed parents do spank/hit their children, and they include some very good advice and thought-provoking ideas for those who do. They also offer alternatives to spanking/hitting. This book covers important issues from birth through age ten. You'll learn how to say no in a positive manner; deal with temper tantrums; provide structure as well as freedom; deal with biting, hitting (how can we condemn children for hitting if we hit them?), whining, sibling rivalry, morals, and manners; and use discipline for special times and special children (the hyperactive child, the special-needs child, the shy child, etc.). Very thorough, very compassionate.

Manners count. We almost always use them interacting with people outside our families. We found that using the same manners within the family isn't always easy, but they make the business of day-to-day living a lot smoother. Sometimes a simple "please" or "thank you" or "would you mind?" is all it takes to avoid hard feelings.

I think I might be getting cranky in my old age. I have less tolerance for misbehavior than I used to have. I've remarked elsewhere in this book that at homeschool fairs and conferences I generally see happy families with happy children. Even though it's rare, sometimes I do see children misbehave. Freedom to explore and grow is essential. I do not think it includes the right to interfere with the freedom of others. It's nice when children can learn from experience and natural consequences, but I see no reason not to give them some guidelines. I have no quarrel with parents who will allow a child to do what he wants within their own home. My house is something else. It's mostly child-proof, but over the years it has become less so. When visiting my house I do not want kids to maul my animals or take things without asking, and I do not want to feel it is up to me to supervise other people's children. With that said, you are all welcome to come and visit most any time. Calling first is not only good manners but will ensure that I am home at the right time.

***KIDS CAN COOPERATE: A PRACTICAL GUIDE TO TEACHING PROBLEM SOLVING,* by Elizabeth Crary.** An innovative, inspiring, and very practical approach to learning how to help children listen, consider, and cooperate. Crary writes clearly about why kids quarrel and offers concrete ways to help kids learn to settle problems. There is a section for working with preschoolers and a separate one for school-age children, recognizing that issues change and older children can use more complex problem-solving skills. There is also an excellent section about child-parent conflicts. I think this book has many excellent ideas for coping and resolving family conflicts. I highly recommend this book to all imperfect parents with imperfect children. I didn't agree with everything, but that shouldn't surprise anyone.

***BEING YOUR BEST: CHARACTER BUILDING FOR KIDS 7-12,* by Barbara Lewis.** All of us strive to do our best. That includes kids too, even when they squabble with each other, refuse to cooperate, or get mad at us. When kids act inappropriately they are learning what works and what doesn't work in a given situation. In writing this book Lewis has given us valuable tools for helping our kids sort out important ideas and clarify their thinking about many important issues that will affect them throughout their lives. As homeschooling parents we should pursue goals beyond teaching the three R's and include models for good living — for being good people, good neighbors, and good citizens of the world. Lewis's book is a practical approach to developing these skills with quizzes, cartoons, and practical writing exercises. If your kids don't want to write, you can discuss the topics, which is a good idea anyway. Subjects covered in this book are caring, citizenship, cooperation, fairness, forgiveness, honesty, relationships with family and friends, respect, responsibility, and safety. Included are positive examples of real kids making a difference. This book — the younger sibling of *What Do You Stand For?*, mentioned in the "Philosophy and Religion" chapter — will help your kids see that what they do can make a real difference.

Need repairs? Do you hate paying someone for doing something you know you could do if you just knew a little more? Try asking the www.repairclinic.com online. You'll feel like a genius!

Recreation and Special Summer Ideas

PETERSON'S SUMMER PROGRAMS FOR KIDS & TEENAGERS. Wondering what will make the summer memorable for your kids? This annual guide, which was published as *Peterson's Summer Opportunities for Kids & Teenagers* through 2006, reviews more than 1,000 possibilities. Travel the U.S., Canada, or Europe; be a camper, a counselor, or a guide; learn new skills, develop talents, improve your sports or academics; get ready for college; and make new friends. Something for everyone, including the gifted and specially challenged. Details given on day and residential programs, courses, special activities, costs, financial aid, accreditations, and more. You can search a selection of the book's listings for free online at www.petersons.com/summerop/code/ssector.asp.

SUMMER ACTIVITIES FOR TEENS AND UP. Are you looking for constructive projects that will challenge your older children and give them a unique opportunity to work with others their own age, under supervision? For projects near home or overseas write the Quaker Information Center, 1501 Cherry St., Philadelphia, PA 19102, or phone 215-241-7024. Request information about short- and long-term youth programs and additional learning opportunities with the American Friends Service Committee and other organizations. Programs last a weekend or months. Some programs pay and others don't. Most programs have no religious orientation.

CANYONLANDS FIELD INSTITUTE. A remarkable place to enjoy and study the Southwest. Take part in their programs as an individual, group, or family. They offer special programs for teens and even courses for university credit. Canyonlands Field Institute, P.O. Box 68, Moab, UT 84532; 800-860-5262.

WILD QUEST. An Outward Bound-type program with more emphasis on environmentally ethical travel through the wilderness and a natural science/history focus. Learn wilderness skills for safe, comfortable, environmentally ethical travel through areas of the U.S., Canada, and Mexico. Staff is primarily made up of educators. Cost is about half what the other outfits charge. Free catalog and information. 888-217-8226; applications@wildquest.org; www.wildquest.org. The Outward Bound wilderness program offers a special scholarship rate for first-time participants if they need assistance. Maybe Wild Quest does too.

INTERESTED IN WORKING ABROAD? Write for free information from Work Abroad, CIEE, 305 E. 42 St., New York, NY 10017; 212-661-1414, ext. 1126.

***KIDS CAMP! ACTIVITIES FOR THE BACKYARD OR WILDERNESS,* by Laurie Carlson and Judith Dammel.** Lots of activities to help young campers build an awareness of the environment, learn about insect and animal behavior, and enjoy the outdoors, whether near or far from the back door.

AU GRAND BOIS is a family camp offering a variety of outdoor activities as well as crafts, etc., for the entire family. Au Grand Bois, Ladysmith, Quebec J0X 2Q0, Canada; 819-647-3522; bm567@freenet.carleton.ca; mha-net.org/users/agb. Comment from a reader who has been there for a women's retreat: "Great food! Great place!"

***THE KIDS CAMPFIRE BOOK,* by Jane Drake and Ann Love,** is full of great ideas for fun around the campfire. Lots of related activities.

Looking for a camp? The **AMERICAN CAMP ASSOCIATION** has a website (find.acacamps.org) where you can search by location, special needs, specific activities, or other characteristics for camps that meet or exceed industry standards for safety, programming, staffing, health care, food, and more.

Gardening

***ROOTS, SHOOTS, BUCKETS, & BOOTS: GARDENING TOGETHER WITH CHILDREN,* by Sharon Lovejoy.** A wonder book of theme gardens, bean tunnels, a moon garden, a sunflower house, a flowery maze, a snacking and sipping garden, and much more. There's a how-to section that will assist the beginning gardener, myths and stories related to growing things that will intrigue young and old, and snippets of information about wildlife that will be attracted to your garden creation. It's winter, but this book makes me want to grab the nearest kid and start planning summer fun. This book goes well beyond just growing flowers and vegetables. It's about having fun in the garden.

***GREEN THUMBS!,* by Laurie Carlson,** is the perfect way to begin gardening with children ages 5 to 12. Lots of good advice and information is slipped into many projects that you can do with your children or they can do on their own. Easily understood text and lively illustrations.

GARDENING WITH KIDS has many useful books and project materials. Available from National Gardening Association, 1100 Dorset St., South Burlington, VT 05403; www.kidsgardening.com; or call 800-538-7476.

Going Somewhere?

***AUTO REPAIR FOR DUMMIES,* by Deanna Sclar.** Auto repair is conventionally in the male domain, and I'm a total ignoramus once the hood is up, and here's a book by a woman that makes it almost clear to me. Boy, am I embarrassed. This book is the answer for those of us (male or female) not born with wrenches in our hands. Concise, direct, simple explanations help the reader understand the major systems of an automobile and take the fear out of dealing with maintenance and repair. If you don't like greasy hands, at least you'll be able to talk to a mechanic as if you know what you're talking about, but probably, with this book, you won't need a mechanic. More than 300 illustrations. 480 pages, comb-bound so it will lie flat while you refer to it as you work, so you won't get grease all over it.

Free maps and travel information about any state. Call directory assistance for toll-free numbers (800-555-1212) and ask for the state tourism office. Easy!

To find recreation or historic sites, outdoor fun, national parks, and more activities in your area or in an area you'd like to visit or study, try www.recreation.gov.

AMERICAN STUDENT TRAVEL, 16225 Park Ten Place, Suite 450, Houston, TX 77084, 800-688-1965; www.astravel.com. Fun and educational trips in various parts of the U.S. with well-supervised groups for kids ages 10 to 18. Be a chaperone and travel free!

Colleges frequently have empty rooms during the summer. Call the university housing office. Rooms can be as little as $15 a night.

Drive cross-country for free (and maybe get paid) as an auto transporter. Check the yellow pages for Automobile Transporters. Good driving record required, and frequently a $200 refundable deposit. You pay only for food, fuel, and lodging.

INTERVAC U.S. (415-435-3497). For a $35 annual fee, they'll provide three directories — with more than 7,000 contacts in all 50 states and 25 countries — of people who want to trade homes for a vacation.

At **HOMEEXCHANGE.COM** you can search for home exchange listings and contact owners directly at no cost.

Looking for a different kind of vacation? Try house sitting or being caretakers. Send a SASE to The Caretaker Gazette, P.O. Box 540-Z, River Falls, WI 54022. Online: www.caretaker.org.

If you'll be traveling with grandparents through the national parks, and they are members of AARP, they are entitled to a 10 percent discount on admission. If they are over 62 they can call 888-467-2757 for information about a $10 lifetime pass (called a Golden Age Passport).

BIRTHING AND BABIES

PREGNANCY — NURSING — EARLY PARENTING PRO/ANTI-CHOICE

Our ideas about parenting have frequently differed from the norm. Our ideas about childbirth are our own. The piece below, "Our Way," is our story. It is intended as something to consider and think about. Our approach was right for us in the late '60s and early '70s, and we would probably take this approach again now. Today, you have many more birthing options available to you than we had more than thirty years ago. Currently, midwives are reputable and available, doctors and medical attitudes about birth have changed, and the special birthing facilities at hospitals no longer seem to be holdovers from the Middle Ages. The most important decision you'll make about how you want to give birth should be based upon what will make you feel the most comfortable.

Our Way

When Jean and I were expecting our first baby, in 1966, there was very little literature about natural birth. We had read enough to know that we wanted an undrugged birth, but we took for granted the "necessity" of birth in a hospital.

From the beginning, we felt that both the pregnancy and the birth were ours, together. All we asked was permission for me to be present during the labor and delivery.

"Oh, no," the doctor said. "We have enough problems without having fainting husbands all over the floor."

So Jean and I decided, tentatively, to have the baby at home. We began studying all the books we could find on childbirth, gynecology, and relaxation techniques (mainly yoga). We left the question of "where" open to the last minute. We bought and familiarized ourselves with the few supplies necessary for a home birth, but kept our suitcases packed, ready to throw into the car. If either of us felt even a little insecure or worried about having the baby at home, we'd go to the hospital.

The time came and we felt fine. We tingled with anticipation and quiet excitement. The labor was a typical 18-hour, first-baby labor: tiring, but completely without pain. Throughout the labor, I stayed with Jean, rubbing her back, moistening her lips, and being a brace for her legs — except for the few times when I tried to find food for myself. Each time I put on a pot of coffee or a pan of beans, another contraction began and I ran back to help.

Cathy was born in a little log cabin in northern Vermont, forty miles from the nearest hospital. She began nursing right away, while I massaged Jean's uterus to reduce the possibility of excessive bleeding. The only thing that went wrong with Cathy's birth was that I burned three pans of beans and boiled away six pots of coffee.

Karen was born in 1968 in our home in Vermont, with six feet of snow drifted outside the windows. This birth was not only painless, but very actively pleasurable. We had never read about this aspect of birth, and it took us both by surprise. What a long way from the pain and agony of conventional myth! (Years later, a sympathetic doctor said, "Yes, I've seen it a few times. It may even be that many women have orgasms during birth, but interpret them as pain, because the sensations are more intense than anything they've experienced previously, and because they have been conditioned to expect pain.")

Susan was born in 1970 and Derek in 1972, both in a log cabin in the mountainous Central Interior of British Columbia, also forty miles from the nearest hospital. Both births were work, but relatively easy, completely painless, and physically pleasurable.

Funny story: Three days after Susan was born, the government of British Columbia took Donn to fight a forest fire for three days. (They can do that if you are considered to have a "nonessential" job. They can pull you out of a restaurant, grocery store, or your home or off the highway if they need firefighters. They pay minimum wage and provide tools, sleeping bags, and very good food.) During that time the RCMP showed up, having heard that someone out our way had had a baby at home. The poor guy took one look at me, in my regular clothes, with the baby, and I think he wondered either about my sanity or if we'd kidnapped the kid. He didn't think it was possible to have given birth, look so good, and in the absence of a husband be caring for two older children and, among other various chores, be milking a dozen goats. He also, I think, wondered about our ability to care for a baby and so sent a nurse to check things out. In retrospect we figured out that the RCMP was contacted by the butcher at the local grocery store because we officially weighed Susan, albeit the day after, on his meat scales.

I was lucky. With each of our four children, I had a period of about a month with Braxton-Hicks contractions coming about every other day and lasting about an hour or two — gentle practice, warm-up exercises for the labor to come. The only problem with these contractions was deciding if I was truly in labor or not. Did we dare go to town or go visiting, or should we stay at home, just in case?

Cathy came easily. I worked hard, but the labor was so gradually progressive that I stayed completely relaxed, totally focused inward and aware of all the new and different sensations and of all the muscles working in harmony, performing the job they were designed to do, without interruption or interference.

We put the camera out with the birth supplies and forgot about it! My only regret over the years is that I didn't take a picture of Donn holding Cathy right after she was born. Like a variation of the Madonna and child, Donn glowed. He was totally enraptured. He was so caught up in the wonder of the experience that when I asked him if we had a girl or a boy, he just stared at me, his face suddenly, totally, blank. To him, at that moment, it was completely irrelevant. He hadn't looked!

Cathy came gently and gradually into this world; Karen, I swear, came into this world pushing with her feet! I had the usual warm-up contractions on and off for a month. The day she was born, I had contractions just before lunch, and knowing we were close to the birthing time, I didn't eat but fixed lunch for Donn, Cathy, and Mother (Donn's). We expected this second labor to be shorter, but didn't feel we could give Cathy, two and a half years old, all the attention she might need without interrupting my concentration. Mother was good enough to come and stay with us.

I decided that labor was "for real" while cleaning up after lunch. Mother took Cathy to the neighbor's and planned to come back in an hour or two. Shortly after they left,

I began to feel the urge to push. I told Donn and he laughed at me! He said he'd start getting things ready soon. I told him I didn't think we should wait. He looked at me and decided this wasn't the time for a debate; he would just "humor me" — and I knew he was humoring me. As we started fixing the bed together, I told him that with the next contraction I was going to lie down and he could just humor me a bit more and take a look to see what, if anything, was happening. With the next contraction, I did, and he did, and I will admit that both of us were surprised to find that the baby's head was beginning to crown. We did get the bed set, just barely in time. Now the contractions were really strong. I love the urge to push. I don't think there is anything else in the world that is so totally compelling and feels so completely right. I had two pushing contractions on the bed and Karen came into the world — and with the most incredible orgasm. This took Donn and me by surprise. Just like our lovemaking, it was a feeling of Life celebrating Life. It seemed so very unfair that Donn couldn't be a part of that, too.

We tried telling people about our experience. Many thought us liars. A few women patted me condescendingly on the shoulder and told me I didn't have to make up stories. To those who were truly interested and asked what made the experience so extraordinary for me, I've always answered: my ability to feel completely relaxed and at one with myself, my sexuality, the natural process of birth, my husband, and the order and wonder of the universe.

Some people have wondered how we could let our young children witness birth. Brought up to see birth as a natural process, and having witnessed animal births, with only minimal explanation they understood what they might hear and see. As children will do, they adopted our attitude and found there was nothing to fear — there was only the wonder and magic of seeing a baby come forth. See how the girls have their hands out?

Here's Derek before he's even a minute old.

Here are a few of our favorite resource books.

***HUSBAND-COACHED CHILDBIRTH,* by Robert A. Bradley, M.D.; foreword by Ashley Montagu.** In 1966, when our first daughter was born, a husband's participation in childbirth was considered very radical; today, in many areas at least, it has become common. This book is one of the very best in discussing the father's role and the ways in which his presence and participation contribute during both pregnancy and childbirth. We recommend this book very highly to all couples expecting a baby.

This was the book I relied on the most. I read and reread it before the birth of each of our children. Bradley has great common sense and a natural, relaxed approach to birthing; he conveys confidence in the naturalness of pregnancy and birth, and the rightful place of the father during this time. The new edition has added sections about different birthing methods, natural prevention and healing for common problems associated with pregnancy, and a chapter called "Daddy Helped Born Me." To find out more about the Bradley Method of birthing, write: American Academy of Husband-Coached Childbirth, Box 5224, Sherman Oaks, CA 91413; 800-4ABIRTH; www.bradleybirth.com.

THE BIRTH BOOK: EVERYTHING YOU NEED TO KNOW TO HAVE A SAFE AND SATISFYING BIRTH, by William Sears, M.D., and Martha Sears, R.N. This is wonderful and very complete guide to birthing. Many approaches are examined, including VBAC (vaginal birth after cesarean). A history of birthing; choices in childbirth; getting your body ready; tests, technology, and other interventions that happen on the way to birth; cesarean births; easing pain in labor; why birth hurts and why it doesn't have to; relaxing for birth; how the doctor can help; best birth positions; labor and delivery; composing your birth plan; and real birth stories. This book is up-to-date and thorough. I'd use it if I were ever going to have another baby.

MOTHERING MAGAZINE, P.O. Box 1690, Santa Fe, NM 87504; 800-984-8116; www.mothering.com. One of the leading international magazines devoted to natural childbirth, breastfeeding, child-rearing, and midwifery. Covers family issues, pros and cons of vaccination, dental care, discipline, childhood illnesses, and baby supplies. Bimonthly.

LA LECHE LEAGUE INTERNATIONAL (P.O. Box 4079, Schaumburg, IL 60168; www.lalecheleague.org) is an international organization with branches in more than 50 countries. They offer a wonderful array of books and information about breastfeeding, birthing, and parenting, with some special books for fathers, whole foods, and other related subjects. Among many other excellent books, they have the classic *The Womanly Art of Breastfeeding*, which I highly recommend. If you live in Canada, ask about their main Canadian office and resources in your province.

Our children are born trusting us. We don't want to lose that, ever. If we treat our children with respect from the time they are born we will not lose it. We are so much bigger, and we need to remember that in our children's eyes we have a natural authority. We need to use it with care and thought. It is all too easy, without thought, sometimes only in response to our own conditioning, to force our ways on our young impressionable children.

INVASION!
Should No Child Be Left Behind????

I don't think it's farfetched to say that babies learn, in utero, the sound of their parents' voices. You can pipe in (so to speak) music — and that doesn't seem too bad, depending on the music — with speakers on your belly; classical music is highly recommended by those who do this. What else can your baby learn before birth? It seems to me that in a rapidly growing body baby is learning something new all the time. Think about that for a while.

Indulge me for a bit longer, please. Did you know that for just under $200 you can now educate your unborn child? (They do suggest that you wait until the eighteenth week of pregnancy to start. Why then? Why not the seventeenth week or the nineteenth week?) BabyPlus® is a sixteen-week set of audio lessons that introduces "a series of sixteen scientifically designed rhythmic sounds that resemble a mother's heartbeat. The rhythm of the sounds increases incrementally and sequentially as the pregnancy progresses ... [which] introduces your child to a sequential learning process." Now why would anyone think this is better than what happens naturally? Why would anyone buy this? Why would you want to interfere with a process that is so miraculous that no one understands it? There is no money-back guarantee with this program. Now that's thoughtful of them, isn't it?

California is about to vote on a bill mandating preschool for all children. At this rate, by 2010 will there be mandatory in-utero classes?

MISSION IMPOSSIBLE

THE SPIRIT IS WILLING, BUT ...

See the blank box above? It's there in memory of a nice idea. I'd planned several pages, at this point in the book, for the kids to write and share their thoughts and feelings about their experiences with homeschooling and moving out into the world. For the most part they are very willing to share their thoughts, but getting something in writing from them was impossible. They have their own lives, and this is, after all, my book, not theirs. Here's an update.

As the kids left home, one by one, at first for very short periods, then for increasingly longer periods, they continued to find that the entire world was their school, and no matter where they were, life was learning. It's been exciting and challenging, and sometimes has been very different from what they or we had expected.

Cathy had tentatively planned to work in Third World countries after high school, and spent several months living, traveling and volunteering in Mexico. Following a disappointing notification that the organization she had planned to work with was unable to establish work permits for ongoing programs, she settled in southern Vermont. She was familiar with the town after visiting her grandmother and spending several summers as a camp counselor in a nearby town during high school. She obtained a position as a full-time librarian, based on her experience at our local library. After a few years, she wanted to see another part of the country and moved to Virginia, where she was a project manager for a company that raised money for volunteer fire departments and emergency services. Desiring a warmer climate, she moved to Northern California, visited some old family friends, worked in a school library, drove the school bus, and fell in love. She and her husband, Michael, married in Scotland and now live in Northern California with their son, Jacob. Before Jacob was born, Cathy was the personal assistant to the owner of a high-end residential and retail real estate developer.

When Jacob was born she wanted to stay at home with him, so she went through the process of becoming a licensed home childcare provider. When Jacob entered preschool, Cathy returned to her position as personal assistant, where she remained for several years. Choosing to follow her passion to help people live happier, healthier lives, Cathy now enjoys being a personal trainer at a family-centered health club. She has studied business, health, nutrition and fitness. She holds national certification as a Personal Fitness Trainer. Cathy is now a regular and dynamic participant at Jacob's school, a CERT (Community Emergency Response Team) volunteer, a CAPS (Citizens Assisting Public Safety) volunteer working with her local police and fire departments, and an American Cancer Society volunteer, and in her spare time studies tai chi.

Karen finished her high school academic studies in two years (her idea, not ours) and went to New York City to study art. Although we felt she wasn't ready to cope with full independence, especially in a large city, we couldn't hold her back. We felt her months in New York were a learning experience, some of it very good and some not so good. After a short time back at home she moved to Florida, lived with my mother, and entered college, where she received very high marks and was on the dean's list. Since then she has worked in the advertising department of a newspaper, in a high-tech optical company, and as an office manager and in accounting. She has gone back to college for advanced computer training and later taught college courses in HTML, JavaScript, VBScript, CSS, software development, designing client/server applications, and design concepts following the Windows paradigm, and an Introduction to MS Office at an adult education center. She is currently an integral part of a large financial investment firm. Karen is an active part of her two daughter's schooling and she loves to travel and go on special excursions with her two beautiful and wonderful daughters.

Susan spent her last two years of high school at the Meeting School in New Hampshire. Donn's impressions of the school when he visited with Susan before enrolling her were good and she came away with much of value, including some lifelong friends, and she feels the Meeting School was a good experience for her. She spent the next year working, saving money, and traveling around the country with friends in a car, which almost made it back home. She decided to pursue a career in outdoor education, participating in programs such as Outward Bound. She was accepted at Prescott College in Arizona, which she attended for two years. She enjoyed her first year but left after the second because of extreme frustration at not being able to get the courses she really wanted. During the years she remained in the Prescott area she studied Intrinsic Breathwork and became a trained leader, enabling her to lead workshops and give individual counseling. Using these skills, she has worked as a behavioral health technician with abused and delinquent teens at Mingus Mountain, a residential treatment center for delinquent girls. After seven years in Arizona she moved to New York State and attended Mercy College as a part-time student while working full time at Green Chimneys, another residential treatment center for inner city youth. She then moved back to Arizona and completed her studies, earning a place on the honor roll and earning her B.A. in Counseling Psychology in the adult degree program at Prescott College while she worked, again, at Mingus Mountain and continued her private Intrinsic Breathwork counseling work. Susan now lives in Baltimore with her active young son. She works as a clinical research coordinator at a clinical pharmacology center conducting phase one pharmaceutical trials.

Derek always wanted to work with horses. He began working in various stables while still in junior high school. To put foundations under his dreams, he cleaned numerous stalls (at the rate of $2 an hour) in exchange for lessons, and eventually was asked to begin giving lessons. At times stable owners left him in charge of a barn, with thousands of dollars worth of horses, while they went on vacation. He learned to manage lessons, complex feeding routines, stable management, clients, veterinary problems, and vets. He has worked as a barn manager, trainer, and riding instructor, and has competed in horse shows in Vermont, Quebec, North Carolina, Florida, Kentucky, Colorado, Virginia, Vermont, and Georgia. He has also worked and trained horses in Germany, and that was a very different type of learning experience. Lest your kids read this and think it's all very glamorous, they should keep in mind that it involves an incredible amount of physical work. Derek frequently spends his days in the barn from 6:30 a.m. to 9:30 p.m. He doesn't mind. He loves his work, and he and his wife, Sulu, and their daughter, Addison, live on their farm in Virginia when they are not on the road competing in numerous horse shows.

I have deliberately left out information about whether or not any of our grown children will homeschool their children. Donn and I made the decision to homeschool our children, and it was right for us. I will be extremely pleased if our kids homeschool their children, but not disappointed if they choose differently. I expect some of them will homeschool and some of them won't. It's not my decision to make. Our children, with their life partners, will make their own decisions based on what is right for them. They know the options, and I have complete faith that they will choose to do what is best for their families.

REFLECTIONS

Donn (1994)

After all the years of raising children and teaching them at home, Jean and I stand back (as we have done frequently through the years) and ask ourselves if we have achieved what we had hoped to achieve. Have we prepared our children adequately for life on their own? Has the education they have received with us really been a better preparation for them than public education would have been? We made many mistakes, although we watched for them and tried to correct them. Sometimes we set our goals too high for our children and for ourselves; other times, our goals may not have been high enough. We listened to our children constantly, and watched them, trying to anticipate and meet all their needs — academic, intellectual, social, physical, and spiritual, both immediate and eventual. Most of the time, I think, we succeeded, although we always wished we could have done better. We aimed for perfection, for ourselves and for our children, knowing it would never be reached, but also knowing that the higher our aim, the higher our achievements would be.

Despite setbacks, problems, and occasional disappointments, we have enjoyed these twenty-four years, and have no regrets about having chosen to teach our children at home. Not to have done so would have left us with much less meaning and happiness in our lives, then and now. We and our children continue to be very close. That alone is great success and wealth. With the wisdom of hindsight, we know there are many changes we'd make, but the decision to home-school would stand.

"By their fruits ye shall know them," says the Bible, which I guess means the final judgment rests not with us, but with our children, and with the people who will know them through their lives. The real measure of our children's education at home will be the degree to which they achieve success and happiness in their own lives, and in the influence they have on the world around them. Jean and I are confident that they will continue to make us proud of them, and we'll feel honored to be judged according to the people our children are and are still becoming.

I think that's the best any parents can hope for.

Jean (2000)

Our goal as parents (and teachers) was to raise healthy, happy, loving children into caring and independent adults, capable of caring for themselves and others and able to make positive contributions to the world around them.

As I sit here in our woodsy home, surrounded by memories of smiling faces and shared laughter and tears and embraced by the house we built, I feel an immense amount of satisfaction. I, too, feel there is much we could have done differently, better, but I know we did the best we could at the time. I feel intensely grateful for the years we all spent together. Would we do it again? Absolutely.

No one knows what the future will bring to any of us, but with over 15 years for retrospection since the last fledgling left home, I feel the time and experiences we had in living and growing together are beyond price and more valuable than any tangible reward. Our children are good people and doing well with their own lives. I am immensely proud of all of them for what they have made, and are making, of their lives with their families. Of greater importance than anything else, our children are my friends. When Donn died, I don't think I could have survived without their love and support. Each in their own way has given and continues to give me strength and love and encouragement. Donn and I gave them life and brought them into this world. They, in turn, have made it possible for me to continue without him. I could ask for no more.

Jean (2009)

It's now 2009 and I have been given more. With spouses and grandchildren we now number thirteen in all, and it is a continuing joy to be with all these wonderful adults and their children. I have had the privilege of watching my children grow and create their own loving families and differing ways of life, each special and each unique. I am truly blessed.

I MET HER ON THE BUS

She was going two hundred miles, back to college from a weekend visit with her grandmother. I was going ten miles, home from the store. Her guitar case was on the luggage rack and she had long blond hair and I sat beside her. Three months later, on Groundhog Day, 1963, we were married.

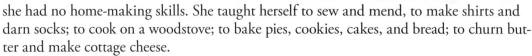

When we built our first home, we worked together, hauling and lifting logs, fitting, chinking, and nailing on the roofing. We've built other homes since then, and we've worked together to make them strong and warm.

With an affluent, suburban childhood, she had no home-making skills. She taught herself to sew and mend, to make shirts and darn socks; to cook on a woodstove; to bake pies, cookies, cakes, and bread; to churn butter and make cottage cheese.

When we decided to start a family, we wanted to share the experience of childbirth, but every doctor we consulted refused my presence in the delivery room: "We can't have fainting husbands all over the floor."

We went to the bookstore and the library, and we studied obstetrics, gynecology, and yoga breathing. We delivered our first child, Cathy, in a small log cabin, miles from the nearest neighbor. In following years, we delivered Karen, Susan, and Derek, all at home, all four without complication or pain.

She nursed each of the children at least a year, and we carried them everywhere, and they always knew they were loved and wanted.

We've worked together in the garden, the hayfield, the barn. She can milk a cow, nurse a sick calf, pitch hay, shovel manure, catch runaway pigs, and be midwife for a pig.

Her pie crusts are light and flaky, a slice of her bread makes a meal complete, and her doughnuts are my special reward.

She has stood spellbound by the Northern Lights, entranced by the call of wild geese flying north, and breathlessly excited by the musical howl of northwestern timber wolves.

Her fingers fly on her guitar and her singing is magic, whether playing classical or folk, Bach or Dylan, loving or growling.

She's five-foot-five, still slim and shapely, and becoming more beautiful every day. Her golden hair is silvery now, but still falls free and long, like spring rain and the morning mist. Her eyes sparkle, she smiles, she laughs, she works and plays, she hugs our children, and she's the best there is. She's a natural woman, whose love flows like a river, warm as summer, strong as a mountain.

With her, my fields are always green, my skies are blue; she nourishes me, feeds my soul. We are two shafts of grain, blown by the wind, north or south or east or west, leaning together, in sunrise and sunset, under clouds and rain and storms, under clear skies and stars, sunlight, moonlight, darkness, whispering together in the breezes, our roots intertwined in the earth, our stalks together in the air, our heads together in the sky.

Sometimes I think I will burst with the awesome mountain of love I have for her; and when I feel her love, I am grateful: Thank you, Jean.

And humble: Bless me, wife.

And glad: Let's dance! Dance! Dance!

And proud: Look, world, look at this woman of mine. There's no better woman anywhere; she's the one I'll take to the stars with me —

Oh yes oh yes oh yes.

That Bus Ride

That bus ride changed my life, making unexpected tours and stops for thirty-seven years. I'm still on the bus. Donn was taken off fourteen years ago, but my life is far more than I imagined it would be because he sat next to me.

Tall and thin, he had hair that came down over the collar of a leather jacket with a large peace symbol on the back. He was soft-spoken and poetic, analytic, philosophical, and mysterious, with a mind-blowing wit and sense of humor and fun.

With a gentle hand and loving heart he led me out of the wilderness of my adolescent rebellion. I felt cherished and safe. I fell into unconditional love with the man and with our challenging and adventurous life.

He was blessed with an irrepressible love and reverence for all life. The days were not long enough, the nights too short. There was never enough time to turn all the dreams into reality. But, oh! He taught me to slow down, to cherish the dreams and savor the moment.

We were blessed with four healthy children, and I was blessed with a man who taught me what a parent should be. The babies were ours, together — all things shared except the nursing, and he often complained that he wished he could do that too!

Thank you, Donn, for your love. For the joy of living that you shared and inspired in me. For making me laugh at myself. For showing me, when discouraged, that the glass was half-full, not half-empty. For leaving me a living legacy of love in our children, by creating a work of love that allows me to continue working with you.

Thank you, Donn, for giving me so much in life that I cry with joy for what we had — and still have.

Thank you, life, for giving me a man to fill my days and nights with wonder and love.

I am waiting for the stars, Donn, and you.

If a man does not keep pace
with his companions,
perhaps it is because he hears
a different drummer.
Let him step to the music
he hears,
however measured or far away.

Thoreau

IN MEMORY

DONN REED TWO or DONN REED, TOO

Daring to be, with fierce integrity, friend.
Open to truth universal. Ready to go
Nebula hopping and shopping for stars and stopping for fun
Anywhere people are silly or batting their cilia.
Long, lanky, loony, loving, learned and loyal.
Dawn dawns on Don; Don dons Donn; I'll be doggoned!

Buck-naked boys bound through woods, each with stone club,
Ready to kill the nearest wolf or deer or bear,
Unless, of course, a small horse or cow would do in lieu.
Cowed and cold we quit, redressed, empty-handed, non-bucolic.
Ecstasies of starlight and laughter surrounded our campfire.

Recalling that we mingled blood one distant yesteryear
Evokes in me an atavistic urge,
Empowers me with mystic-fingered grace,
Delivers me again to archetypal brotherhood, friend.

Leonard J. Nadeau,
Lifelong friend
December 20, 1995

The Sweet Music of Good Neighbours:
Jean and Donn and Their Rare Love Affair

my life is shot through with
silk moiré watermarks of his presence
memories of early seventies tapestry days
his sense of humour
the ability to go to extremes in
ridiculousness to make us laugh
or learn

I was sorry when they moved away
haven't seen him for thirty years but I am often
surprised at the number of things he taught
just by being himself

it was he who taught me the danger
to satisfactory discussion posed by the non sequitur
and to be wary of letting it slip into one's own thoughts
continuing not only to miss the point forever
but never notice its loss, thus becoming
a first-class bore to oneself

which led us to discuss syllogism
the putting of the literary cart before the
metaphorical horse

I found their new location recently and wrote to
congratulate them on a book they published
his wife writes to say he died of cancer
some years ago

the depth of the grief I feel surprises me
I feel furious that he has died so young because
they were two who got love right
not fair that he has died at fifty-seven leaving her
their children, grandchildren, and the world, without him
it was he and his wife who taught us about love in the way
Quakers teach: by example

Jean and Donn knew what it meant for each partner to care
unconditionally, unreservedly for the
spiritual growth and well-being of the other
to throw themselves body and soul, toward the
fulfillment, the enrichment of their beloved

this is my hymn of rejoicing and sorrow
my song of praise, farewell, and deep sympathy

By Jacqueline Baldwin
Prince George, British Columbia, Canada
2005

BROOK FARM BOOKS WEBSITE: WWW.BROOKFARMBOOKS.COM

On our website you will find everything reviewed in this book and hundreds more, all that I have found to be effective creative learning tools for the whole family. Yes, you'll find books (including reference books and a wealth of classic literature), but you'll also find games, kits that your kids can make, models that demonstrate important ideas or make it easy to visualize the human body, maps and globes that illustrate our world, audiocassettes, and DVDs.

Our promise to you is that we will do our best to give you the best deal possible. We understand that monetary resources may be hard to stretch. If we can give you the best price then we'll sell it to you. If we can't then we'll either give you the information you need to get it on your own or provide a link to a site or the address where you will get the best deal. There are times you will find it more convenient to order from us if your choices are from a number of different sources (that information is on the web). I think you will find that frequently the deciding factor in this decision is the cost of shipping and handling. You'll figure it out.

You will find that many books on our site have a link to Amazon.com (or you can use Amazon.ca). Frequently they can sell a book for less than we can. I've found it useful and economical to pay the yearly fee to join what they call Amazon Prime. This fee covers all shipping (to you or someone else if you do the ordering) of stock from Amazon for a year. It does not cover items sold by a third party.

TO ORDER MORE COPIES OF THIS BOOK

Additional copies of *The Lifetime Learning Companion* may be ordered from Brook Farm Books, P.O. Box 246, Bridgewater, ME 04735, or Brook Farm Books, Box 101, Glassville, NB E7L 4T4, for $19.95 plus $2 postage. All orders must be paid in U.S. funds; checks or money orders are fine. If you wish to send a Canadian check, that's fine as long as you write the following clearly right under the line where you write out the amount of your check: "Payable in U.S. funds." Visa/MasterCard orders are accepted through our toll-free order number: 877-375-4680. You may also purchase copies from your local bookstore. If they don't have it, they can order it through Baker & Taylor, IPG, or their regular wholesaler.

WISH LIST

The first ten commandments are called "the Bill of Rights" because they are— What's so funny?
U.S. HISTORY

WISH LIST

I met a kid today and he said, "Where do you go to school?" and I said, "I have school at home," and he said, "Really? I do, too!" and we just looked at each other for a minute until we both realized there was nothing we had to explain, so we went and played ball!

NOTES

Aw, Mom! Don't you remember that quotation from Mark Twain? "Soap and education are not as sudden as a massacre, but both are more deadly in the long run." You agree with him about education. Why don't you agree with him about soap?

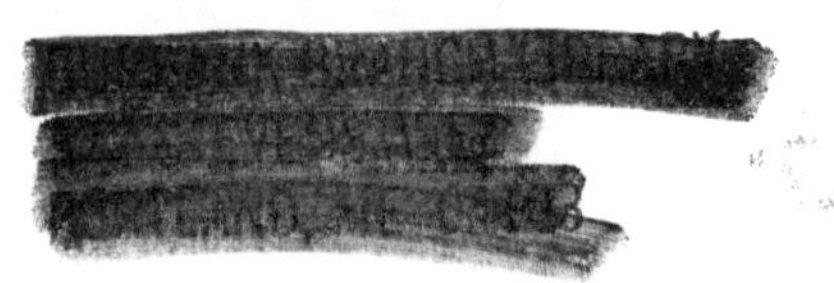

A cartoon book? About home-schooling?
Shouldn't you learn how to draw first?
Dad's going to be another Grandma Moses.
I know a lot of knock-knock jokes you can use.
What's so funny about home-school?